THE ART OF
WALLPAPER
MORRIS & CO. IN CONTEXT

Mary Schoeser

ACC ART BOOKS

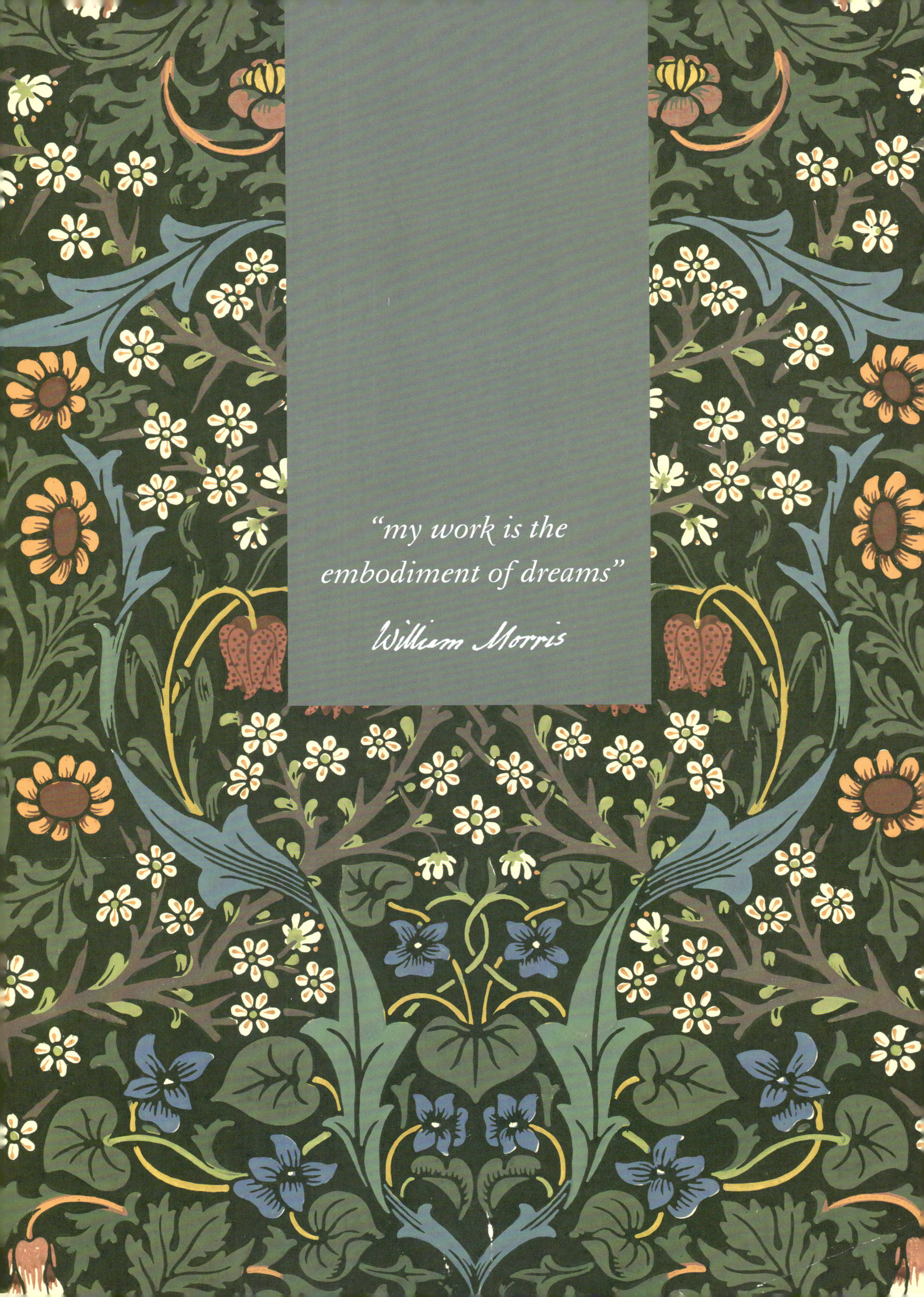
"my work is the
embodiment of dreams"
William Morris

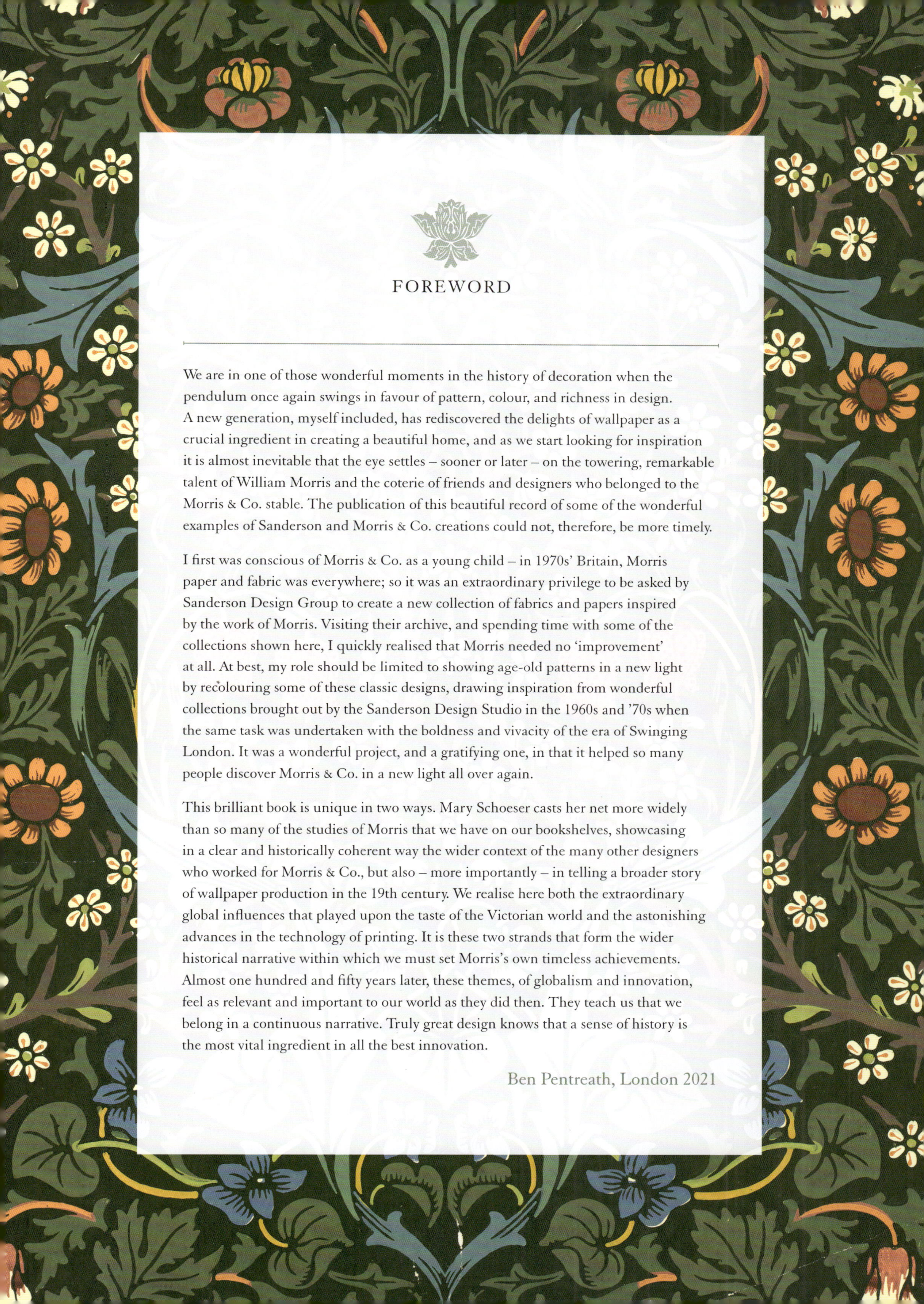

FOREWORD

We are in one of those wonderful moments in the history of decoration when the pendulum once again swings in favour of pattern, colour, and richness in design. A new generation, myself included, has rediscovered the delights of wallpaper as a crucial ingredient in creating a beautiful home, and as we start looking for inspiration it is almost inevitable that the eye settles – sooner or later – on the towering, remarkable talent of William Morris and the coterie of friends and designers who belonged to the Morris & Co. stable. The publication of this beautiful record of some of the wonderful examples of Sanderson and Morris & Co. creations could not, therefore, be more timely.

I first was conscious of Morris & Co. as a young child – in 1970s' Britain, Morris paper and fabric was everywhere; so it was an extraordinary privilege to be asked by Sanderson Design Group to create a new collection of fabrics and papers inspired by the work of Morris. Visiting their archive, and spending time with some of the collections shown here, I quickly realised that Morris needed no 'improvement' at all. At best, my role should be limited to showing age-old patterns in a new light by recolouring some of these classic designs, drawing inspiration from wonderful collections brought out by the Sanderson Design Studio in the 1960s and '70s when the same task was undertaken with the boldness and vivacity of the era of Swinging London. It was a wonderful project, and a gratifying one, in that it helped so many people discover Morris & Co. in a new light all over again.

This brilliant book is unique in two ways. Mary Schoeser casts her net more widely than so many of the studies of Morris that we have on our bookshelves, showcasing in a clear and historically coherent way the wider context of the many other designers who worked for Morris & Co., but also – more importantly – in telling a broader story of wallpaper production in the 19th century. We realise here both the extraordinary global influences that played upon the taste of the Victorian world and the astonishing advances in the technology of printing. It is these two strands that form the wider historical narrative within which we must set Morris's own timeless achievements. Almost one hundred and fifty years later, these themes, of globalism and innovation, feel as relevant and important to our world as they did then. They teach us that we belong in a continuous narrative. Truly great design knows that a sense of history is the most vital ingredient in all the best innovation.

Ben Pentreath, London 2021

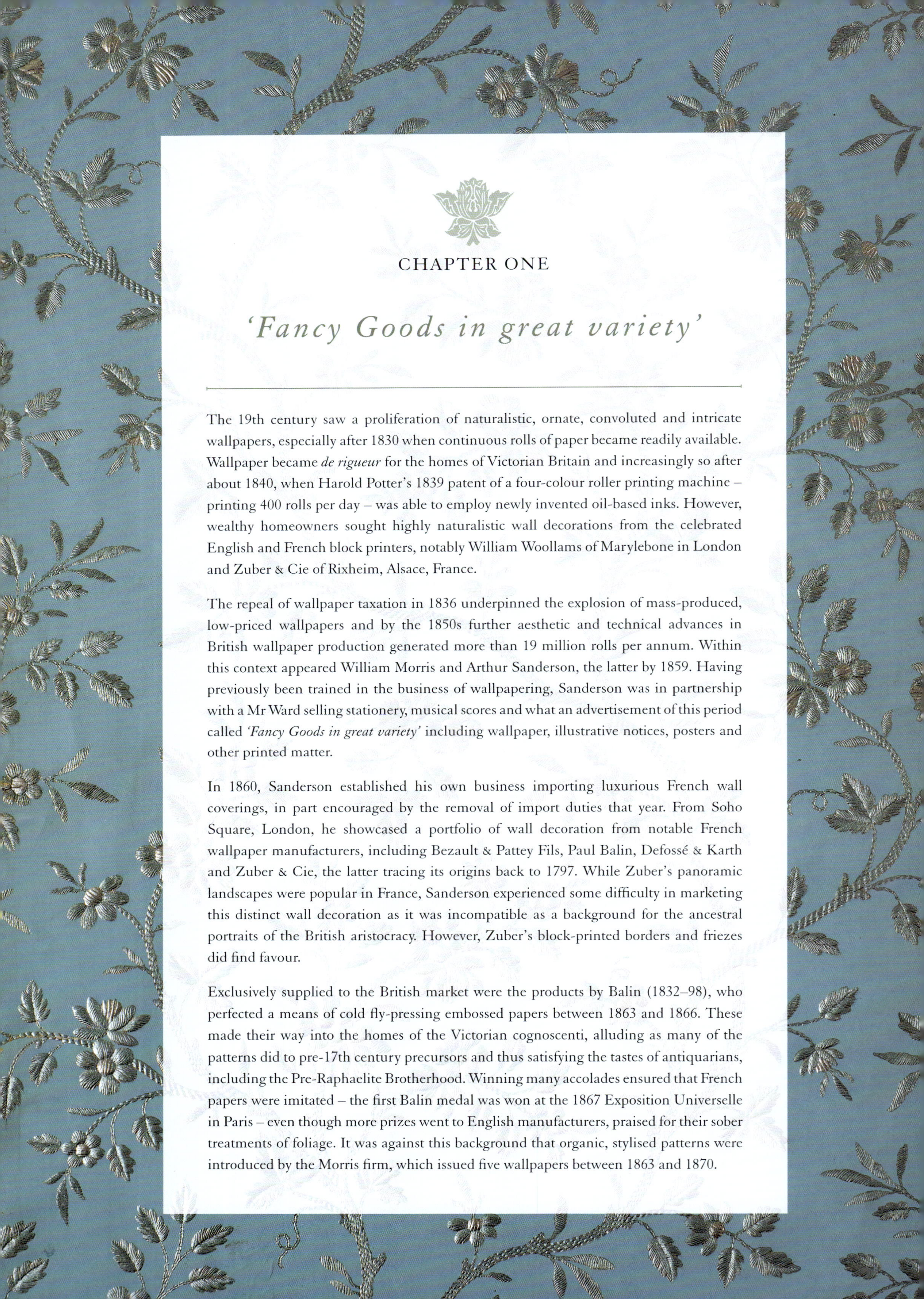

CHAPTER ONE

'Fancy Goods in great variety'

The 19th century saw a proliferation of naturalistic, ornate, convoluted and intricate wallpapers, especially after 1830 when continuous rolls of paper became readily available. Wallpaper became *de rigueur* for the homes of Victorian Britain and increasingly so after about 1840, when Harold Potter's 1839 patent of a four-colour roller printing machine – printing 400 rolls per day – was able to employ newly invented oil-based inks. However, wealthy homeowners sought highly naturalistic wall decorations from the celebrated English and French block printers, notably William Woollams of Marylebone in London and Zuber & Cie of Rixheim, Alsace, France.

The repeal of wallpaper taxation in 1836 underpinned the explosion of mass-produced, low-priced wallpapers and by the 1850s further aesthetic and technical advances in British wallpaper production generated more than 19 million rolls per annum. Within this context appeared William Morris and Arthur Sanderson, the latter by 1859. Having previously been trained in the business of wallpapering, Sanderson was in partnership with a Mr Ward selling stationery, musical scores and what an advertisement of this period called *'Fancy Goods in great variety'* including wallpaper, illustrative notices, posters and other printed matter.

In 1860, Sanderson established his own business importing luxurious French wall coverings, in part encouraged by the removal of import duties that year. From Soho Square, London, he showcased a portfolio of wall decoration from notable French wallpaper manufacturers, including Bezault & Pattey Fils, Paul Balin, Defossé & Karth and Zuber & Cie, the latter tracing its origins back to 1797. While Zuber's panoramic landscapes were popular in France, Sanderson experienced some difficulty in marketing this distinct wall decoration as it was incompatible as a background for the ancestral portraits of the British aristocracy. However, Zuber's block-printed borders and friezes did find favour.

Exclusively supplied to the British market were the products by Balin (1832–98), who perfected a means of cold fly-pressing embossed papers between 1863 and 1866. These made their way into the homes of the Victorian cognoscenti, alluding as many of the patterns did to pre-17th century precursors and thus satisfying the tastes of antiquarians, including the Pre-Raphaelite Brotherhood. Winning many accolades ensured that French papers were imitated – the first Balin medal was won at the 1867 Exposition Universelle in Paris – even though more prizes went to English manufacturers, praised for their sober treatments of foliage. It was against this background that organic, stylised patterns were introduced by the Morris firm, which issued five wallpapers between 1863 and 1870.

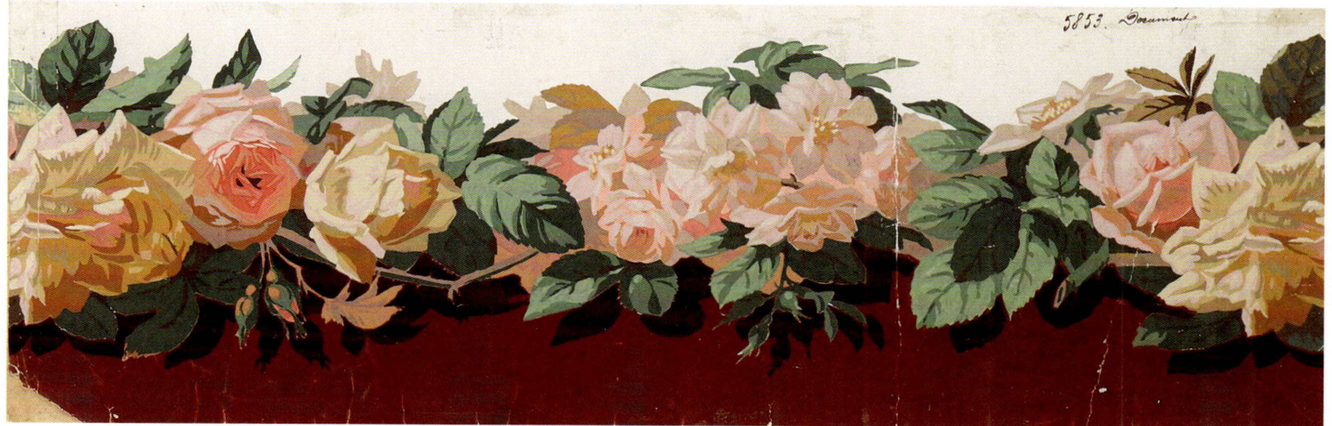

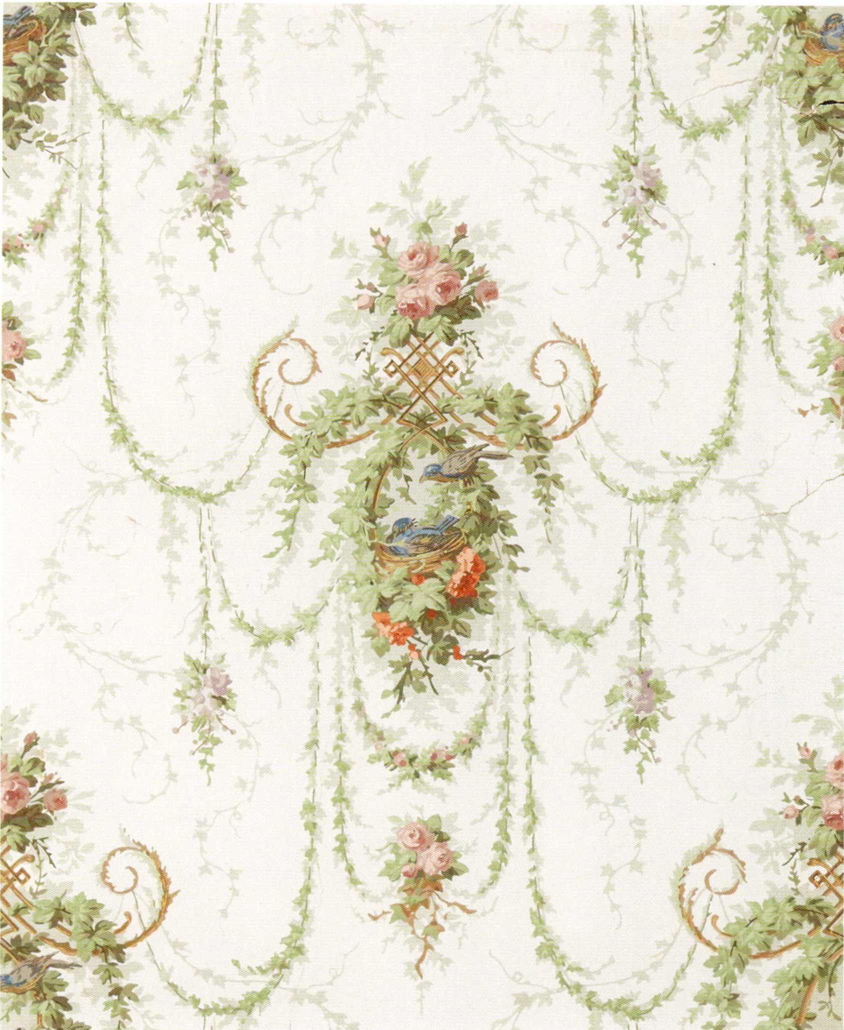

001 | Charles-Louis Müller (attributed), *Rose Border*, c.1848–70

At least three different techniques have been used to produce this elaborate frieze. The paper has been polished before being printed with wooden blocks, then flocked in two colours to create *trompe-l'oeil* shadows beneath the roses. A very similar, smaller-scale design is attributed to the French designer Müller and found in a pattern book dated c.1848–70.

This paper, numbered '6474', is mounted on inexpensive paper, suggesting it too came from a manufacturer's pattern book. It pre-dates the opening of the Sanderson factory in 1879, suggesting that it was purchased by Arthur Sanderson to be used as a design reference in the new factory studio.

002 | *Swags and Scrolls with Flower Baskets*, c.1855, French

Swags and clusters of pink and blue flowers were fashionable motifs for wallpapers used to decorate boudoirs, bedrooms and other feminine domestic spaces. The exquisite detail in this finely wrought design, particularly its use of grey foliage trails to suggest three-dimensional form, marks it as a virtuosity of drawing and printing.

For William Morris, such designs represented the worst influence of bourgeois taste. Within ten years, his own work had entirely rejected such descriptive naturalism. In an 1884 lecture on pattern design, he argued for the rejection of 'sham real flowers, casting sham real shadows on your walls'.

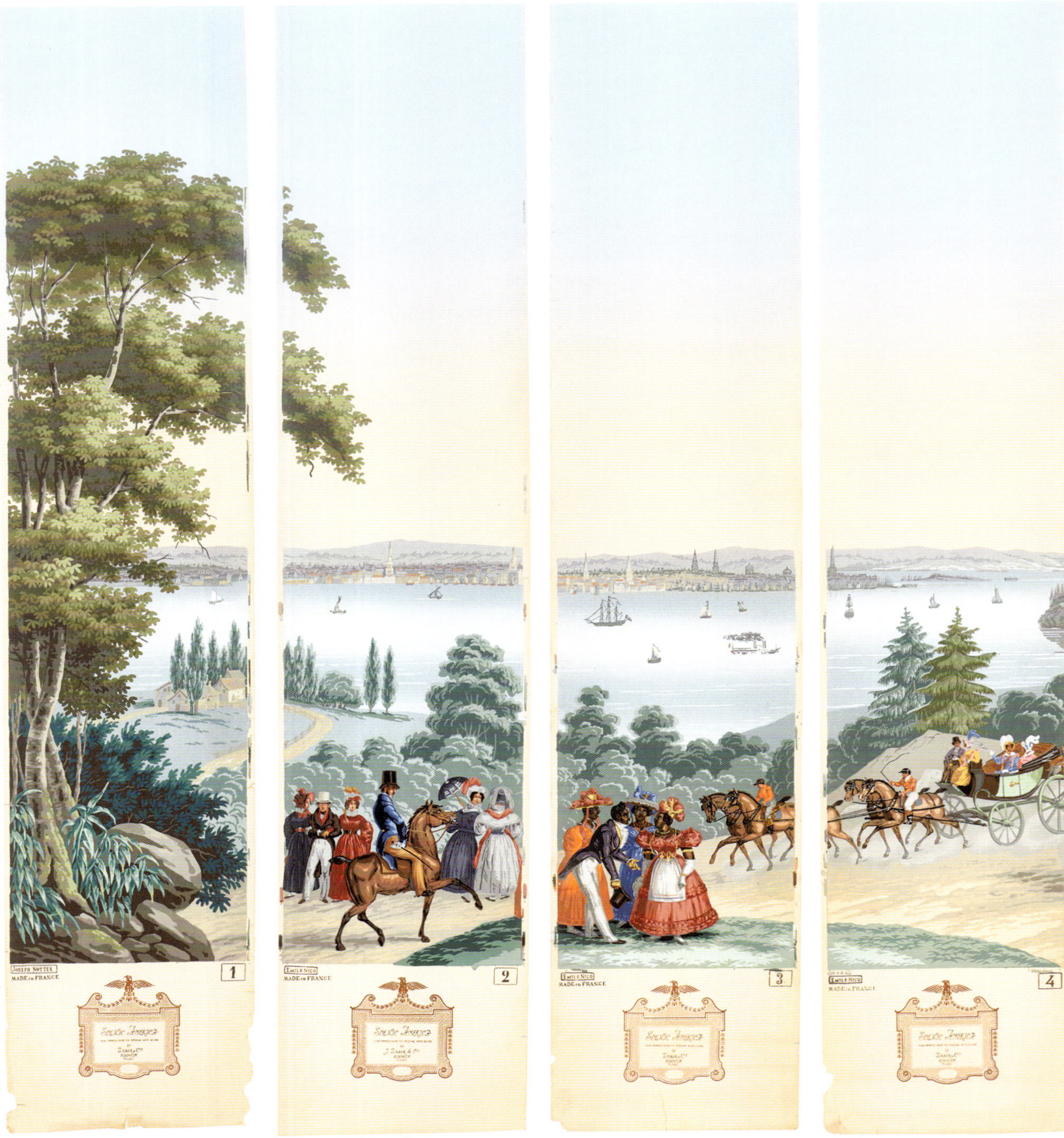

003 | Jean-Julien Deltil, *Les Vues d'Amerique Du Nord*, 1833, Zuber & Cie

Scenic papers emerged in the early-19th century to showcase the capabilities of their manufacturers. Several rose to fame when exhibited at national and later international exhibitions. *Les Vues d'Amerique Du Nord* was first printed in 1834. Its full design spans 49 feet across 32 drops. It includes 223 colours and takes 1,690 blocks to print.

Foreign lands were a common theme in scenic papers, which often took their imagery from the accounts of famous travellers or artists. This panorama has been used in a number of important interiors, most notably the Diplomatic Reception Room in the White House, where it was installed by the First Lady, Jacqueline Kennedy, in 1962.

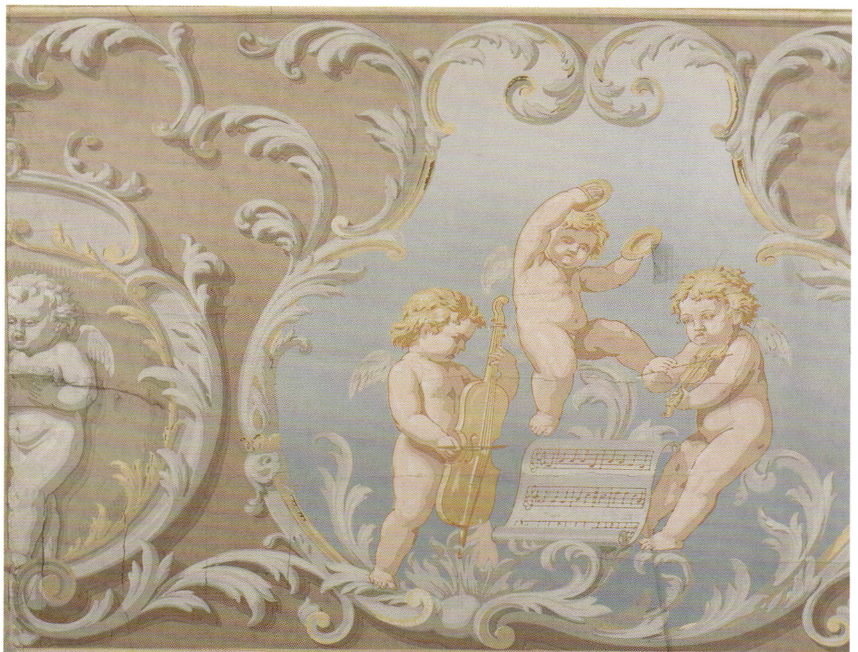

004 | *Music Frieze*, c.1850–75, French

This fragment shows a design of putti (cherubs) playing musical instruments in an elaborate arrangement of rococo, faux plasterwork scrolls. Its large scale and allegorical content suggest use for a public space, perhaps a music room or other interior used for entertaining. Wallpaper was an effective alternative to the more expensive, hand-painted mural decoration.

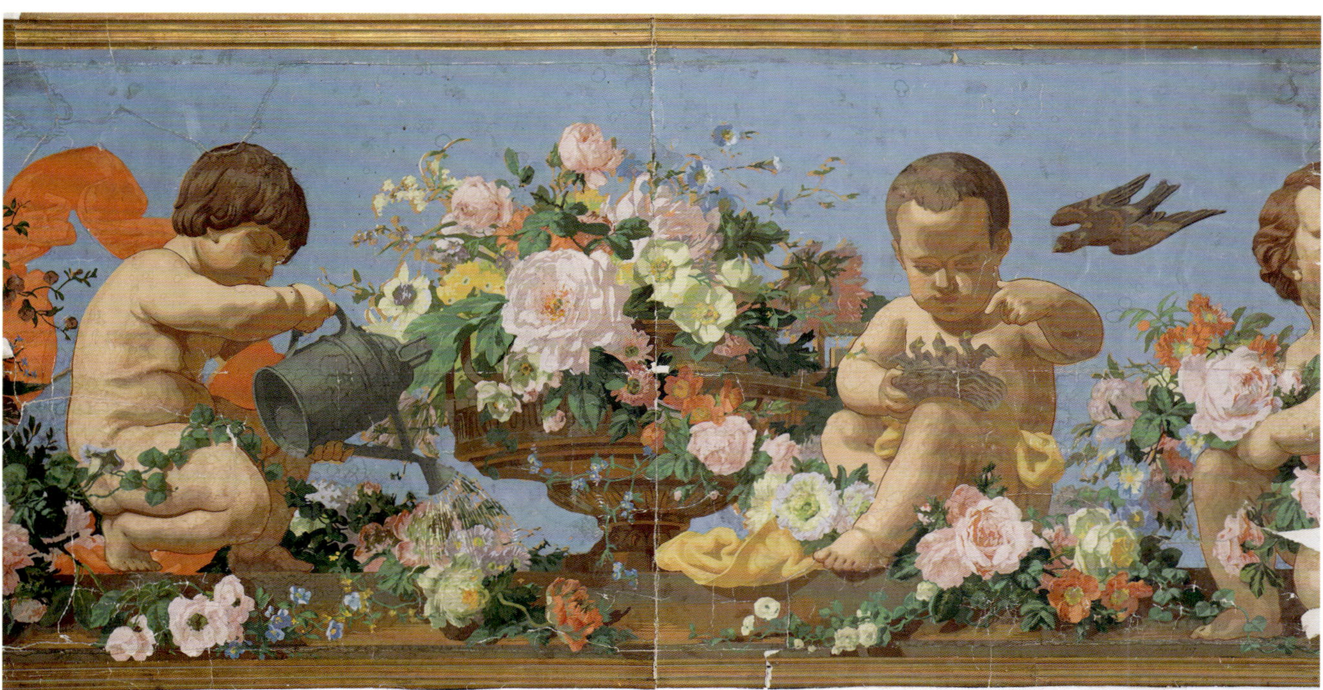

005 | Charles-Louis Müller, *Frieze with Putti and Jardinières*, c.1865, block-printed, Zuber & Cie

This impressive frieze was printed by Zuber & Cie in Rixheim, France's second city of wallpaper in the 19th century after Paris. Elaborate floral friezes were used to decorate rooms intended for socialising and entertaining, particularly billiard rooms or restaurants. By 1865, such friezes were in Sanderson's new Berners Street showroom.

006 | *'Louis XIII' Embroidery Wallpaper*, c.1887, Paul Balin

Balin owned a large collection of valuable textiles and also used museum examples as source material for his elaborate wallpapers. This example, taken from a 17th-century Italian embroidery, shows the effect of highly detailed metallic stitch work. It is block-printed, gilded and embossed to replicate laid-and couched-work embroidery.

Balin used a high-relief screw-press to emboss the pattern, which was then over-printed with bronze powder pigment. The expense involved in such elaborate construction was reflected in the cost of Balin's papers: 100 francs a roll was a typical price for papers imitating textiles with flock or metal finishes, when a roll of simple wallpaper could be had for a few francs.

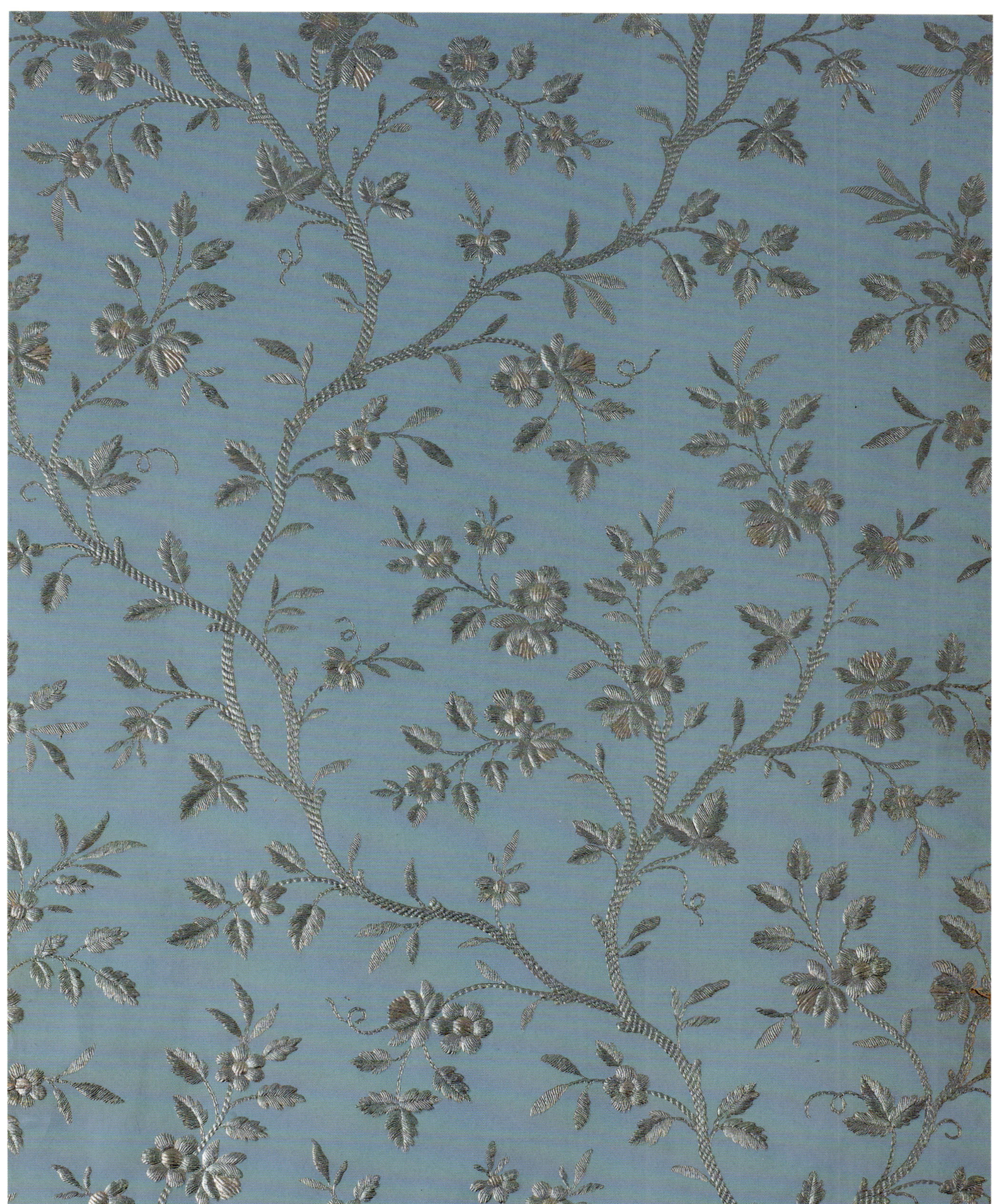

007 | *untitled wallpaper*, 1863–73, Paul Balin

Balin's ability to imitate even the most subtle of textiles is epitomised by this example. It was inspired by a 17th-century Persian silk satin with metal thread embroidery. The three-dimensionality of this wallpaper was one of the notable features of Balin's wallpapers, which for centuries offered the elite in society an alternative to expensive cloths for cladding walls.

Exhibited at the Vienna Exhibition of 1873, an example of this wallpaper was donated to the South Kensington Museum (now V&A) the following year. The donor was Paul Balin himself, who presented the museum with 58 examples of his work, which took inspiration from textiles dating back to the 13th century.

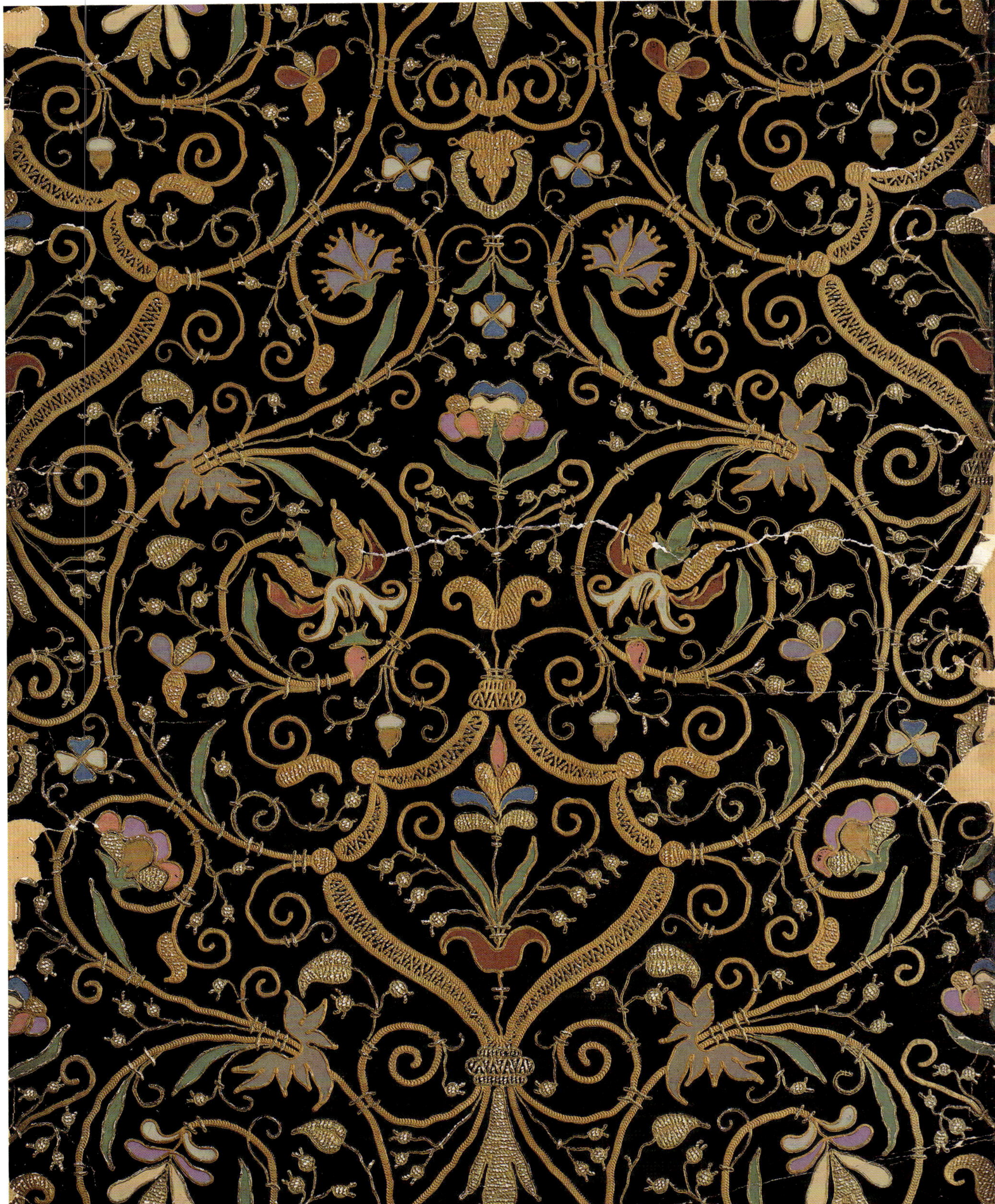

008 | *'Henry II' Embroidery Wallpaper*, 1877-85, Paul Balin

Balin purchased the Parisian factory of Genoux & Bader in 1863, becoming notable for his unrivalled imitations of silks, velvets, brocades and leather. This embossed paper was created to resemble a 16th-century embroidery in his personal collection. The handwritten label reads: '5327 executed after a brocade fabric from the time of Henry II France.'

Balin filed at least seven different patents to protect his inventions, but his work was widely copied during his lifetime. This design was also among the Balin papers exhibited at the 1873 world exhibition in Vienna, where he was awarded a grand diploma of honour in recognition of his contribution to the art of wallpaper manufacturing.

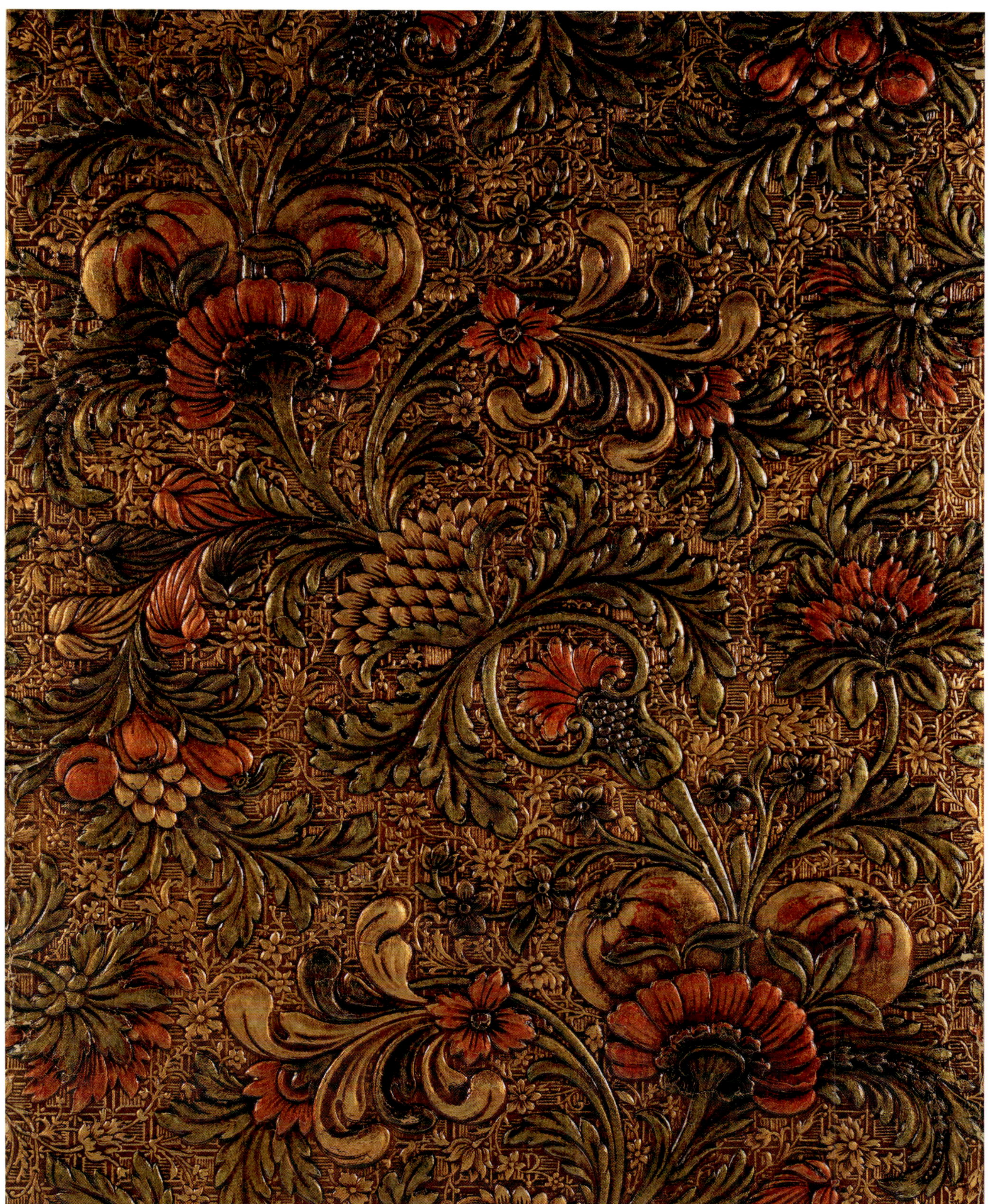

009 | *Louis XVI*, c.1878–85, Paul Balin

Balin's expensive imitation leathers were made from block-printed paper that was painted, gilded, embossed and varnished. This design, stamped 'Louis XVI', was developed from an 18th-century Italian leather in his personal collection. Two versions survive. One has a plain ground while this example has the addition of an embossed Japanesque pattern.

The appearance of *Louis XVI* mimics gilt leather, in which silver leaf was applied to the prepared calf hides that were then covered by a yellow varnish, making it resemble gilding. However, it also shows an awareness of the new fashion for embossed, sized, metalled (typically with tin foil), lacquered and finally stencilled Japanese *kinkarakawakami*.

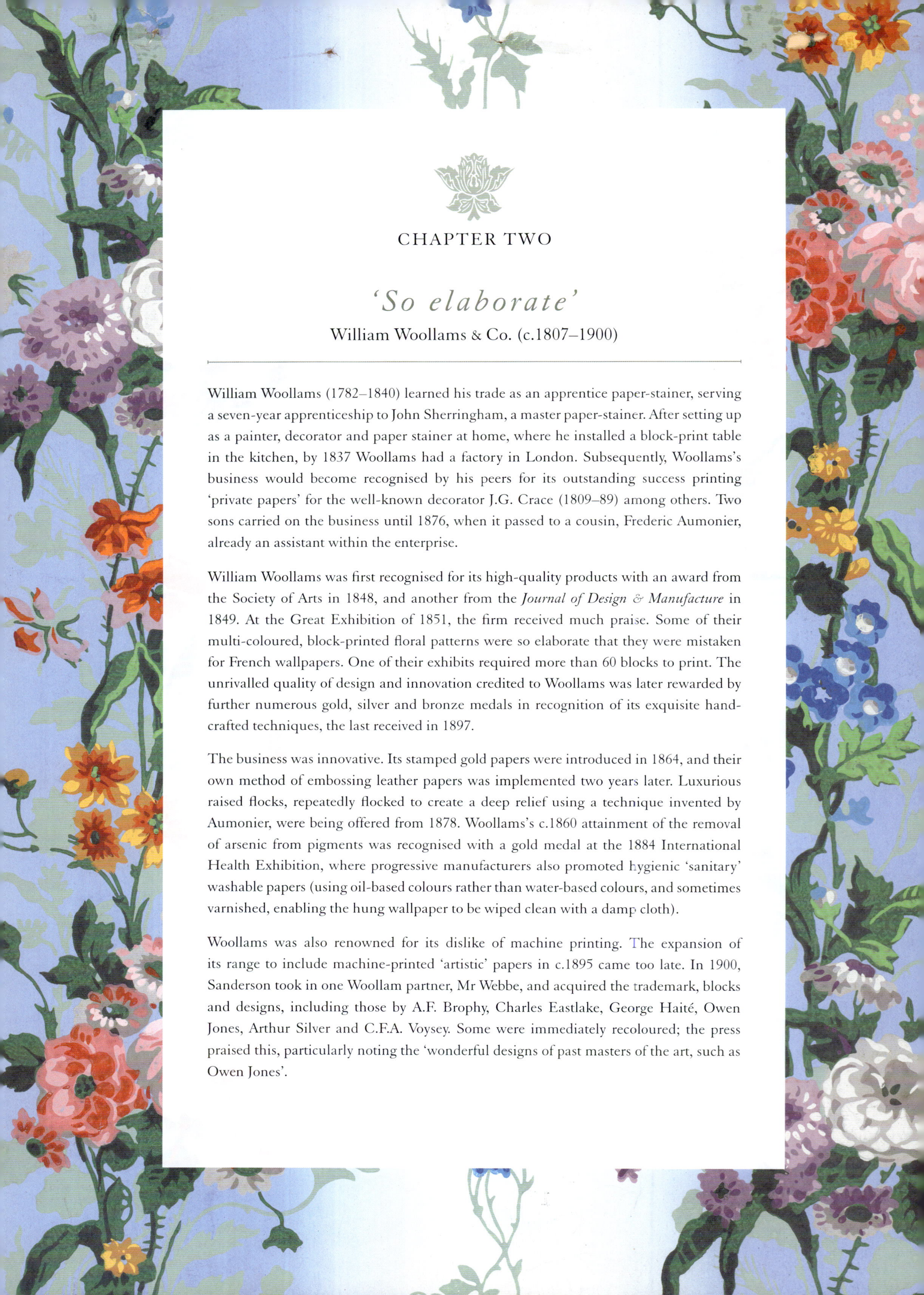

CHAPTER TWO

'So elaborate'

William Woollams & Co. (c.1807–1900)

William Woollams (1782–1840) learned his trade as an apprentice paper-stainer, serving a seven-year apprenticeship to John Sherringham, a master paper-stainer. After setting up as a painter, decorator and paper stainer at home, where he installed a block-print table in the kitchen, by 1837 Woollams had a factory in London. Subsequently, Woollams's business would become recognised by his peers for its outstanding success printing 'private papers' for the well-known decorator J.G. Crace (1809–89) among others. Two sons carried on the business until 1876, when it passed to a cousin, Frederic Aumonier, already an assistant within the enterprise.

William Woollams was first recognised for its high-quality products with an award from the Society of Arts in 1848, and another from the *Journal of Design & Manufacture* in 1849. At the Great Exhibition of 1851, the firm received much praise. Some of their multi-coloured, block-printed floral patterns were so elaborate that they were mistaken for French wallpapers. One of their exhibits required more than 60 blocks to print. The unrivalled quality of design and innovation credited to Woollams was later rewarded by further numerous gold, silver and bronze medals in recognition of its exquisite hand-crafted techniques, the last received in 1897.

The business was innovative. Its stamped gold papers were introduced in 1864, and their own method of embossing leather papers was implemented two years later. Luxurious raised flocks, repeatedly flocked to create a deep relief using a technique invented by Aumonier, were being offered from 1878. Woollams's c.1860 attainment of the removal of arsenic from pigments was recognised with a gold medal at the 1884 International Health Exhibition, where progressive manufacturers also promoted hygienic 'sanitary' washable papers (using oil-based colours rather than water-based colours, and sometimes varnished, enabling the hung wallpaper to be wiped clean with a damp cloth).

Woollams was also renowned for its dislike of machine printing. The expansion of its range to include machine-printed 'artistic' papers in c.1895 came too late. In 1900, Sanderson took in one Woollam partner, Mr Webbe, and acquired the trademark, blocks and designs, including those by A.F. Brophy, Charles Eastlake, George Haité, Owen Jones, Arthur Silver and C.F.A. Voysey. Some were immediately recoloured; the press praised this, particularly noting the 'wonderful designs of past masters of the art, such as Owen Jones'.

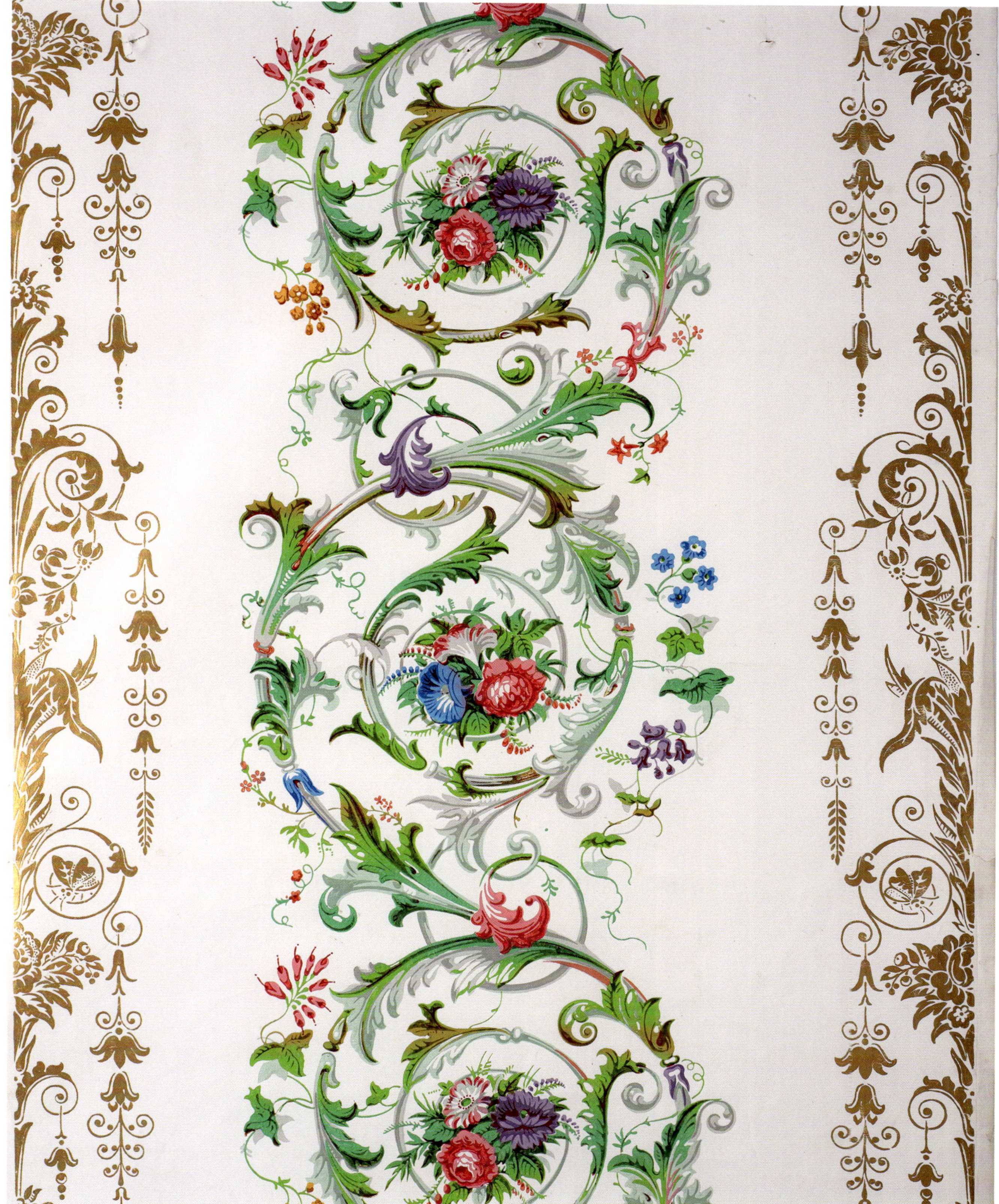

010 | *Flowers and Rococo Scrolls*, c.1850, William Woollams & Co.

This block-printed wallpaper has a design of popular garden flowers, including roses, morning glory, campanula and fuchsias. Arranged in delicate, scrolling rococo foliage, a framework in a more neo-classical arrangement completes what, on the wall, would have been a double-columned pattern. Woollams had a factory near Manchester Square in London.

Manufacturers diversified their ranges by printing the same design on differently grounded papers. This paper was printed in two versions by William Woollams & Co. The alternative version follows the fashion for imitation textiles by being printed on paper embossed to resemble moiré silk.

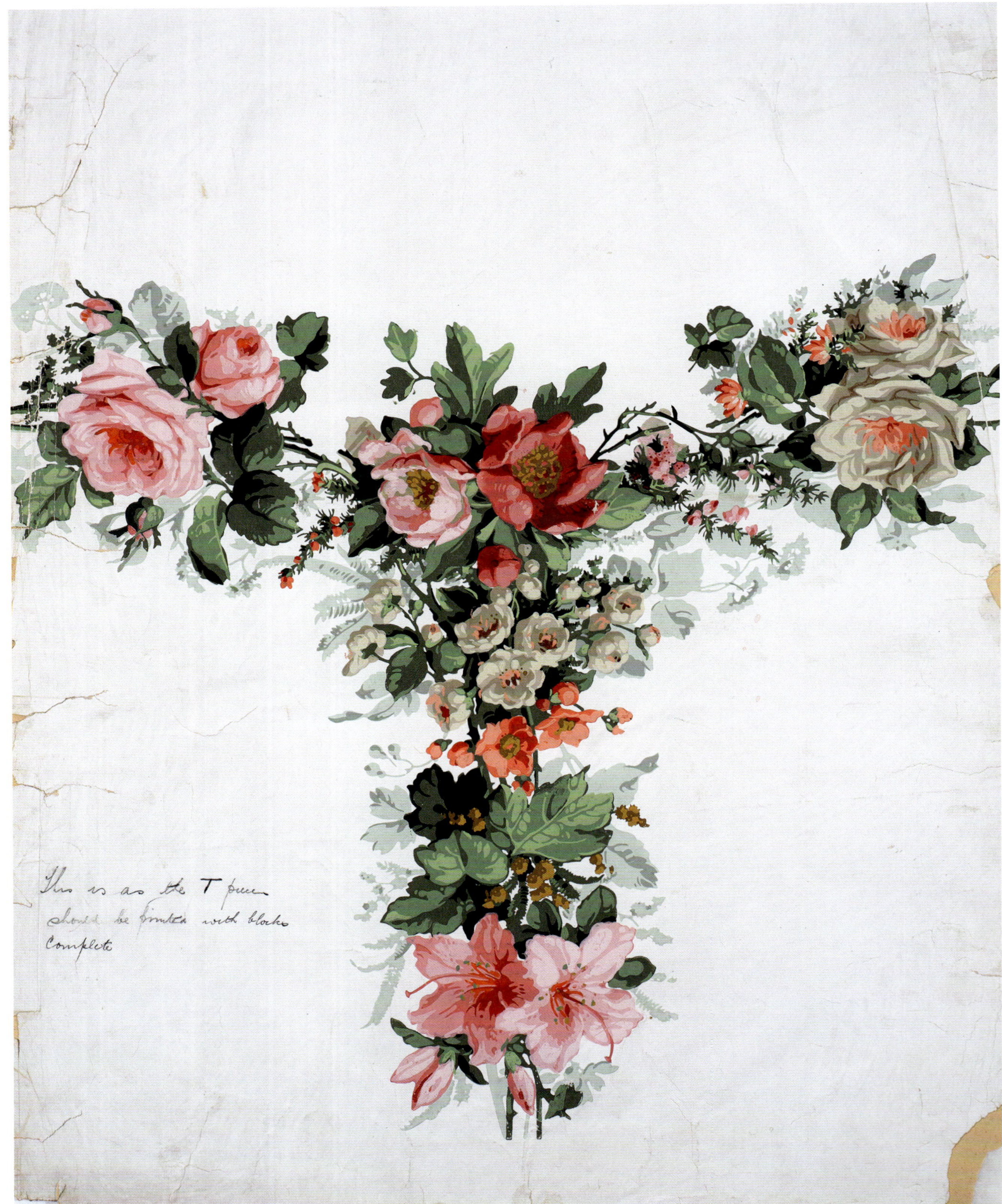

011 | *'T' piece with roses and azaleas*, c.1846, William Woollams & Co.

As one of England's oldest and most accomplished block-printing firms, Woollams was renowned for the quality of its printing. More than 22 printing blocks and a great deal of skill were needed to achieve the naturalistic three-dimensionality of this floral garland. Such elaborate borders were a conspicuous display of the taste and wealth of their owners.

'T'-shaped garlands such as this formed part of the borders used to create the effect of an indoor flowering arbour. They could also form part of a larger pilaster-and-panel decoration that mimicked carved architectural details. One such decoration requiring more than 60 blocks was exhibited by Woollams at the Great Exhibition of 1851.

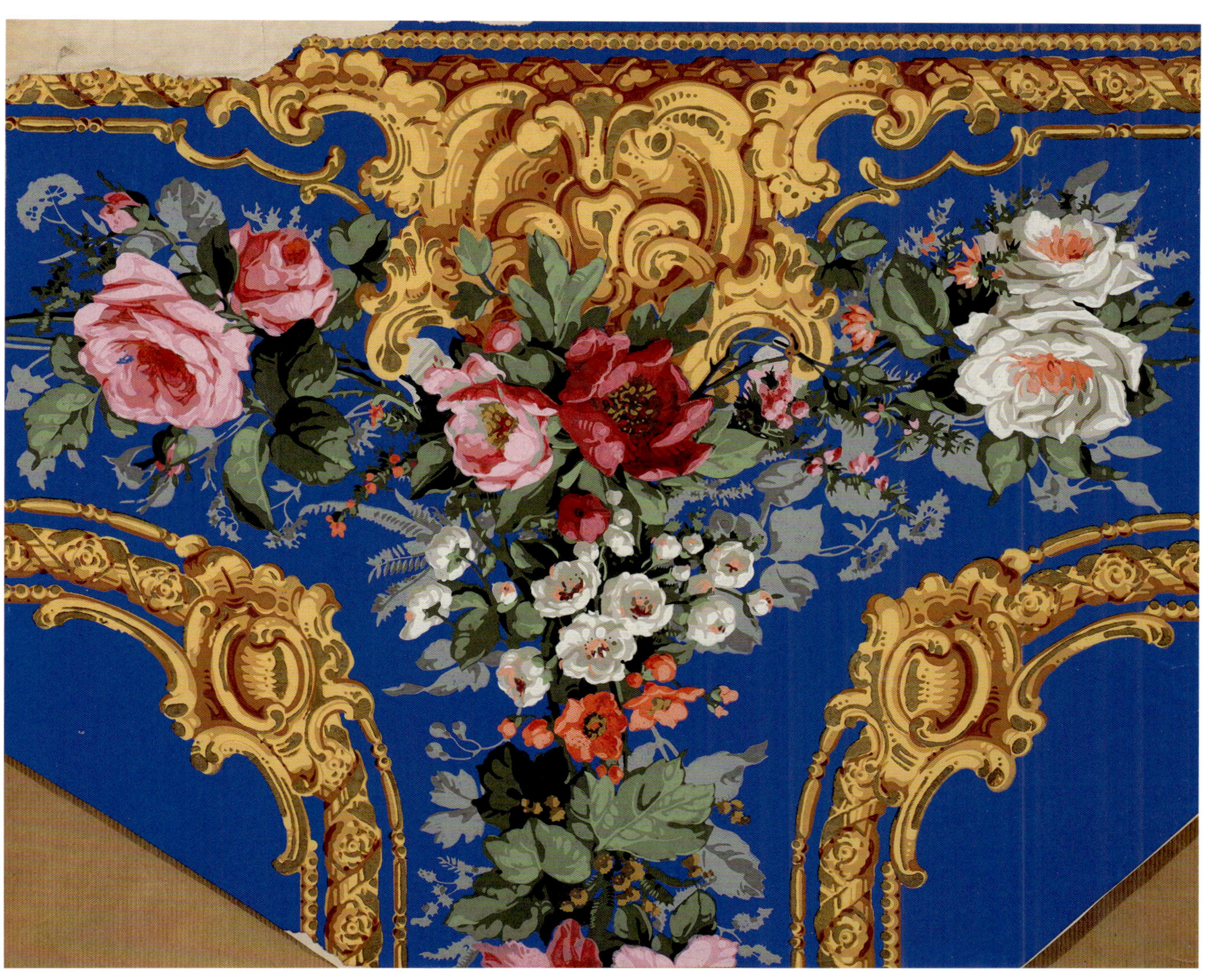

012 | *Border of roses and azaleas with gold rococo decoration*, c.1846, William Woollams & Co.

The flexibility of block-printing meant that designs could be printed with additional blocks. Here, you can see an alternative version of the 'T' piece shown left, this time printed with a rich lapis-blue ground and using additional blocks to create an ornate frame of rococo-style, gilded decoration.

Louis XIV-style decoration was one of the most popular historicist styles used in fashionable households in the mid-19th century. Typical of many such designs, it includes a combination of wild and cultivated roses and secondary flowers, including azaleas. The English design reform from the 1850s would call into question the taste for such elaborate papers.

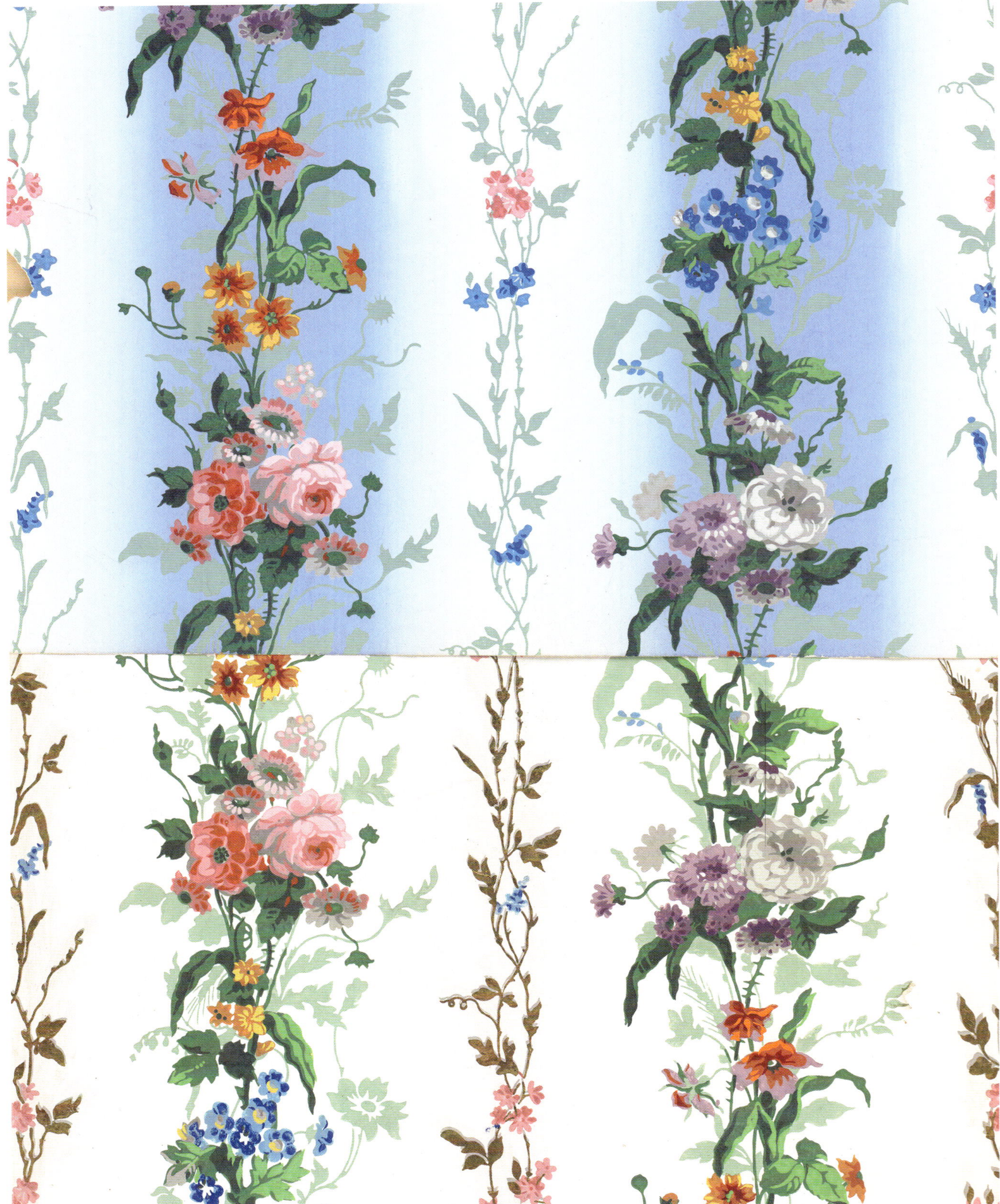

013 | *Flowers with irisé stripe*, c.1850, William Woollams & Co.

The term *irisé* refers to the upper paper's blue shading. It was created using a hand-brushing technique developed in c.1819 and perfected by French manufacturers who used it to create shaded areas on single ground-colour papers as seen here, or rainbow-effect papers with grounds blended with many colours.

Novelty and choice were significant factors in selling wallpapers. The lower example is an alternative version of a wallpaper using the same printing blocks but on a simple, polished ground. Its climbing trails of barley and wildflowers have been embellished with gold pigment.

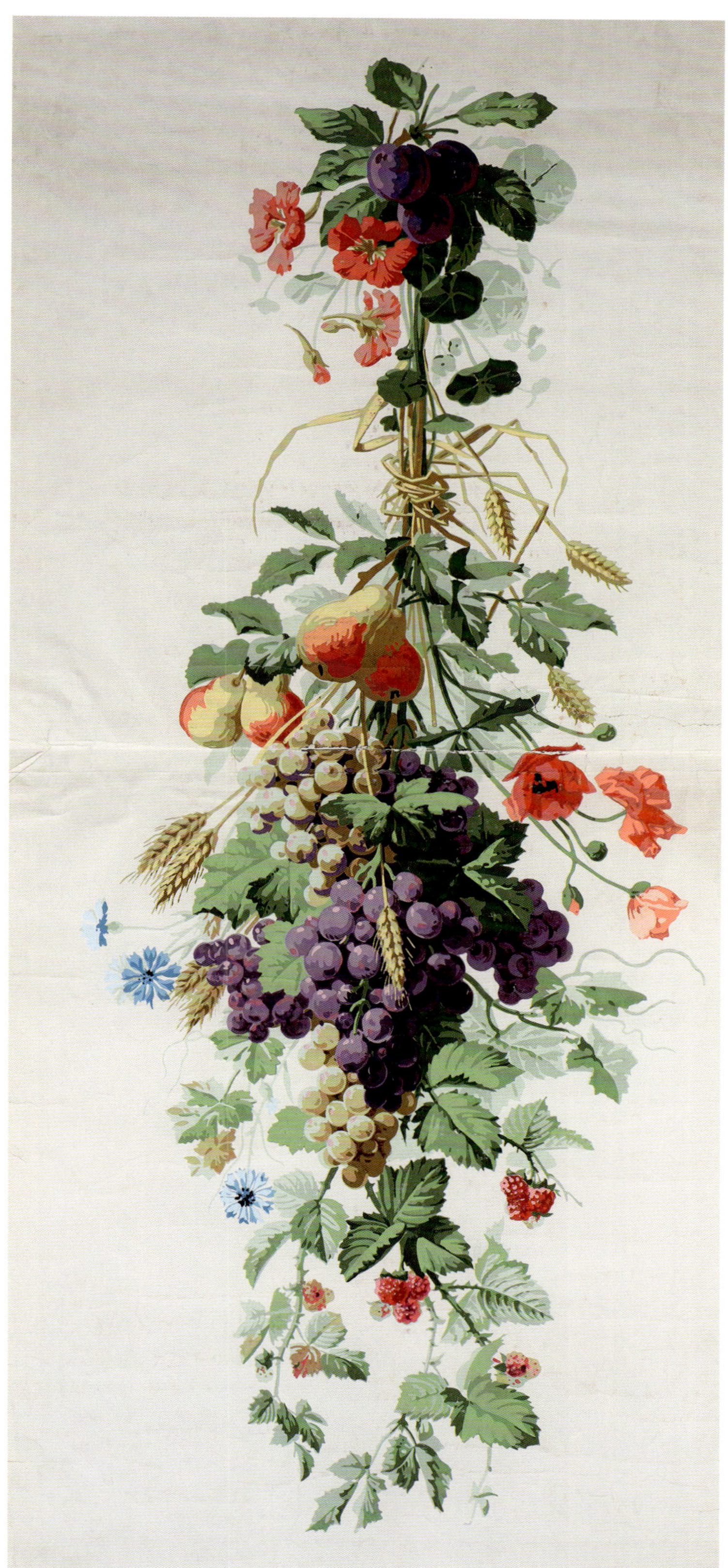

014 | *Four Seasons Panel*, 19th or early 20th century, attributed to William Woollams & Co.

This panel decoration with a design of seasonal fruit and flowers, probably 'Autumn', is part of a sequence of four seasonal prints. The scale and naturalistic detail of this paper suggests a date of c.1865 but valuable printing blocks frequently changed hands, so this sample may be a much later printing.

In 1900, Sanderson acquired the Woollams archive containing papers remarkable for realistic designs. The Edwardian era (1901–10) in England brought renewed popularity for mid-19th century chintzes, and the elements of this design, with its harvest-themed motifs, align with a romanticism in interior decoration that endured into the early-20th century.

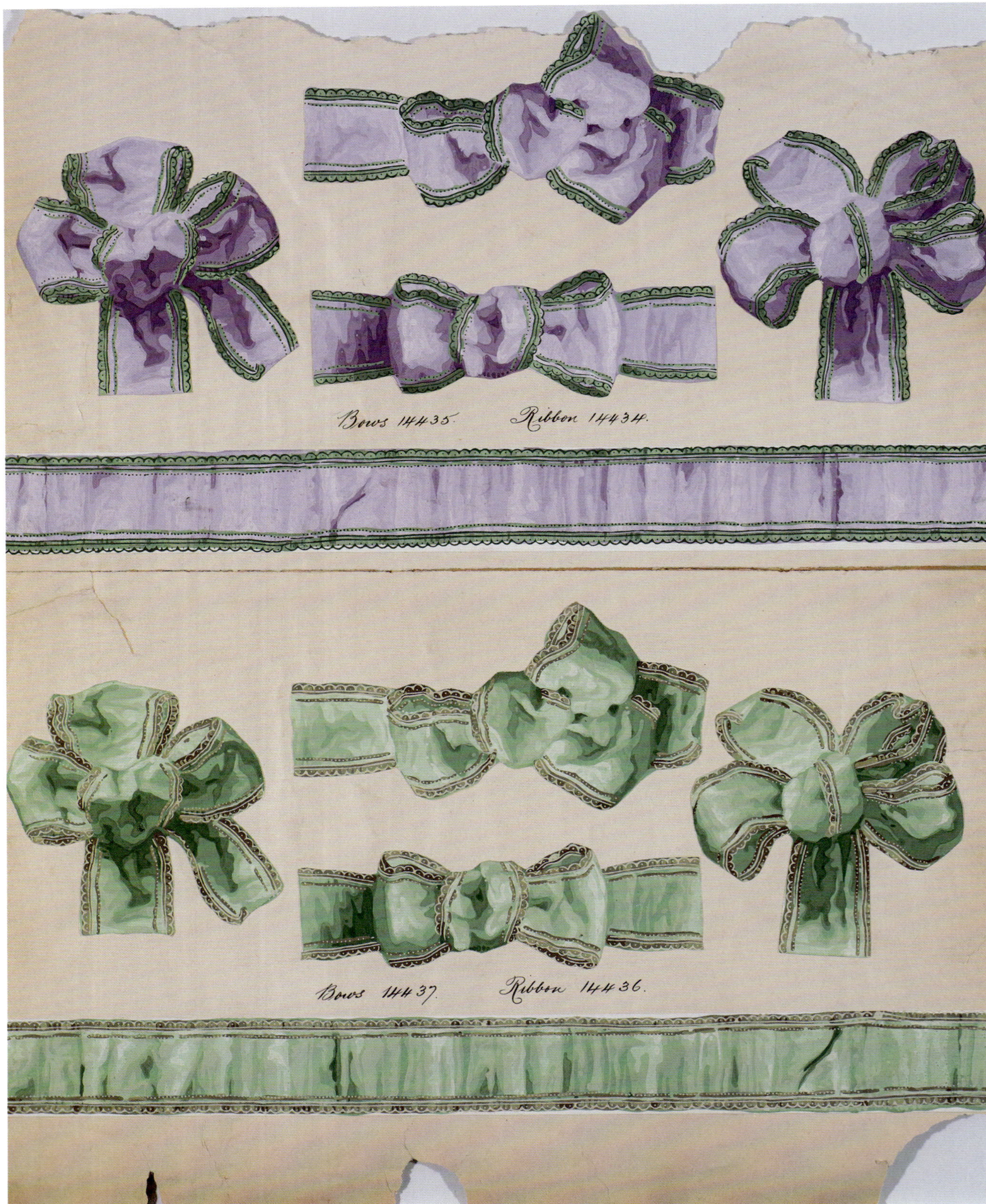

015 | *Ribbons and Bows*, early-19th century, William Woollams & Co.

Papers that mimicked the swags and folds of drapery were a response to the early-19th-century European fashion for 'tent rooms', created by the head-to-toe draping of rooms with fabrics. Such realism extended to ribbons and bows, seen here printed as 'cut-outs' to be used as simple borders on their own or as companions to striped or more elaborate wallpapers.

These have been mounted together on a page from a pattern book, are of exceptional quality and were printed using 11 different blocks. Woollams continued to print versions of these bows until their demise at the end of the 19th century, but earlier versions employ more tones of colour and are very finely detailed, as seen here.

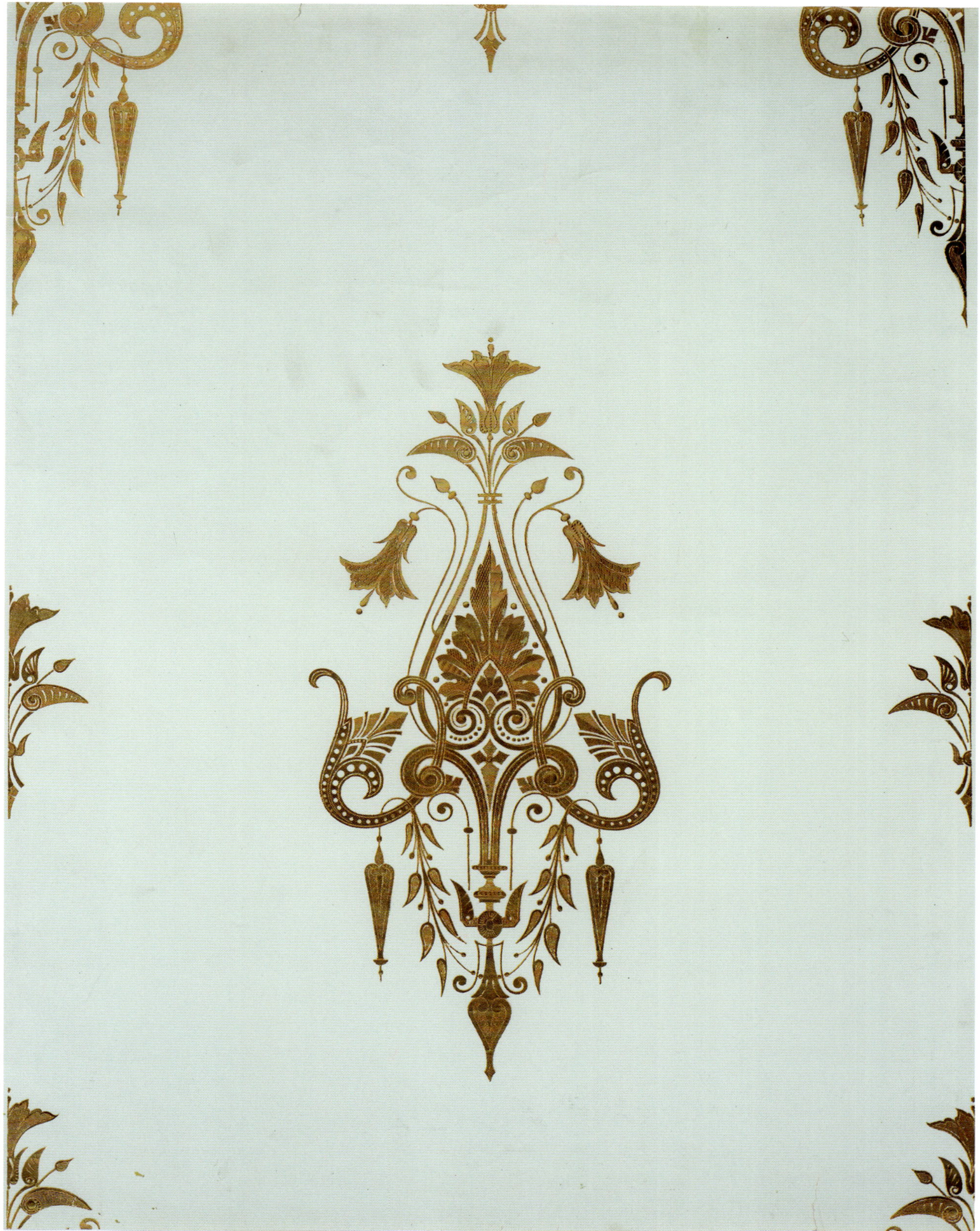

016 | *Stamped-Gilt Wallpaper*, c.1850, William Woollams & Co.

The soft colouring of stamped-gilt wallpapers was favoured particularly for sitting rooms and parlours. This paper's ground was coloured by hand before being block-printed with varnish. Metal leaf was then applied to the areas of pattern before being stamped under high pressure with cut metal dies that created highly detailed impressions.

Neo-classical styles of this type were particularly suitable for the gilding process, but floral sprigs and lace designs were also printed in this manner between about 1850 and 1875. All were part of Woollams's repertoire of luxury papers aimed at a growing, gentrified market during a period when the number of newly built houses in Britain doubled.

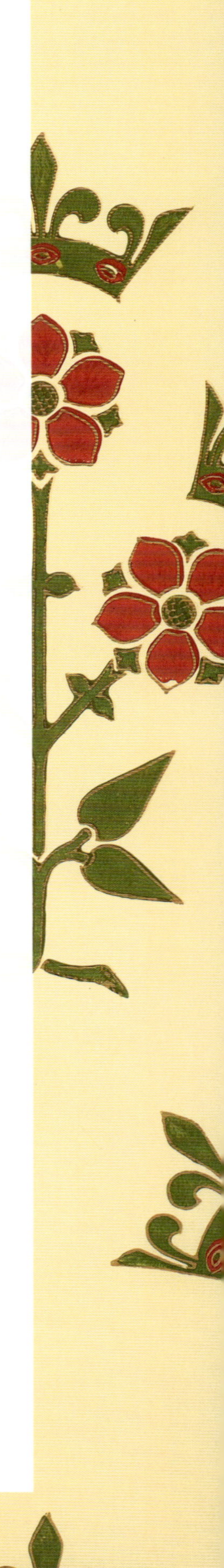

CHAPTER THREE

The Reform Movement

By the mid-1850s, contemporary-minded design reformers began to condemn wallpapers replicating naturalistic florals embellished with rococo motifs, much loved by most English households. For the reformers, their crusade was against such multi-coloured ornamental decoration, described by them as 'design debauchery'. These reformers strived to encourage the new generation of middle-class homeowners to create not only artistic but also hygienic, germ-free homes, endorsed by Charles Locke Eastlake's authoritative 1868 publication *Hints on Household Taste*, which also promoted the division of interior walls into dado, filling and frieze.

The two leading protagonists of the Reform Movement were the architect-designers Augustus Welby Northmore Pugin (1812–52) and Owen Jones (1809–74). Pugin is today most famous for his contribution to the neo-Gothic interiors of the Palace of Westminster (itself designed by architect Charles Barry and completed in 1860 with additions by Sir George Gilbert Scott). Pugin became synonymous with true British Gothic style, advocating the concepts of 'honesty and propriety' in ornament and design. His book *Contrasts, or, A parallel between the noble edifices of the fourteenth and fifteenth centuries, and similar buildings of the present day* (1836) was critical of the 19th-century tendency in architecture and interior design to borrow indiscriminately from historical styles.

In two other influential books, *On the Present State of Ecclesiastical Embroidery* (1843) and *Glossary of Ecclesiastical Ornament* (1844), Pugin illustrated juxtapositions of vivid colours and decorative patterns. Owen Jones also intended his patterns to work together. An influential architect, he is now remembered for his oft-reprinted book *The Grammar of Ornament* (1856), which changed the language of decorative art in Britain. Along with Henry Cole and Richard Redgrave at the South Kensington (now Victoria and Albert) Museum, Jones was a leading proponent of the British design reform movement.

Jones argued that good design followed rules of representation and colourings found in non-Western pattern, rejecting the naturalistic floral forms found in French wallpapers and traditional English chintzes. Among other points, these 37 'principles' specified ideal colour proportions and the importance of the use of outlines to underpin an impression of natural growth, both of which can be seen in many patterns by William Morris, who himself used Jones's designs as illustrations when lecturing. Of the two reformers, Owen Jones's wallpapers gained broader popularity as his patterns were more suited to the domestic interior than Pugin's. In 1900, when Sanderson acquired the entire portfolio of William Woollams's designs and blocks, most notable were those of Owen Jones.

017 | A.W.N. Pugin, *Palace of Westminster Wallpaper*, c.1848, Samuel Scott for J.G. Crace

This paper, block-printed with wool flock, is one of several produced to Pugin designs for the Palace of Westminster, where some survive in their style to the present day. The original palace was destroyed by fire in 1835, resulting in the commission of Westminster-born architect Charles Barry, who worked closely with Pugin on the Palace's neo-Gothic interiors.

William Morris shared A.W.N. Pugin's pre-occupation with medieval art, although Pugin's designs more closely emulate the stylisation of the Gothic originals. This design features a typically medieval arrangement of two-dimensional motifs, in this case roses and coronets, arranged within a vertical ogival pattern.

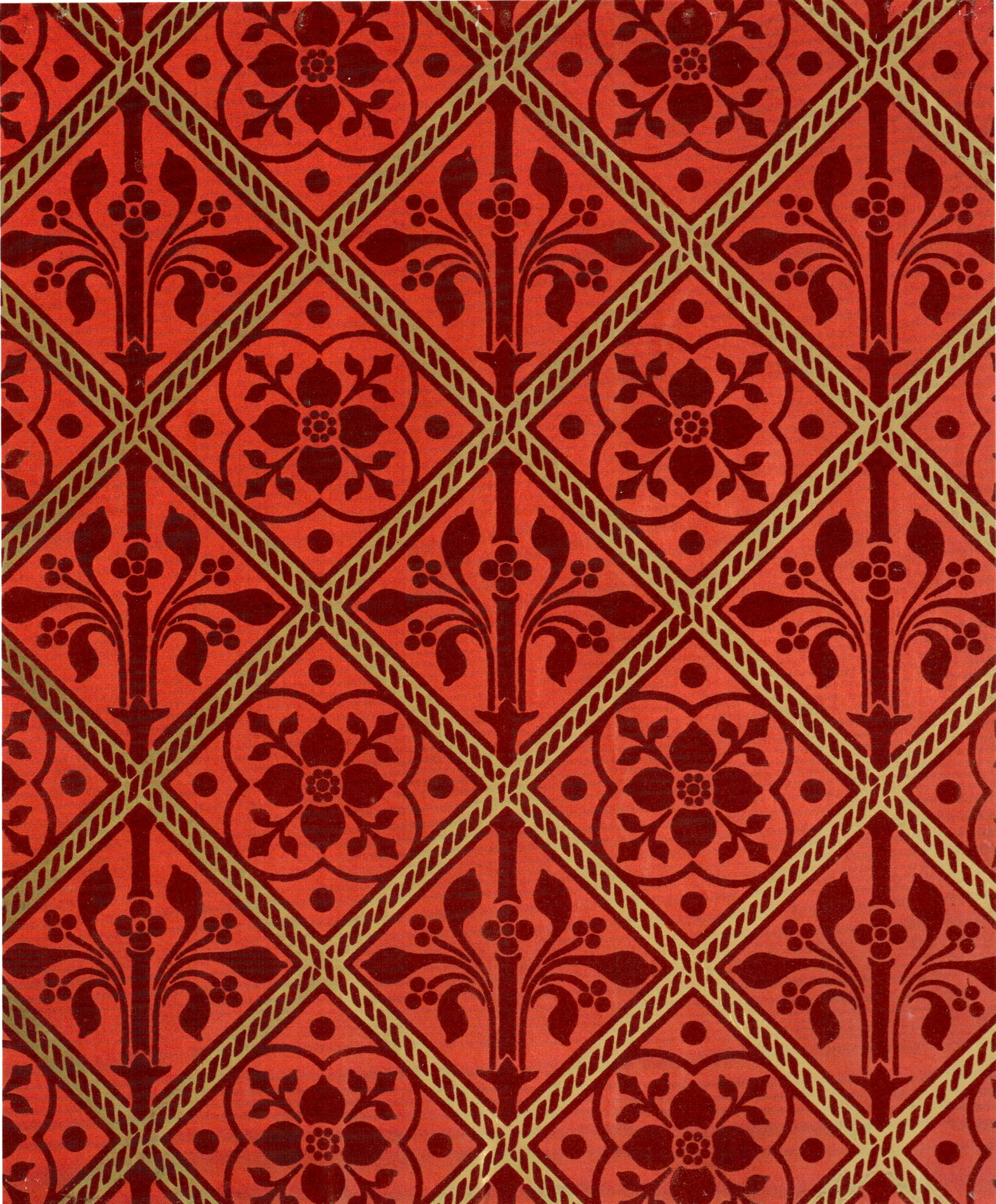

018 | A.W.N. Pugin, *Palace of Westminster Wallpaper*, c.1848, Samuel Scott for J.G. Crace

Simple diaper (diamond) patterns designed by Pugin appear in the pattern book of wallpapers supplied for the decoration of the Palace of Westminster between 1851 and 1859. Rich colours, in this case red and gold, and wool flocking create a sumptuous effect with a relatively modest design of repeating quatrefoils and foliate motifs.

Pugin converted to Catholicism in 1835 and wrote widely on the beauty of the simple geometric patterns carved into the stonework of medieval churches. For Pugin, design reform in Britain depended on the wide-scale adoption of Gothic ornament as a morally superior and truthful form of artistic and spiritual expression.

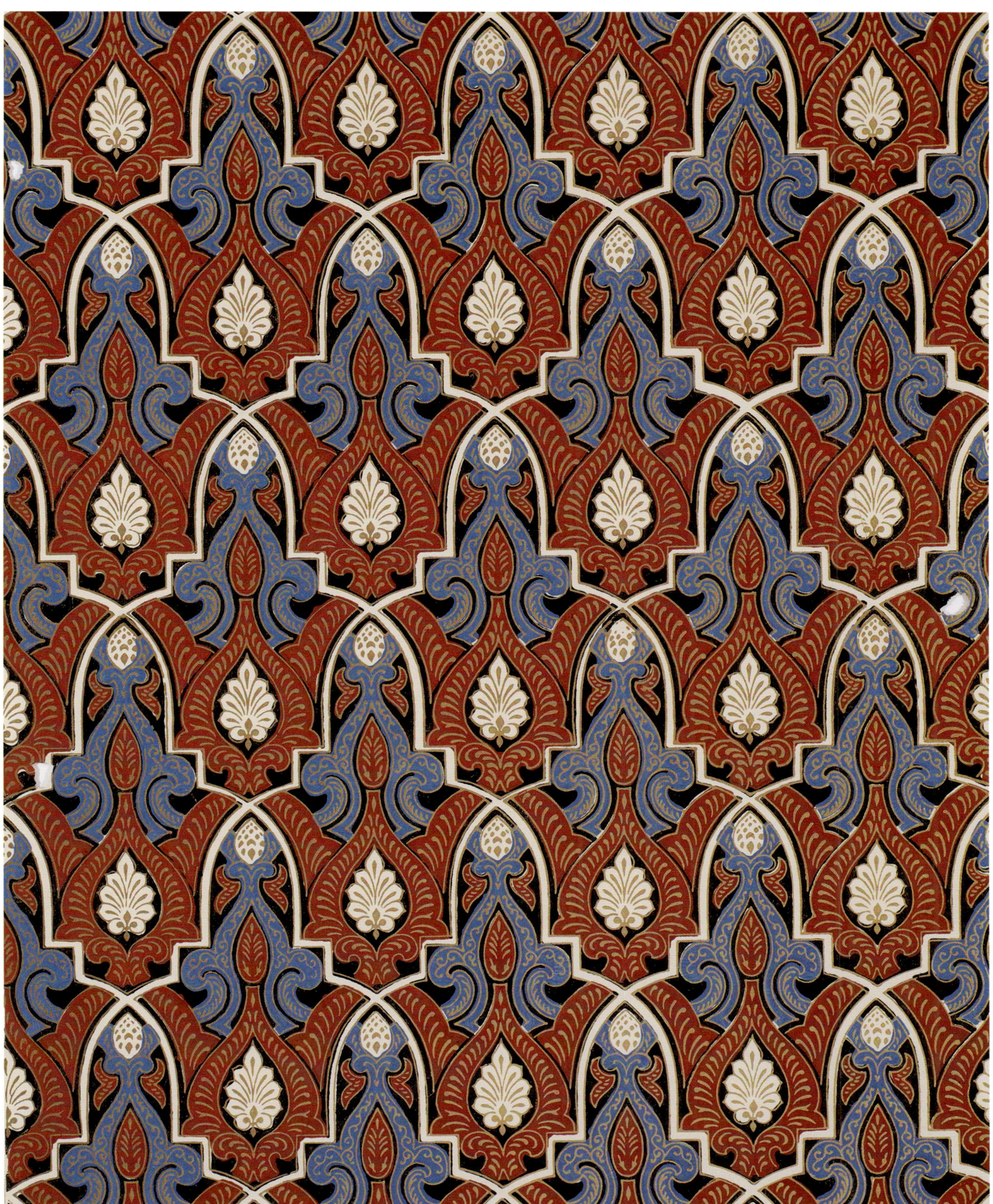

019 | Owen Jones, *Alhambra*, 1852, William Woollams & Co.

Block-printed in pigments and gold, the source of this design can be found in Jones's visual record of his visits to the Alhambra Palace in Granada, Spain in 1834 and 1837. He and the French architect Jules Goury (who died during the 1834 trip) were the first to study the Alhambra as a masterpiece of Islamic design.

Plans, Elevations, Sections and Details of the Alhambra was published by Jones in two volumes, the first in 1842 and the second in 1845. These publications were the first to be produced employing chromolithographic plates, the only process that could provide the necessary colour rendition. Note the use of line and contrast to create rhythmic movement.

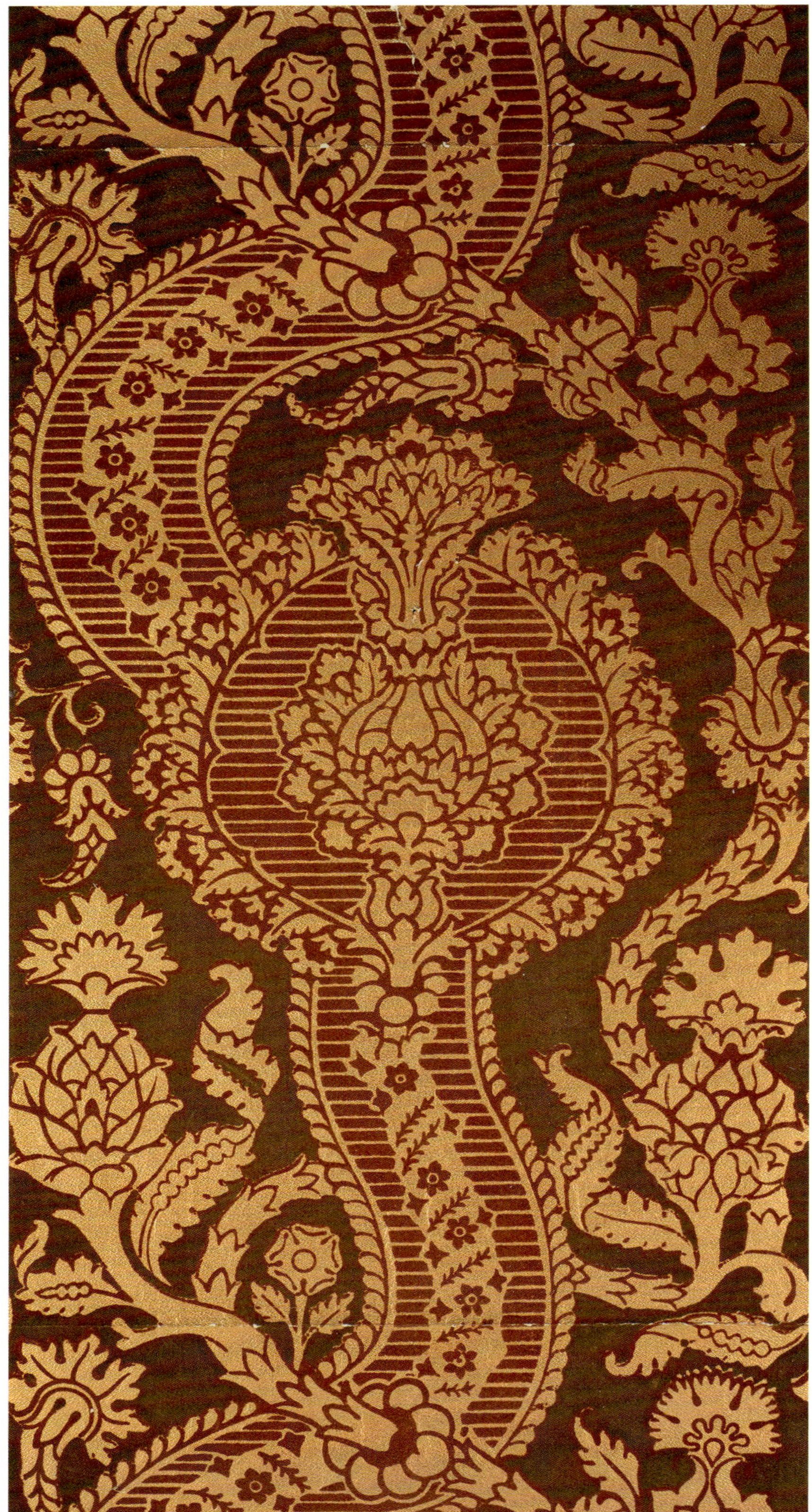

020 | A.W.N. Pugin, *Palace of Westminster 'Robing Room' Paper*, 1951 reproduction from c.1848 original, Arthur Sanderson & Sons Ltd

Woven textiles were also an inspiration to Pugin. Here, he has drawn upon a Flemish 15th-century silk design of thistles and Tudor roses arranged within a serpentine foliate structure. Probably first printed by Woollams, Sanderson reprinted this sample from a fragment taken from the Palace of Westminster. It remains today on the walls of The Queen's Robing Room.

Although only requiring two print blocks to create the pattern, such was the skill involved in printing this embossed and double-flocked wallpaper that a Perivale block-printer was brought out of retirement in 1970, when a further 76 replacement rolls were needed to refurbish the House of Lords committee rooms.

021 | C.F.A. Voysey, *The Aldworth*, c.1910 (designed), c.1918 (printed), Arthur Sanderson & Sons Ltd

Illustrated in the *Art Journal* in 1910, and unusually showing neo-Gothic influences, this design reflects Voysey's early training with John Pollard Seddon, a Gothic Revival architect who was influenced by John Ruskin. Pugin was also an early influence on Voysey: both shared the belief in the social, moral and spiritual value of the 'lesser arts' (decorative arts).

Unlike any of Pugin's wallpapers, all of which were block-printed, this sample is machine-printed in dark colours on linen-effect paper. The Sanderson stamp on the reverse shows that it was printed at the Sanderson factory in Chiswick. The paper sold for 20 shillings per roll, the equivalent of around £115 today.

022 | A.W.N. Pugin, *The Brinton*, c.1900 reproduction from c.1848 original, Samuel Scott for J.G. Crace

This is one of Pugin's most understated patterns with its design of simple repeating, stylised roses and coronets. The embossed surface and evidence of pattern book mounting of this sample suggest a later printing, perhaps dating from the early-20th century when Percy Heffer took over Scott's business, transferring the printing blocks in 1912 and becoming Heffer Scott & Co.

The original Palace of Westminster papers were printed by the wallpaper manufacturer Samuel Scott (of Scott, Cuthbertson & Co., founded as Hinchliff in 1796) under commission of the decorating firm of J.G. Crace, which built its reputation furnishing British royal households from the time of George III.

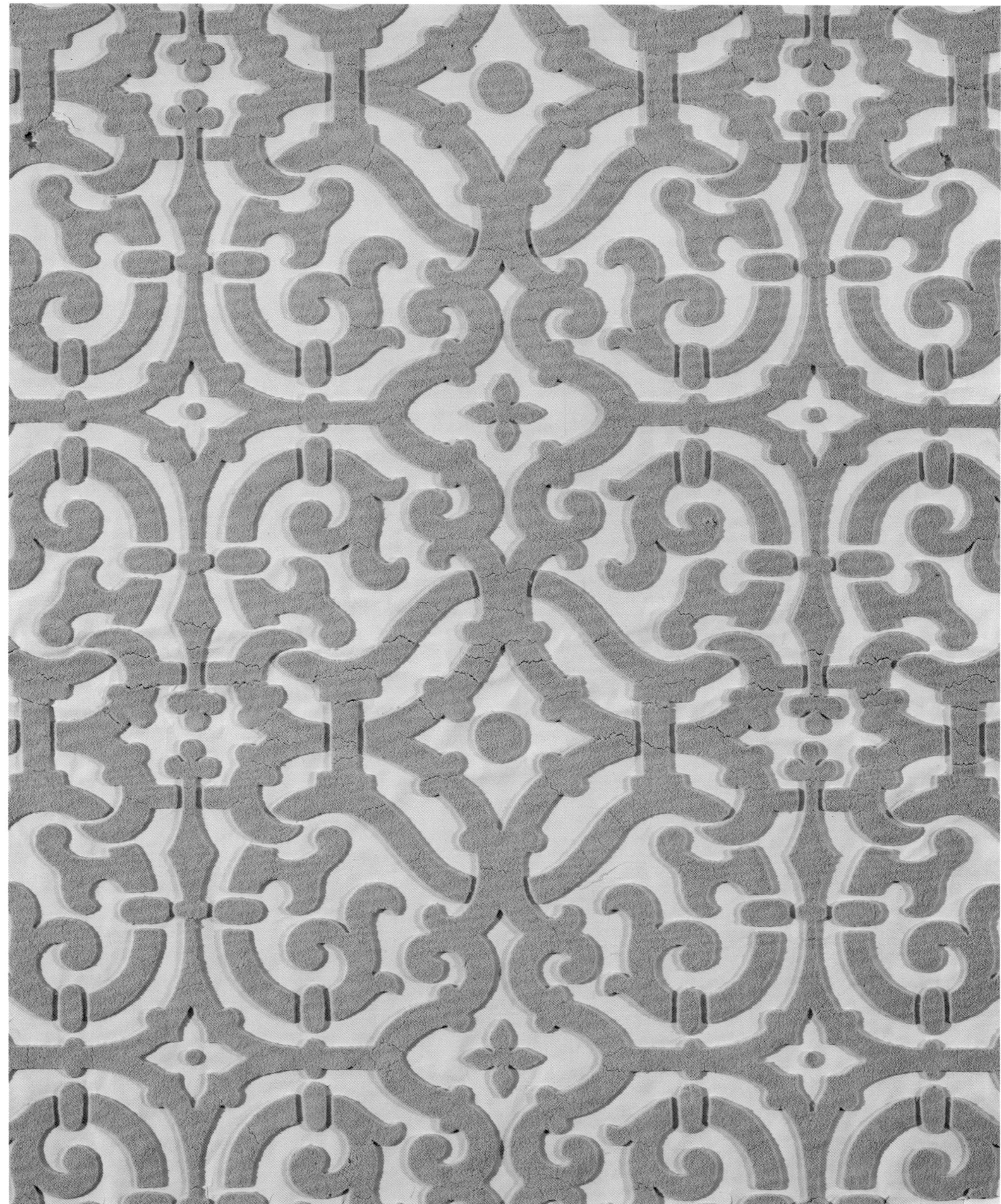

023 | *Flocked Ceiling Wallpaper*, c.1895, Percy Heffer

Wallpapers with non-directional, fretwork patterns like this were used as ceiling papers. This example has been block-printed and then flocked. Fretwork patterns printed in one or two colours mimicked the architectural detail of the plasterwork (stucco) used to ornament 17th-century ceilings.

Ceiling papers were replaceable and offered a practical and decorative solution to maintaining the appearance of cleanliness in rooms lit by gas and heated with coal fires. The textured surfaces of flock papers were notoriously difficult to keep clean, a problem resolved by neutral colour papers like this one that were suitable for over-painting.

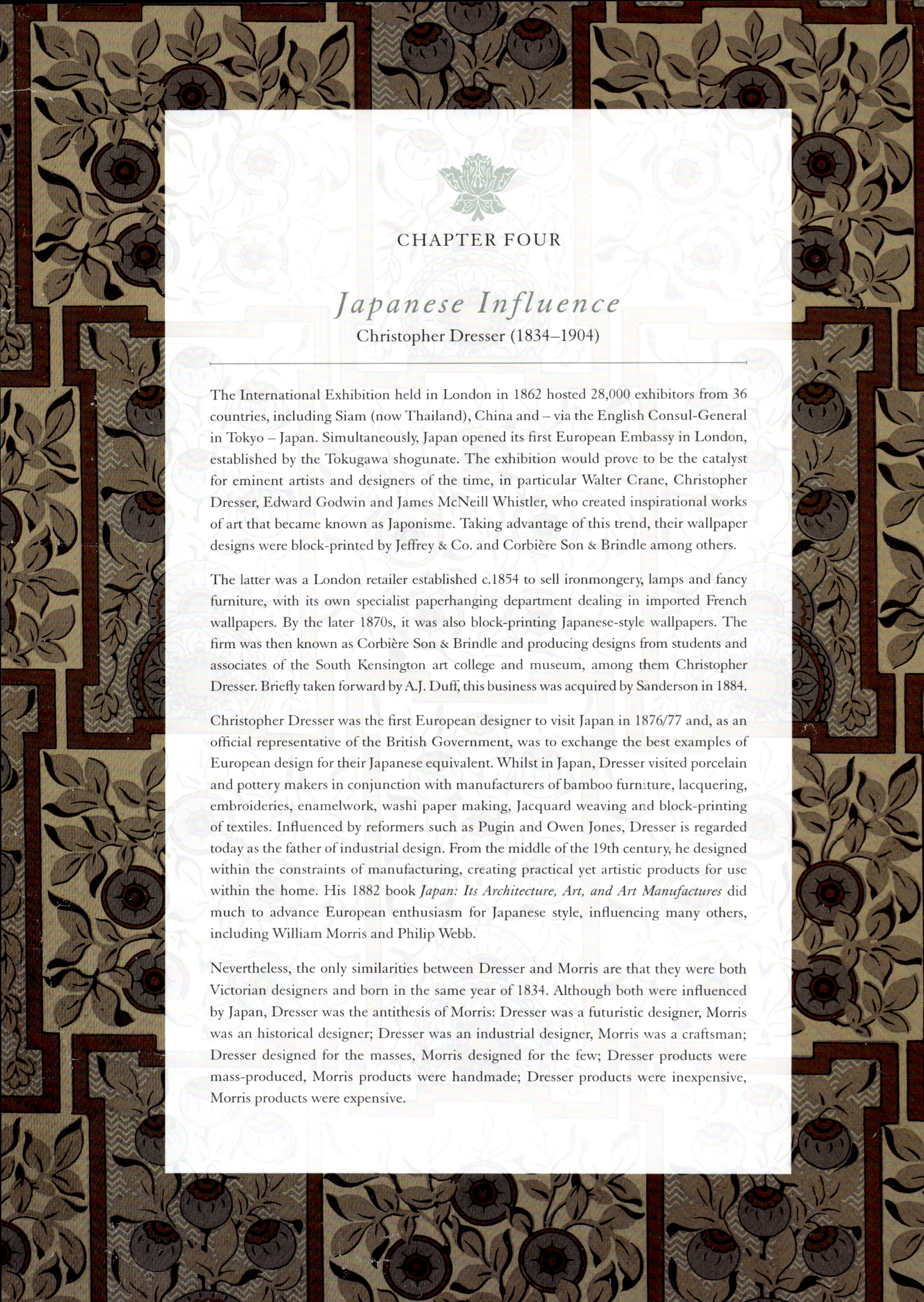

CHAPTER FOUR

Japanese Influence

Christopher Dresser (1834–1904)

The International Exhibition held in London in 1862 hosted 28,000 exhibitors from 36 countries, including Siam (now Thailand), China and – via the English Consul-General in Tokyo – Japan. Simultaneously, Japan opened its first European Embassy in London, established by the Tokugawa shogunate. The exhibition would prove to be the catalyst for eminent artists and designers of the time, in particular Walter Crane, Christopher Dresser, Edward Godwin and James McNeill Whistler, who created inspirational works of art that became known as Japonisme. Taking advantage of this trend, their wallpaper designs were block-printed by Jeffrey & Co. and Corbière Son & Brindle among others.

The latter was a London retailer established c.1854 to sell ironmongery, lamps and fancy furniture, with its own specialist paperhanging department dealing in imported French wallpapers. By the later 1870s, it was also block-printing Japanese-style wallpapers. The firm was then known as Corbière Son & Brindle and producing designs from students and associates of the South Kensington art college and museum, among them Christopher Dresser. Briefly taken forward by A.J. Duff, this business was acquired by Sanderson in 1884.

Christopher Dresser was the first European designer to visit Japan in 1876/77 and, as an official representative of the British Government, was to exchange the best examples of European design for their Japanese equivalent. Whilst in Japan, Dresser visited porcelain and pottery makers in conjunction with manufacturers of bamboo furniture, lacquering, embroideries, enamelwork, washi paper making, Jacquard weaving and block-printing of textiles. Influenced by reformers such as Pugin and Owen Jones, Dresser is regarded today as the father of industrial design. From the middle of the 19th century, he designed within the constraints of manufacturing, creating practical yet artistic products for use within the home. His 1882 book *Japan: Its Architecture, Art, and Art Manufactures* did much to advance European enthusiasm for Japanese style, influencing many others, including William Morris and Philip Webb.

Nevertheless, the only similarities between Dresser and Morris are that they were both Victorian designers and born in the same year of 1834. Although both were influenced by Japan, Dresser was the antithesis of Morris: Dresser was a futuristic designer, Morris was an historical designer; Dresser was an industrial designer, Morris was a craftsman; Dresser designed for the masses, Morris designed for the few; Dresser products were mass-produced, Morris products were handmade; Dresser products were inexpensive, Morris products were expensive.

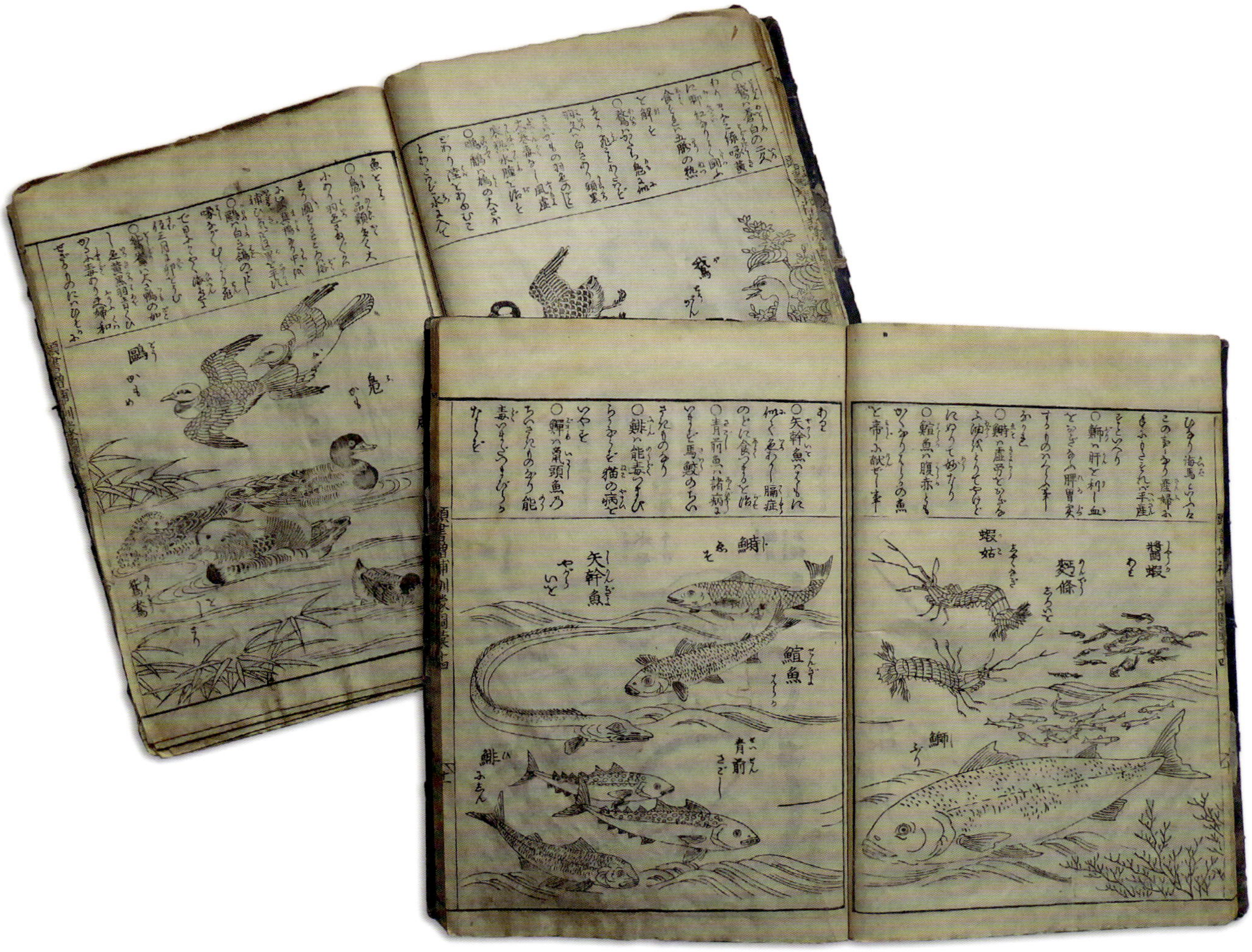

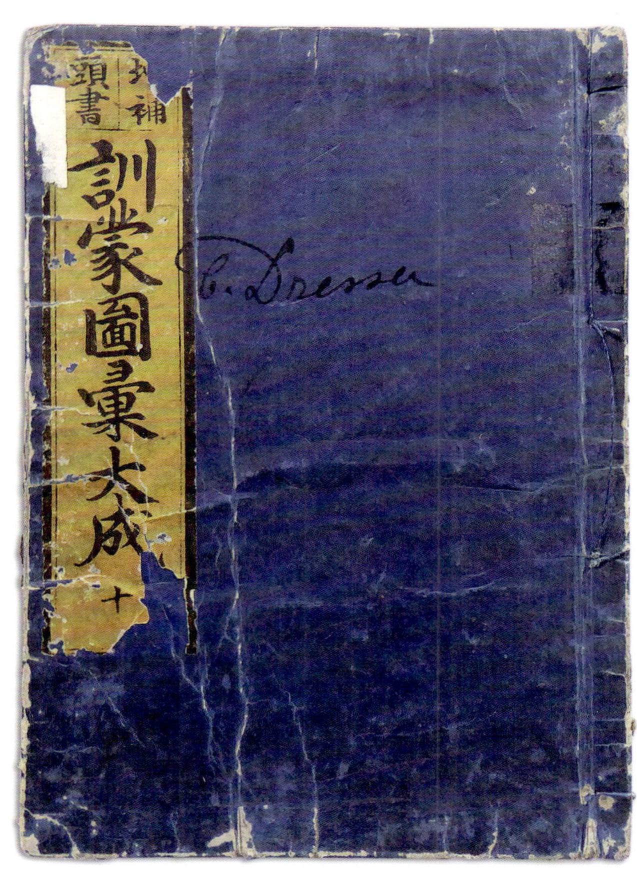

024 | *Dr. Dresser's reference books*, c.1800, Japanese Wood Cuts

During his trip to Japan in 1876/77, Christopher Dresser acquired a number of block-printed books, each illustrating various decorative 'topics', such as fish and fruit. Following his exhilarating but exhausting visit, his resultant design style would be one of elegant simplicity based on these topics and artefacts he acquired.

In 1882, Dresser's book *Japan: Its Architecture, Art, and Art Manufactures* was published by Longmans Green & Co. In it, he wrote: 'Many will be surprised when I say that as yet the English know almost nothing, and even our architects very little, of Japanese architecture.' That this ceased to be the case was in part due to Dresser's promotion of Japonisme.

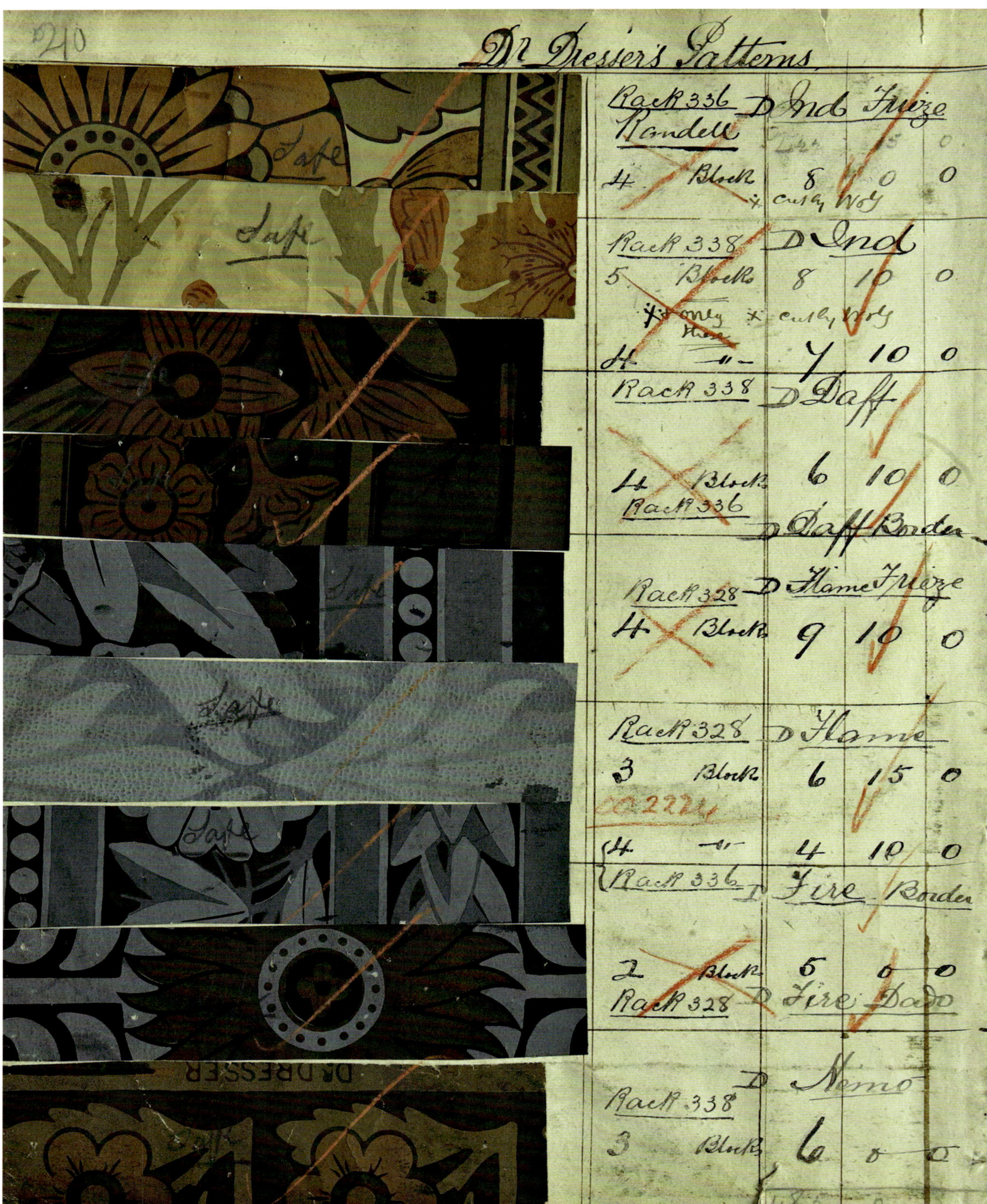

025 | *Dr Dresser's Patterns Page*, 1873, Jeffrey & Co.

Apart from printing the entire Morris & Co. collection of wallpapers, Jeffreys also printed 'private' patterns by notable designers, including Walter Crane, Owen Jones, C.F.A. Voysey and, of course, Christopher Dresser. This page from one of many Jeffrey & Co. logbooks presents the original approved samples of various *Dr Dresser Patterns.*

The small cuttings show the near-perfect colours of the first printing. Each cutting has a notation providing essential details. For example, given for the sample at the top of the page are the print block location (Rack 336), the number of blocks (4), the block maker (Mr Randall), the design name (*Indian Frieze*) and the cost of making the set of blocks (£8.00).

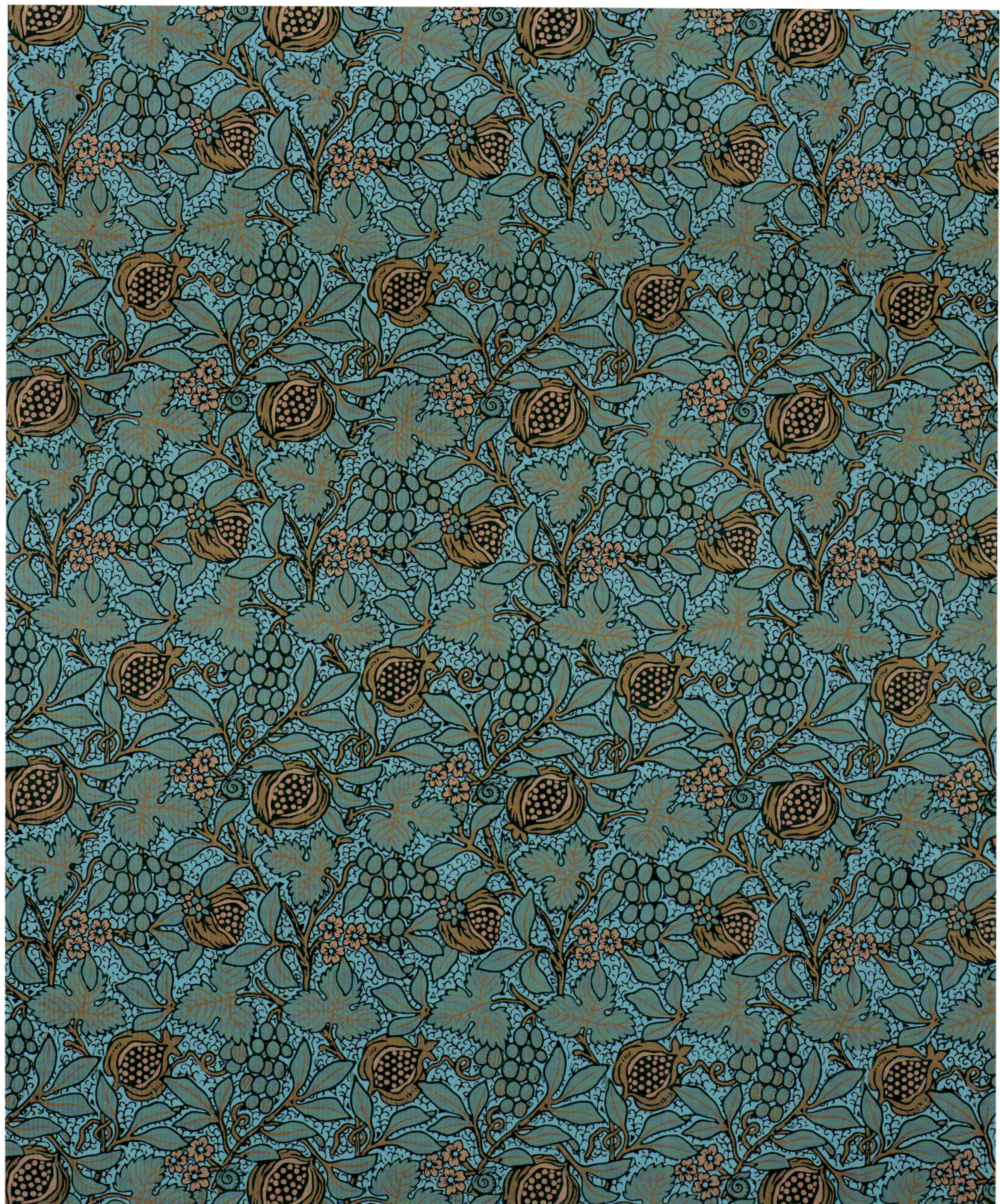

026 | In the style of Christopher Dresser, *Pomegranate*, 1876, Corbière Son & Brindle

Christopher Dresser was one of a number of designers commissioned by Corbière to design novel wallpapers. Although not directly attributed, stylistically this design suggests Dresser's work, or that of another designer who was strongly influenced by patterns from Japan. It was one of several similarly styled papers produced by Corbière at this time.

The Ornamental Design Act of 1842 gave manufacturers the ability to register original designs with the British Board of Trade, and to protect their right to be the sole producer for up to three years. This richly coloured design was one of several designs copyright registered by Corbière Son & Brindle on 25 and 26 September 1876.

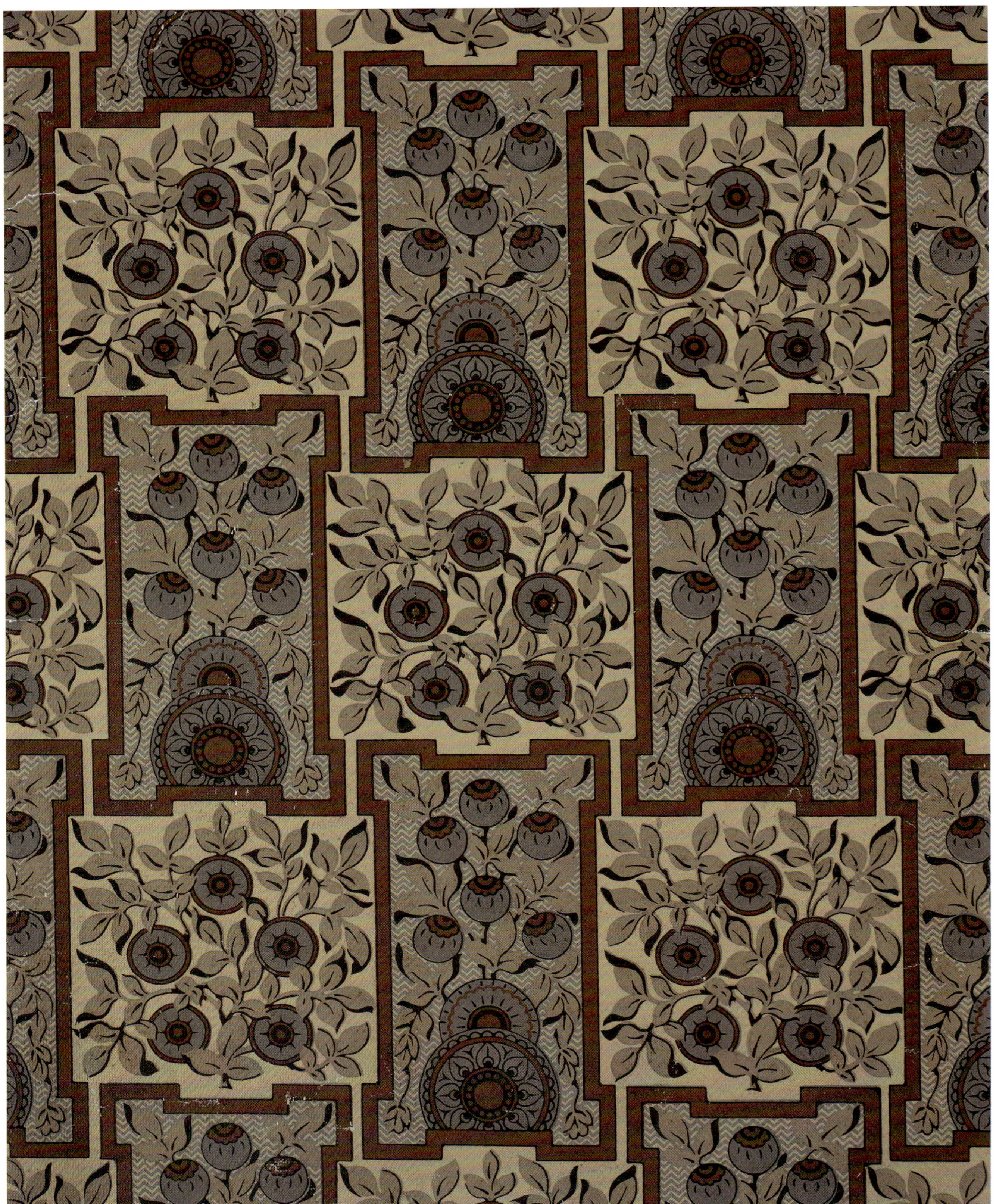

027 | Attributed to Christopher Dresser, *Anglo-Japanese Wallpaper*, 1876, Corbière, Son & Brindle

This flamé-embossed block-print with its tile layout perfectly illustrates the fusion of geometric and natural form that incorporates both Japanese-influenced motifs and an 'architectural' layout more reflective of Dresser's interaction with Owen Jones, whom he met and worked with while teaching at the South Kensington schools from 1855–68.

A freelance designer, Dresser created wallpapers, textiles and carpets for over 30 firms in Britain, Ireland, France and the United States, as well as ceramics and cast-iron furniture and metalwork. His Art Furnishers' Alliance opened in 1880 in London on New Bond Street, with Morris & Co., Liberty's, the Fine Art Society and the Grosvenor Gallery all nearby.

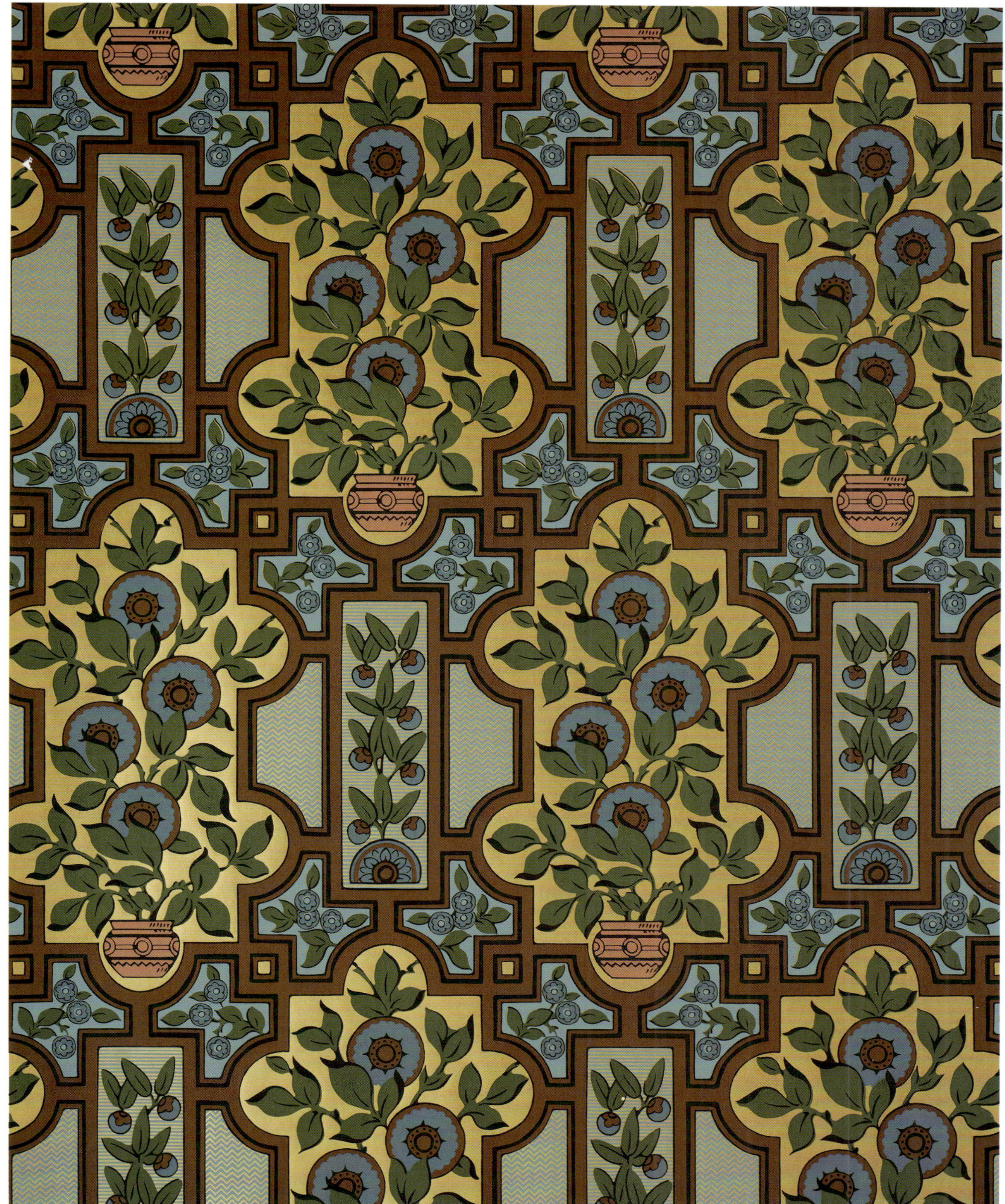

028 | Christopher Dresser (attrib.), *The Glenview Paper*, 1999 screen print (from 1876 design), Arthur Sanderson & Sons Ltd

This wallpaper is a screen print adapted from the original manufactured by Corbière Son & Brindle in 1876 and thought to be by Christopher Dresser. The screen-printed version was created by Sanderson at its Brook Mill print works on commission for architect Page Ayres Cowley, as part of her restoration of Glenview House, in Yonkers, New York.

The commission involved producing two papers, a frieze and a border as replacements for the papers installed at the house in the 1870s by its owner, the banker John Bond Trevor. Gold pigment gave the design a three-dimensionality enlivening the pattern when seen in gas-lit rooms. The 1999 screen print was colour-matched to the original papers at Glenview.

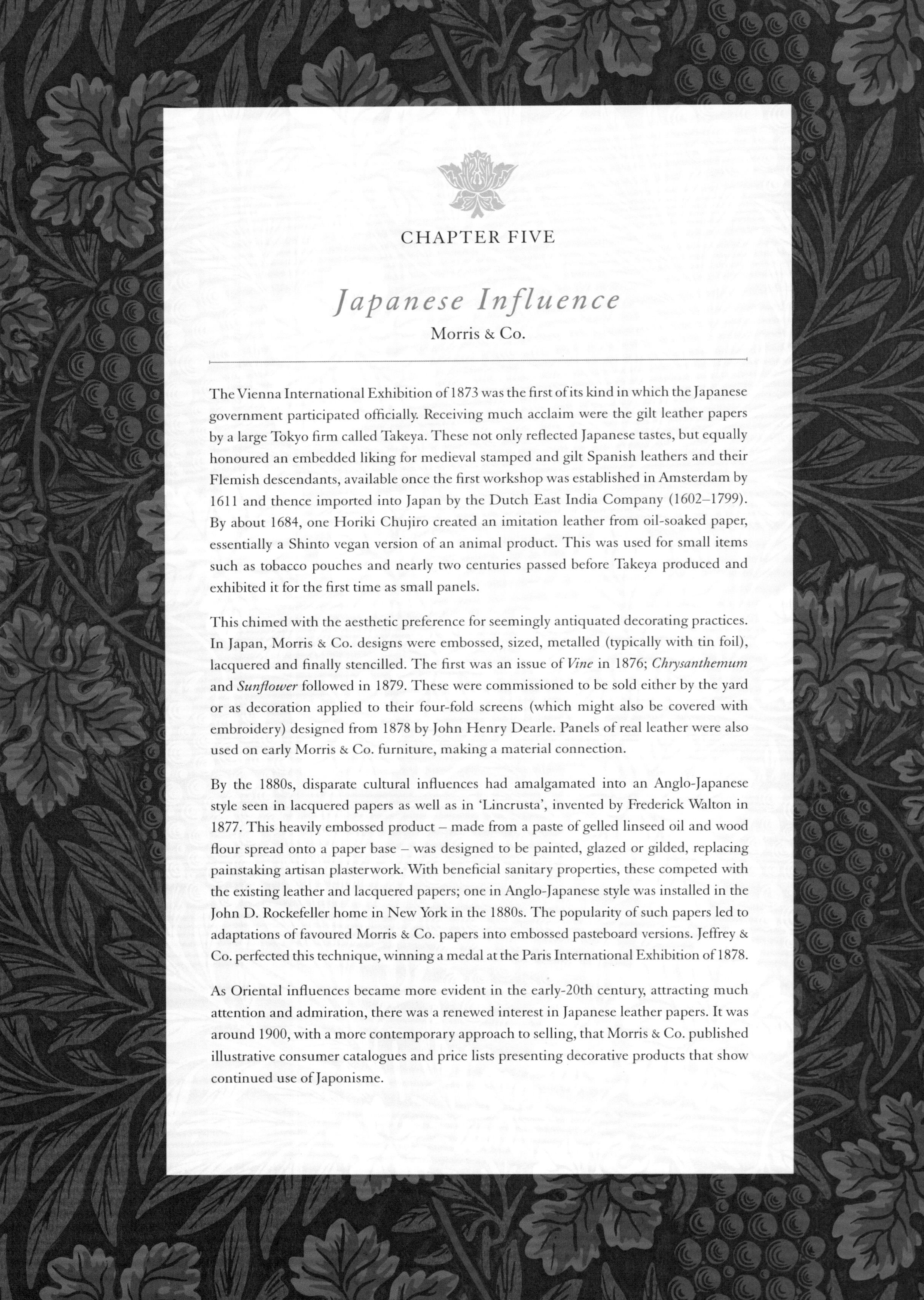

CHAPTER FIVE

Japanese Influence

Morris & Co.

The Vienna International Exhibition of 1873 was the first of its kind in which the Japanese government participated officially. Receiving much acclaim were the gilt leather papers by a large Tokyo firm called Takeya. These not only reflected Japanese tastes, but equally honoured an embedded liking for medieval stamped and gilt Spanish leathers and their Flemish descendants, available once the first workshop was established in Amsterdam by 1611 and thence imported into Japan by the Dutch East India Company (1602–1799). By about 1684, one Horiki Chujiro created an imitation leather from oil-soaked paper, essentially a Shinto vegan version of an animal product. This was used for small items such as tobacco pouches and nearly two centuries passed before Takeya produced and exhibited it for the first time as small panels.

This chimed with the aesthetic preference for seemingly antiquated decorating practices. In Japan, Morris & Co. designs were embossed, sized, metalled (typically with tin foil), lacquered and finally stencilled. The first was an issue of *Vine* in 1876; *Chrysanthemum* and *Sunflower* followed in 1879. These were commissioned to be sold either by the yard or as decoration applied to their four-fold screens (which might also be covered with embroidery) designed from 1878 by John Henry Dearle. Panels of real leather were also used on early Morris & Co. furniture, making a material connection.

By the 1880s, disparate cultural influences had amalgamated into an Anglo-Japanese style seen in lacquered papers as well as in 'Lincrusta', invented by Frederick Walton in 1877. This heavily embossed product – made from a paste of gelled linseed oil and wood flour spread onto a paper base – was designed to be painted, glazed or gilded, replacing painstaking artisan plasterwork. With beneficial sanitary properties, these competed with the existing leather and lacquered papers; one in Anglo-Japanese style was installed in the John D. Rockefeller home in New York in the 1880s. The popularity of such papers led to adaptations of favoured Morris & Co. papers into embossed pasteboard versions. Jeffrey & Co. perfected this technique, winning a medal at the Paris International Exhibition of 1878.

As Oriental influences became more evident in the early-20th century, attracting much attention and admiration, there was a renewed interest in Japanese leather papers. It was around 1900, with a more contemporary approach to selling, that Morris & Co. published illustrative consumer catalogues and price lists presenting decorative products that show continued use of Japonisme.

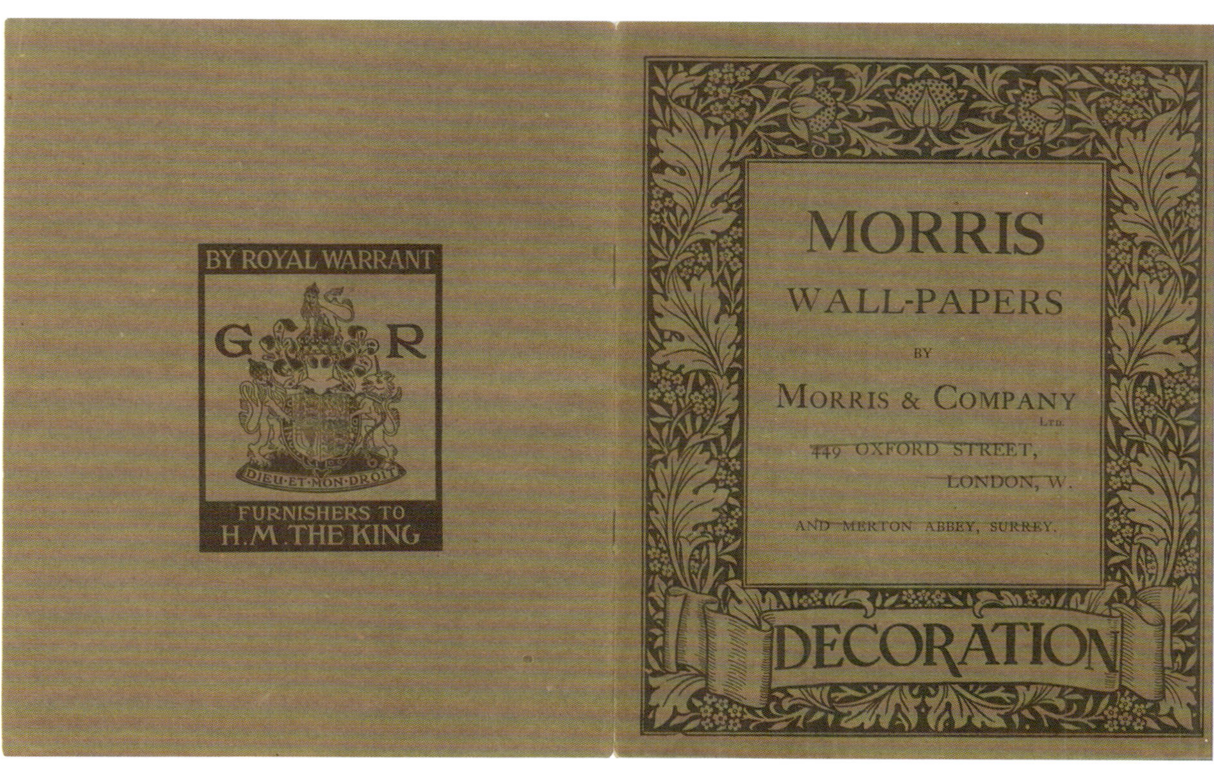

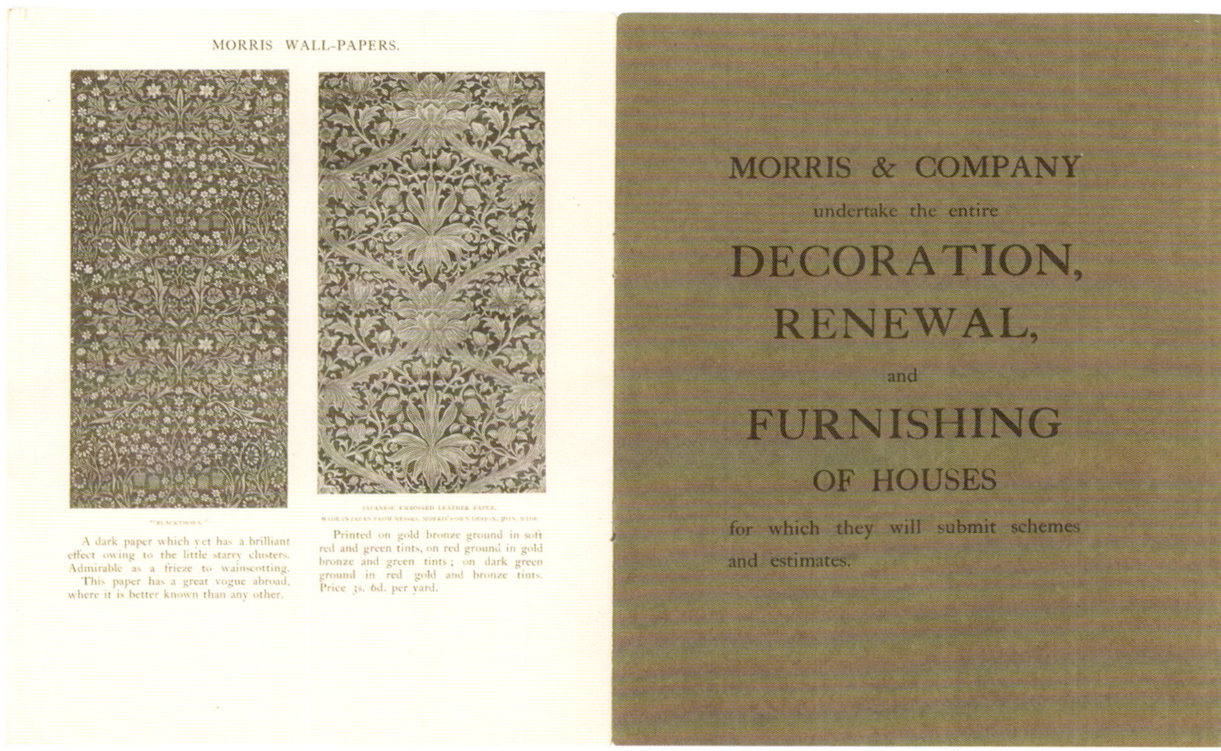

029 | *Decoration: Morris Wallpapers*, c.1906, Morris & Co.

Now styled Morris & Co. Decorators Ltd (1905–17), this publication stresses the identity of 'Morris wallpapers' at a time when only Liberty and Voysey could command the same brand recognition. Other individual catalogues promoted Morris embroidery, upholstered furniture, furniture and interior decoration, house decorating and furnishing, and tapestries.

Included are block-printed wallpapers such as *Blackthorn* (left), noted as enjoying 'a great vogue abroad, where it is better known than any other'. Also illustrated is one of the exclusively commissioned Japanese-style embossed papers, in this instance (right) printed in three colourways, including one on a 'gold bronze ground in soft red and green tints'.

030 | William Morris, *Chrysanthemum*, 1877, Jeffrey & Co. for Morris & Co.

The chrysanthemum, called *kiku* in Japanese, symbolises the autumn season but has other auspicious meanings, namely longevity, rejuvenation and nobility. The latter arises from its use since the 5th century on the imperial crest. The monarchy is called the 'Chrysanthemum Throne'; the yellow mum remains the symbol of the Japanese emperor today.

1877 was, perhaps, one of the busiest and most creative periods for William Morris, with the opening of his London showroom in Oxford Street and designing for block-printed wallpaper and fabrics as well as those for Jacquard weaving. Aside from penning lectures and prose, it was in this year that he co-founded the Society for the Protection of Ancient Buildings.

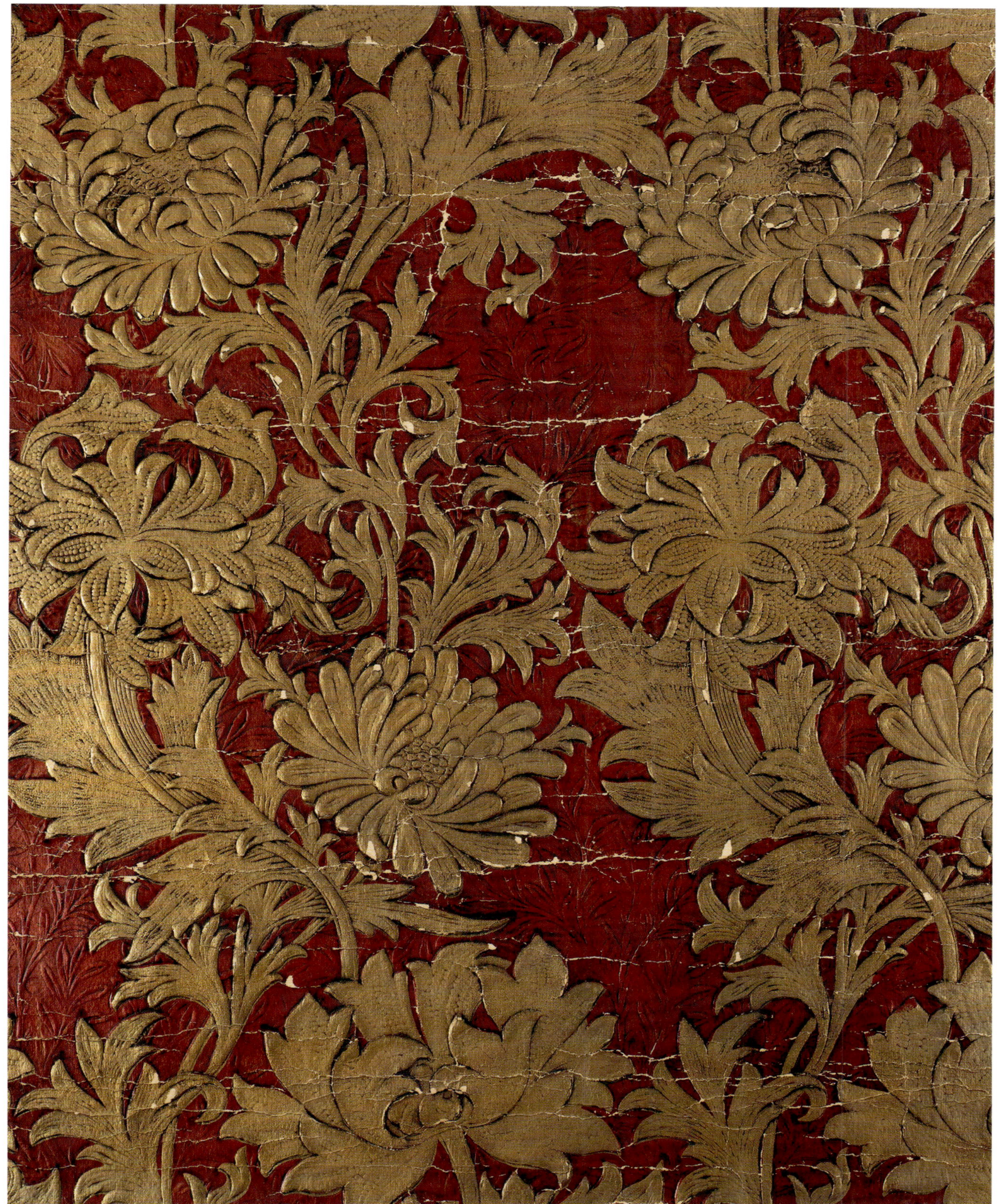

031 | William Morris, *Chrysanthemum*, 1879, Jeffrey & Co. for Morris & Co.

This embossed pasteboard version has colouring that reflects the demand for Japanese-style leather papers using metallic pigments over richly coloured grounds. It was hung in the drawing room at 1 Holland Park, the home of Alexander Ionides, as part of a sumptuous decor created by Morris & Co. and including work by Walter Crane and William De Morgan.

In the entry written with Professor Middleton describing 'Mural Decoration', included in the 1884 edition of *Encyclopaedia Britannica*, William Morris endorsed and complimented such imitation leather papers. Although he never visited Japan, his teachings, art and philosophy nevertheless have been held in high regard there since the early-20th century.

032 | *Chrysanthemum Match-Piece*, [1877], 2018 re-creation for Morris & Co.

The name 'match-piece' refers to the very first signed and dated sample of wallpaper approved prior to production. The match-piece serves as a blueprint, or master sample, on which each individual colour is identified, the coloured ground is presented and an imprint from each printing block is shown. A match-piece, therefore, is the recipe from which the colour matcher and block-printer are able to complete the pattern in repeat throughout the entire length of the paper.

Prior to printing *Chrysanthemum*, the seven print blocks are placed on wet woollen blankets to be soaked for 36 hours (a process of expanding the cracked wooden sycamore blocks before printing the pattern), after which the blocks are 'laid up' in printing order and sequence. Preceding printing, the colour mixer blends a base of titanium white water-based emulsion with prime colours to replicate the original colours shown on the match-piece.

The hand-printing process starts with the first block being placed on a woollen 'pad' impregnated with colour; the coloured block is then positioned on the base 'grounded' paper and pressed firmly down to imprint the image. On completion of printing, the entire roll of paper is then hung on rails to dry. When dry, the second block repeats the same printing process, which is replicated for all remaining blocks until the complete pattern is realised. The skill and judgement of the block-printer determines the signature of individual printings.

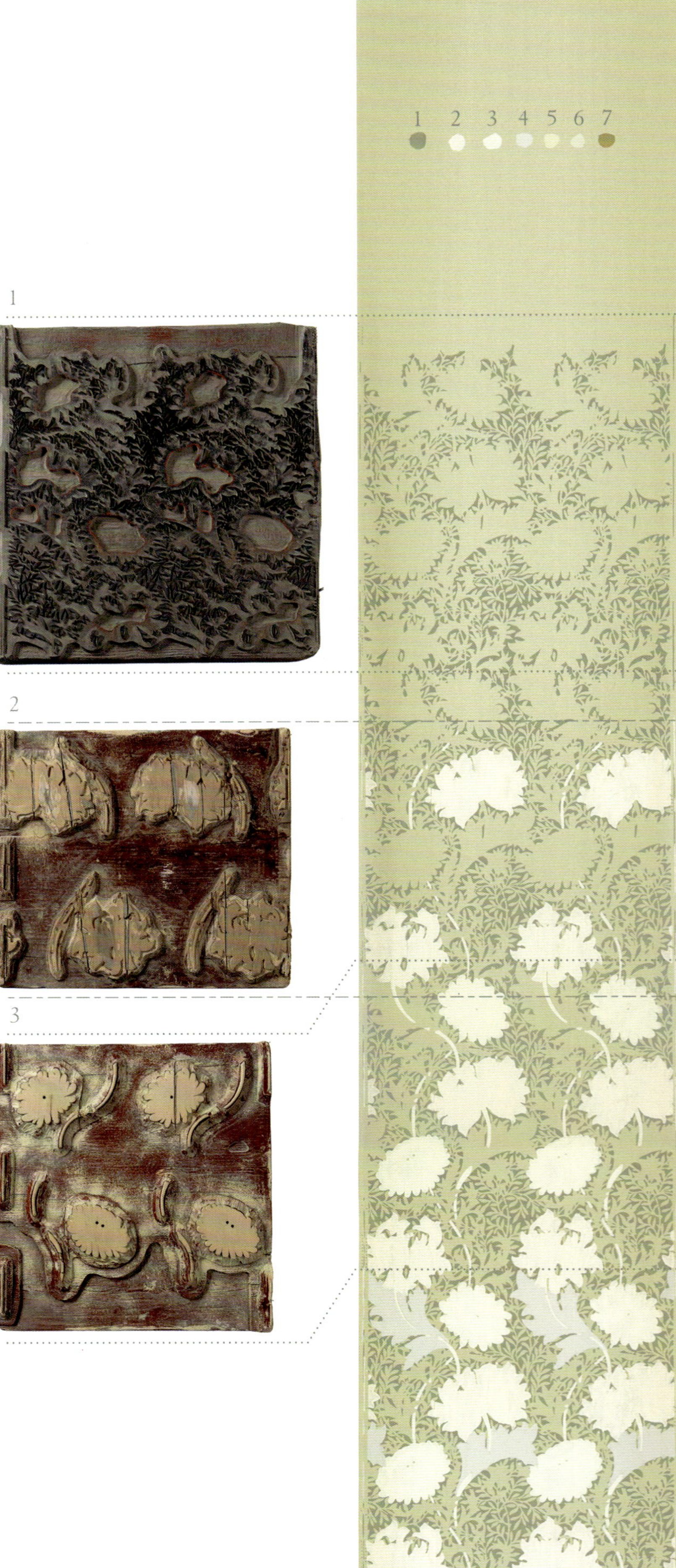

032a-g | *Chrysanthemum Printing Blocks 1-7, 1877, Alfred Barratt (originals), Arthur Sanderson & Son (reproductions)*

These are the printing blocks used to create the *Chrysanthemum* wallpaper. The original blocks, made by Alfred Barratt of 489 Bethnal Green Road, London, include the diamond registration mark embedded in the paper's selvedge. Some of these blocks were recreated from the originals by Sanderson, probably in the 1960s when Morris & Co. patterns were still often in block-printed production.

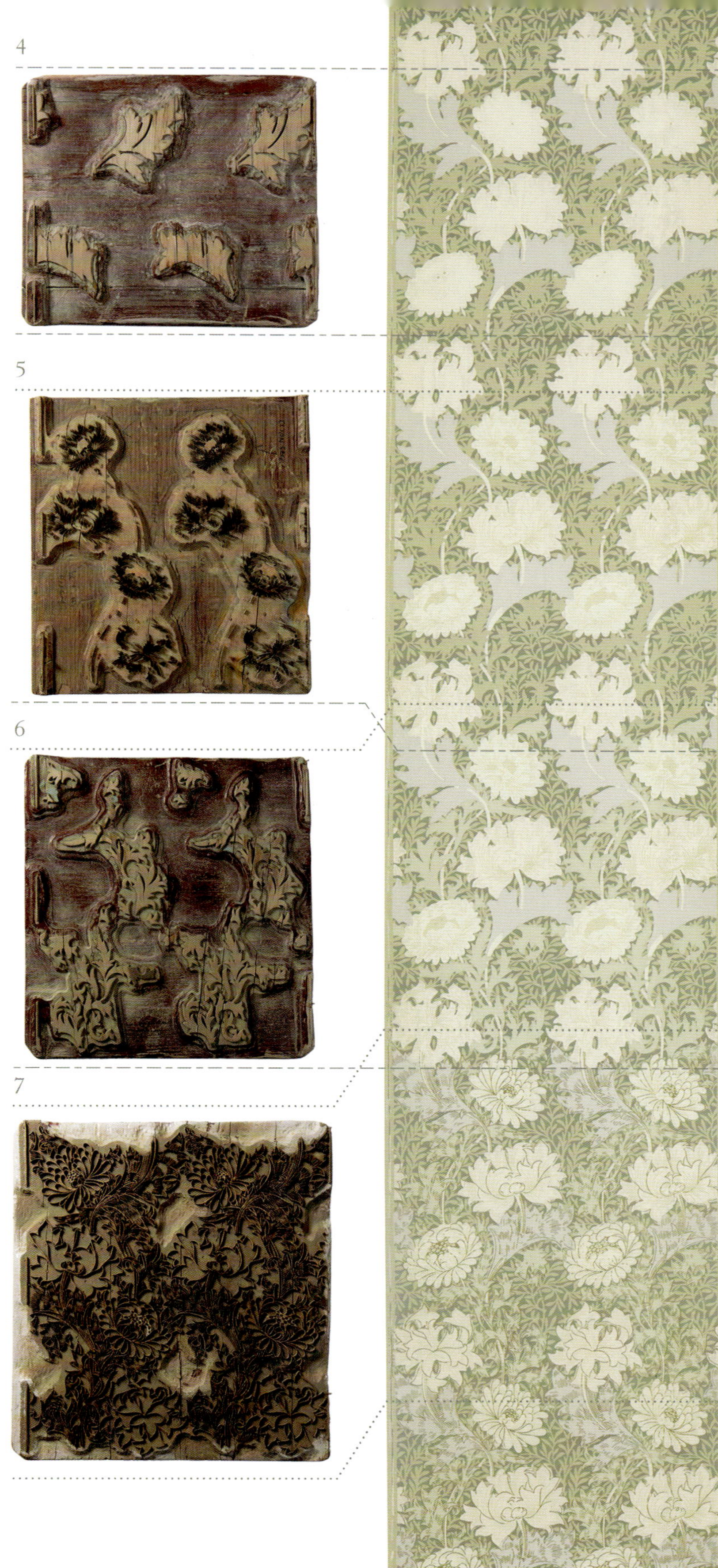

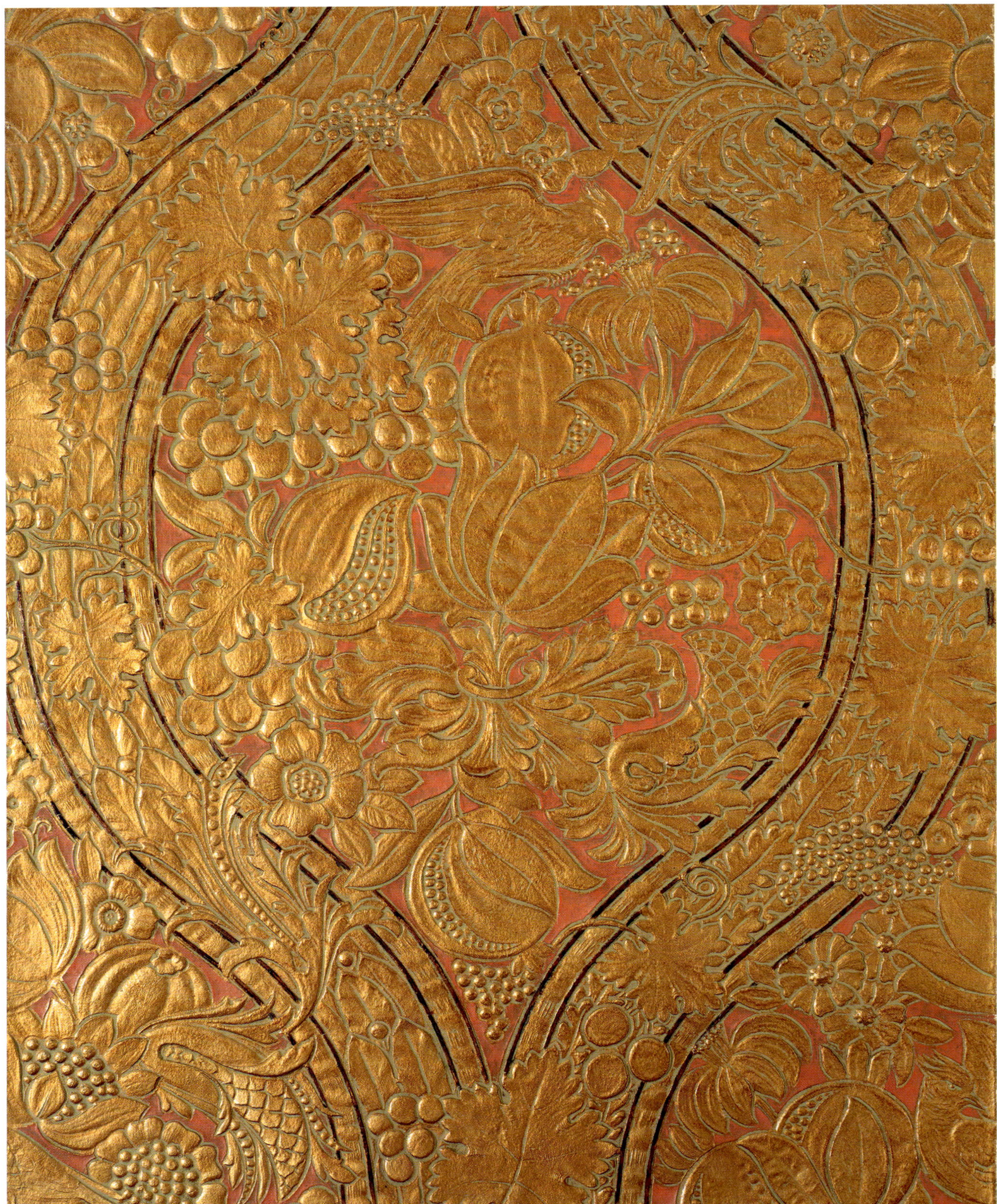

033 | Designer unknown, *Embossed Pasteboard*, 1880s, Jeffrey & Co.

In 1871, Metford Warner became sole proprietor of Jeffrey & Co. Japanese leather papers and Frederick Walton's 'Lincrusta' could well have been Warner's motivation to work with Bruce J. Talbert in the creation of embossed pasteboard designs imitating *kinkarakawakami* leather papers.

By 1878, Jeffrey & Co. issued a Talbert wallpaper pattern of foliage, fruit and birds not too dissimilar from Japanese originals. Over a 15-year period, Jeffrey & Co. issued several more embossed, gilded and hand-coloured pasteboard designs, including this example, offering a decorative, competitively priced alternative to Japanese leather papers.

034 | William Morris, *Vine*, 1873/74 (printed), Jeffrey & Co. for Morris, Marshall, Faulkner & Co.

This is one of the patterns that was also produced in Japanese leather paper form, in 1876. Although Morris believed that the traditions of Western art were essential to give meaning to a pattern, and that the Middle Ages provided the truest exemplars, he nevertheless acknowledged that the Japanese were 'admirable naturalists'.

The characteristics of Japanese patterns were, in fact, not that dissimilar to Morris's approach to design. Both shared the use of restrained, flattened motifs, as well as the incorporation of natural forms that were familiar – in Morris's case most often inspired by wildflowers or traditional garden flowers and fruits.

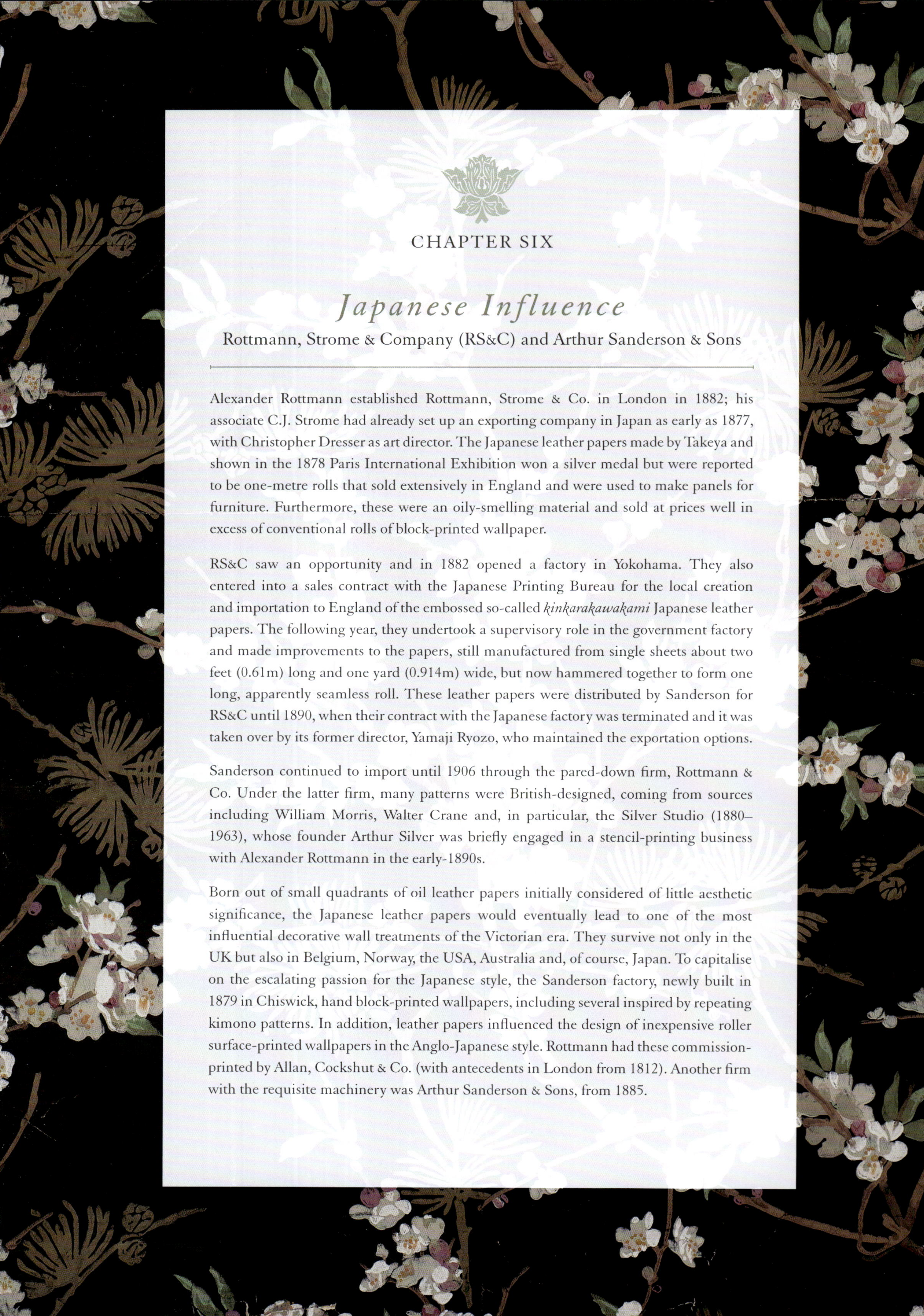

CHAPTER SIX

Japanese Influence

Rottmann, Strome & Company (RS&C) and Arthur Sanderson & Sons

Alexander Rottmann established Rottmann, Strome & Co. in London in 1882; his associate C.J. Strome had already set up an exporting company in Japan as early as 1877, with Christopher Dresser as art director. The Japanese leather papers made by Takeya and shown in the 1878 Paris International Exhibition won a silver medal but were reported to be one-metre rolls that sold extensively in England and were used to make panels for furniture. Furthermore, these were an oily-smelling material and sold at prices well in excess of conventional rolls of block-printed wallpaper.

RS&C saw an opportunity and in 1882 opened a factory in Yokohama. They also entered into a sales contract with the Japanese Printing Bureau for the local creation and importation to England of the embossed so-called *kinkarakawakami* Japanese leather papers. The following year, they undertook a supervisory role in the government factory and made improvements to the papers, still manufactured from single sheets about two feet (0.61m) long and one yard (0.914m) wide, but now hammered together to form one long, apparently seamless roll. These leather papers were distributed by Sanderson for RS&C until 1890, when their contract with the Japanese factory was terminated and it was taken over by its former director, Yamaji Ryozo, who maintained the exportation options.

Sanderson continued to import until 1906 through the pared-down firm, Rottmann & Co. Under the latter firm, many patterns were British-designed, coming from sources including William Morris, Walter Crane and, in particular, the Silver Studio (1880–1963), whose founder Arthur Silver was briefly engaged in a stencil-printing business with Alexander Rottmann in the early-1890s.

Born out of small quadrants of oil leather papers initially considered of little aesthetic significance, the Japanese leather papers would eventually lead to one of the most influential decorative wall treatments of the Victorian era. They survive not only in the UK but also in Belgium, Norway, the USA, Australia and, of course, Japan. To capitalise on the escalating passion for the Japanese style, the Sanderson factory, newly built in 1879 in Chiswick, hand block-printed wallpapers, including several inspired by repeating kimono patterns. In addition, leather papers influenced the design of inexpensive roller surface-printed wallpapers in the Anglo-Japanese style. Rottmann had these commission-printed by Allan, Cockshut & Co. (with antecedents in London from 1812). Another firm with the requisite machinery was Arthur Sanderson & Sons, from 1885.

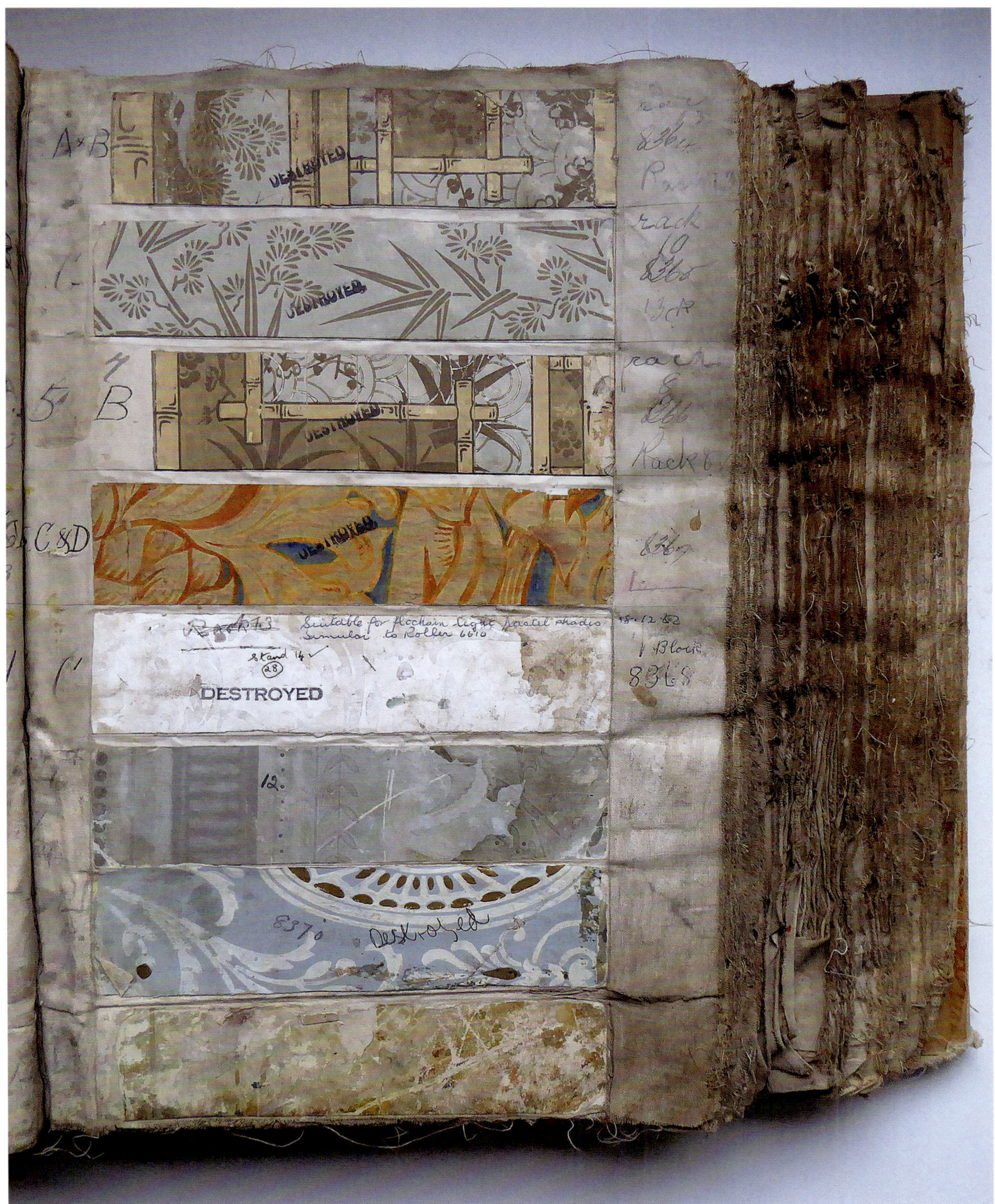

035 | *Logbook*, 1882 (printed entries), Arthur Sanderson & Sons, Chiswick Factory

This page from the earliest Chiswick wallpaper *Logbook* shows original entries for Sanderson's block-printed wallpaper designs, some of which were inspired by the new trend for Japonisme. This style became part of the Aesthetic Movement, which privileged the beautiful over the doctrinal and was named by the writer Walter Hamilton in 1882.

The top three paper samples show related patterns incorporating bamboo leaves and canes, a plant that was being introduced into Britain from Japan during this period. Such suites of wallpapers allowed for the creation of interiors that could be living artworks, thus allowing the decorative arts to be aesthetic and utilitarian simultaneously.

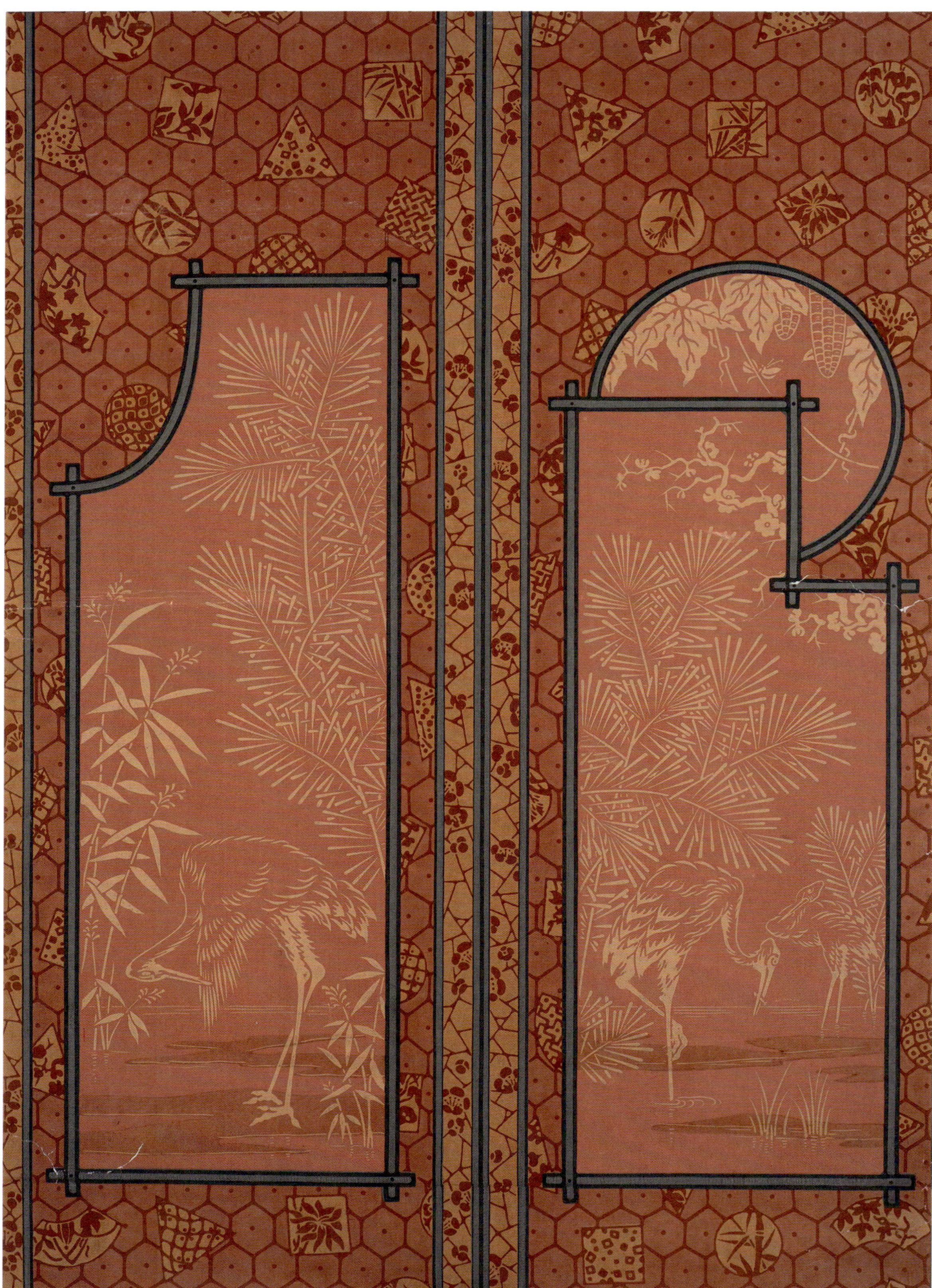

036 | Chiswick Design Studio, *Japanese Staircase*, c.1888, Arthur Sanderson & Sons

This block-printed wallpaper was designed specifically for staircases. The design of bamboo, cherry blossom and crane motifs within the panels is heavily influenced by kimono repeating patterns. Such Anglo-Japanese styles, with rich but limited tones, reflect the 1880s' trend towards subdued, harmonious colours.

Staircase papers would be cut down the centre to the width of a stair tread (approximately 25.5cm deep), ensuring the pattern was consistent throughout the flight of stairs. A border would be applied to the staircase wall to create an optical illusion of a dado rail. The Sanderson triangle logo is printed on the reverse together with the reference number 23387.

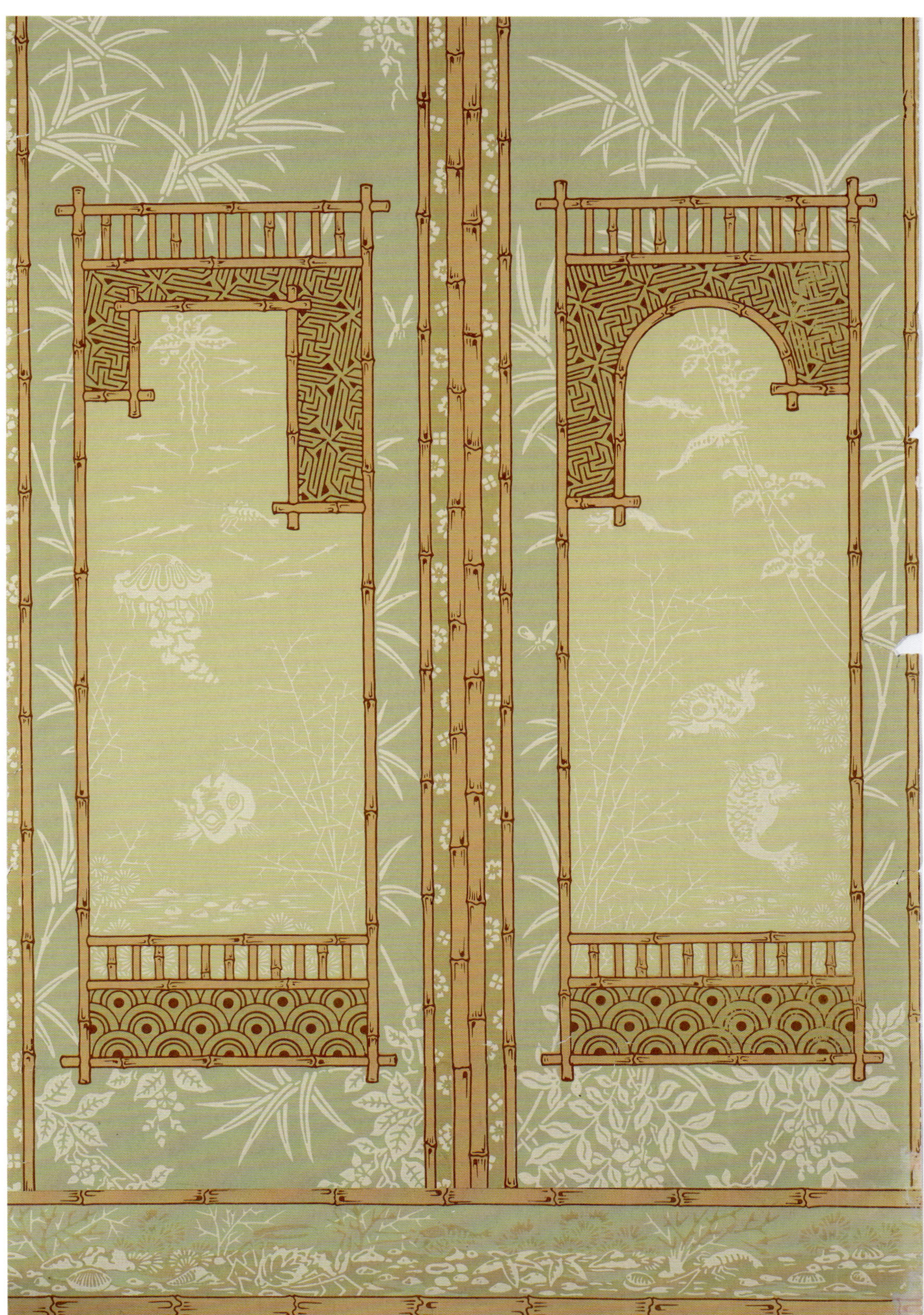

037 | Chiswick Design Studio, *Japanese Staircase*, c.1888, Arthur Sanderson & Sons

This second Sanderson block-print for staircases was inspired by marine life and is shown with an inner border derived from *Seigaiha*, a pattern of overlapping circles, symbolic of waves and the ebb and flow of life. The Sanderson triangle logo is printed on the reverse together with the reference number 23387 for the wallpaper and 23370 for the border.

The 1880s saw many changes at Sanderson, not least the untimely death of its founder Arthur Sanderson in 1882 who, as late as 1890, was 'still held in affectionate esteem by the whole of the decorating trade, many of whose members owe much to his assistance and advice'. As for the Anglo-Japanese style, it remained fashionable well into the early-20th century.

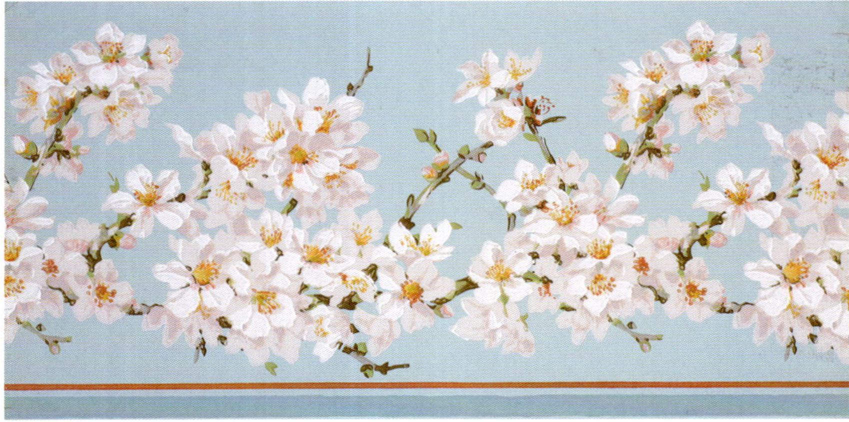

038a | Chiswick Design Studio, *The Almond Blossom Frieze*, 1896, Arthur Sanderson & Sons

From the mid-1800s, fashionable wall decoration comprised three sections – dado, filling and frieze – but by the end of the century Sanderson was marketing a form of decoration that was less complicated to install. Its popular floral wallpapers were partnered by a single frieze, thereby negating the use of dado papers.

This uncomplicated form of wall decoration, made popular by Sanderson, was also more economical, being produced by surface-roller printing. *The Almond Blossom* wallpaper (2/-shillings per roll) and border (6d pence per roll) designs were offered in a variety of light, bright and cheerful colours facilitating harmonious decoration.

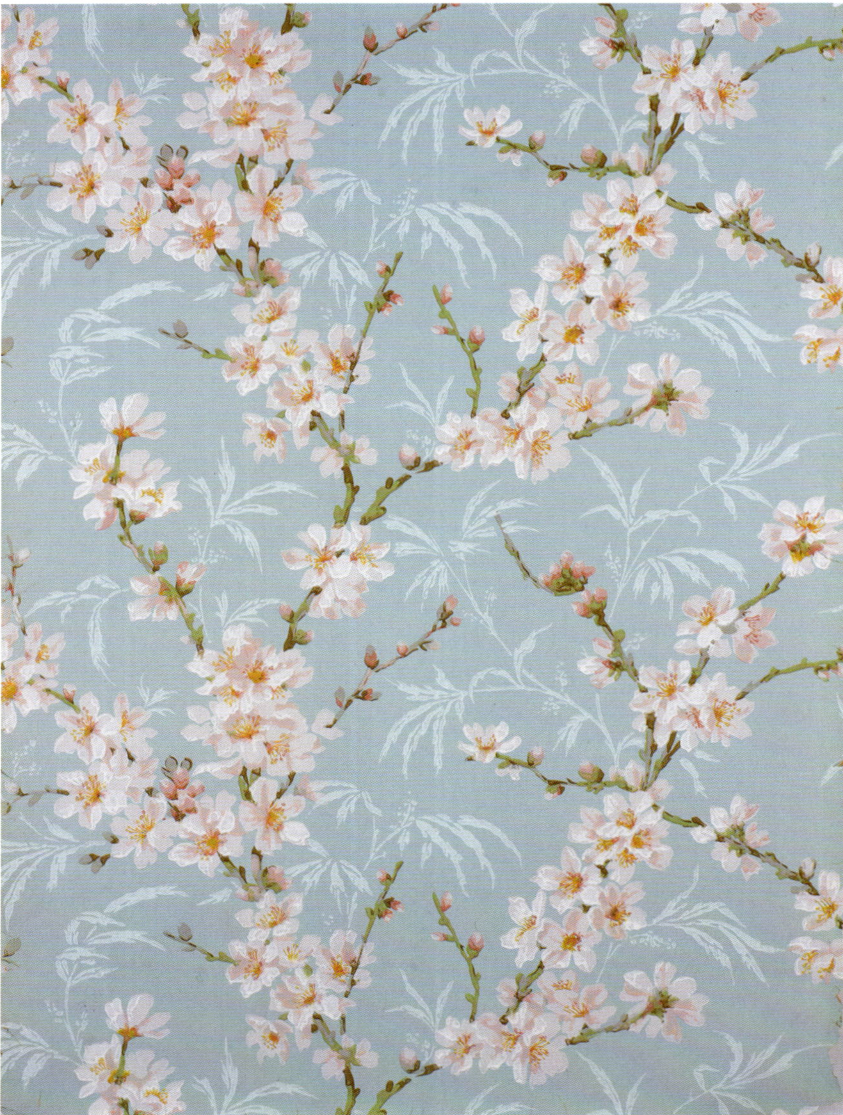

038 | Chiswick Design Studio, *The Almond Blossom*, 1896, Arthur Sanderson & Sons

By this time, the earlier impact of Japanese art and design had become assimilated fully into British interiors. Such patterns contributed to the popularity of Sanderson wallpapers, which were seen as being of 'exceptional quality and taste'. Many were printed on surface-roller machines. Here, ten rollers were required.

Arthur Sanderson's third son, Harold, oversaw the manufacturing and also design, seeking inspiration from diverse cultural sources. *The Almond Blossom* wallpaper combines the impressionistic style of James Abbott McNeill Whistler with the naturalistic realism of Japanese wood cuts.

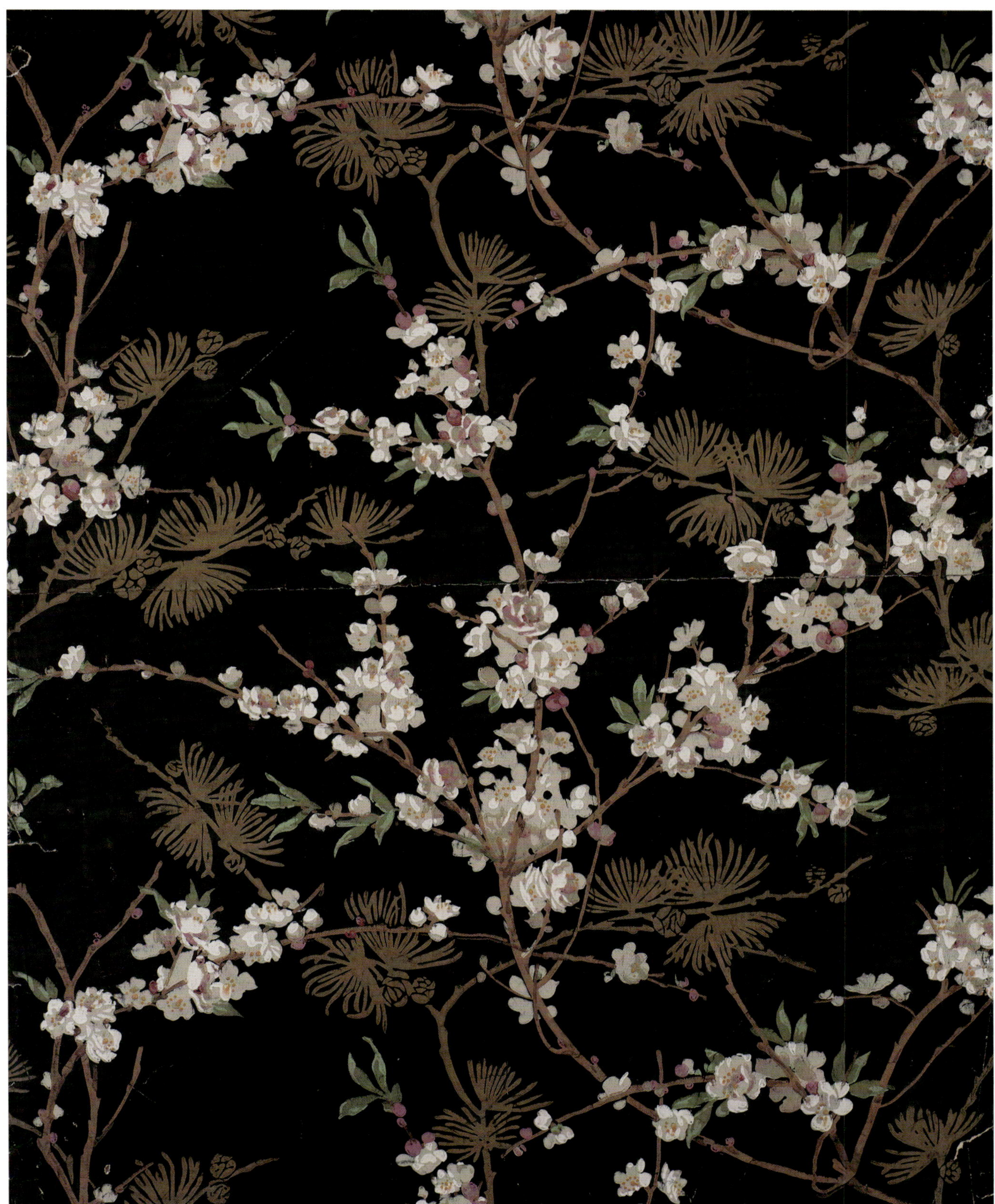

039 | Harry Watkins Wild, *Blossom*, 1917/18, Arthur Sanderson & Sons Ltd

One long-serving designer who influenced the Sanderson style was Harry Watkins Wild, who joined the Chiswick Design Studio in 1893 and remained in place for 46 years. Wild created many 'authentic' Japanese designs, the result of having previously worked in the studio of William Cooke & Sons, known as Christopher Dresser's most prolific collaborator.

This Wild design, surface-roller printed on a black pre-grounded paper, was compatible both with fashionable Western kimono dresses, in vogue well into the 1920s, as well as lacquered furniture. The latter was both new – that is, in Art Deco style – and remained in place from the fashion for ebonized furniture associated with the Aesthetic style of the later 19th century.

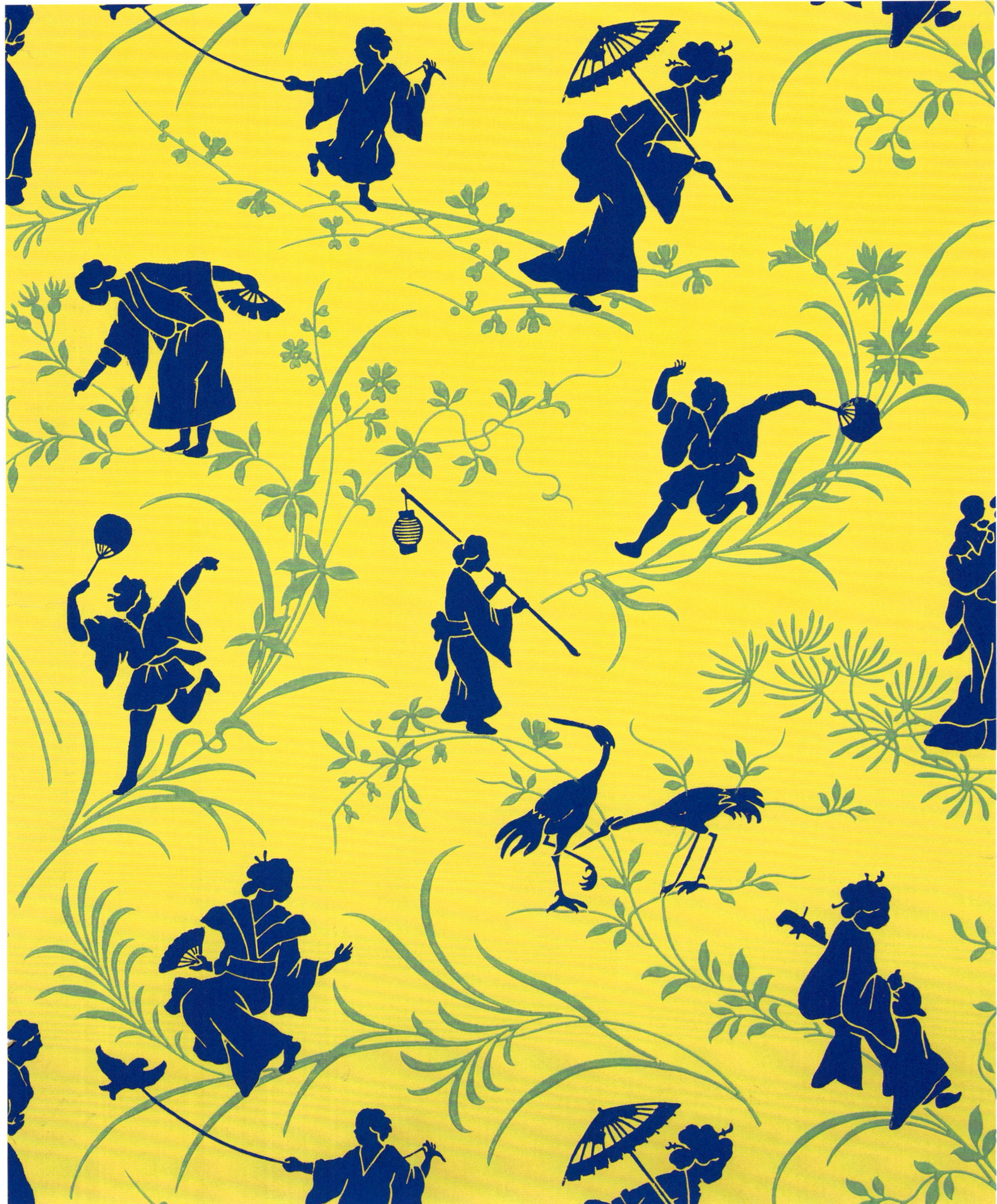

040 | Designer unknown, *Silhouette Wallpaper No.202/10*, early-20th century, SDG Archive

The Sanderson Design Group Archive contains innumerable documents and works of art, some of which have yet to be researched. However, this unusual machine-printed paper, the reverse of which is referenced '202/10', features Western interpretations of Japanese motifs in striking colours with oriental figures, cranes, blossom, honeysuckle/pine and cornflowers.

This colourful wallpaper was possibly acquired by Harold Sanderson during a visit to Paris ateliers in the early-1920s. Its use of silhouetted figures is in line with the modernised 'toile' style as developed by the French décorateurs Süe et Mare (Louis Süe and André Mare) and André Groult, who worked with the prolific designer André Saglio.

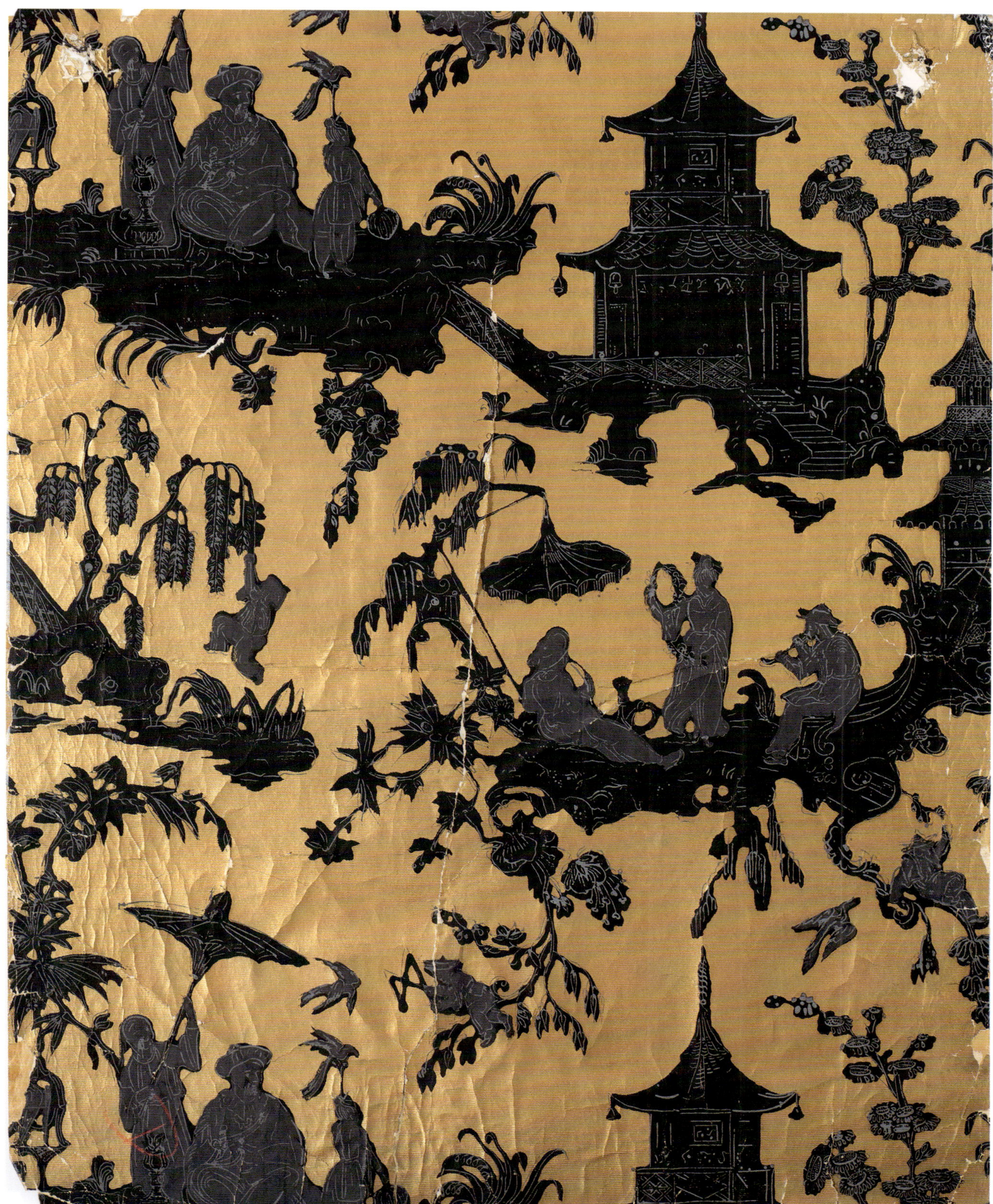

041 | Attributed to Louis Stahl, *The Mandarin*, c.1915, Arthur Sanderson & Sons Ltd

The Mandarin wallpaper epitomises the revival of more authentic 18th-century toile patterns, perfectly suited to the Edwardian taste for neo-Georgian architecture and decor. As was the case in the originals, sources were often illustrations and the design for this block-printed paper employs adaptations of European 18th-century engravings depicting Japanese scenes.

German-born Louis Stahl joined the Sanderson Chiswick wallpaper studio at the beginning of the 1900s; aside from his work as a designer, he also conducted the Sanderson Bleak House Band. By late-1914, Stahl had left to become chief designer for Heffer Scott & Co., creating in particular 'oriental subjects'.

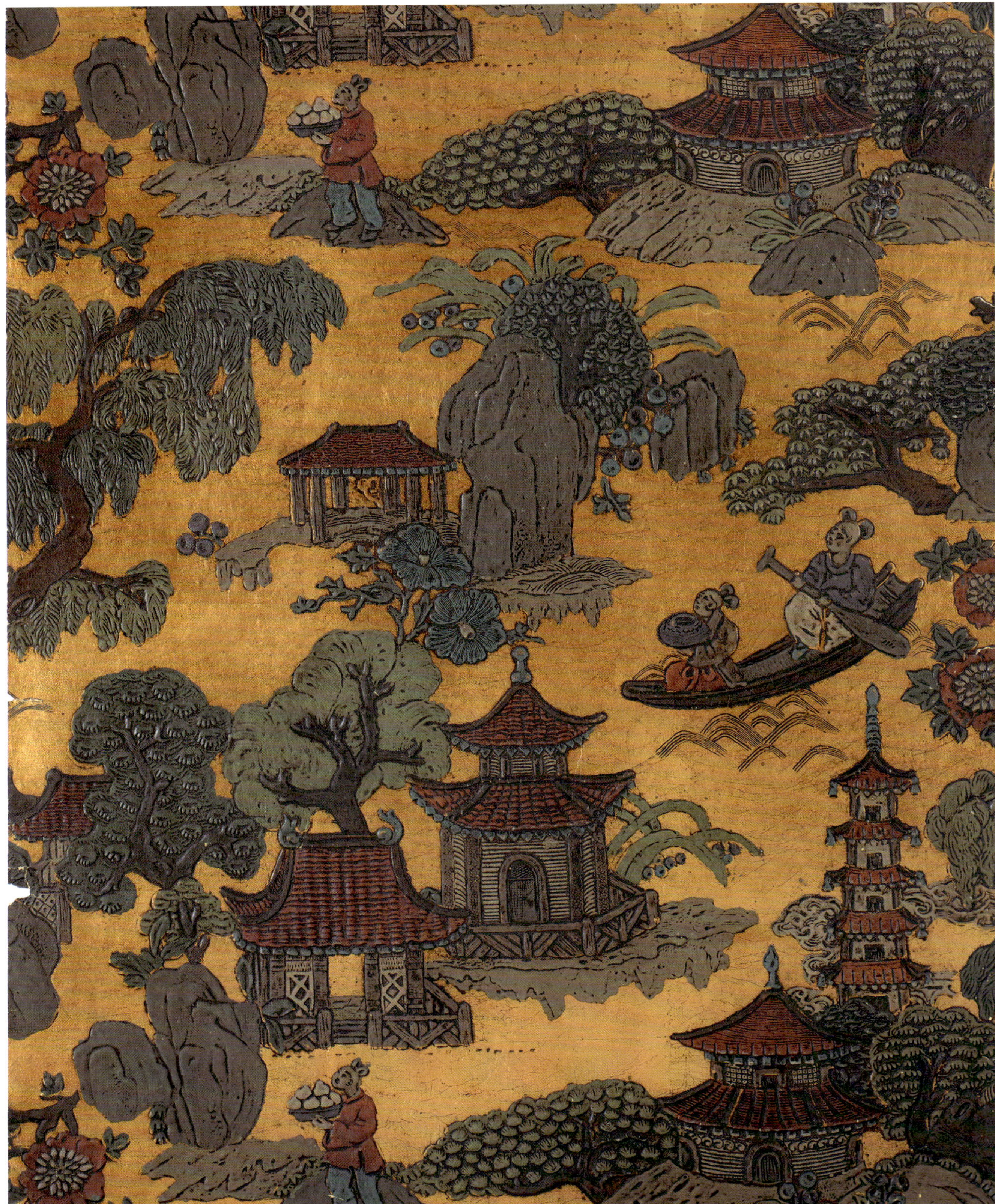

042 | Chiswick Design Studio, *Oriental Scene Wallpaper*, c.1919, Arthur Sanderson & Sons Ltd

Some exhibition pieces were orchestrated by Harold Sanderson. Here, Design 87189, a limited-edition hand block-printed paper, has a hand-applied gold leaf ground, on to which Chinese images were block-printed, with in-register embossing creating three-dimensional decoration. It was 11 times more expensive than conventional wallpaper.

The dawning of the 20th century saw the Sanderson showrooms in Berners Street crowned 'the largest wallpaper showroom in London'. Within was a then-novel swinging-screen system developed by Arthur Bengough Sanderson, allowing clients to view longer drops and the full widths of papers.

043 | *The Buzzing Wood*, *kinkarakawakami* leather paper, c.1897, Rottmann & Co.

The Buzzing Wood was one of the papers imported by Arthur Sanderson & Sons, the craftsmanship in the making of such high-quality, intricate papers made them expensive to produce and purchase. They sold for 35/- (shillings) per roll (equivalent to £225 today) compared to 6d (pence) a roll for more every day, machine-printed wallpaper.

This paper illustrates the complex patterning found on the finest examples of *kinkarakawakami* leather papers, featuring a myriad of insects, birds and botanical motifs. It was created by a process of embossing that used carved wooden rollers or blocks, and staining with burnished metallic pigments on to washi paper.

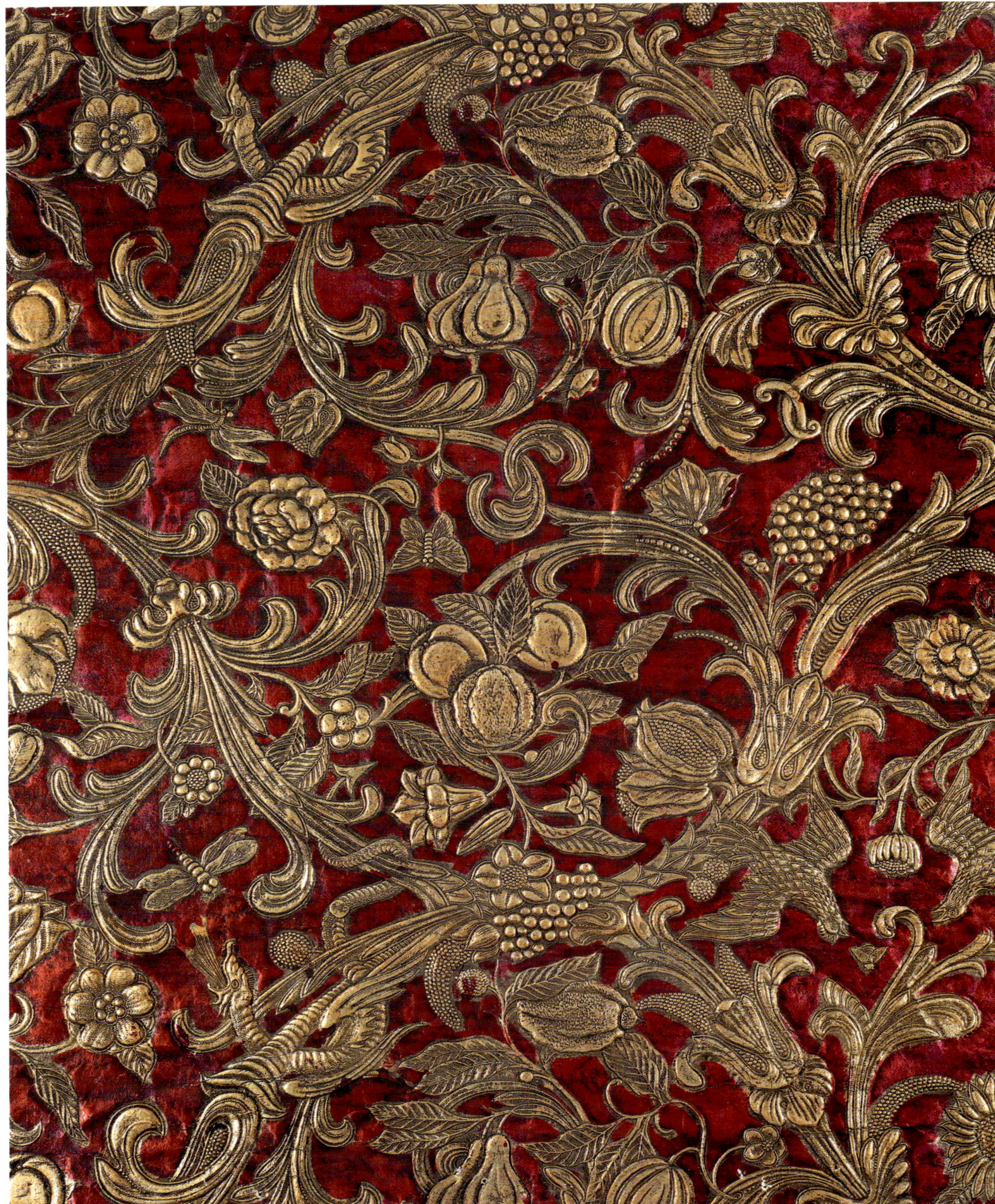

044 | *Kinkarakawakami* leather paper, c.1885, Rottmann, Strome & Co.

Through its office in Yokohama, Alexander Rottmann ensured that newly produced leather papers continued to be lacquered, a treatment that was advantageous because they remained impervious to both gaslight and heat. This also rendered them washable, a feature leading to a gold medal at the International Health Exhibition in London in 1884.

The *kinkarakawakami* leather paper shown here was one of the most sought-after. Its design content of curling vines, grapes, sunflowers, pomegranates and birds stands comparison with designs by William Morris. Created in rich colours of ox blood and bronze, it offered an ideal palette for use with oak panelling in aristocratic country houses.

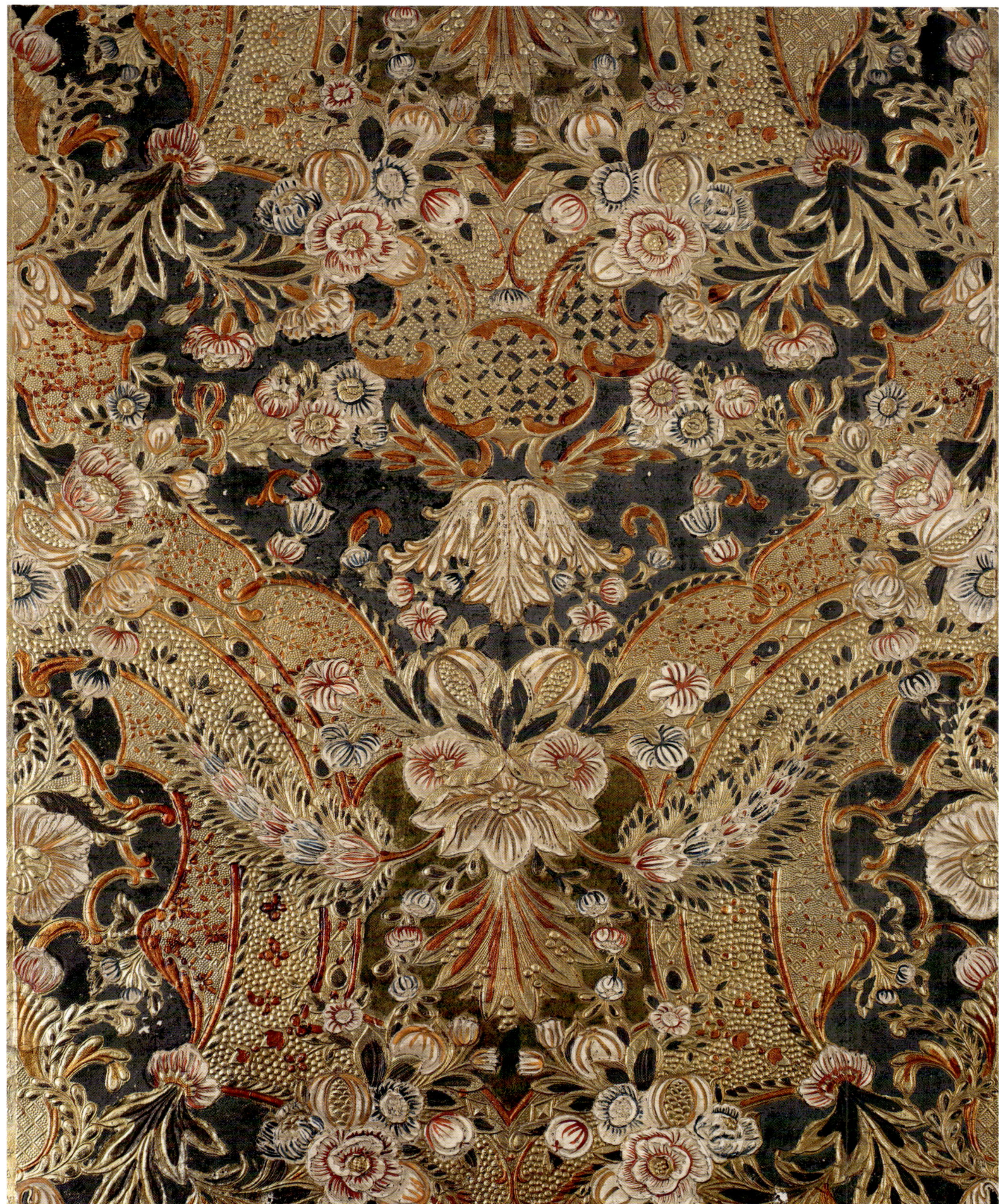

045 | *The Alicante, kinkarakawakami* leather paper, 1897, Rottmann & Co.

The Alicante, as befits the long history of trade from the Netherlands to Japan, is European in style, replicating Spanish tooled leatherwork. The formal, symmetrical pattern is based on Cordovan leather patterns of Muslim origin that were richly dyed and polished to an enduring finish, intended for use as both upholstery and wall decoration.

Both Morris & Co. and Sanderson commissioned exclusive *kinkarakawakami* leather paper patterns from Rottmann, Strome & Co. and its successor, Rottmann & Co. This example, registered in the Patents, Designs and Trademarks Office, was most likely for Sanderson, although it could have been obtained with their acquisition of Rottmann in 1913.

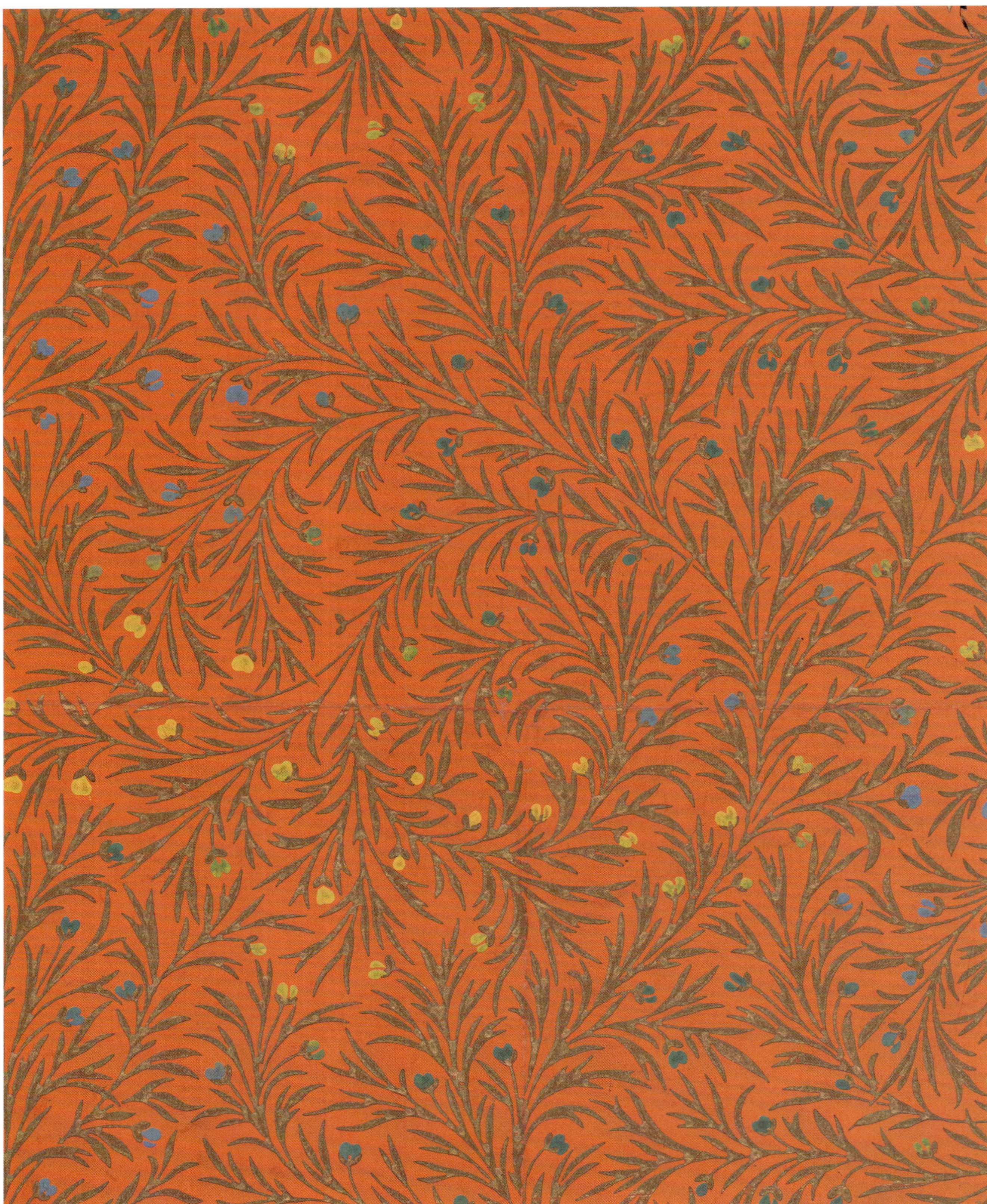

046 | *The Flax*, filling paper, c.1880, Jeffrey & Co.

Intended for a drawing room decorated in aesthetic style, the small-scale design of simplified trailing foliage and flowers takes its influences from Japan. Oscar Wilde and Charles Eastlake were among those advising the use of such wallpapers as a backdrop to rooms of antique furnishings and blue and white porcelain from Japan and China.

Filling papers were used on the upper half of walls divided into dado (bottom), filling (middle) and frieze (top). While filling papers offered unobtrusive designs principally required to provide colour, the patterns for Anglo-Japanese dados and friezes were larger in scale, employing ornamental bosses or geometric motifs emblematic of non-Western design.

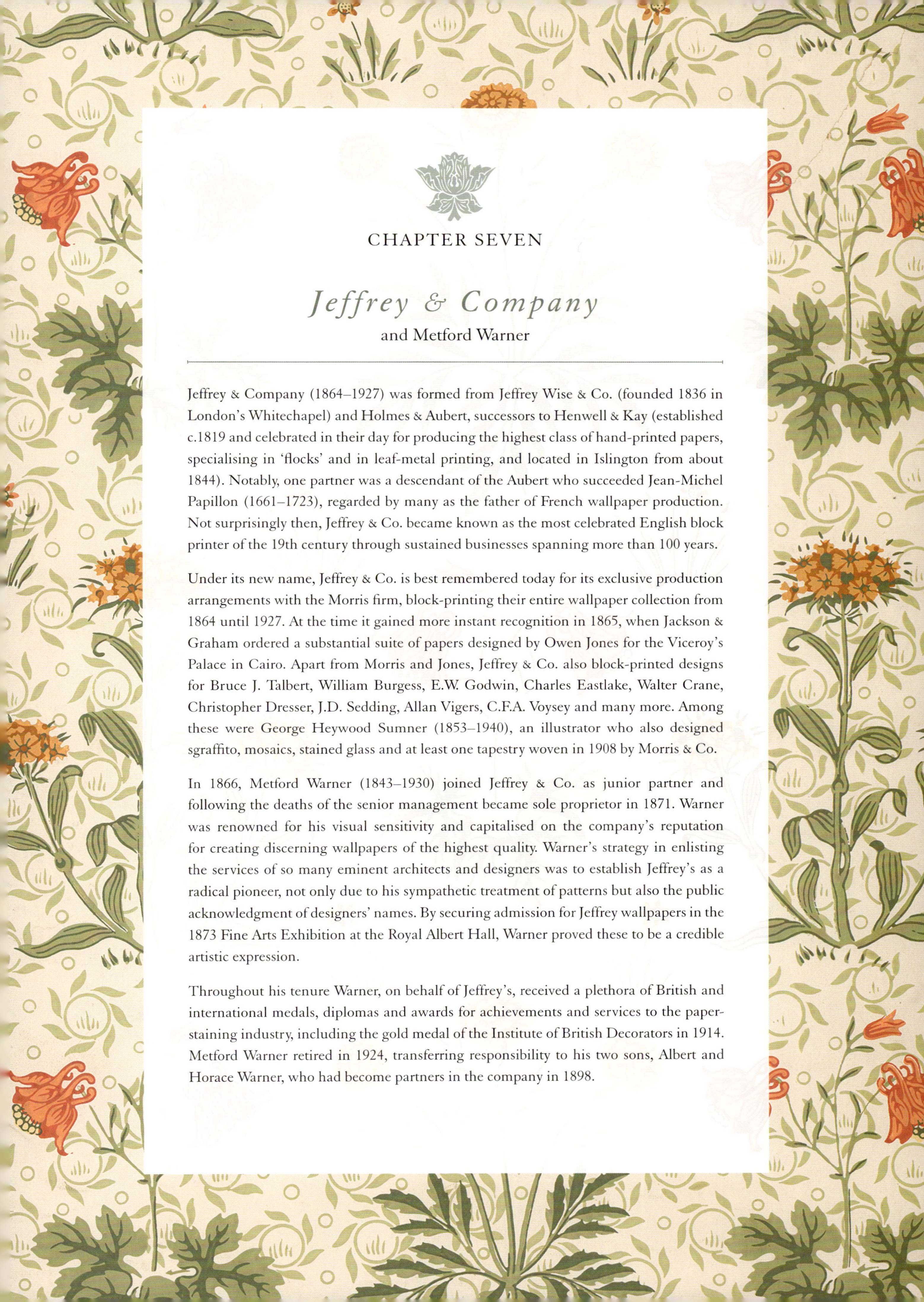

CHAPTER SEVEN

Jeffrey & Company

and Metford Warner

Jeffrey & Company (1864–1927) was formed from Jeffrey Wise & Co. (founded 1836 in London's Whitechapel) and Holmes & Aubert, successors to Henwell & Kay (established c.1819 and celebrated in their day for producing the highest class of hand-printed papers, specialising in 'flocks' and in leaf-metal printing, and located in Islington from about 1844). Notably, one partner was a descendant of the Aubert who succeeded Jean-Michel Papillon (1661–1723), regarded by many as the father of French wallpaper production. Not surprisingly then, Jeffrey & Co. became known as the most celebrated English block printer of the 19th century through sustained businesses spanning more than 100 years.

Under its new name, Jeffrey & Co. is best remembered today for its exclusive production arrangements with the Morris firm, block-printing their entire wallpaper collection from 1864 until 1927. At the time it gained more instant recognition in 1865, when Jackson & Graham ordered a substantial suite of papers designed by Owen Jones for the Viceroy's Palace in Cairo. Apart from Morris and Jones, Jeffrey & Co. also block-printed designs for Bruce J. Talbert, William Burgess, E.W. Godwin, Charles Eastlake, Walter Crane, Christopher Dresser, J.D. Sedding, Allan Vigers, C.F.A. Voysey and many more. Among these were George Heywood Sumner (1853–1940), an illustrator who also designed sgraffito, mosaics, stained glass and at least one tapestry woven in 1908 by Morris & Co.

In 1866, Metford Warner (1843–1930) joined Jeffrey & Co. as junior partner and following the deaths of the senior management became sole proprietor in 1871. Warner was renowned for his visual sensitivity and capitalised on the company's reputation for creating discerning wallpapers of the highest quality. Warner's strategy in enlisting the services of so many eminent architects and designers was to establish Jeffrey's as a radical pioneer, not only due to his sympathetic treatment of patterns but also the public acknowledgment of designers' names. By securing admission for Jeffrey wallpapers in the 1873 Fine Arts Exhibition at the Royal Albert Hall, Warner proved these to be a credible artistic expression.

Throughout his tenure Warner, on behalf of Jeffrey's, received a plethora of British and international medals, diplomas and awards for achievements and services to the paper-staining industry, including the gold medal of the Institute of British Decorators in 1914. Metford Warner retired in 1924, transferring responsibility to his two sons, Albert and Horace Warner, who had become partners in the company in 1898.

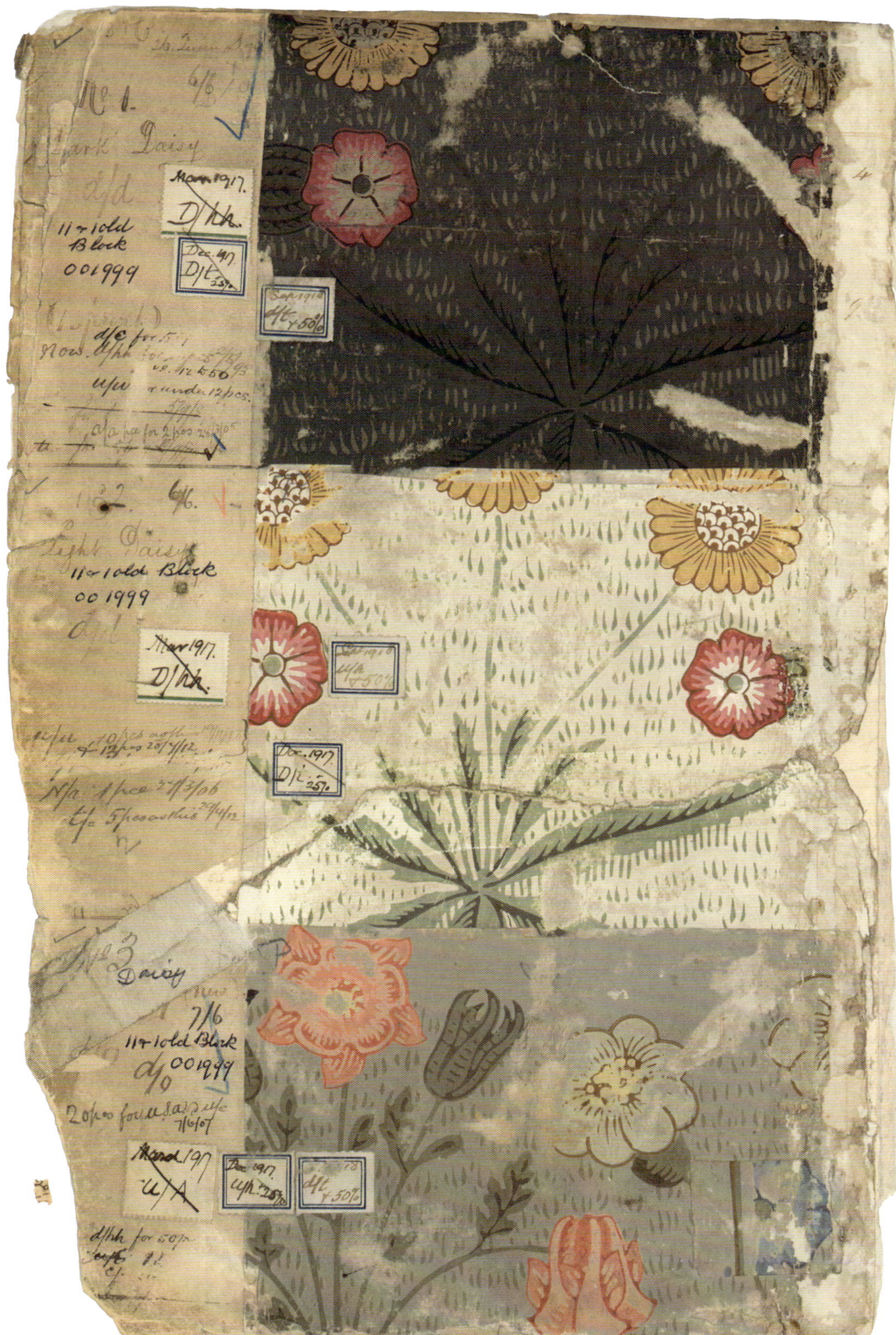

047 | William Morris, *Logbook page*, 1864, Jeffrey & Co. for Morris & Co.

Jeffrey & Co. printed all the wallpapers issued by Morris & Co. As part of this process, they kept chronological logbooks to record each of the colourways that had been printed. Wallpaper samples were pasted into old account books, providing the block-printers with an accurate 'match-piece' identified by name and number, together with comments.

Here, one can see three different colourways of *Daisy*, first produced in c.1864; the numbers indicate how many pieces were to be printed together, with the date of production. In the case of the central sample, called *Light Daisy* due to its off-white ground, the logbook shows that it was available for production until at least December 1917.

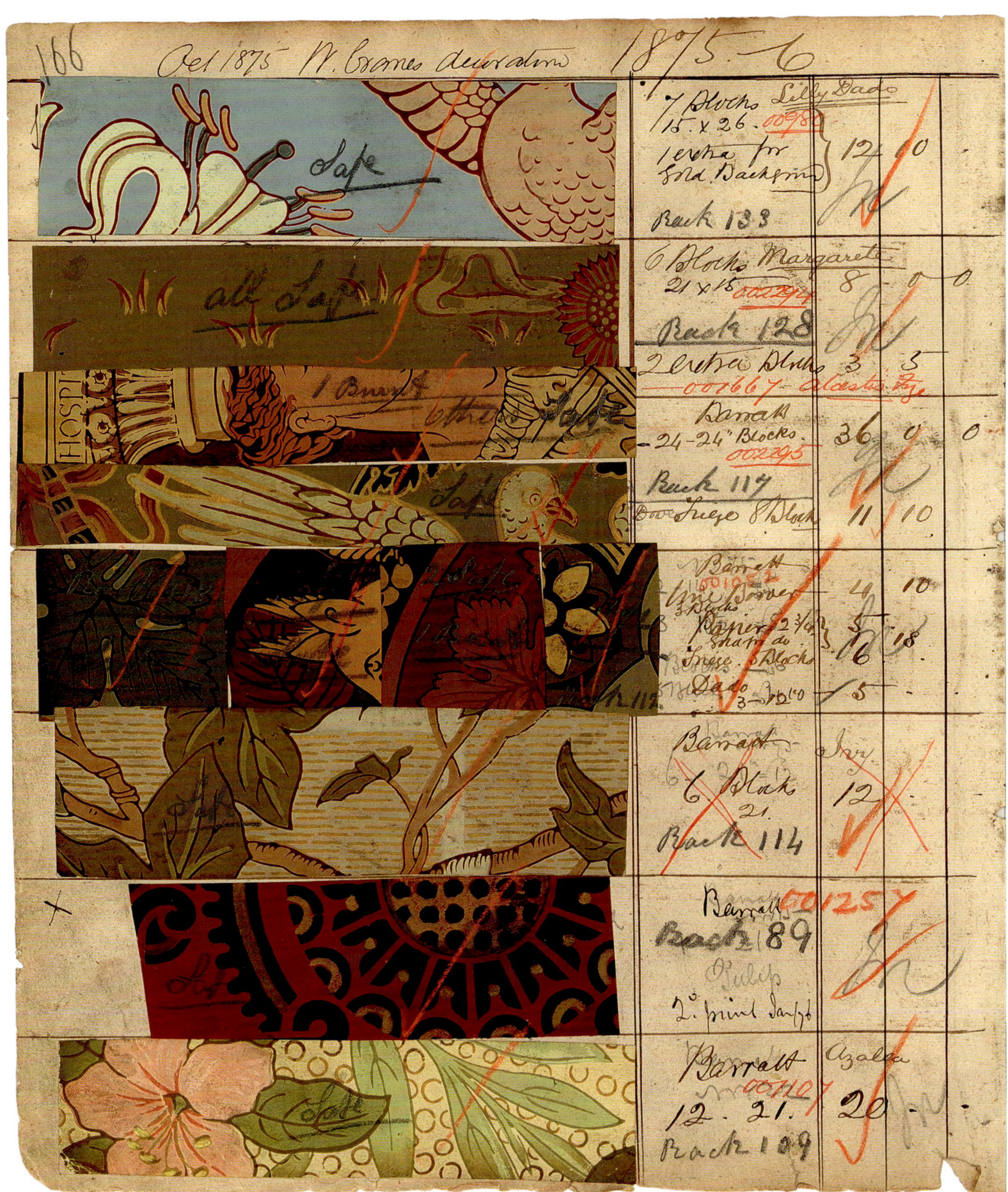

048 | Walter Crane, *Logbook page*, 1875/76, Jeffrey & Co.

This logbook page records the first and subsequent printings of wallpapers designed by Walter Crane and printed by Jeffrey & Co. in 1875/76. Enough can be seen of these snippets to identify the designs as: *Lily Dado*, *La Margarete*, *Alcestis Frieze*, *Dove Frieze*, *Wallpaper Frieze*, *Ivy*, *Tulip* and *Azalea*.

This is one of several logbooks documenting Jeffrey & Co. A sample of each production run was recorded within these books, which are now housed in the Sanderson Design Group Archive at Denham. In total containing 309 samples entered sequentially in order of production from 1864 until 1928, these volumes were conserved during the 1980s.

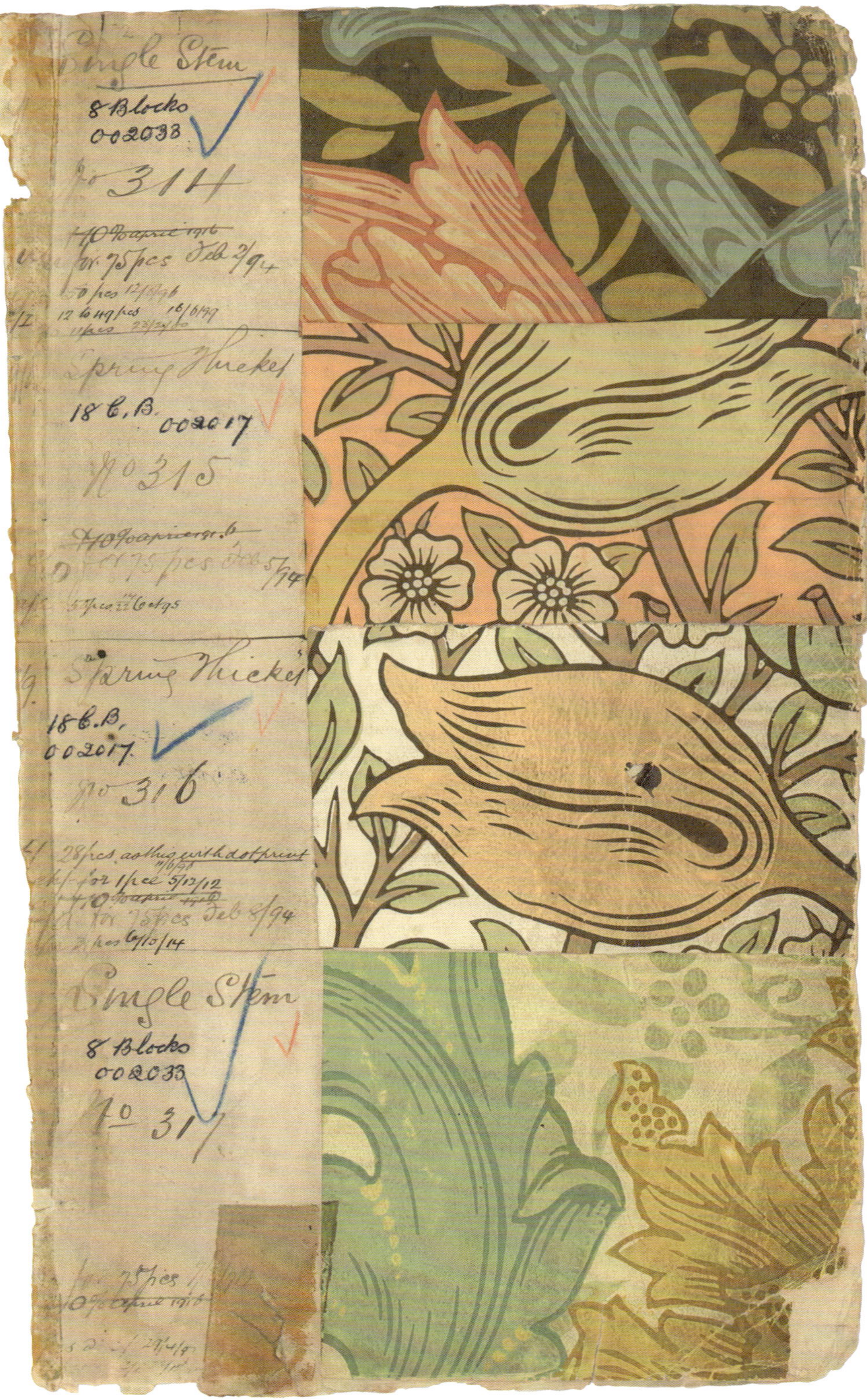

049 | William Morris and John Henry Dearle, *Logbook page*, 1894, Jeffrey & Co. for Morris & Co.

Aside from a subsequent ceiling paper, Morris's last full wallpaper design was *Spring Thicket*, shown in the centre of this page in two colourways. The one numbered '316' has a notation 'as this with dot print' regarding the printing of 28 pieces, meaning it was to have a textural dot incorporated.

Other notations indicate that *Spring Thicket* continued to be in demand much later and No. 316 was printed again in 1912 and 1914. In contrast, Dearle's pattern, *Single Stem*, appears to have had its last printing in 1916 and possibly as late as 1919. Such longevity was an indication of the timelessness of the Morris & Co. style.

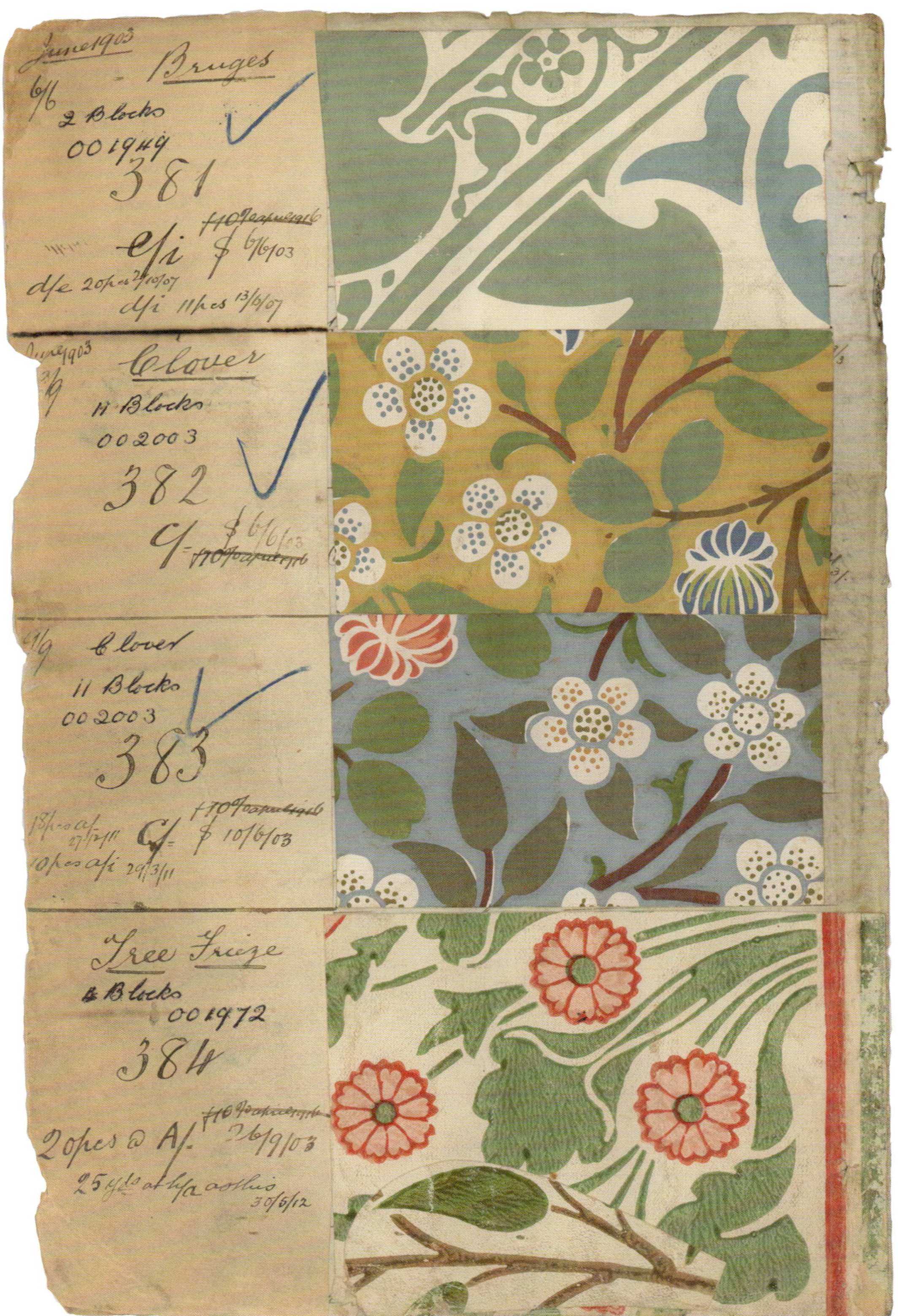

050 | William Morris and unknown designer, *Logbook page*, 1903, Jeffrey & Co. for Morris & Co.

Inscribed 'June 1903', this page documents three designs, one of which is Morris's *Bruge* (top), which was first block-printed by Jeffrey's in 1887. It shows that this design was ordered again, once in 1903 and twice in 1907. It also indicates that it was printed with only two blocks, whereas in Morris's day it was printed with three.

The designers of *Clover* and *Tree Frieze* are unknown. However, they were undoubtedly associated with Morris & Co. since this logbook was kept by Jeffrey's specifically to record their production for The Firm. Both are in the 'sweet' colour palette seen in Dearle's designs of the period and certainly would have been designed under his direction.

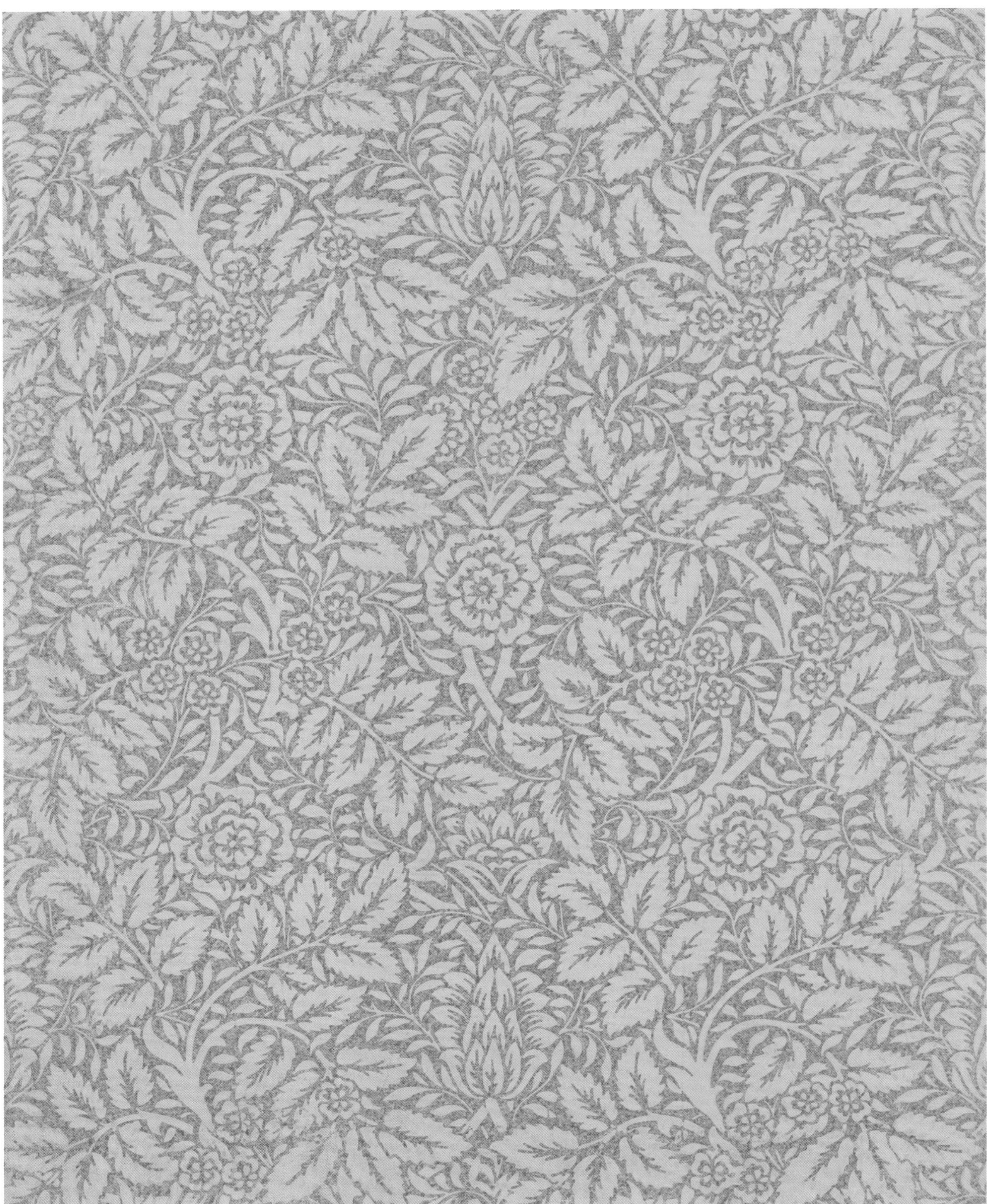

051 | Designer unknown, *Peri*, c.1885, Jeffrey & Co.

This paper is documented in the Jeffrey & Co. printing logbooks. It creates a hand-crafted feel by being printed with a single wood block on a textured, or ingrain, ground. Ingrains were made with two layers of paper and were saturated with colour, in effect dyed in the making. They were popular from the 1880s into the 1920s.

Similar in approach and layout to the 'briar' designs by Walter Crane (1880) and later John Henry Dearle at Morris & Co. (1912), this paper includes an unusual combination of motifs, including stylised Tudor roses and small flowerheads rather like *vinca major*. The latter flowers, commonly known as periwinkle, probably provide the paper with its name.

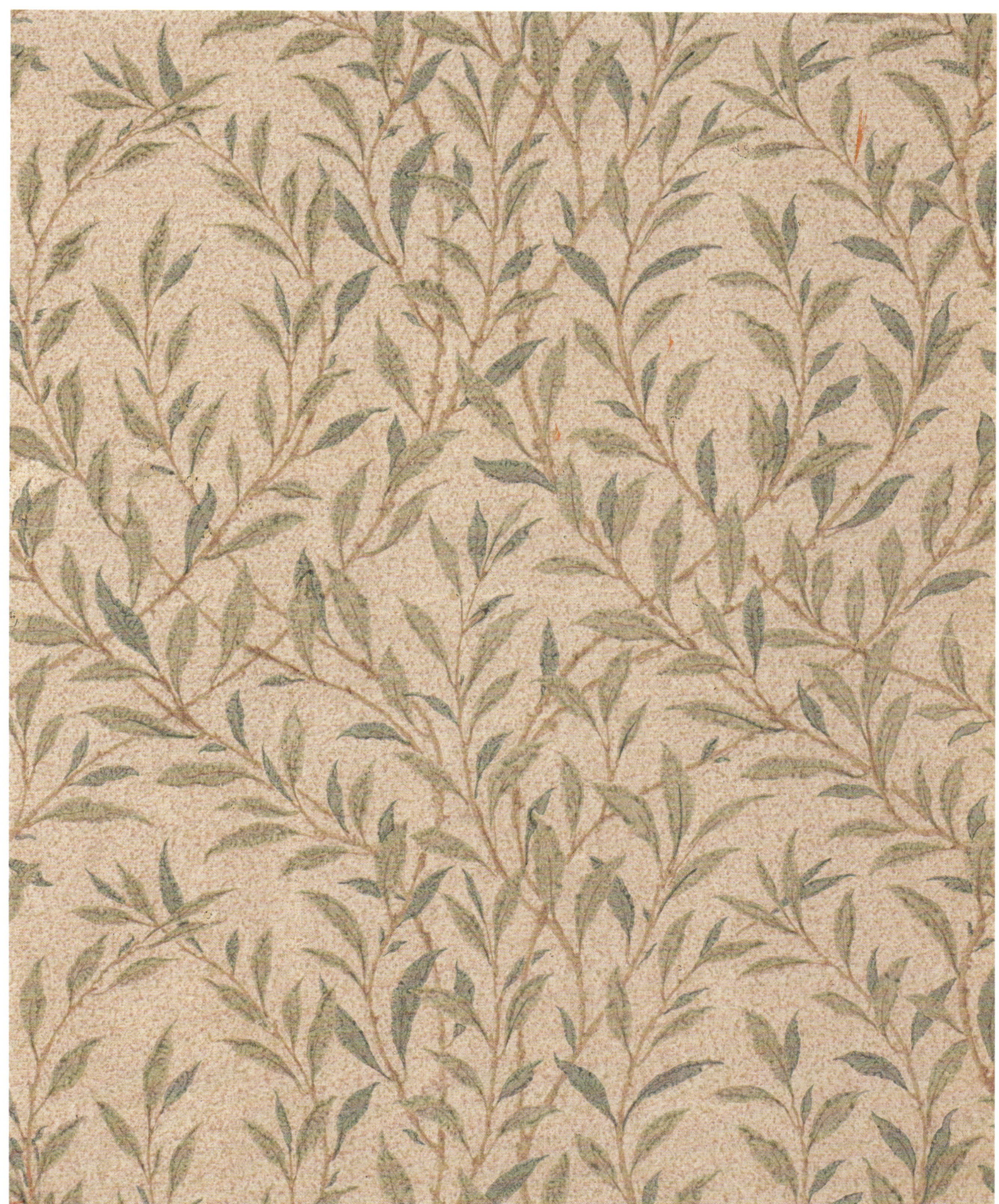

052 | Metford Warner, *The Osier*, 1924, Jeffrey & Co.

This paper shows the design skills of Metford Warner, best known as the man William Morris trusted to print his wallpapers. The design shows a departure from similar foliage patterns in having a symmetrical structure. It is one of the last patterns by Warner, who retired from Jeffrey & Co. the year it was designed.

The osier is a form of willow, an enduring symbol in arts and crafts wallpapers. Its flexible stems, known as withies, were used in traditional British woodland industries, particularly roof thatching and basket making. Both crafts were reclaimed by the rural preservation societies that formed after the First World War and were inspired by William Morris's ideas.

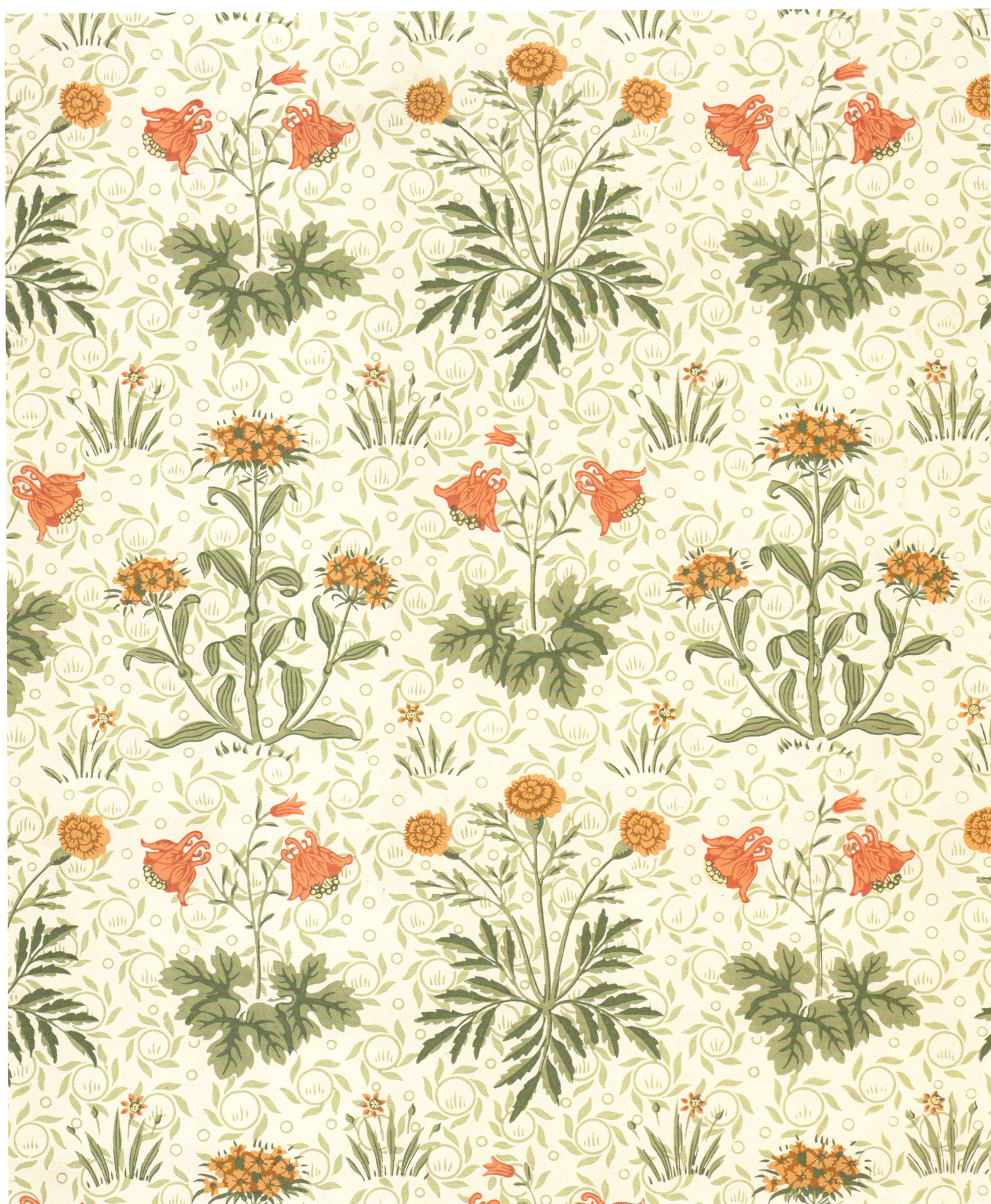

053 | Designer unknown, *Daisy*, c.1885, Jeffrey & Co.

Nearly every late 19th-century wallpaper manufacturer produced its own version of Morris's 1864 *Daisy* wallpaper. This version appears in Jeffrey & Co's book of 'Patent Hygienic Wallpapers', c.1885. 'Hygienic' refers to the paper's washability and the book cover states that its papers 'may be cleaned with soap and water'.

Jeffrey & Co.'s claims also guaranteed papers would be free from arsenic, an increasingly important factor given rising concern about green arsenic-based pigments. Woollams had begun developing arsenic-free papers in 1859–60, but Morris, a director of a large arsenic-producing mine near Tavistock from 1871 to 1875, only ceased using it in 1880.

054 | William Morris, *Daisy*, 1864 (registered), Jeffrey & Co. for Morris, Marshall, Faulkner & Co.

Although *Daisy* was Morris's second wallpaper design, it was the first pattern to be printed by Jeffrey & Co. A fine botanical draughtsman, Morris's inspiration for *Daisy* drew upon Jean Froissart's 1470s' *Chroniques*, Vol. IV, part 1, in which naïve, flat frontal foliate backdrops support gold-decorated initials with figures and animals.

Froissart's illuminated manuscripts reflect decorative wall hangings of the 15th century. It was this type of pattern that Morris himself used when designing *mille fleur* backgrounds for The Firm's tapestries, which were first woven in 1879. However, they also appear in the ceiling painting he designed in 1866 for Jesus College Chapel, Cambridge.

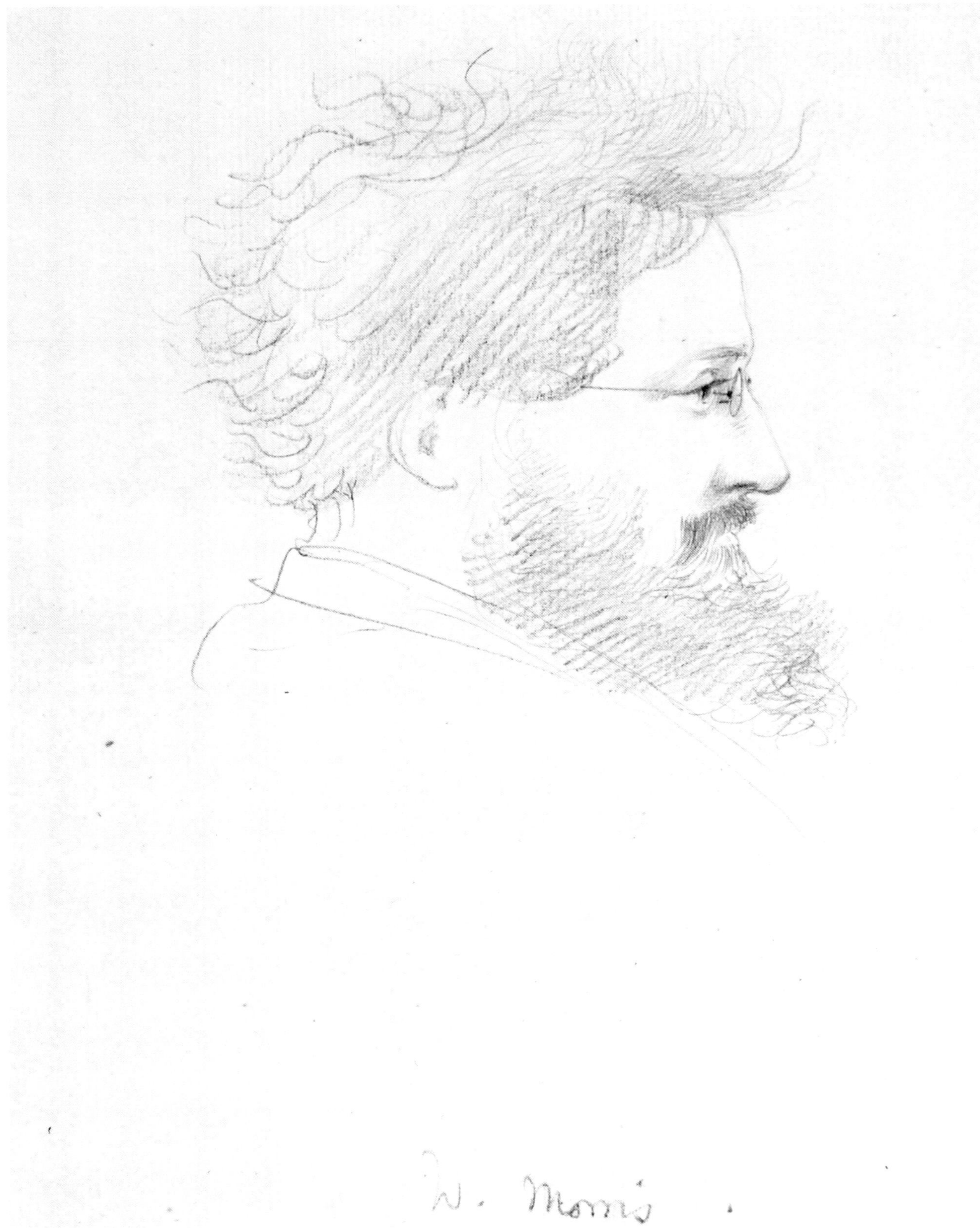

055 | *William Morris*, George Howard, courtesy of Tullie House Museum & Art Gallery Trust

"… Morris is the true prophet of the 20th century. We owe it to him that an ordinary man's dwelling-house has once more become a worthy object of the architect's thought, and a chair, a wallpaper, or a vase, a worthy object of the artist's imagination."

Nikolaus Pevsner, in *Pioneers of Modern Design* (1936)

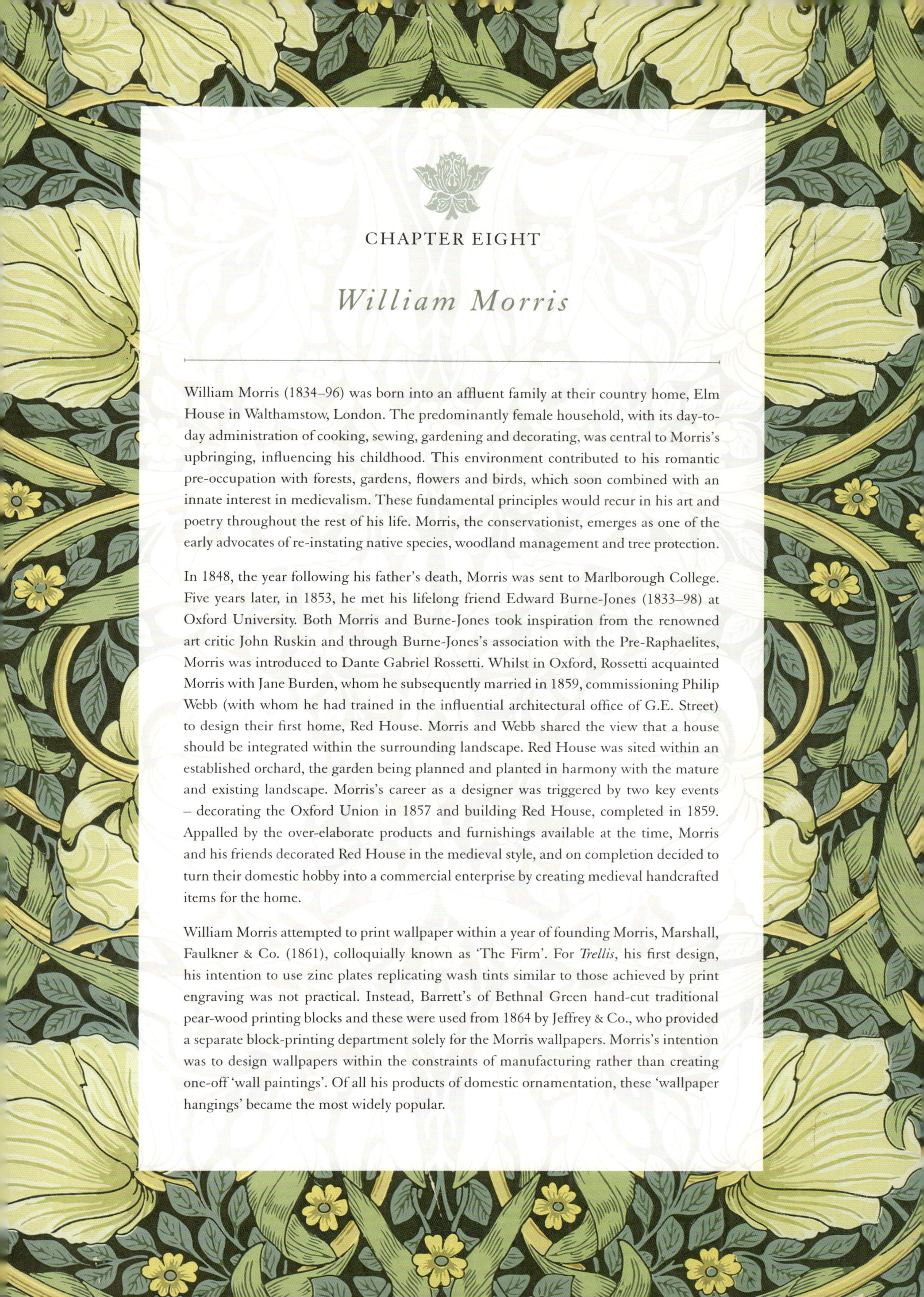

CHAPTER EIGHT

William Morris

William Morris (1834–96) was born into an affluent family at their country home, Elm House in Walthamstow, London. The predominantly female household, with its day-to-day administration of cooking, sewing, gardening and decorating, was central to Morris's upbringing, influencing his childhood. This environment contributed to his romantic pre-occupation with forests, gardens, flowers and birds, which soon combined with an innate interest in medievalism. These fundamental principles would recur in his art and poetry throughout the rest of his life. Morris, the conservationist, emerges as one of the early advocates of re-instating native species, woodland management and tree protection.

In 1848, the year following his father's death, Morris was sent to Marlborough College. Five years later, in 1853, he met his lifelong friend Edward Burne-Jones (1833–98) at Oxford University. Both Morris and Burne-Jones took inspiration from the renowned art critic John Ruskin and through Burne-Jones's association with the Pre-Raphaelites, Morris was introduced to Dante Gabriel Rossetti. Whilst in Oxford, Rossetti acquainted Morris with Jane Burden, whom he subsequently married in 1859, commissioning Philip Webb (with whom he had trained in the influential architectural office of G.E. Street) to design their first home, Red House. Morris and Webb shared the view that a house should be integrated within the surrounding landscape. Red House was sited within an established orchard, the garden being planned and planted in harmony with the mature and existing landscape. Morris's career as a designer was triggered by two key events – decorating the Oxford Union in 1857 and building Red House, completed in 1859. Appalled by the over-elaborate products and furnishings available at the time, Morris and his friends decorated Red House in the medieval style, and on completion decided to turn their domestic hobby into a commercial enterprise by creating medieval handcrafted items for the home.

William Morris attempted to print wallpaper within a year of founding Morris, Marshall, Faulkner & Co. (1861), colloquially known as 'The Firm'. For *Trellis*, his first design, his intention to use zinc plates replicating wash tints similar to those achieved by print engraving was not practical. Instead, Barrett's of Bethnal Green hand-cut traditional pear-wood printing blocks and these were used from 1864 by Jeffrey & Co., who provided a separate block-printing department solely for the Morris wallpapers. Morris's intention was to design wallpapers within the constraints of manufacturing rather than creating one-off 'wall paintings'. Of all his products of domestic ornamentation, these 'wallpaper hangings' became the most widely popular.

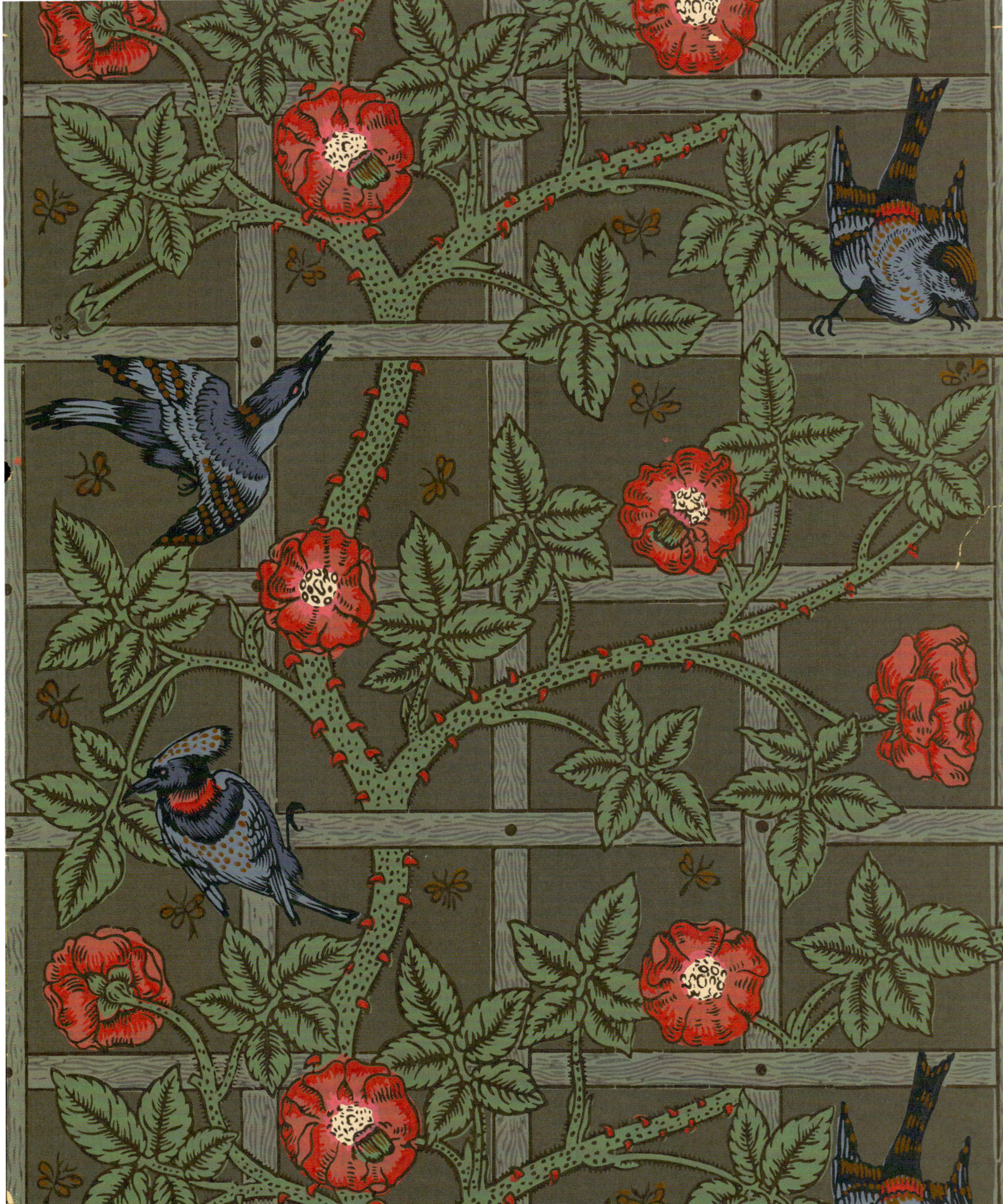

056 | William Morris, *Trellis*, 1864, Jeffrey & Co. for Morris, Marshall, Faulkner & Co.

Trellis was the first wallpaper pattern created by William Morris. It was inspired by the trellis work and rose arbours at his marital home from 1860–65, Red House. Designed for Morris by his friend and collaborator Philip Webb (1831–1915), this house broke with contemporary architectural practice, combining informal living areas with a practical studio space.

Some suggest that the birds were drawn by Webb, but this was disputed by Morris's daughter Jenny. The design for this pattern was created in 1863, but Morris's own experiments with traditional German zinc-plate printing failed. This led to the relationship between Morris & Co. and Jeffrey & Co., confirmed in 1864 and lasting until 1927.

057 | William Morris, *Fruit*, 1864, Jeffrey & Co. for Morris, Marshall, Faulkner & Co.

Morris's original artwork for this pattern featured quadrants of olives, pomegranates, oranges and lemons. In the end, however, the olives were removed and the design modified to include additional pomegranate flowers. Historically, *Fruit* has been labelled incorrectly as 'Pomegranate', perhaps because of this modification.

Fruit was much admired by Morris's lifelong friend Edward Burne-Jones, who used this design to decorate his own dining room at The Grange, North End, Fulham, where he lived from 1867 until his death in 1898. It contained his studio and for at least ten years became a salon for fellow members of the Pre-Raphaelite Brotherhood and The Firm, such as Rossetti.

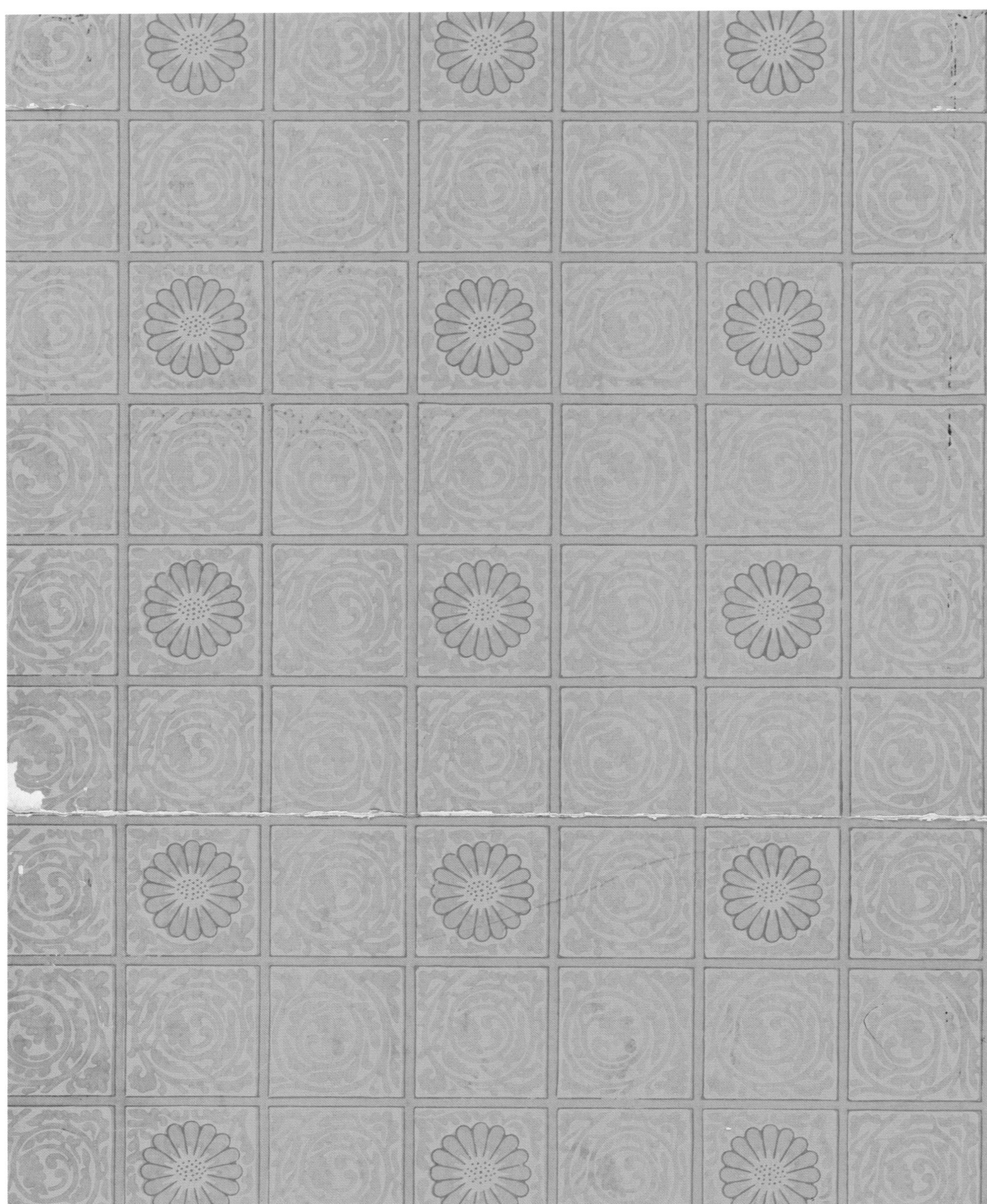

058 | William Morris, *Diaper*, 1870, Jeffrey & Co. for Morris, Marshall, Faulkner & Co.

Designed in 1868, this early block-print takes reference from 'diapering', a decorative treatment using square, chequer, diaper, lozenge or rectangular repeating patterns frequently practised in the creation of medieval stained glass. While not recognisable instantly as a Morris design, *Diaper* demonstrates his knowledge of stylised medieval imagery.

Stained glass was the bedrock on which Morris, Marshall, Faulkner & Co. was founded, and Morris had a detailed understanding of the process, overseeing recreations with the simplicity of medieval examples yet creating something unique. While the figurative work in The Firm's stained glass was done primarily by Burne-Jones, Morris's diaper backgrounds were essential.

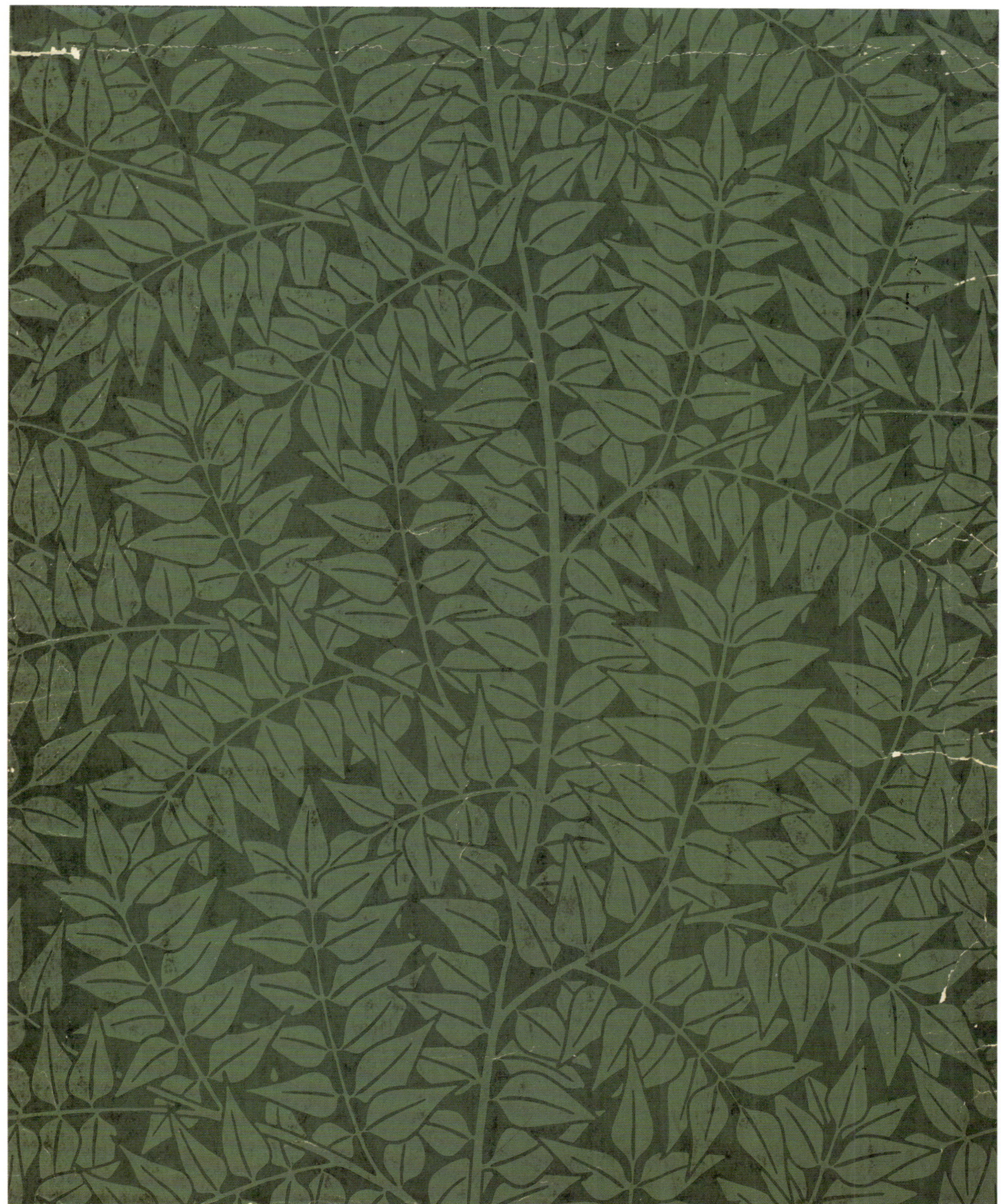

059 | William Morris, *Branch*, 1871, Jeffrey & Co. for Morris, Marshall, Faulkner & Co.

Like *Diaper*, this optically complicated wallpaper design only required two blocks, as opposed to the 11 and 12 needed for *Trellis* and *Fruit* respectively. It was designed as a back-print or 'under-print' for *Scroll* – which required a further ten blocks to complete – but in addition provided a richly toned surface in its own right.

Morris aimed in his designs to suggest the richness and growth found in nature itself, without creating a restless effect. In his view, the main challenge for designers when organising patterns for wallpapers was in finding a balance between what he called 'mystery' and 'clarity'. The result was to be stimulating and refreshing but not overtaxing.

060 | William Morris, *Scroll*, 1871, Jeffrey & Co. for Morris, Marshall, Faulkner & Co.

The use of back-prints in support of a feature design would subsequently become a Morris & Co. trademark and *Scroll*, sometimes referred to as *Scroll & Flower*, is an early example of this characteristic style. Although uncomplicated and elementary in character, *Scroll* was, at the time, one of The Firm's most expensive wallpapers.

In developing designs of this sort – with two layered patterns that together produced the impression of depth without being realistically three-dimensional in their representation – Morris pioneered a creative style diametrically opposed to the naturalistic appearance that had dominated wallpaper patterns of the mid-Victorian era.

061 | William Morris, *Jasmine*, 1872, Jeffrey & Co. for Morris, Marshall, Faulkner & Co.

In 1871, William Morris stumbled across [what he described as] 'a little house out of London' with delightful gardens: Kelmscott Manor in the Cotswolds. Observing the flowers in the countryside and absorbing the delicate scent of the jasmine climbing the walls of his country retreat led Morris to create the all-over block-printed pattern seen here.

Morris wrote of his garden in many letters to Thomas Wardle (1831–1909), a skilled textile dyer; in the latter's Hencroft works in Leek, he taught Morris everything he could about dyeing and printing with natural dyes. In 1875 and 1877, Morris travelled to Leek, staying with the Wardle family. By 1876, Wardle was printing a range of 14 Morris textiles.

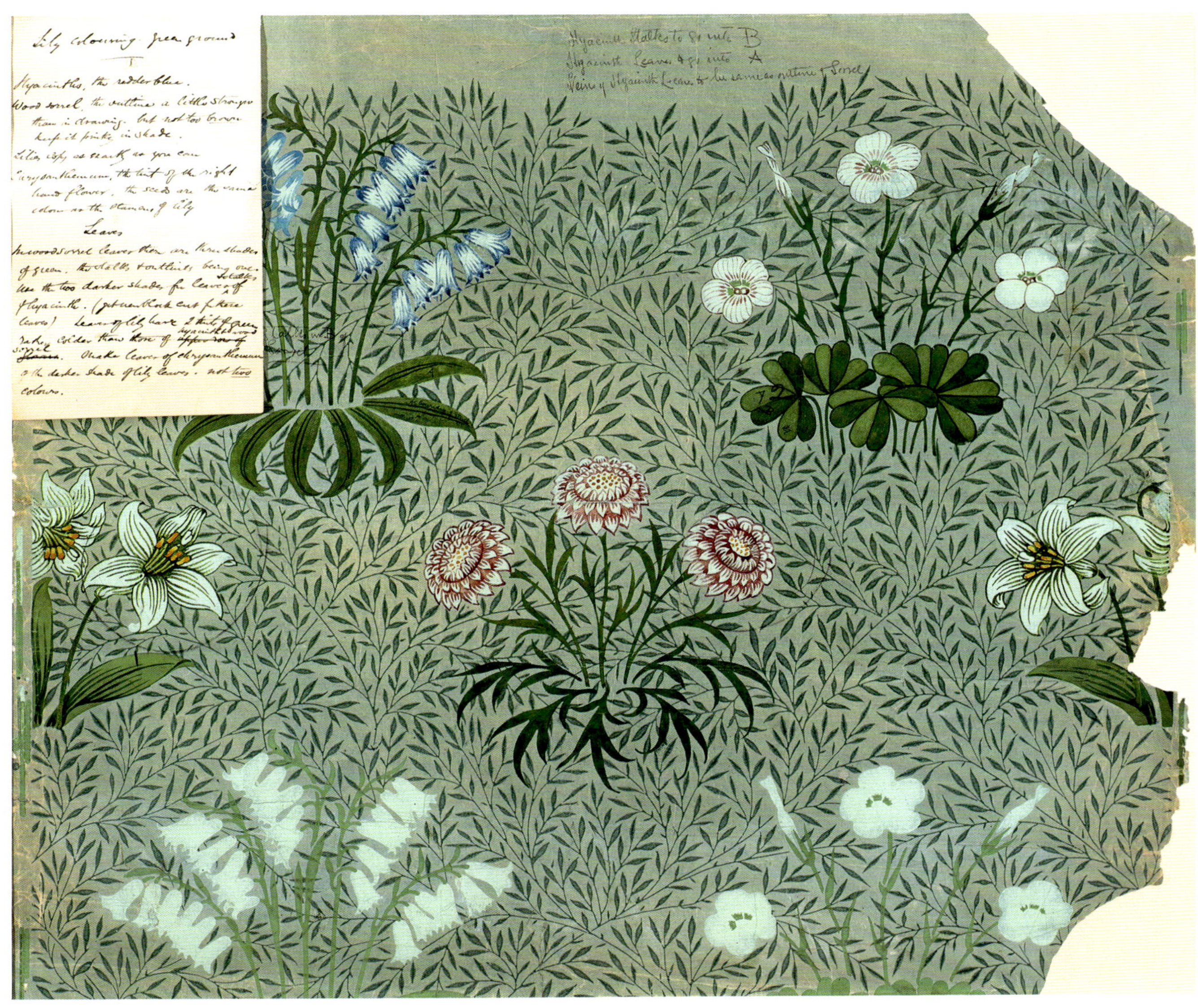

062 | William Morris, *Lily*, 1874, Jeffrey & Co. for Morris, Marshall, Faulkner & Co.

This unique, remarkable colour 'trial sample' was sent to William Morris by Jeffrey & Co. After several abortive attempts and the receipt of detailed handwritten notes regarding the colouring and details of the shapes, also shown here, Jeffrey finally received Morris's approval. Such attention to detail was to underpin all of Morris's creative endeavours.

During 1874, William Morris finalised his partition from his business partners in order to establish his own company, writing: 'I should very much like to make the business quite a success, and it can't be unless I work at it myself.' This and much else can be found in *The Collected Letters of William Morris, Volume I: 1848–80* (p.178).

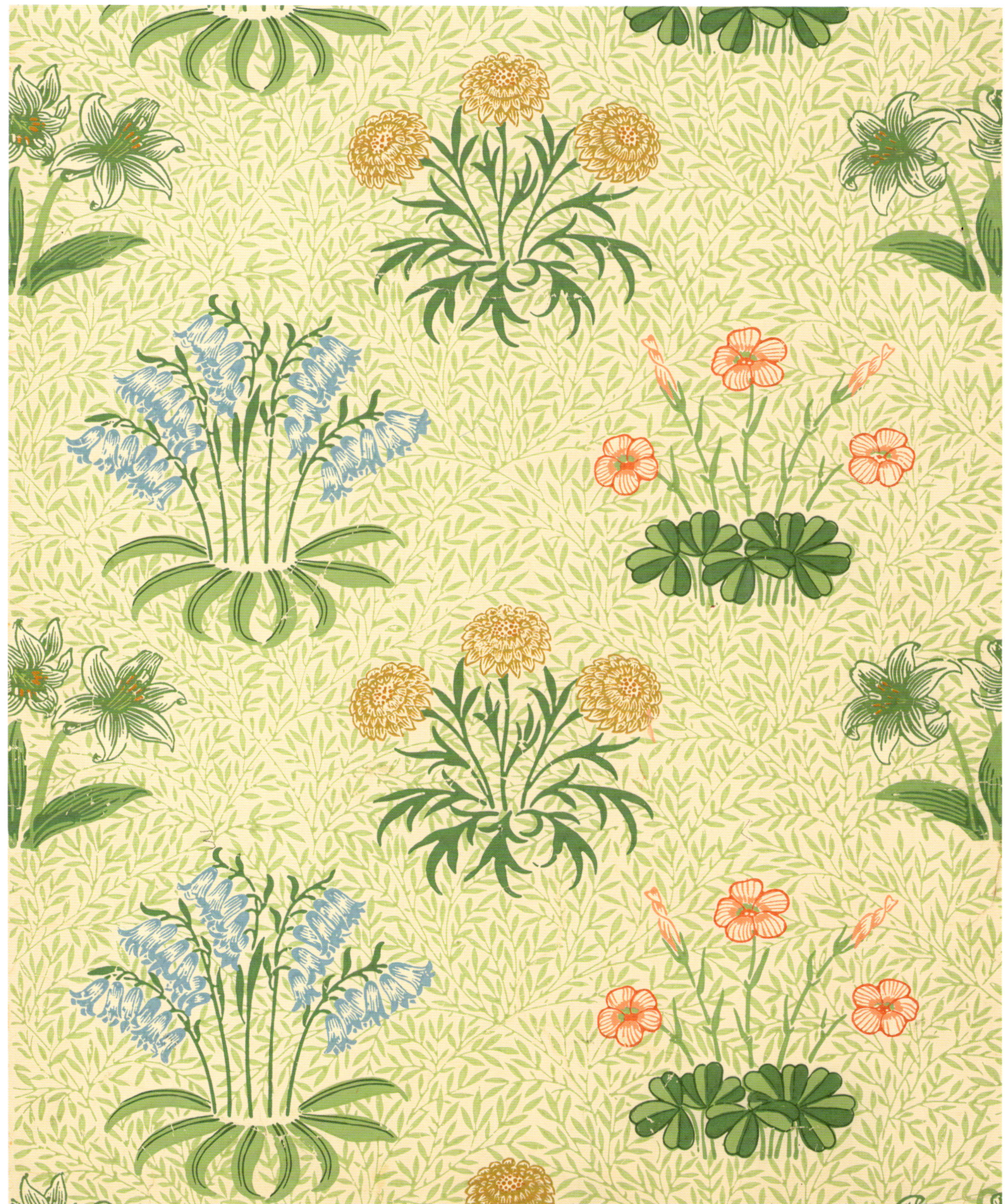

063 | William Morris, *Lily*, 1874, Jeffrey & Co. for Morris, Marshall, Faulkner & Co.

Morris designed only two wallpapers with repeating millefleurs-style motifs of the type seen in the medieval tapestries. *Lily* adheres to and observes the sensitivity and essence of *Daisy*, created some ten years earlier. It was designed for use in bedrooms, including Morris's own at Kelmscott Manor in Oxfordshire.

It would appear from entries in the Morris & Co. factory logbooks that *Lily* was reprinted less frequently than the more popular *Daisy* wallpaper. Nevertheless, Morris's fascination with medieval tapestries bore fruit in 1879, when he taught himself tapestry-weaving and set up a tapestry workshop with his apprentice John Henry Dearle at Queen Square, Bloomsbury.

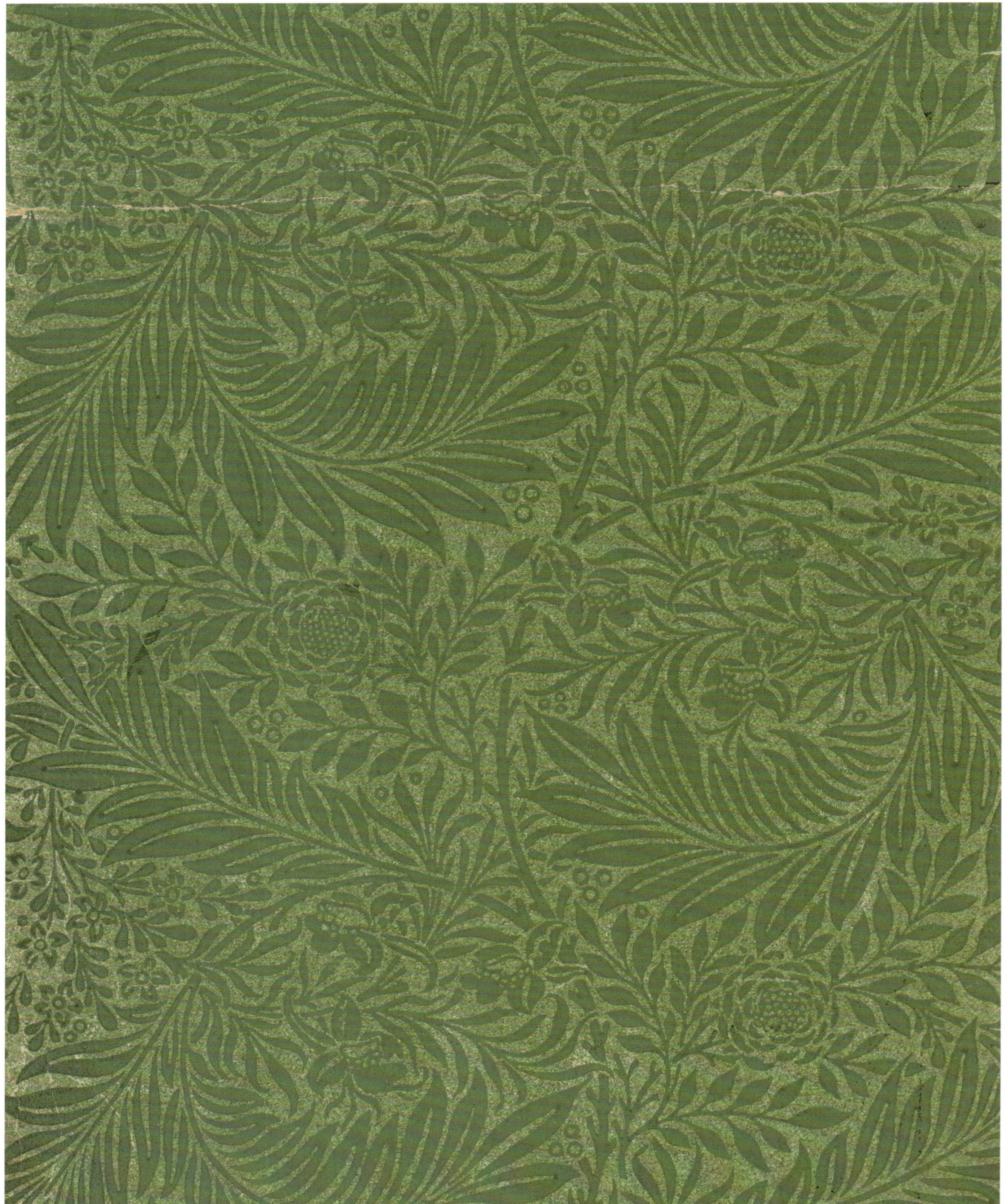

064 | William Morris, *Larkspur*, 1872, Jeffrey & Co. for Morris, Marshall, Faulkner & Co.

Morris named this block-print after the Greek flower delphinium, subsequently named larkspur by the British. The first in a series of monochrome block-printed wallpapers, it proved to be well received. Sought after by middle-class Victorian homeowners, it sold at the low end of The Firm's price range of 3 shillings (about £10 today) to 16 shillings a roll.

It also had a broadening audience. From the early-1870s, Morris & Co. wallpapers, fabrics and carpets became available to American consumers through the firm's authorised agent in New York, as well at stores in Boston, Philadelphia and the then-largest department store in the world, Marshall Field & Co., Chicago. It decorated the home of W.A.S. Benson in c.1898.

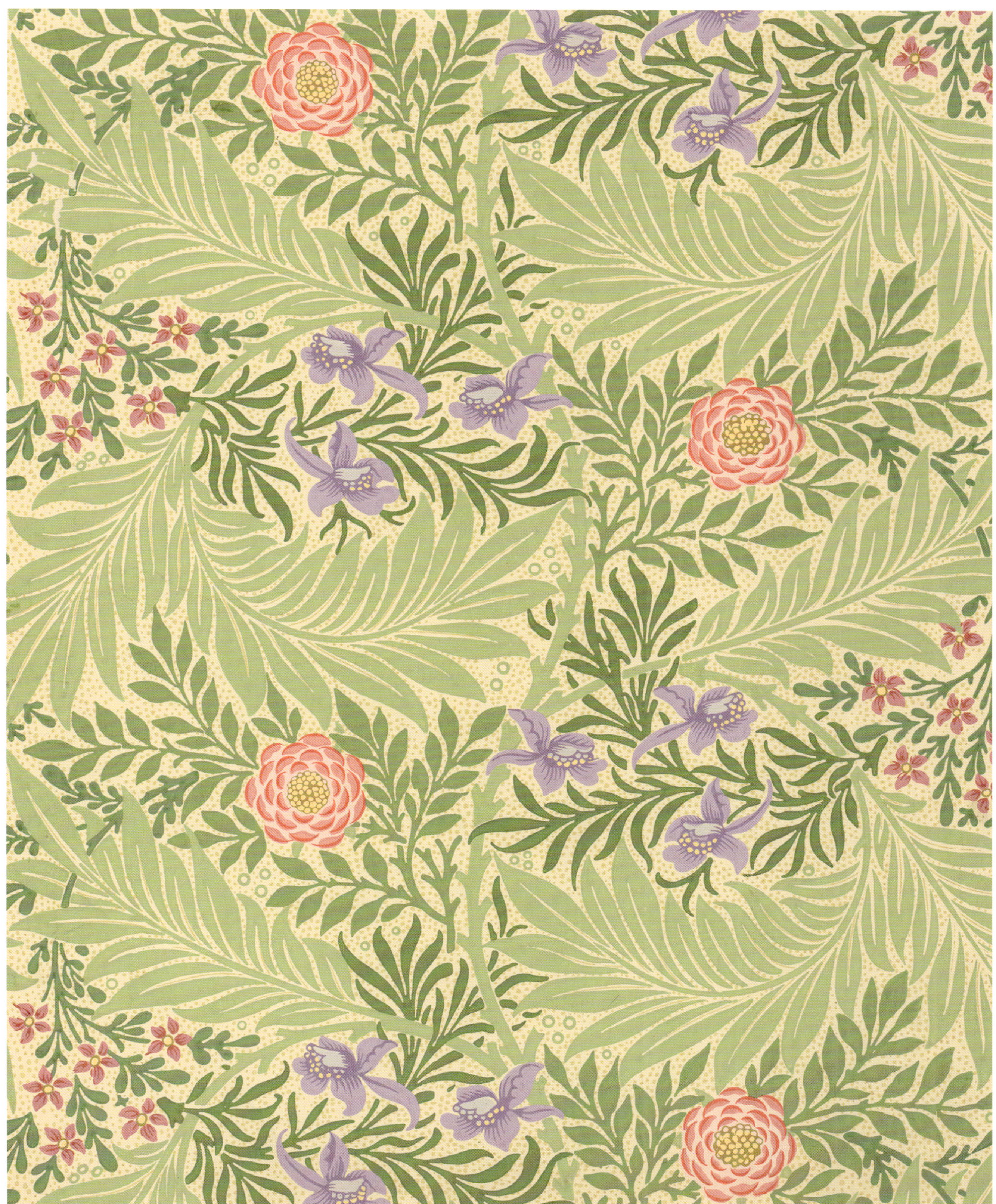

065 | William Morris, *Light Larkspur*, 1875, Jeffrey & Co. for Morris & Co.

Following the apparent success of *Larkspur*, Morris created the multi-coloured variation seen here, which was registered at the same time as *Marigold* in April 1875. Printed on light grounds with colourful, clear and bright water-based emulsions, *Light Larkspur* offered clients of the newly formed Morris & Co. an instantly appealing decorative wallpaper.

Light Larkspur is also the first fully resolved expression of what would become a signature of Morris's interpretation of the curves of living plants. The composition employs a meandering line that provides a subtle structure suggestive of vine-like movement. Here casting off coiling leaves, this device can be seen in many later Morris patterns.

066 | William Morris, *Willow*, 1874, Jeffrey & Co. for Morris, Marshall, Faulkner & Co.

In 1874, The Firm launched four new block-printed wallpaper patterns, including *Willow*, which added a new dimension to wall decoration. The first *Willow* design reflected simple amassed foliage on a pastel ground; subsequently Morris & Co. would re-issue the design block-printed on a complex ground of small hedgerow berries, as seen here.

The English wallpaper industry flourished during the 19th century, with both block-printed and machine-printed papers saturating the market. Since launching its first block-printed wallpaper ten years earlier, Morris, Marshall, Faulkner & Co. created only 12 wallpapers plus three adaptations of traditional designs, a total considered insignificant at the time.

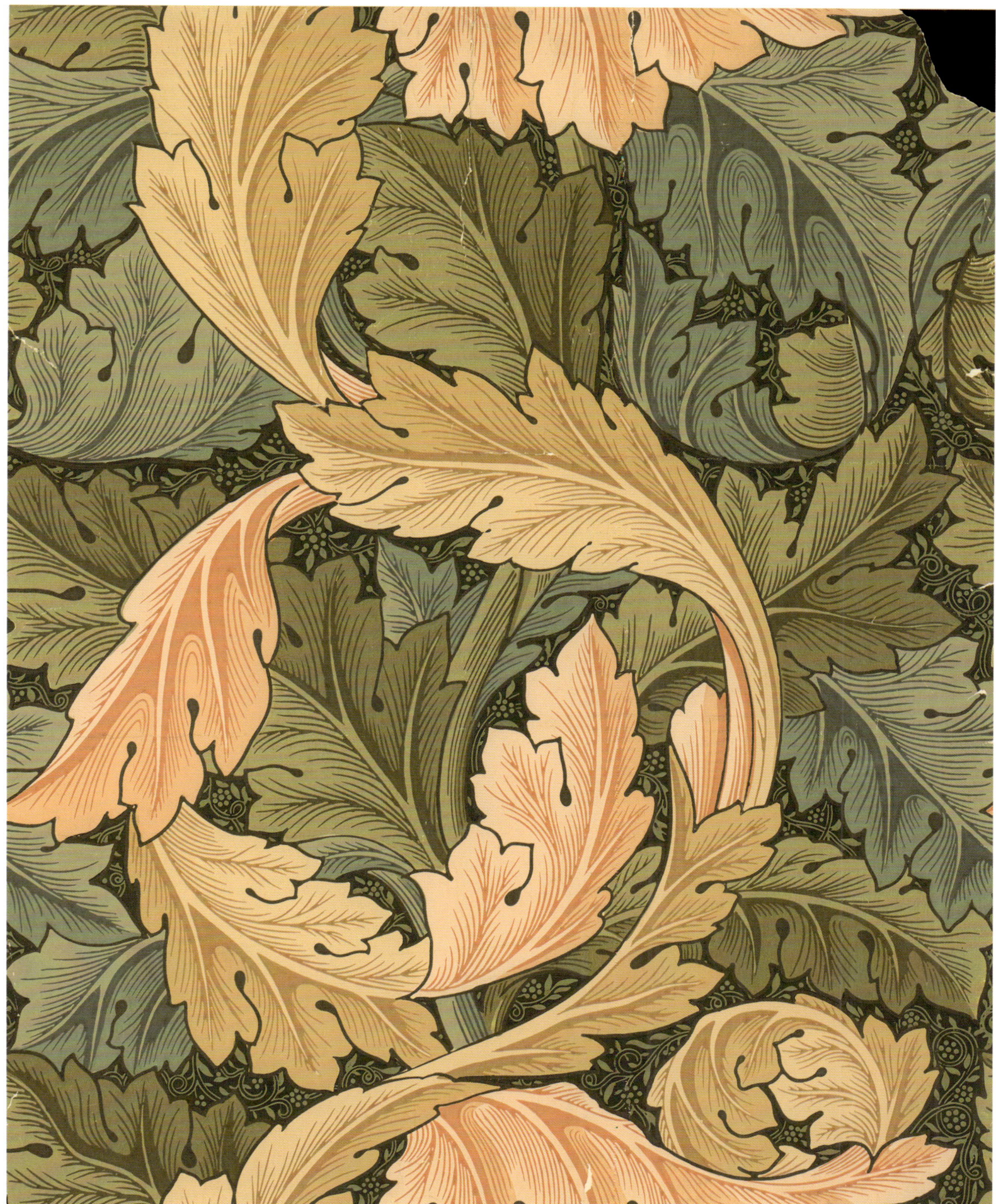

067 | William Morris, *Acanthus*, 1875, Jeffrey & Co. for Morris & Co.

Morris's first design for the reconfigured Morris & Co., *Acanthus*, reflects his now-famous layering technique, creating depth without three-dimensional imagery. The appeal of this pattern proved far reaching. It decorated many *nouveau riches* homes, including Wightwick Manor, home to a Pre-Raphaelite art collection and now cared for by the National Trust.

Acanthus was the first wallpaper to be issued following the dissolution of Morris, Marshall, Faulkner & Co. in March 1875; the new company, Morris & Co., was managed and controlled by William Morris, assisted by Edward Burne-Jones. Essentially self-taught, the latter as a painter, designer and illustrator was one of the last of the Pre-Raphaelites.

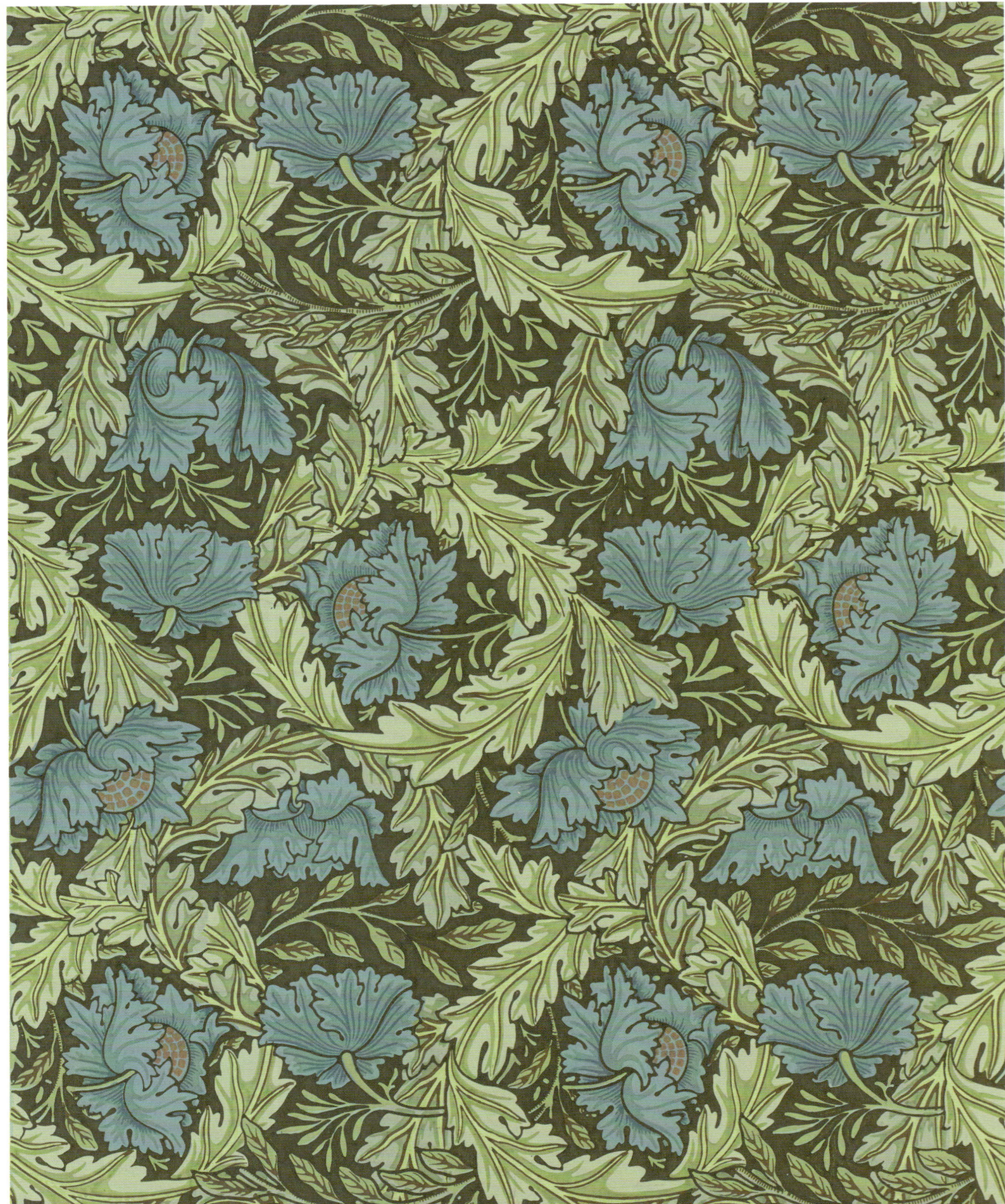

068 | William Morris, *Wreath*, 1876, Jeffrey & Co. for Morris & Co.

Optically, this pattern is of a smaller scale but similar design layout to that of *Acanthus* and, whilst the impact may be less dramatic, the design requires 22 print blocks to complete the extended height repeat, nearly twice the number of many seemingly more elaborate patterns such as *Scroll* (1871).

The *Wreath* wallpaper block print follows similar characteristics to Morris's first carpet patterns – registered the same year – in which inter-twined poppy heads and foliage are embraced by acanthus leaves. Some five years later, Morris & Co. carpet-weaving was established as part of the manufacturing complex at Merton Abbey Mill (see p.89).

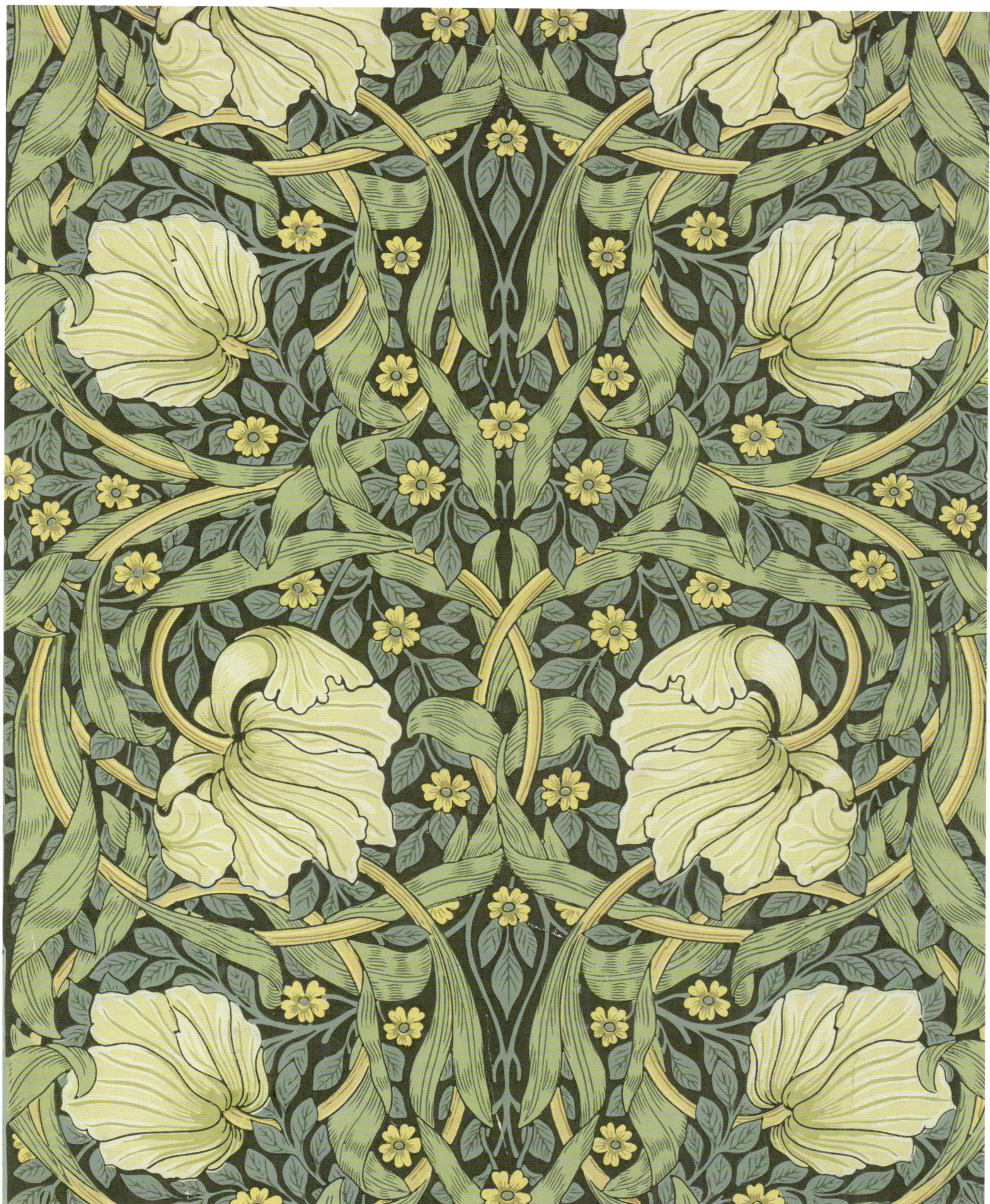

069 | William Morris, *Pimpernel*, 1876, Jeffrey & Co. for Morris & Co.

This bold design features large-scale, scrolling tulip flowers yet, typically, Morris named the design after the secondary flower, in this case the tiny yellow pimpernel. *Pimpernel* was used by Morris in the dining room of his London home, Kelmscott House, in a space described by Sydney Cockerell as Morris's 'enchanted interior'.

In 1887, Sir Geoffrey Mander and his wife decorated their entire family home, Wightwick Manor, Wolverhampton, with furnishings purchased from Morris & Co. Sir Geoffrey's billiard room walls were decorated with the *Pimpernel* wallpaper. When extended in 1893 by the architect Edward Ould, further Morris & Co. decor graced the Great Parlour.

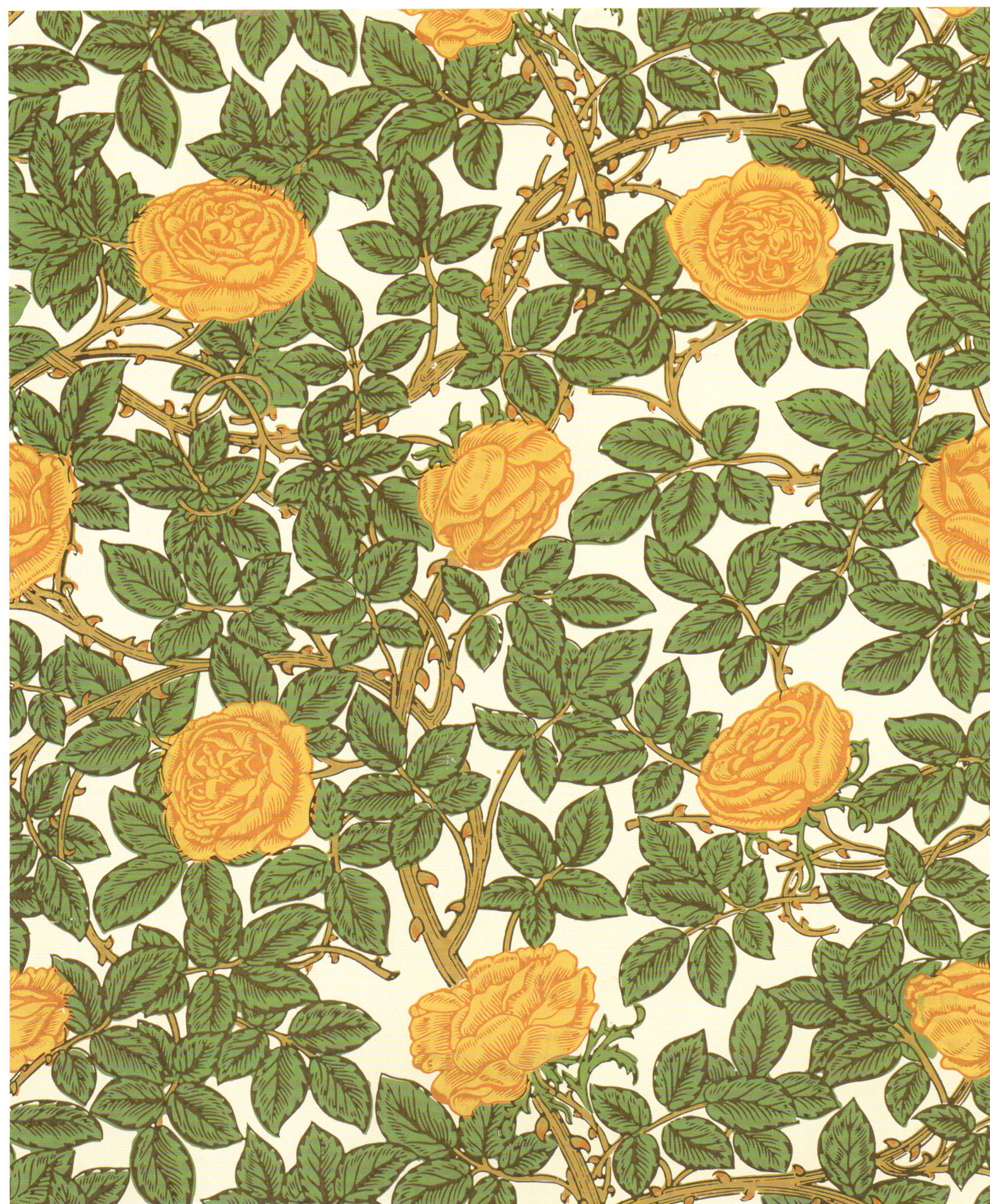

070 | William Morris, *Rose*, 1877, Jeffrey & Co. for Morris & Co.

Morris based his *Rose* wallpaper on the medieval rose, which symbolised not only Christianity's Virgin Mary but also secular earthly love and beauty. Returning Crusaders brought back to Europe a heightened appreciation of the rose, prized for its beauty and fragrance, as well as its culinary and medicinal value.

While the rose motif was frequently employed by Morris within the designs created for Morris & Co. carpets, tapestries and textiles, it occurred less often in his wallpapers. Nevertheless, it appeared throughout his lifetime as a wild rose in his first design, *Trellis*, as seen here, and in *Pink and Rose*, which he designed in about 1890.

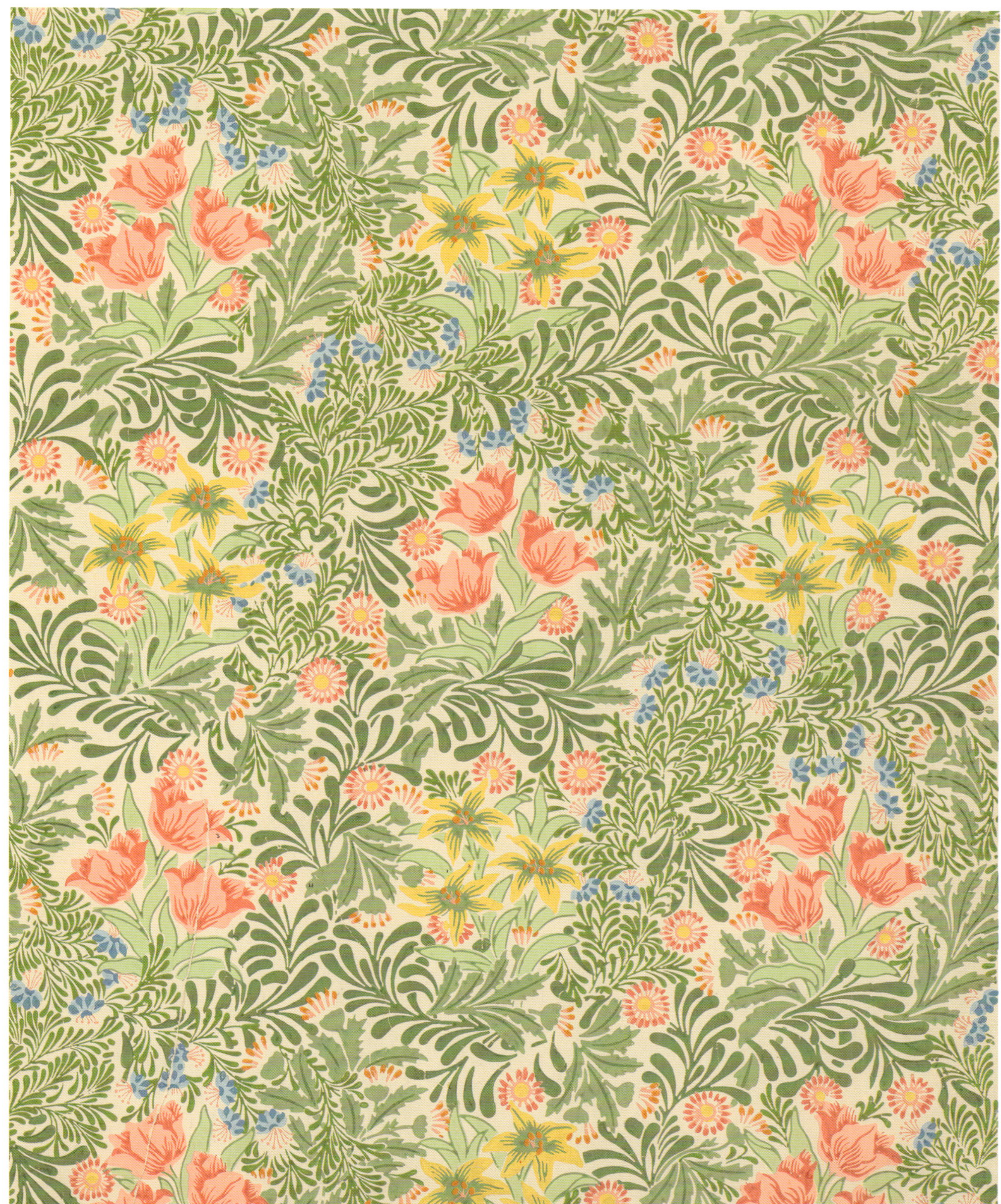

071 | William Morris, *Bower*, 1877, Jeffrey & Co. for Morris & Co.

The dense, all-over composition of flowering plants and swirling foliage in *Bower* is also typical of the Morris early designs for textiles that date from 1873 to 1876. It was in this period that a few patterns were used simultaneously for wallpapers and textiles. Among these was *Larkspur* of 1872, which in 1875 became both printed and woven textiles.

Morris was already familiar with convoluted medieval wood carvings and their similarly shallow and stylised motifs. He most certainly saw the carved shrine at St Albans Abbey, Hertfordshire, which became the first project undertaken by the Society for the Protection of Ancient Buildings, for which Morris, Philip Webb and George Wardle wrote the manifesto.

072 | William Morris, *Ceiling*, 1877 (registered), Jeffrey & Co. for Morris & Co.

This is one of five papers created by William Morris for ceiling decoration. Wall and ceiling papers became increasingly popular during the 19th century, and some were considered a cheap and effective means of brightening up cramped and dark rooms. This example would have been inexpensive since it required only one printing block.

Victorian living room walls were divided into three specific sections: dado, filling and frieze. The hard-wearing dado (chair rail) paper provided a practical dark-patterned surface while the filling paper at eye level created a decorative stage, surmounted by either an architectural or foliate frieze. The addition of a multi-directional 'ceiling paper' completed the scheme.

073 | William Morris, *Apple*, 1877, Jeffrey & Co. for Morris & Co.

William Morris's appreciation for and enjoyment in enfolding willow foliage to enhance his designs is perfectly reflected in his *Apple* wallpaper design. Furthermore, the layout of the serpentine acanthus leaves bears a remarkable similarity to those represented in *Chrysanthemum*, designed in the same year.

After Morris sold Red House in 1865, the property changed hands several times until, in 1952, it was acquired by Edward 'Ted' Ernest Hollamby, who embarked upon a major refurbishment and decorated the entrance hall with *Apple* wallpaper. The wallpaper can still be seen by visitors to the house, now owned and managed by the National Trust.

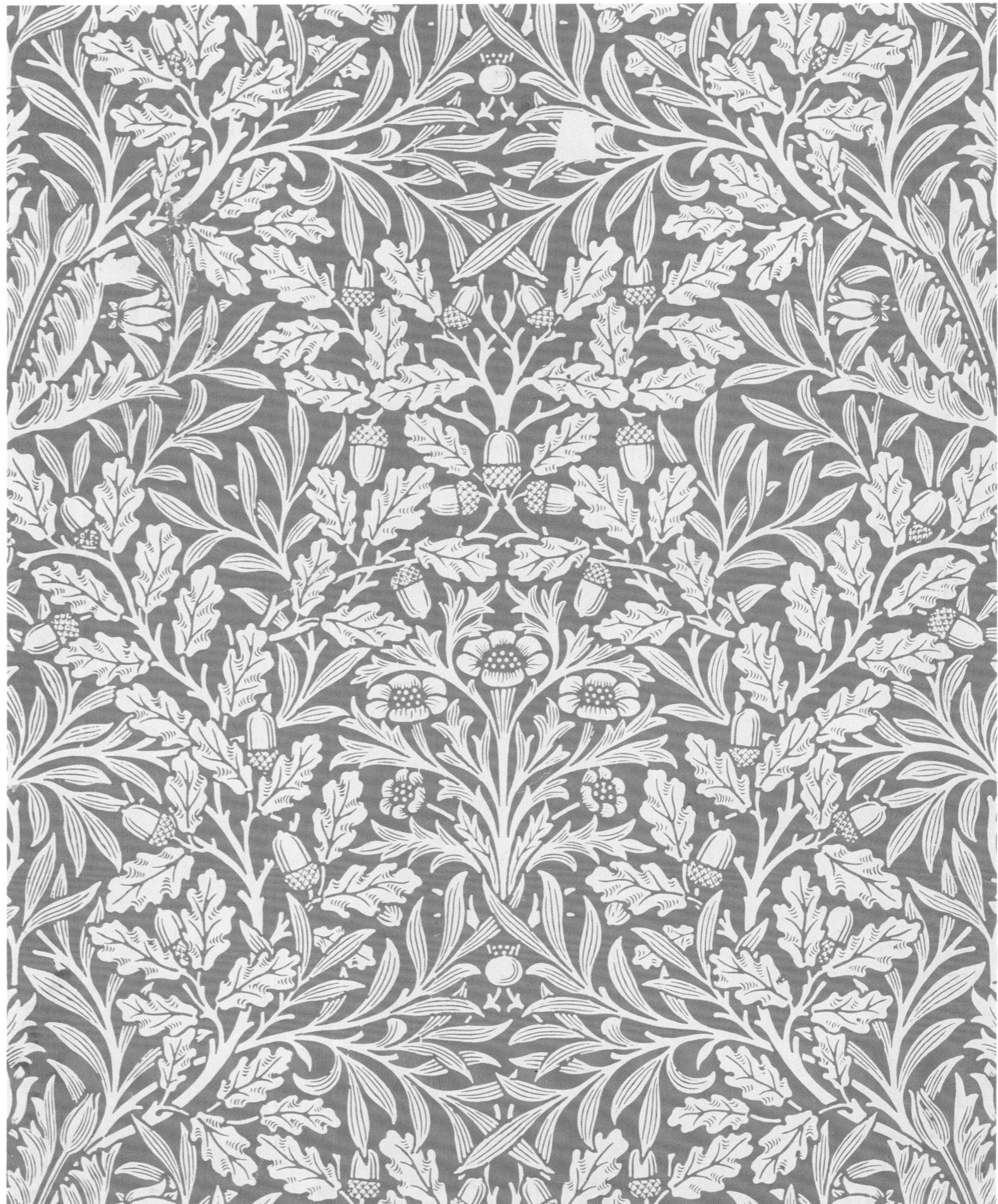

074 | William Morris, *Acorn*, 1879, Jeffrey & Co. for Morris & Co.

On 7 January 1879, William Morris registered both the *Acorn* and *Sunflower* wallpaper designs. Commensurate with several Morris designs, the pattern frequently camouflaged the print image from the ground colour. *Acorn* is no exception to this anomaly: the print image is the dark colour and the delicate light colour is, in fact, the ground.

Acorn symbolises Morris's love of his childhood playground, Epping Forest, where he had visited Queen Elizabeth's Hunting Lodge, standing in an oak-filled ancient woodland hunting forest. Less than five miles (7.4km) away is the William Morris Gallery, located in a Georgian house that was Morris's family home from 1848 to 1856.

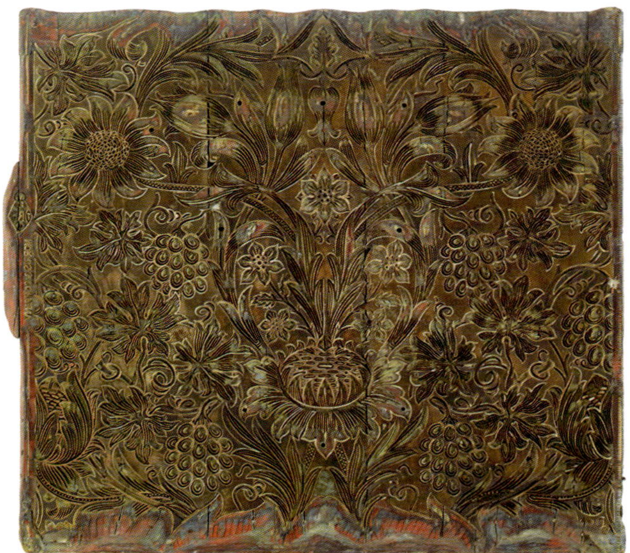

075a | *Sunflower Block*, 1879, Alfred Barratt for Morris & Co

Block-printing was the heart and soul of the Morris & Co. wallpaper business. The pear-wood printing blocks made by Alfred Barratt of 489 Bethnal Green Road, London were supervised by William Morris prior to printing. This block was made with a brass outline in-filled with dense woollen felt.

075 | William Morris, *Sunflower*, 1879, Jeffrey & Co. for Morris & Co.

As a single-colour design, *Sunflower*, along with *Acorn* and *Mallow*, were relatively inexpensive papers to produce and so more affordable to buy. Produced in a range of soft colours, *Sunflower* could be bought for just 4/6d (4 shillings and 6 pence) per piece, considerably less than the 11/- (11 shillings) price tag for multiple-block designs, the equivalent of two days' wages.

This pattern was one of several additionally produced as a foil-ground paper, giving some indication of its popularity. It is not to be confused with another design of the same name that was the work of John Henry Dearle for Morris & Co. The latter was handloom-woven in wool on the Jacquard looms at Merton Abbey Mill and dates from c.1890.

076 | William Morris, *The St James's Ceiling*, 1881, Jeffrey & Co. for Morris & Co.

William Morris created the large-scale, multi-directional, single-colour St James's ceiling paper design to complement the intricate and complex *St James's* wallpaper. Once installed, the ceiling paper created a *trompe l'oeil* effect, replicating the decorative plasterwork of London's historic houses and palaces.

This was the second commission from St James's Palace, which included the decoration and furnishing of the Blue Room and Throne Room. The first commission had been for the Armoury and Tapestry Room, which was undertaken by Morris, Marshall, Faulkner & Co. in 1866/67. The latter was The Firm's first secular commission.

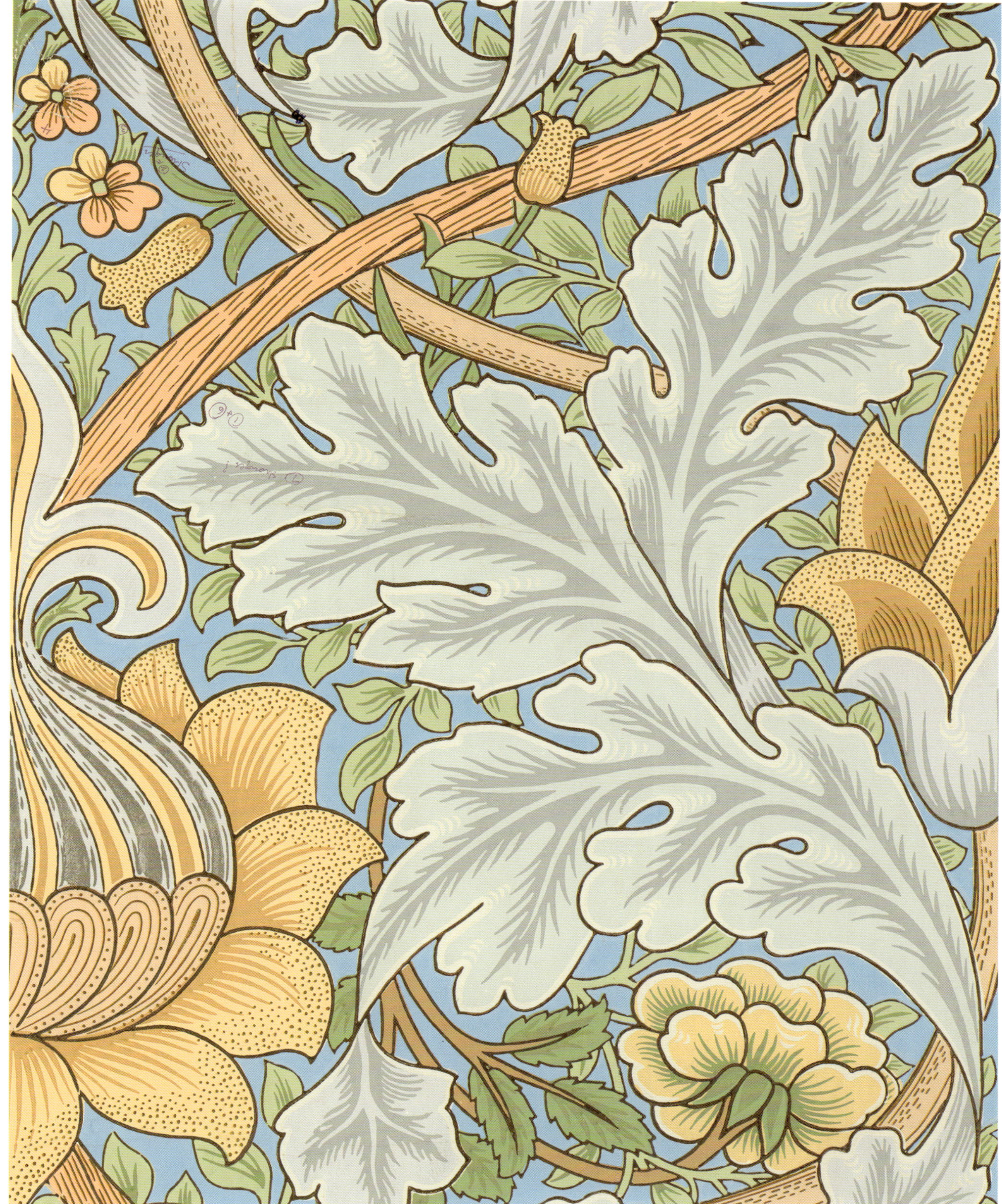

077 | William Morris, *St James's*, 1881, Jeffrey & Co. for Morris & Co.

This, the largest block-printed design ever created by Morris & Co., required two widths of paper and two sets of blocks to create the full pattern repeat. It was designed on commission for the redecoration of the Grand Staircase in St James's Palace, London in 1881. The Firm's scheme elsewhere incorporated a silk damask and a set of embroidered appliqué pelmets.

William Morris met with representatives from the Board of Works on 16 July 1880 to discuss the Grand Staircase decoration. Cutting the print blocks for the paper was carried out with both precision and speed. Following approval of the design schemes, Morris & Co. were challenged to complete the decoration within four months.

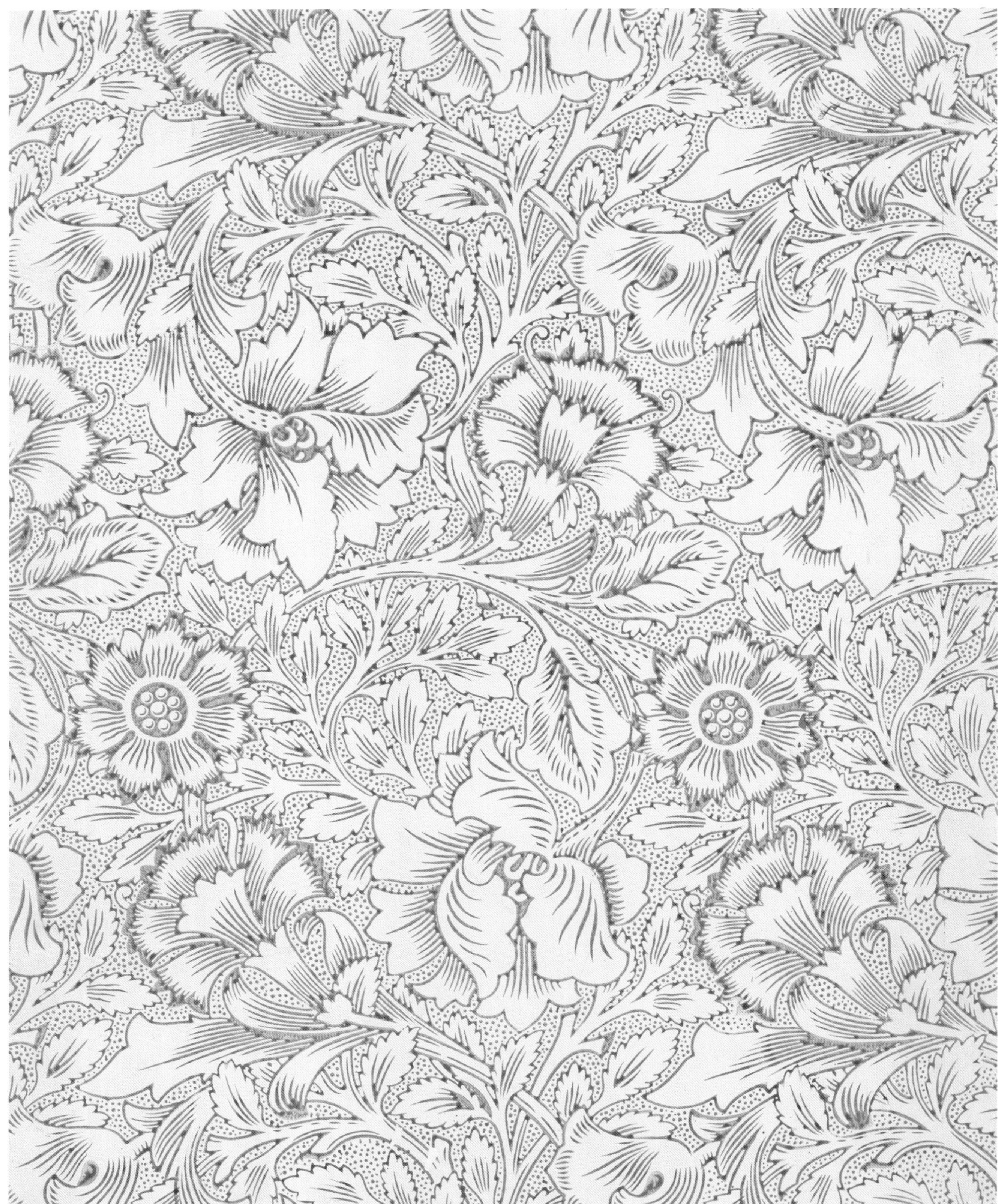

078 | William Morris, *Pink & Poppy*, 1881, Jeffrey & Co. for Morris & Co.

Sometimes known simply as *Poppy*, this design was registered in 1880 as a 'machine wallpaper' but for unknown reasons was never printed by this process. Instead, the first production was block-printed by Jeffrey & Co. in 1881. *Pink & Poppy* proved to be a popular pattern, a fact reflected by the issuing of it in more than ten individual colourways.

Pink & Poppy was selected along with many other wallpapers for inclusion in the decoration and furnishing of 1 Holland Park, the home of the stockbroker and art collector Alexander "Aleco" Ionides. The house itself was designed by Philip Webb and Thomas Jekyll, and housed several paintings by Aleco's friend James Whistler.

079 | William Morris, *Bird & Anemone*, 1882 (registered), Jeffrey & Co. for Morris & Co.

Designed before June 1881 but not registered until the following June, this is one of only two designs – the other is *Marigold* – that were contemporaneously produced, with the scale adjusted for wallpaper and printed textiles. It was conceived by Morris to be printed on cotton using the indigo-discharge method, which was perfected at Merton Abbey Mill in 1882.

On 7 June 1881, Morris signed the lease for the seven-acre site at Merton Abbey on the River Wandle in Surrey. There, since 1600, textile mills had used the river as a source of power but also because its water, a chalk stream, was ideally suited to the washing, dyeing and printing of textiles. Morris & Co. printing continued into the 1930s, by then also using hand-screens.

080 | William Morris, *Grafton*, 1883, Jeffrey & Co. for Morris & Co.

The *Grafton* wallpaper follows Morris's characteristic approach to over-printing a background pattern. However, the design lacks detail, notably in the marigold and sunflower blooms. This most probably reflects Morris's brief immersion in the study of Indian textiles during the mid-1870s while studying dyeing with Thomas Wardle, an authority on these.

Morris was an avid observer of historic textiles, regularly visiting the South Kensington Museum (V&A) and in 1884 joining the museum's Committee of Art Referees. This group helped the institution make decisions on the purchase of new holdings and included painters Sir Lawrence Alma-Tadema, Sir Edward Poynter and Frederic, Lord Leighton.

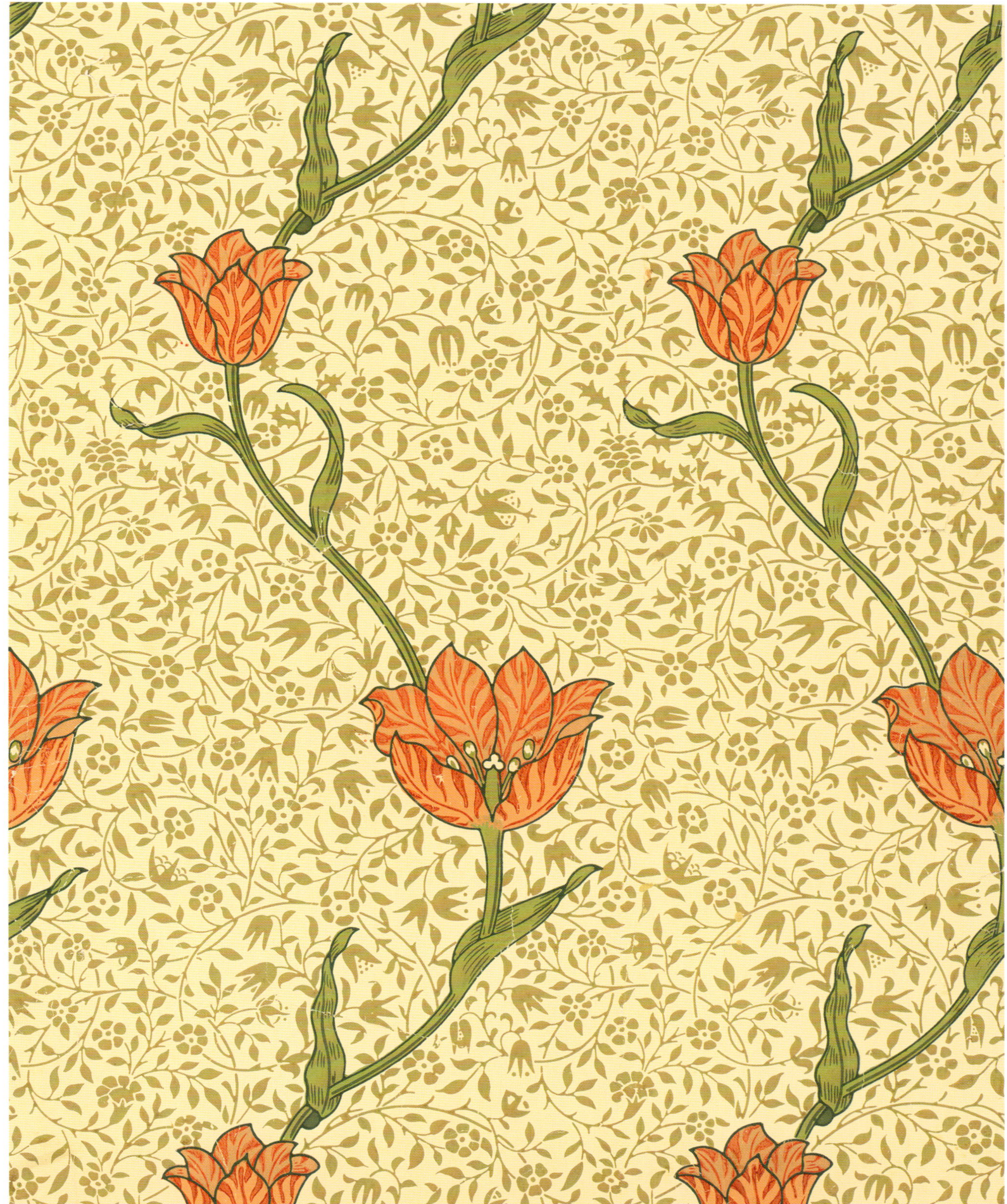

081 | William Morris, *Garden Tulip*, 1885, Jeffrey & Co. for Morris & Co.

This serpentine design of tulips employs the characteristic layout and structure frequently employed by Morris in his wallpaper creations – a random all-over monochrome back-print on which the feature floral design was printed. In c.1897, *Garden Tulip* paper was used in the decoration of Emperor Nicholas II's family apartment at the Winter Palace, St Petersburg.

Nicholas II and his wife, Empress Alexandra (Queen Victoria's granddaughter), were well acquainted with Morris's work following their 1896 visit to Balmoral Castle, which had been decorated by Morris & Co. in 1887. Married in 1894, the Russian royal couple probably referred to the company's illustrated catalogues when furnishing their private apartments.

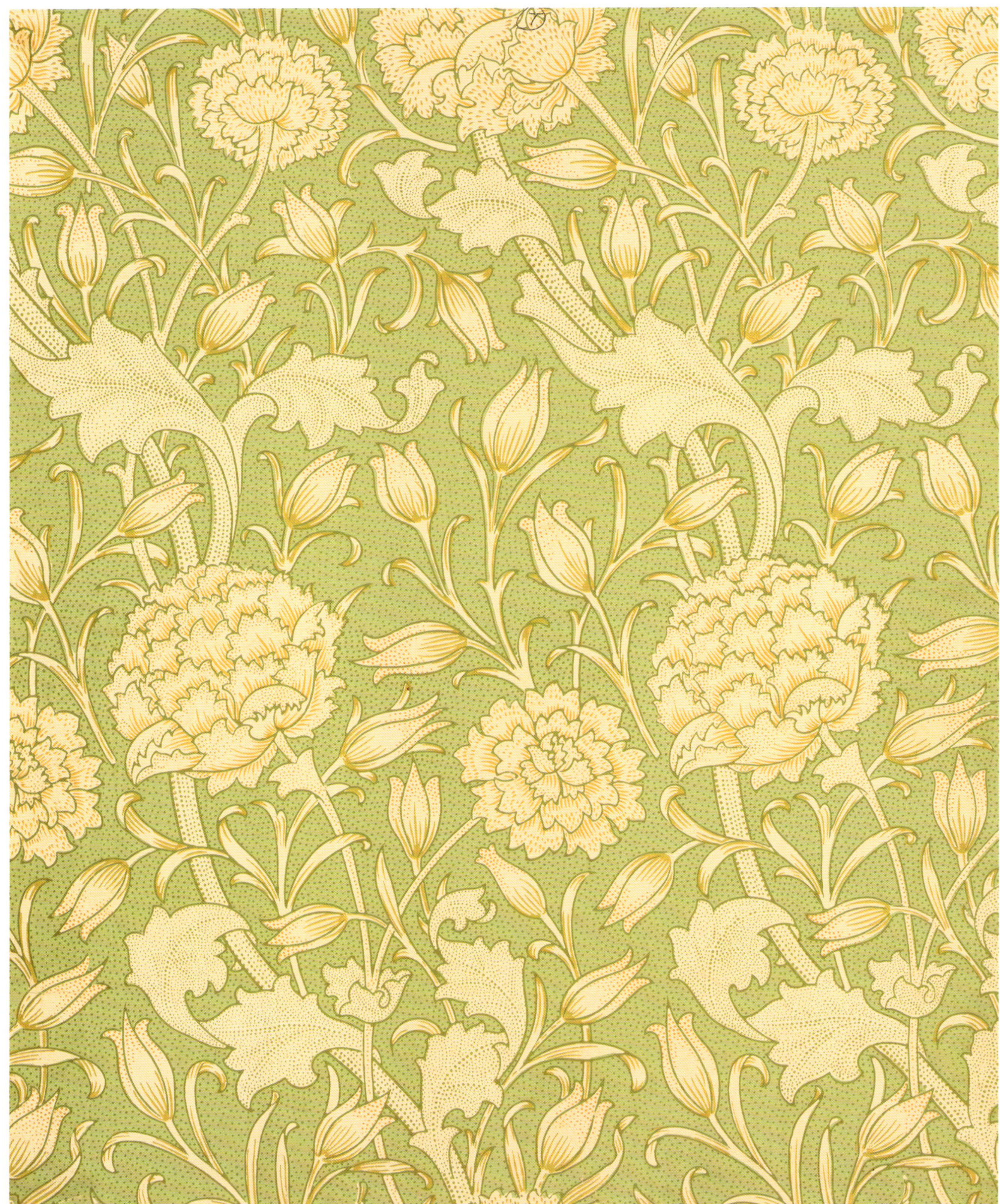

082 | William Morris, *Wild Tulip*, 1884, Jeffrey & Co. for Morris & Co.

This design is nearly identical to *Medway,* an indigo-discharge printed fabric, registered in 1885. The prominent diagonal stem, pin-work ground, characteristic flower heads and scale of *Wild Tulip* also acted as a template for Morris's *Norwich* wallpaper (1888/89) and John Henry Dearle's *Double Boughs* (1890), although these are much more densely figured.

By the end of 1884, Morris had become the leader of the Socialist League. The cover of their manifesto of 1885 featured art by Walter Crane, a league member. It was not a success. Morris wrote of 'that insane talk of immediate forcible revolution, when we know that the workers of England are not even touched by the movement'. He withdrew in 1890.

083 | William Morris, *Willow Boughs*, 1887, Jeffrey & Co. for Morris & Co.

Willow Boughs was inspired by an afternoon walk taken by Morris and his younger daughter, May, along a little stream close to the banks of the river Thames at Kelmscott Manor. She was to write in the 1930s of that 'keenly observed rendering of our willows that has embowered many a London living room'.

During a three-day stay at Kelmscott in September 1887, Morris is quoted as saying: 'I had that delightful quickening of perception by which everything gets emphasised and brightened and the commonest landscape looks lovely: anxieties and worries, though remembered, yet [have] no weight on one's spirits – Heaven in short.'

084 | William Morris, *The VRI Cipher Paper*, 1887, Jeffrey & Co. for Morris & Co.

The VRI Cipher Paper was designed for Queen Victoria. It was installed at Balmoral Castle, the large estate house in Royal Deeside, Aberdeenshire, Scotland, designed in 1856 by the architect William Smith of Aberdeen and Prince Albert. Also called *Balmoral*, it was printed with a coloured mordant on to which fine merino wool flock was applied, brushed and laid.

The design is unusually wide (60cm) due to the imperial scale of The Queen's personal cipher coupled with the royal symbol of Scotland, the thistle. The original design bears a pen note: 'Their Majesties prefer this design with the diamonds as big again... the design to be in flock (not coloured).' This paper is still sourced from Sanderson today.

085 | William Morris, *Bruges*, 1887, Jeffrey & Co. for Morris & Co.

With its large formal foliate pattern of scrolling flora and ornamental diagonal strap-work, *Bruges* is suggestive of a silk damask. Its name pays homage to Bruges, an outstanding example of a medieval historic settlement. There, one finds Stadhuis van Brugge, Belgium's oldest building; Gothic in style, it was constructed between 1376 and 1420.

Morris was familiar with Bruges, having spent his honeymoon there with Jane in 1859. Among later visits was one in 1874, when they visited the mid-12th century Hospital of St John, one of Europe's oldest buildings. Within is the Gothic chapel-shaped shrine of St Ursula (1489) by Hans Memling, in which the Virgin Mary wears a cloak of red damask.

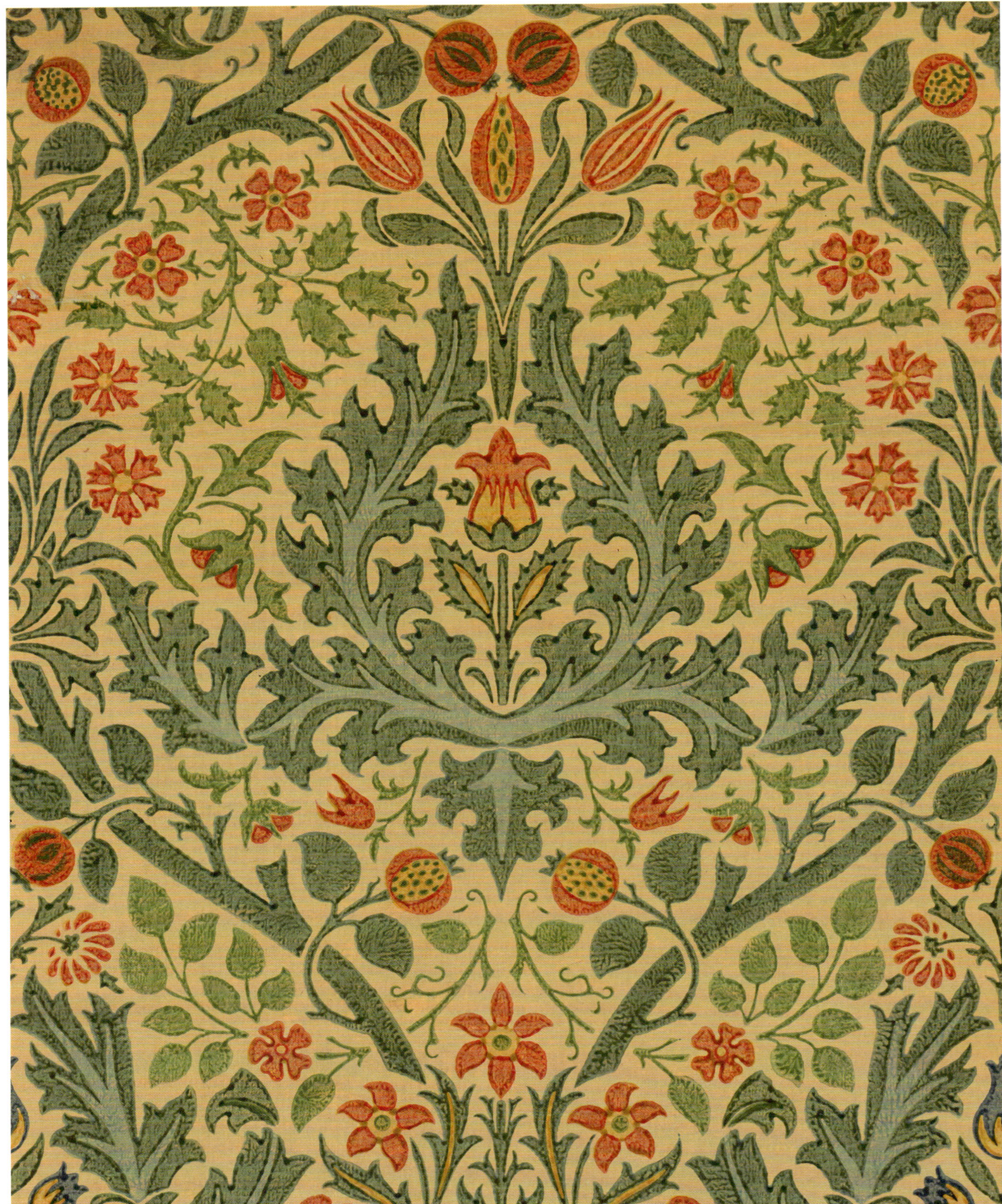

086 | William Morris, *Autumn Flowers*, 1888, Jeffrey & Co. for Morris & Co.

This pattern is unlike others designed by Morris for wallpapers, but it is related to a group of woven textiles produced by Morris & Co. between 1888 and 1890. Two were exhibited at the first London Arts and Crafts Exhibition, including the very similar *Golden Bough*, which was used in Stanmore Hall near Bridgnorth and the Barr Smith homes in Adelaide, Australia.

Such patterns, with medieval inspired 'ogee' outlines, were popular for church furnishings. At its formation in 1861, commissions from churches occupied The Firm. Among these were All Saints Church, Cambridge (1864), designed by G.F. Bodley, who worked with Morris on the stencilled and painted decoration throughout, some showing the same pattern structure.

087 | William Morris, *Norwich*, 1888/89, Jeffrey & Co. for Morris & Co.

The scale and finish of this paper suggests its production for a country house. Mica added to a wash colour was applied to the surface of the ungrounded base paper to create a lustrous effect. Once dried, the glass-grounded paper was block-printed with water-based emulsions. The making of this finish was a constant source of danger to the workers.

After founding the Socialist League in 1884 and becoming editor of *The Commonweal*, Morris began to promote his socialist beliefs through public lectures and literature. His *Norwich* wallpaper was named after the county town of Norfolk, where he gave open-air talks in Provision Market, established on a site thus occupied since the 12th century.

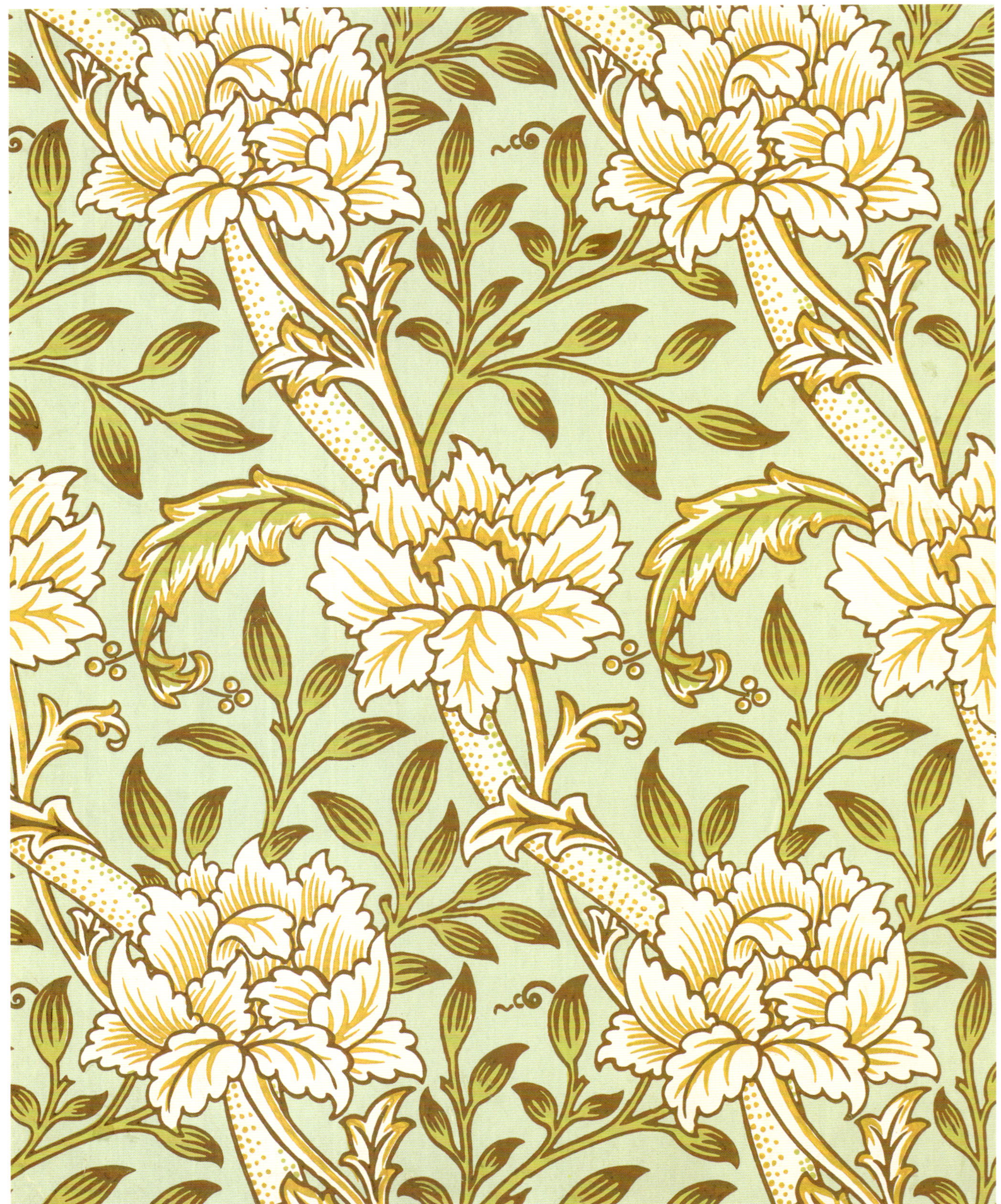

088 | William Morris, *Hammersmith*, 1890, Jeffrey & Co. for Morris & Co.

Having briefly lived in Horrington House on Turnham Green Road, Chiswick in 1878, the Morris family moved to Kelmscott House, Upper Mall, Hammersmith, residing there until William Morris's death on 3 October 1896. *Hammersmith* was named after the location of his London home, where the Hammersmith branch of the Socialist League met.

Today, the William Morris Society operates a small museum in the coach house and basement of Kelmscott House. In 1879, the coach house and adjoining stable were converted by Morris into weaving sheds, dedicated to producing hand-knotted carpets. Today, it holds Morris's Albion printing press on which his Kelmscott Press's *Chaucer* was produced in 1896.

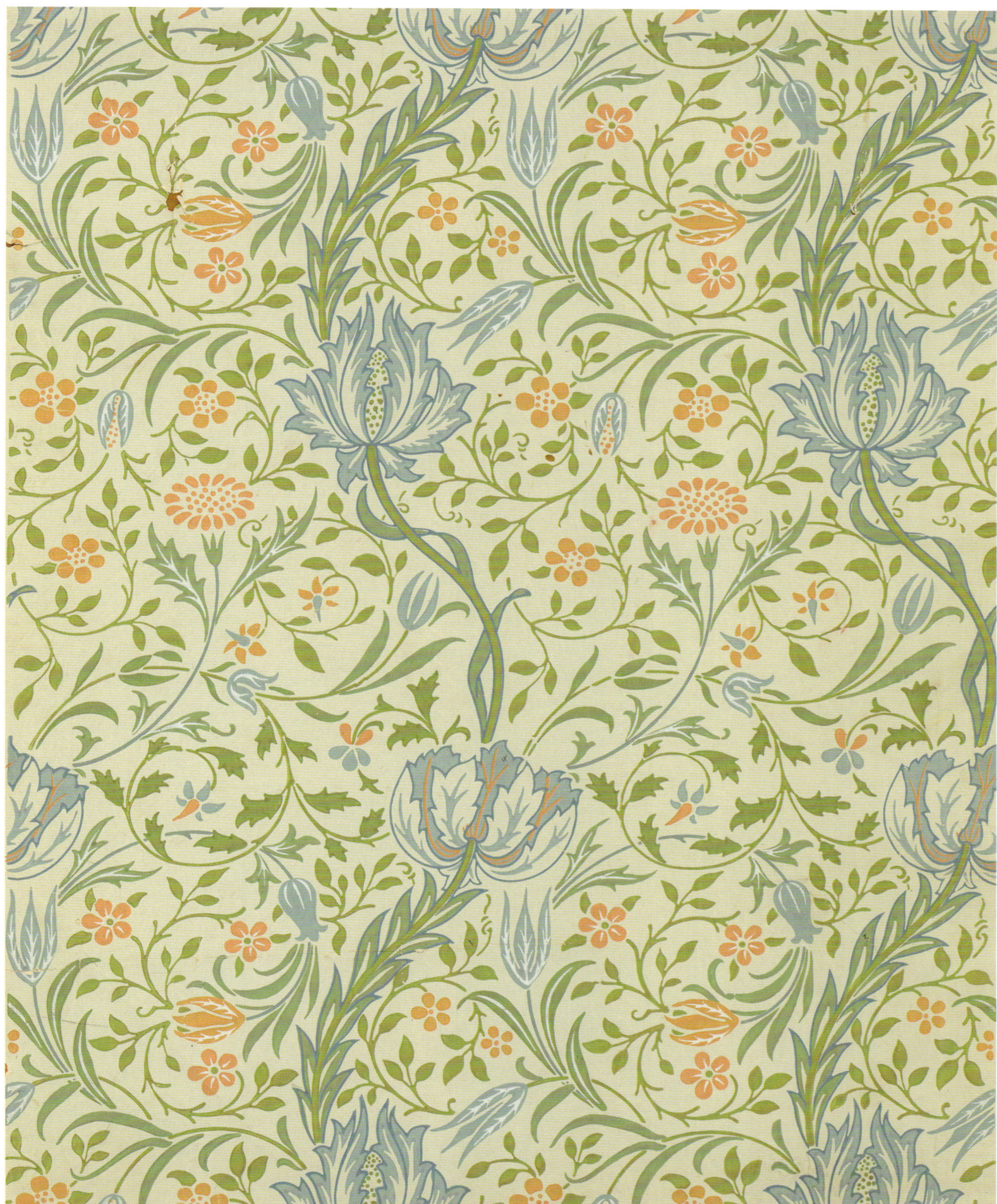

089 | William Morris, *Flora*, 1891, Jeffrey & Co. for Morris & Co.

Flora was produced at the end of the most successful period for Morris & Co. during its founder's lifetime. Throughout the 1880s, its annual net profit was more than £6,000. Estimates of the equivalent value today vary according to the means of calculation, so in 2021 this sum is the equivalent of something between £748,350 and £790,876.

By the 1890s, the Morris & Co. shop at 449 Oxford Street, London was the hub of Morris's business operations. He was now spending less time at Merton Abbey Mill and had ceased designing textiles in about 1888. The shop itself continued until 1917, by which time its small frontage was competing with that of nearby Selfridges, founded eight years earlier.

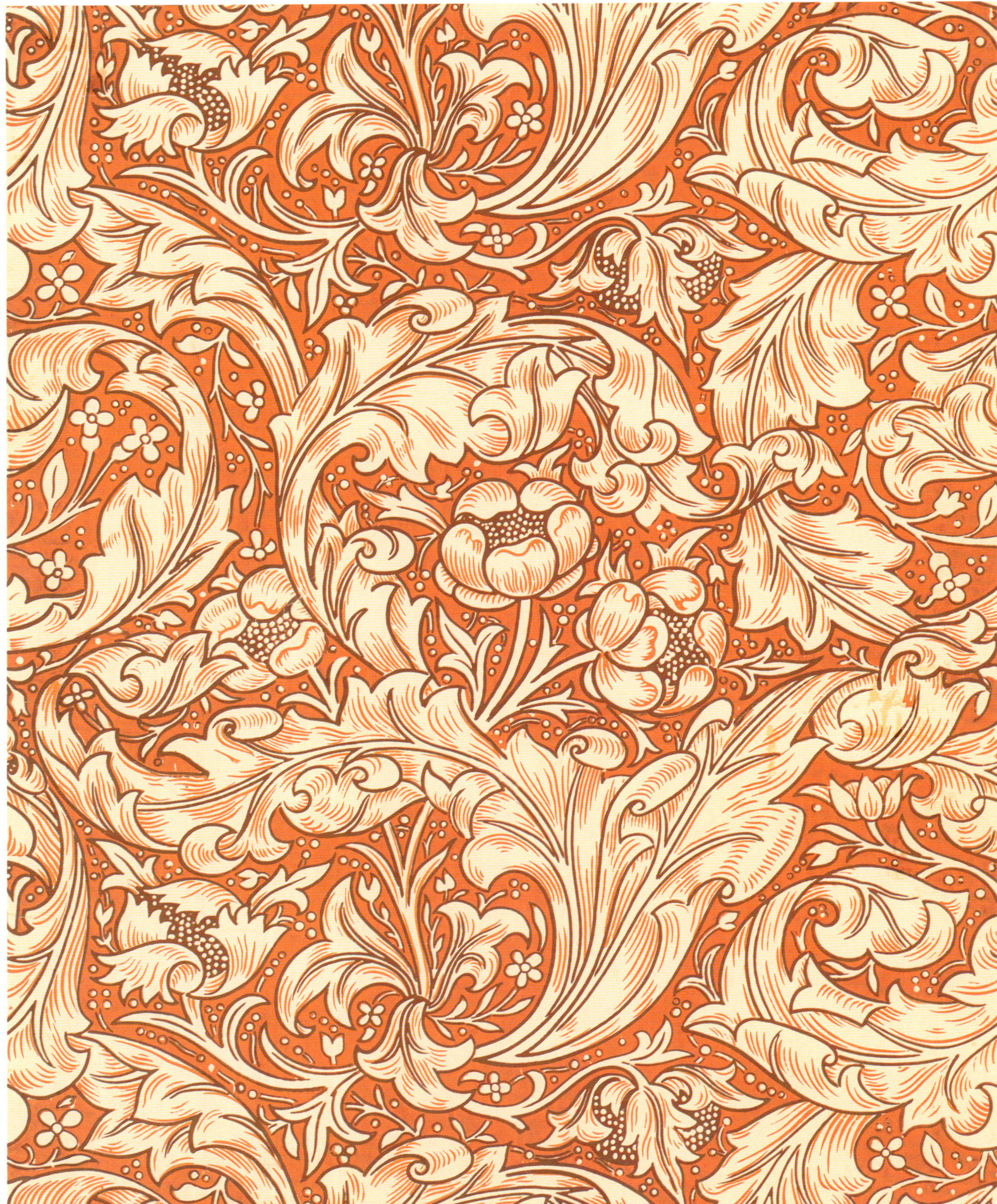

090 | William Morris, *Bachelor's Button*, 1892, Jeffrey & Co. for Morris & Co.

Bachelor's button is the colloquial name for the *Centaurea cyanus*, commonly known as cornflower. Symbolic of requited love, cornflowers were worn by young men in the buttonholes of their jackets; a withering bloom was seen as a bad omen of fast-fading affection from a sweetheart.

This wallpaper followed on quickly from Morris's foundation of Kelmscott Press in 1891. In just seven years, they produced over 22,000 copies of 53 book titles. Admired for their artistry, the dense pattern with coiling acanthus leaves and flowers that were imprinted as borders on the title pages of several volumes bears close comparison to *Bachelor's Button*.

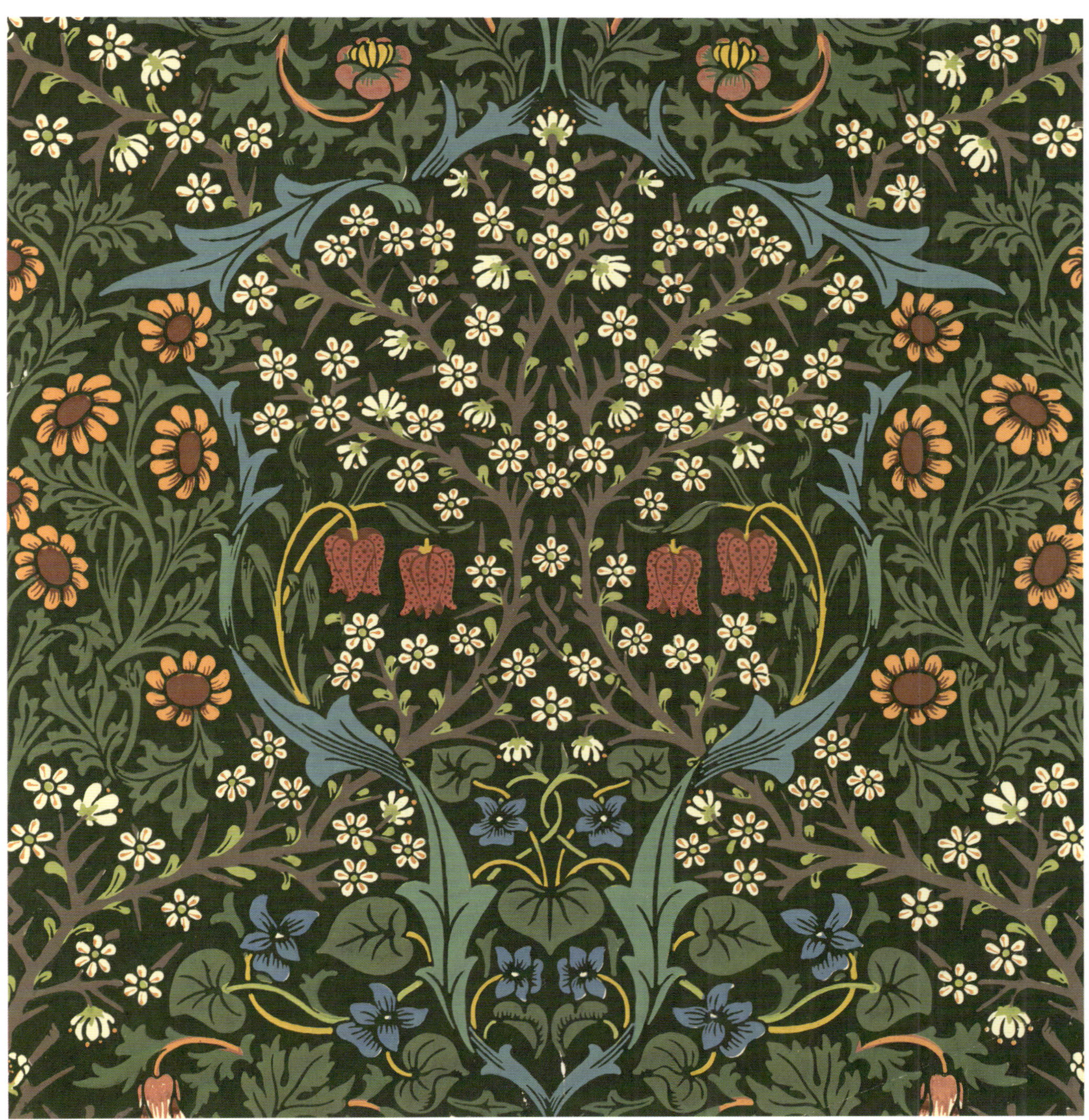

091 | William Morris/John Henry Dearle, *Blackthorn*, 1892, Jeffrey & Co. for Morris & Co.

This overtly complex design captures observations of life in the hedgerows, woodlands and meadows surrounding Kelmscott Manor. However, it has been attributed to both Morris and Dearle as at this time they worked closely together. As late as 1894, Morris wrote to Dearle: 'I am sending back the paper with as much roughed in as I can.'

Kelmscott was also the setting for one of Morris's best-known publications, *News from Nowhere*. Issued in London, New York and Boston in 1890 and in its second edition by 1891, in 1892 and 1893 it was printed at Kelmscott Press. Constantly republished to this day, in it Morris imagines a utopian future where, among other things, people find pleasure in nature.

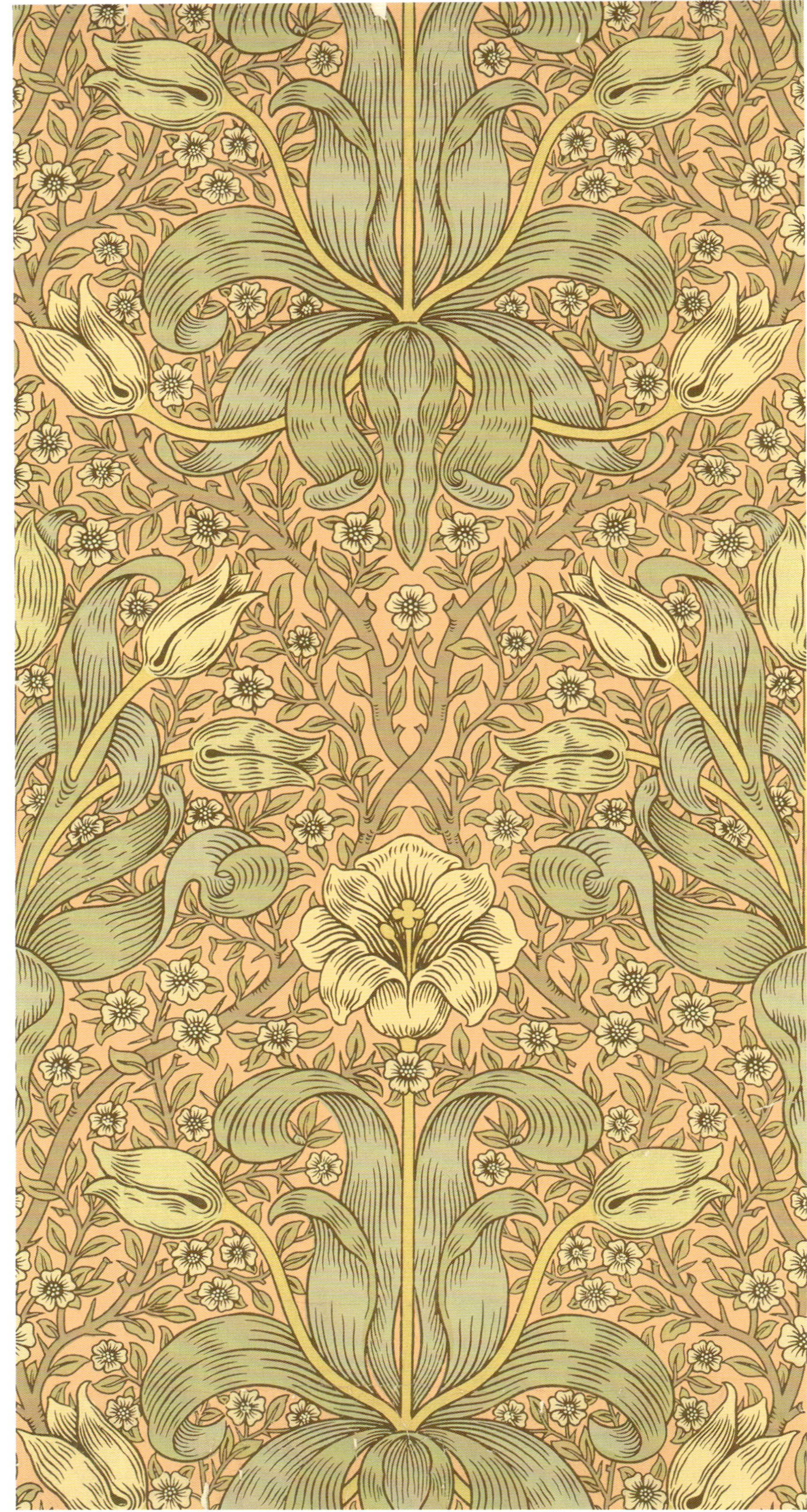

092 | William Morris, *Spring Thicket*, 1894, Jeffrey & Co. for Morris & Co.

Spring Thicket was the last hand-printed paper designed by Morris for walls and drew inspiration from woodland tulips. It harks back to 1840, when William was six and the family moved to Woodford Hall, a Palladian mansion on the edge of Epping Forest, where William lived until his father's death in 1847.

Also in 1894, *The Wood Beyond the World* was published by Kelmscott Press. Morris's prose influenced the burgeoning genre of fantasy literature: C.S. Lewis named Morris as a favourite. Morris's poetry was equally highly regarded. 'The Earthly Paradise' of 1870 made his name, yet he turned down the role of poet laureate when it was offered in 1891.

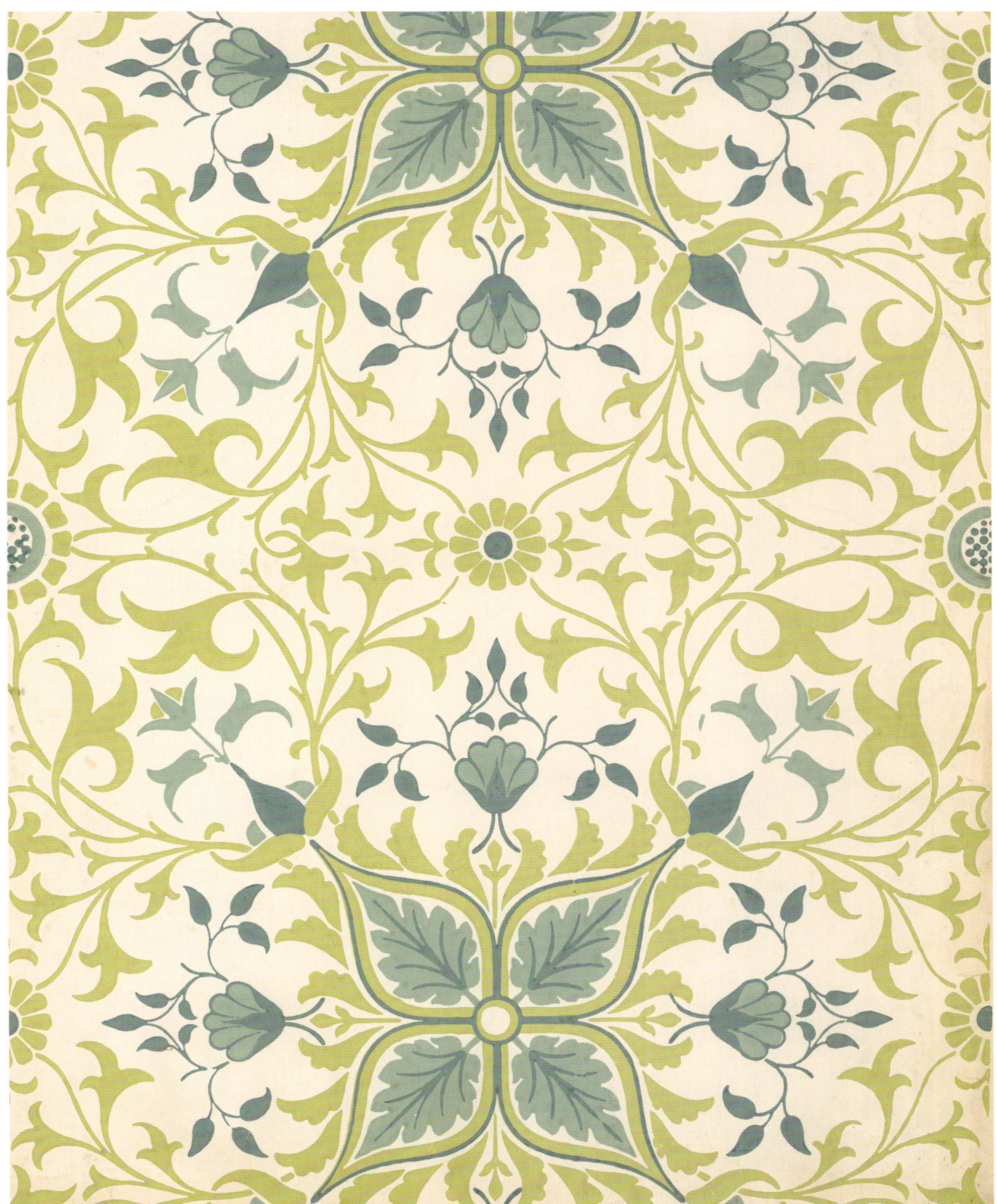

093 | William Morris, *Net Ceiling*, 1895, Jeffrey & Co. for Morris & Co.

Net Ceiling was the last block-print William Morris designed, the year before his death. Ill for a time, he was clearly aware of his declining health, having told his life-long friend Edward Burne-Jones: 'The best way of lengthening out the rest of our days now, old chap, is to finish off our old things.'

He was remembered in the *Manchester Guardian* as 'a rare, a gifted, and a jolly comrade. Nobody liked a good time better than he did, and he always got it. He was at his best with the unlettered and the dolefully inartistic, as he was with those who were thoroughly in touch with the work he most loved. It was a supreme pleasure to visit a great church with Morris'.

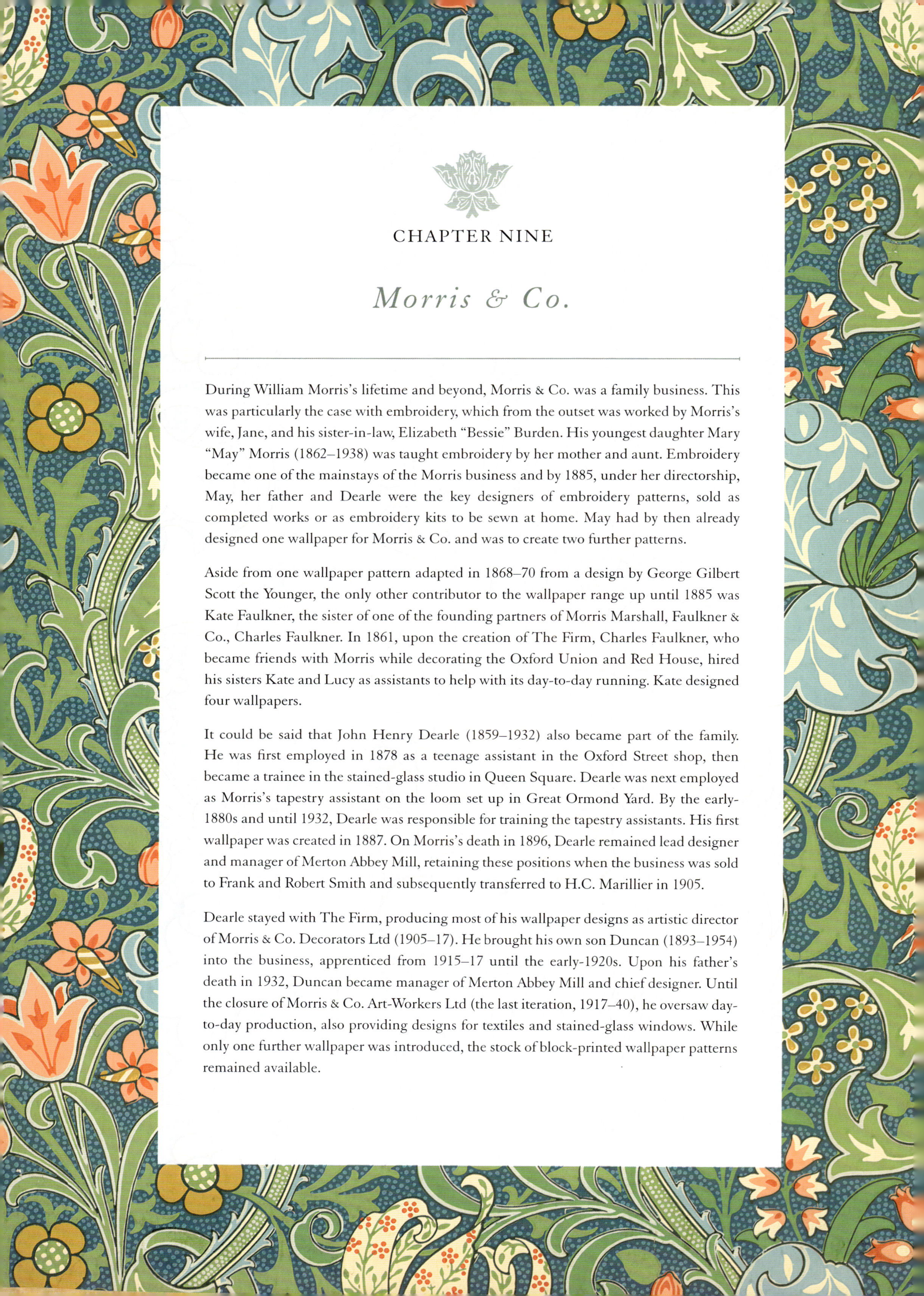

CHAPTER NINE

Morris & Co.

During William Morris's lifetime and beyond, Morris & Co. was a family business. This was particularly the case with embroidery, which from the outset was worked by Morris's wife, Jane, and his sister-in-law, Elizabeth "Bessie" Burden. His youngest daughter Mary "May" Morris (1862–1938) was taught embroidery by her mother and aunt. Embroidery became one of the mainstays of the Morris business and by 1885, under her directorship, May, her father and Dearle were the key designers of embroidery patterns, sold as completed works or as embroidery kits to be sewn at home. May had by then already designed one wallpaper for Morris & Co. and was to create two further patterns.

Aside from one wallpaper pattern adapted in 1868–70 from a design by George Gilbert Scott the Younger, the only other contributor to the wallpaper range up until 1885 was Kate Faulkner, the sister of one of the founding partners of Morris Marshall, Faulkner & Co., Charles Faulkner. In 1861, upon the creation of The Firm, Charles Faulkner, who became friends with Morris while decorating the Oxford Union and Red House, hired his sisters Kate and Lucy as assistants to help with its day-to-day running. Kate designed four wallpapers.

It could be said that John Henry Dearle (1859–1932) also became part of the family. He was first employed in 1878 as a teenage assistant in the Oxford Street shop, then became a trainee in the stained-glass studio in Queen Square. Dearle was next employed as Morris's tapestry assistant on the loom set up in Great Ormond Yard. By the early-1880s and until 1932, Dearle was responsible for training the tapestry assistants. His first wallpaper was created in 1887. On Morris's death in 1896, Dearle remained lead designer and manager of Merton Abbey Mill, retaining these positions when the business was sold to Frank and Robert Smith and subsequently transferred to H.C. Marillier in 1905.

Dearle stayed with The Firm, producing most of his wallpaper designs as artistic director of Morris & Co. Decorators Ltd (1905–17). He brought his own son Duncan (1893–1954) into the business, apprenticed from 1915–17 until the early-1920s. Upon his father's death in 1932, Duncan became manager of Merton Abbey Mill and chief designer. Until the closure of Morris & Co. Art-Workers Ltd (the last iteration, 1917–40), he oversaw day-to-day production, also providing designs for textiles and stained-glass windows. While only one further wallpaper was introduced, the stock of block-printed wallpaper patterns remained available.

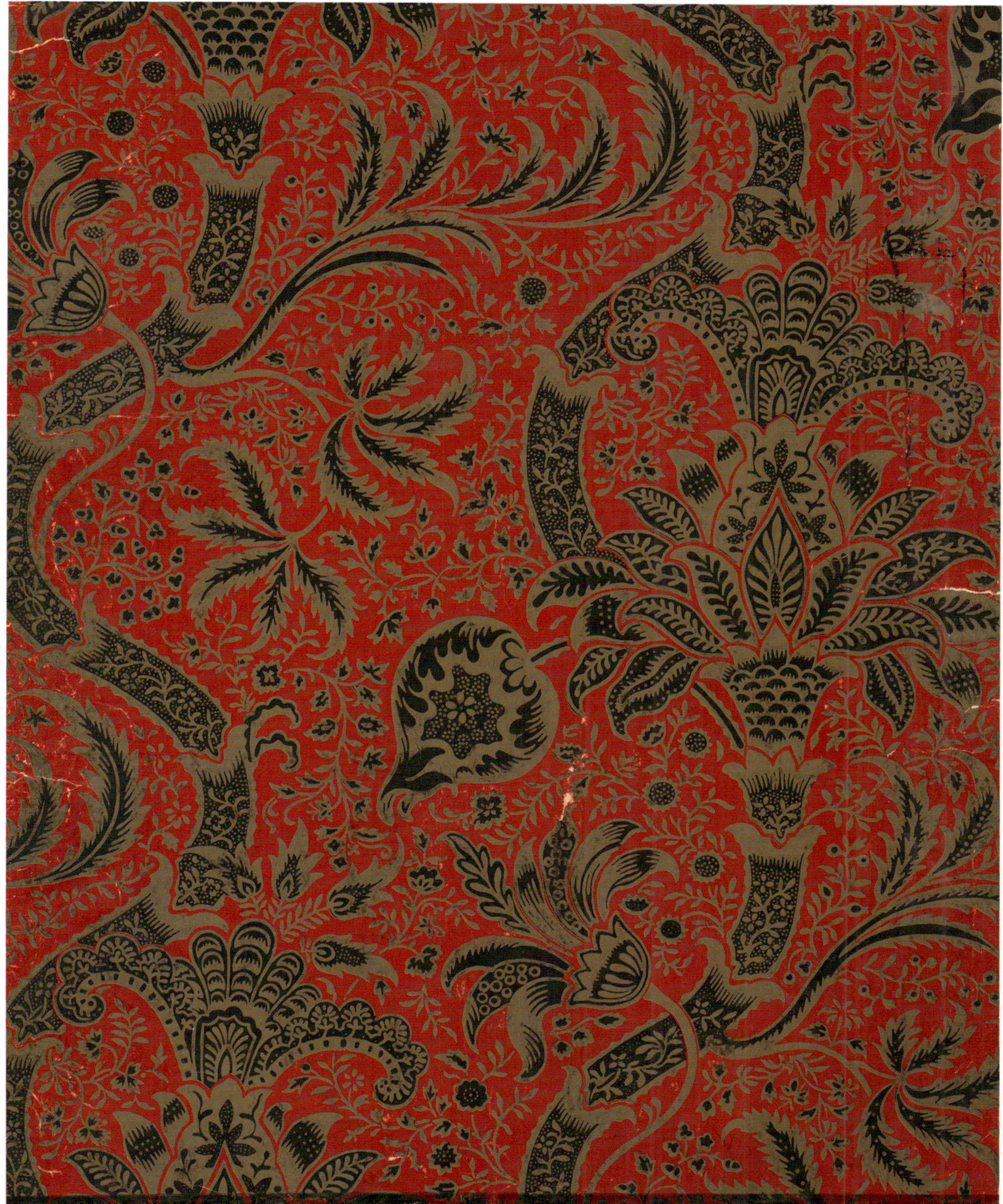

094 | George Gilbert Scott the Younger (1839–97), *Indian*, 1868–70, Jeffrey & Co. for Morris, Marshall, Faulkner & Co.

George Gilbert Scott the Younger was the son of Sir George Gilbert Scott, the Gothic Revival architect. He was himself an architect and also a talented decorator, designing furniture, carpets, metalwork, needlework and, of course, wallpaper. In 1874, he co-founded Watts & Co. with fellow architects G.F. Bodley and Thomas Garner.

One of The Firm's first commissions was from Bodley for the stained glass and interior decoration at St Martin-on-the-Hill, Scarborough. Consecrated in July 1863, the project involved Edward Burne-Jones, Ford Madox Brown, Dante Gabriel Rossetti and Philip Webb, as well as Morris himself, and would have introduced him to the younger Scott.

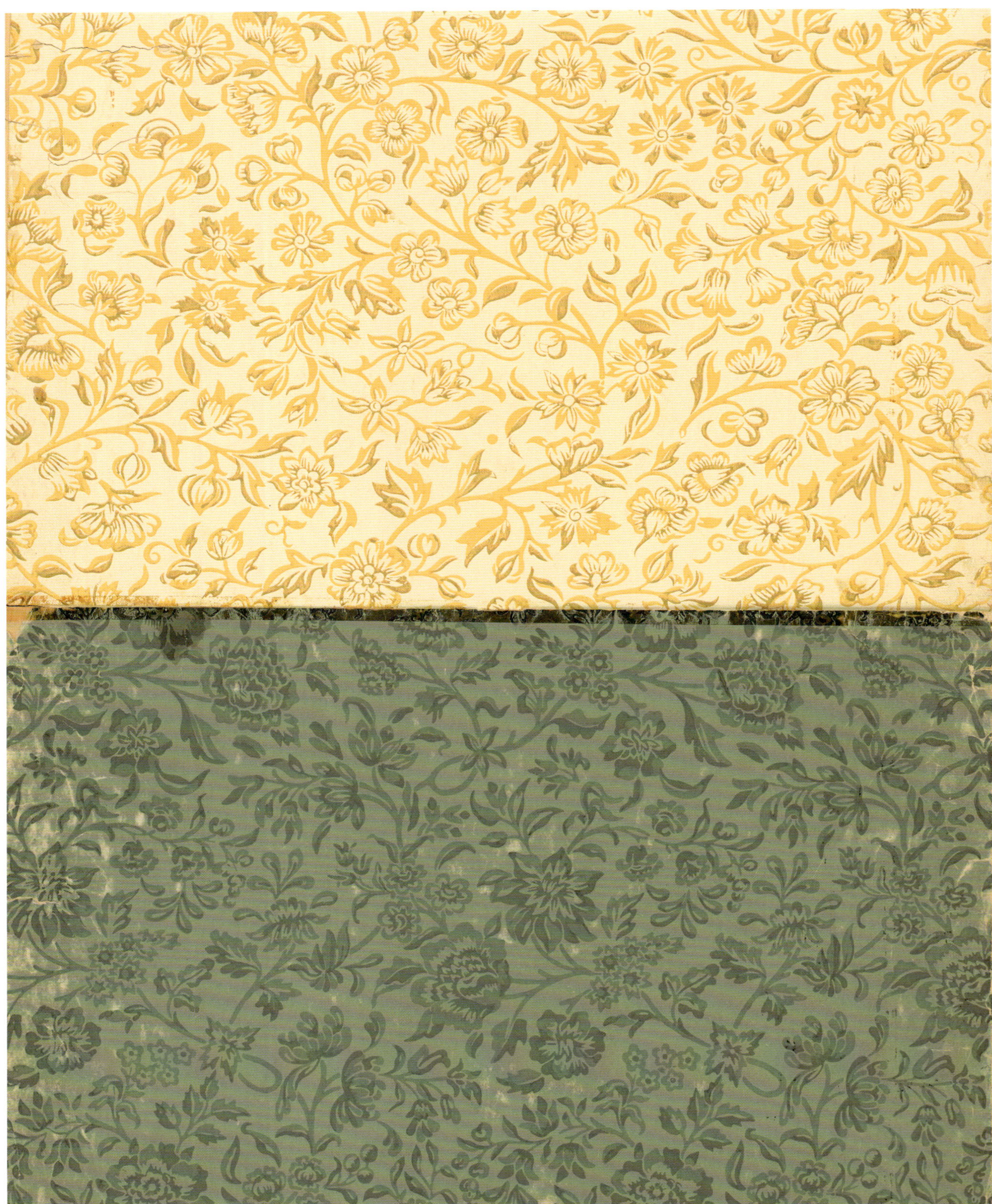

095 | Kate Faulkner, *Loop Trail*, 1877 (registered), Jeffrey & Co. for Morris & Co.

Loop Trail, created by the sister of Charles Faulkner, one of the original partners of Morris, Marshall, Faulkner & Co., was to be Kate Faulkner's (1841–98) first pattern in a series of products bearing The Firm's name. This is also the first Morris & Co. wallpaper that was not designed by William Morris himself.

The small scale, repeat, balance and colour distribution of *Loop Trail* facilitated ease of use in smaller rooms, especially servants' quarters and children's bedrooms. It bears comparison with a large decorative Morris & Co. dish made 'blank' by the Burslem pottery of Pinder, Bourne & Co. and painted by Kate in c.1880.

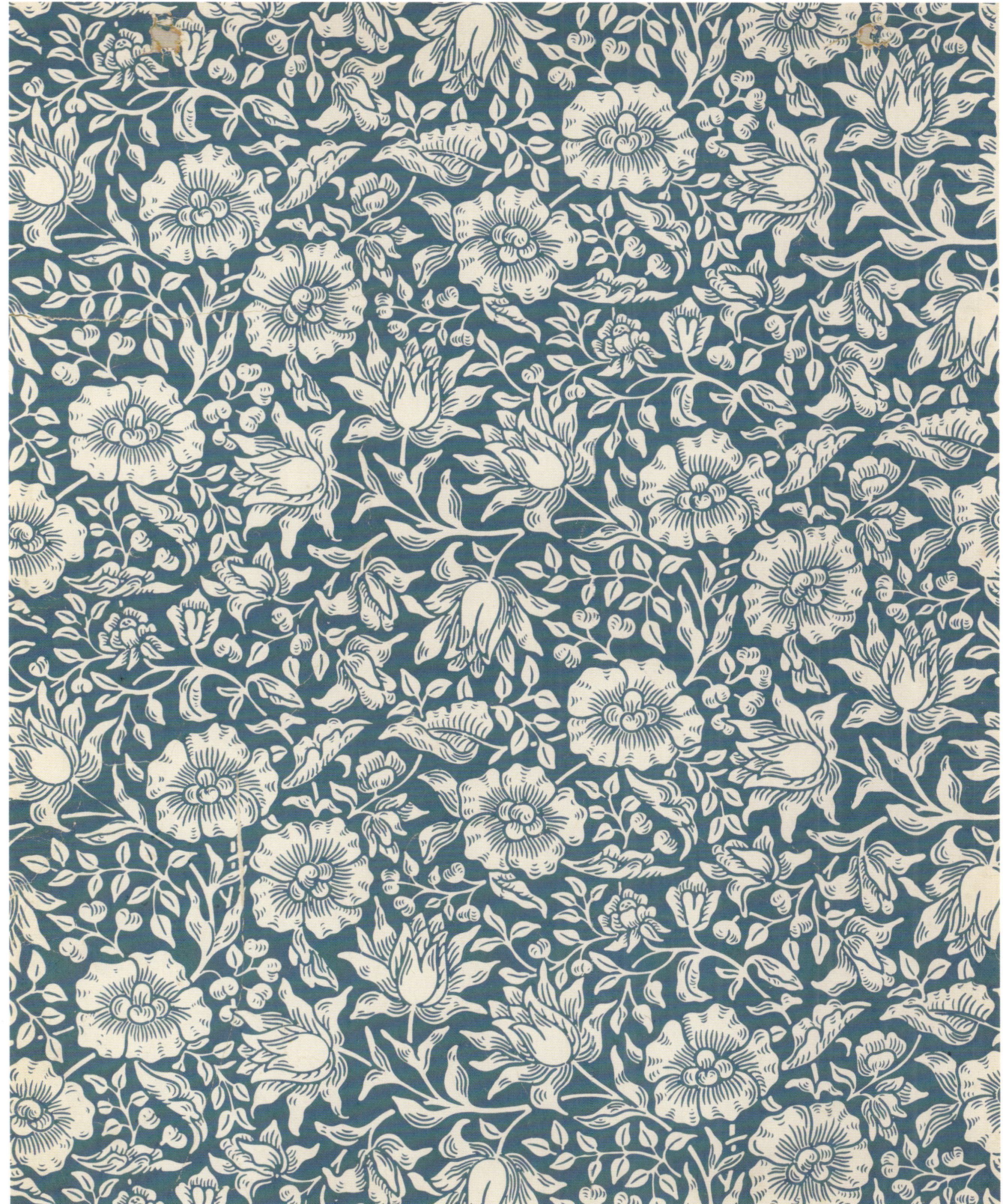

096 | Kate Faulkner, *Mallow*, 1879, Jeffrey & Co. for Morris & Co.

Faulkner's *Mallow* block-print became a design of some importance to Morris & Co. Between 1879 and 1908, they would release more than 11 individual colourways. The celadon green version (Mallow 145 – 1882) was reprinted in 2017 as part of the five-year restoration project carried out by the National Trust at Standen House, West Sussex.

The hand-painted *Peony* tile, designed by Kate in c.1877, was put into production by Morris & Co. some three years later. Her identically titled hand block-printed cotton also dates from 1877 and is in indigo-discharge, the technique taught to Morris by Thomas Wardle during this period. *Mallow* suggests this demanding technique in its colouration.

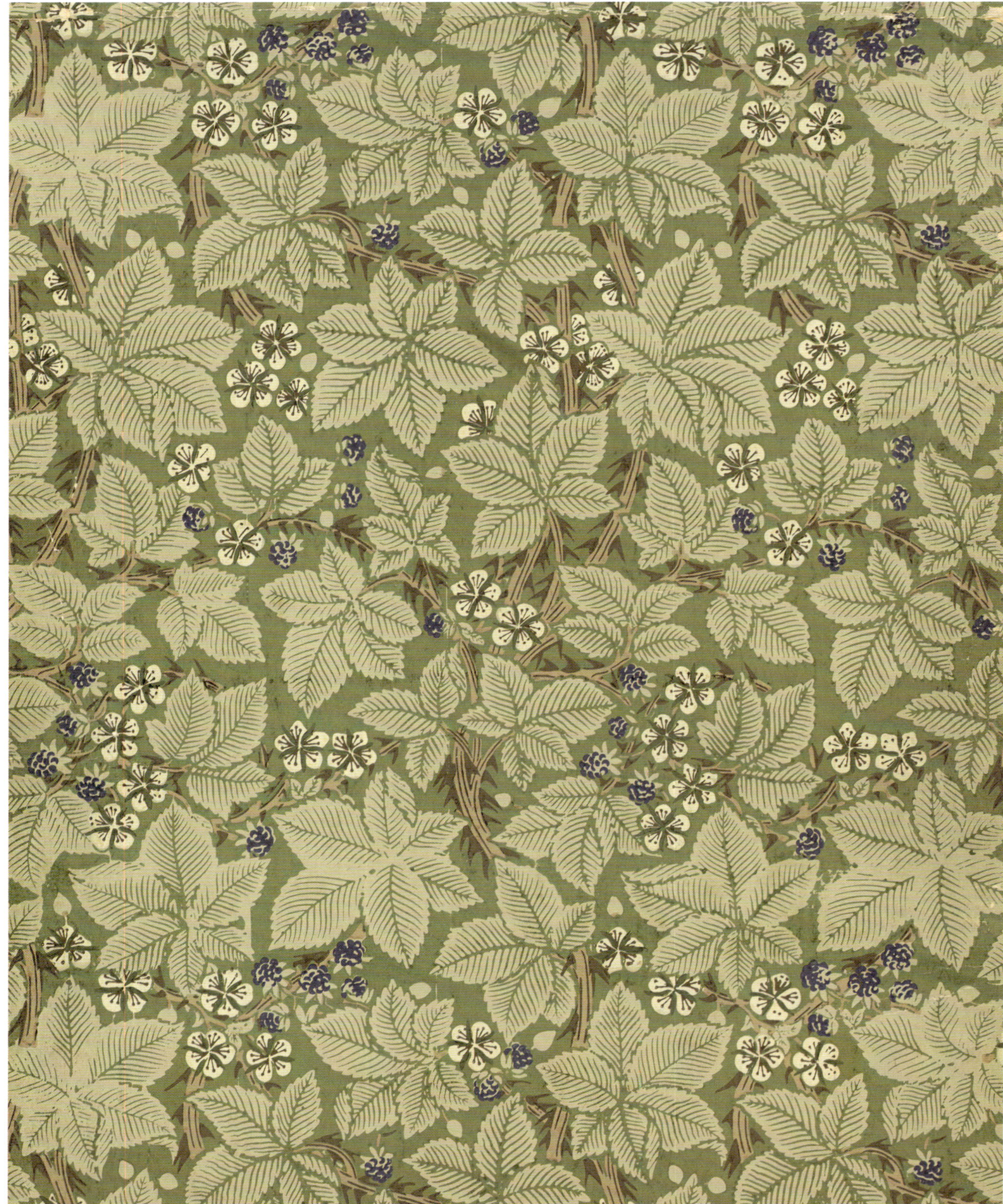

097 | Kate Faulkner, *Bramble*, 1879, Jeffrey & Co. for Morris & Co.

While *Bramble* is one of only four wallpaper designs created by Kate for Morris & Co., her creative aptitude for surface pattern led her to a design career within the embroidery, ceramic tile and pottery industries. Her freelance commissions include wallpaper designs for Metford Warner of Jeffrey & Co. and painted china for Doulton of Lambeth.

An accomplished craftswoman, Kate contributed with her sister Lucy Faulkner Orrinsmith to The Firm's production. Initially, the sisters worked together, although eventually Lucy concentrated on painting and ceramics while Kate contributed designs for painted tiles and pottery as well as embroideries, gesso decoration and block-printed materials.

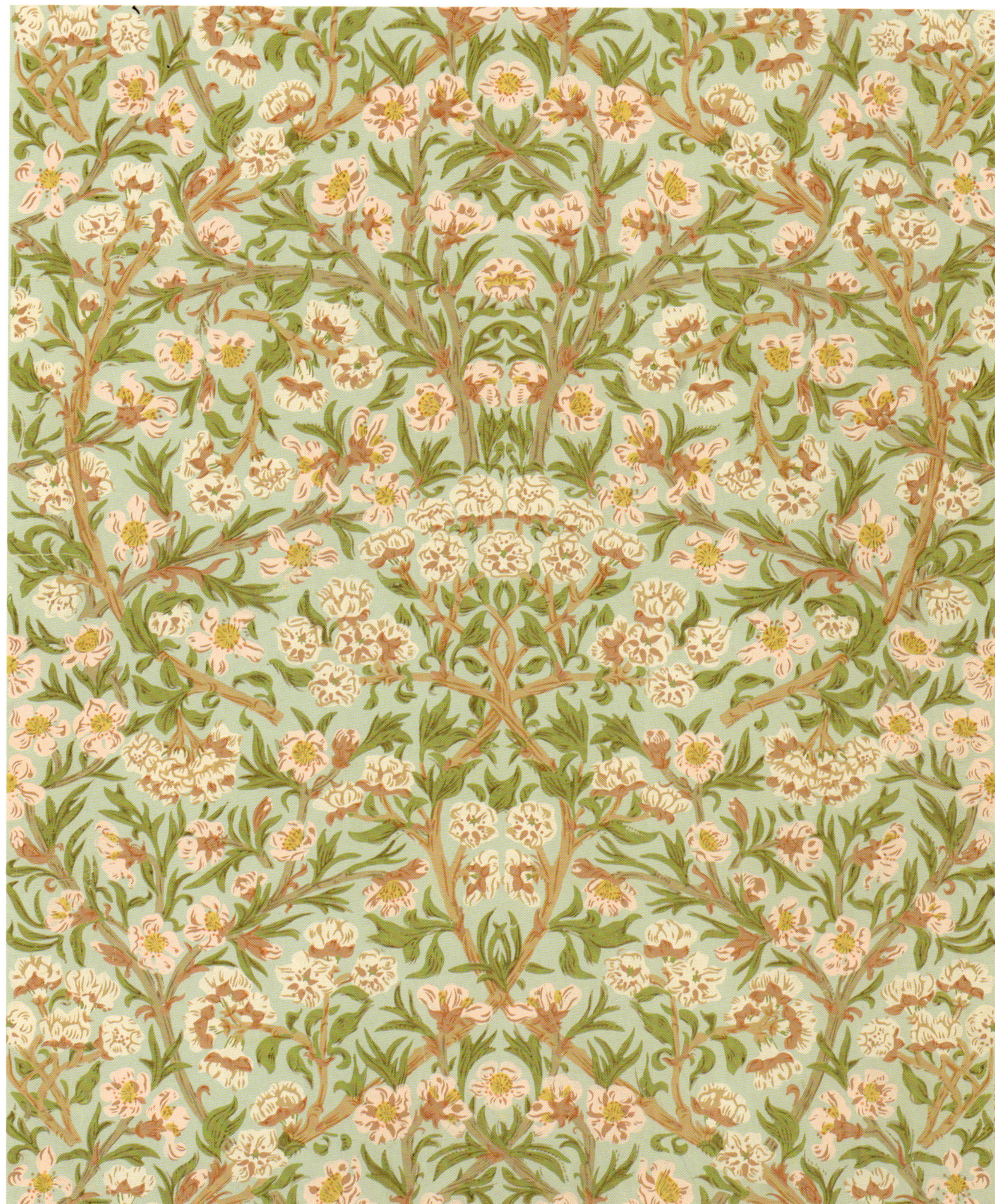

098 | Kate Faulkner, *Blossom*, 1885, Jeffrey & Co. for Morris & Co.

Aside from working with her sister at Morris & Co., Kate had considerable experience of collaborations with others. Both also worked at the wood-engraving firm Smith and Linton's, which re-interpreted the wood block engraving for Dante Gabriel Rossetti's title page design on the second edition of Christina Rossetti's *Goblin Market and Other Poems* (1865).

Just prior to *Blossom*, in 1883, she decorated a piano after a design by Edward Burne-Jones for the home of Alexander 'Aleco' Ionides, one of the major patrons of the Pre-Raphaelite Brotherhood. This design, together with *Bramble*, is one of several reprints of Morris & Co. papers produced by Arthur Sanderson & Sons Ltd in c.1955.

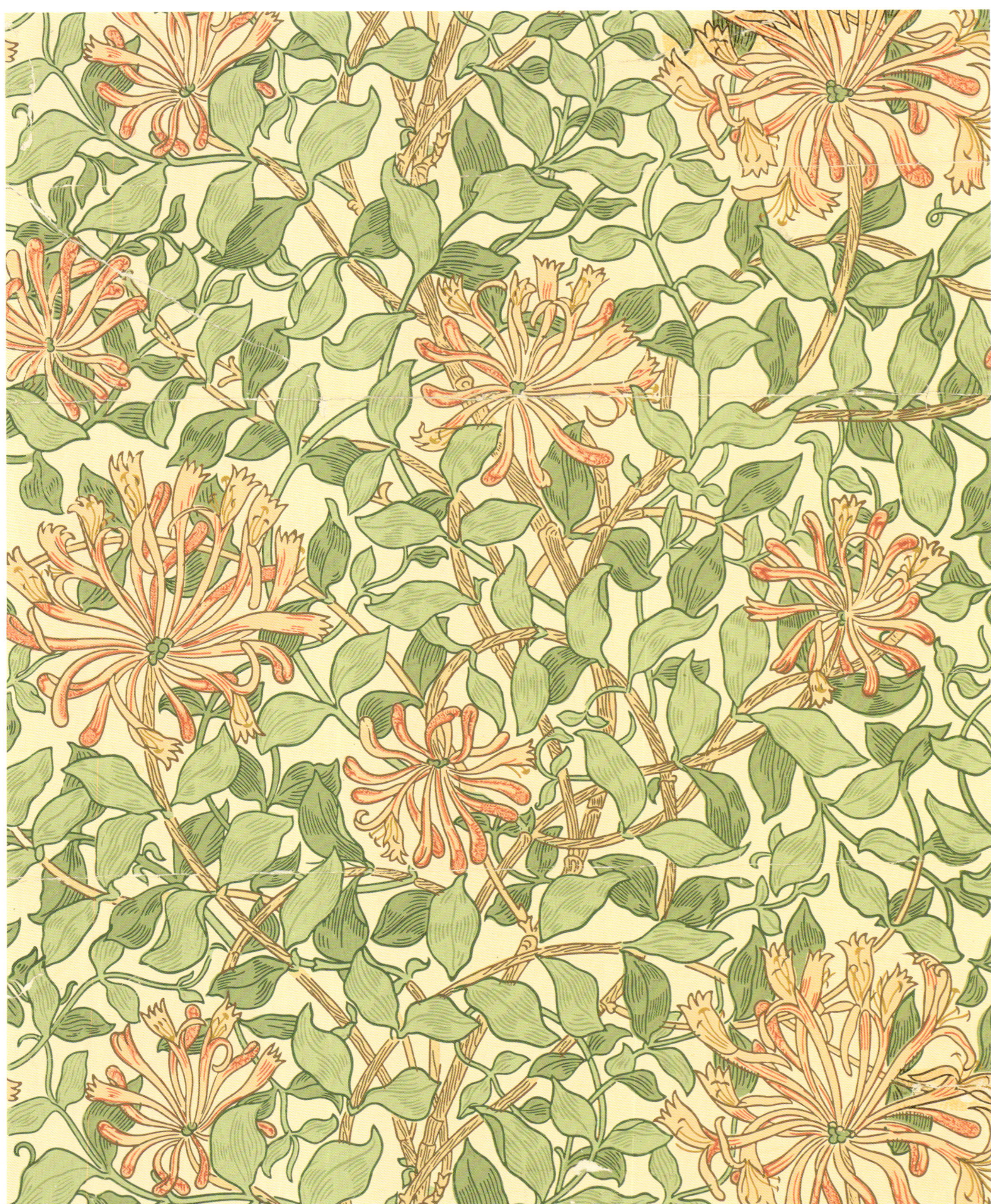

099 | May Morris, *Honeysuckle*, 1883, Jeffrey & Co. for Morris & Co.

May Morris designed very few wallpapers for Morris & Co. Enrolled at the National Art Training School in London's South Kensington to study embroidery from 1878, she is better known for her contribution to the design and production of Morris & Co. embroideries, some of which reflect a similar honeysuckle motif to that of her first wallpaper pattern.

Apart from needlework, May was also a talented water-colour artist and designer of jewellery, book bindings and tapestries. She was active elsewhere too, becoming involved with the Royal School of Art Needlework, where her aunt was chief technical instructor from 1880, and founding the Women's Guild of Arts with Mary Elizabeth Turner in 1907.

100 | May Morris, *Horn Poppy*, 1885, Jeffrey & Co. for Morris & Co.

In 1885, at the young age of 23, May took over the Morris & Co. embroidery department. She was to remain in this position until her father's death in 1896, thereafter acting as an advisor. In addition, she edited her father's *Collected Works* in 24 volumes for Longmans, Green and Company, published between 1910 and 1915.

May also contributed to the preservation of Kelmscott Manor, where her mother lived until her death in 1914 and May remained until her own passing in 1938. She commissioned the Morris Memorial Cottages (1902) and the Morris Memorial Hall (1934) designed by Philip Webb and Ernest Gimson respectively. Gimson designed a second pair of cottages in 1914.

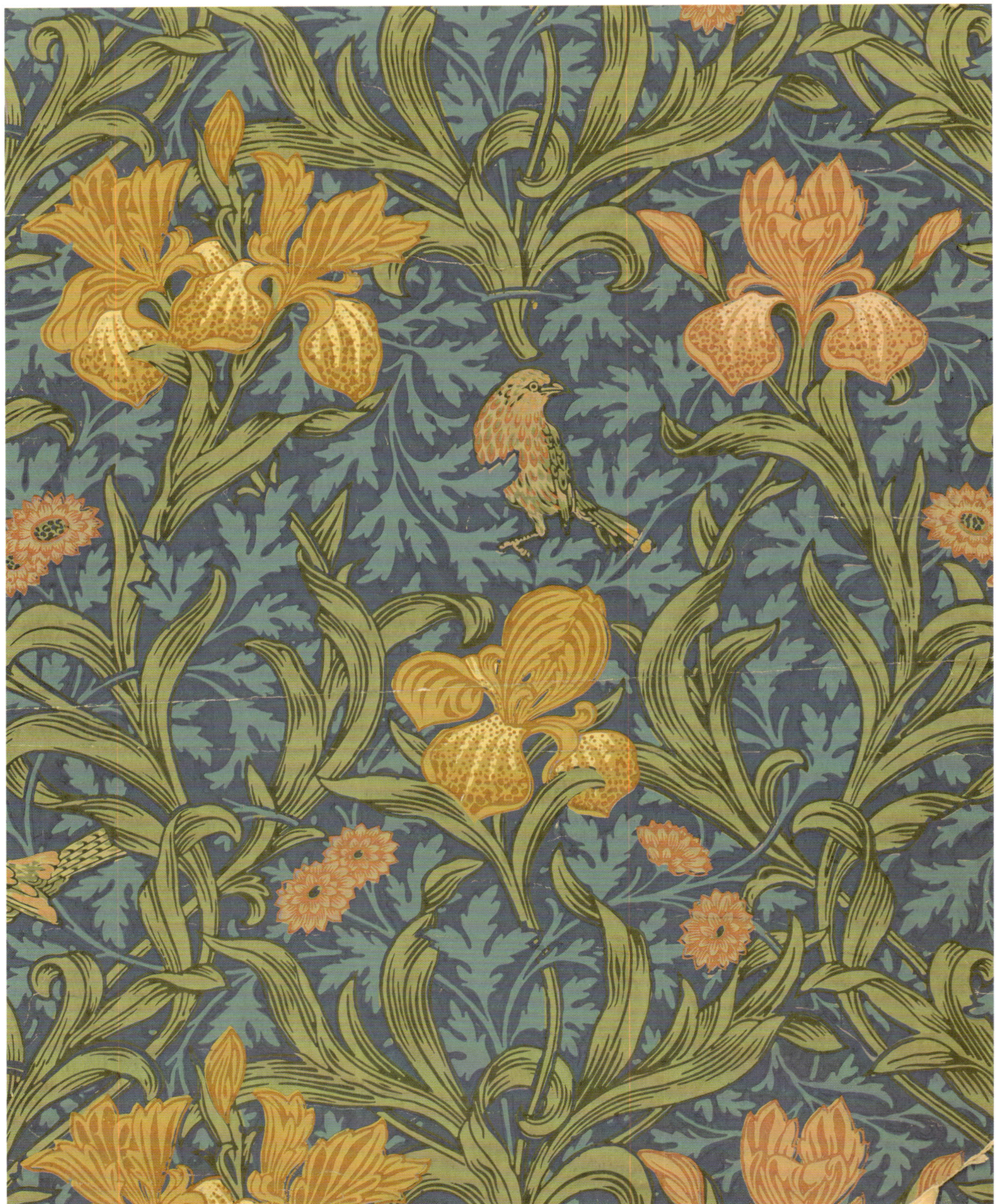

101 | John Henry Dearle, *Iris*, 1887, Jeffrey & Co. for Morris & Co.

In 1878, at the age of 19, John Henry Dearle was employed by William Morris as a shop assistant in the Morris & Co. retail showroom in London's Oxford Street. *Iris*, Dearle's first design for block-printed wallpaper, bears the classic Morris hallmark of blooms and foliage overlaid on a foliate back-print, itself discreetly camouflaging a small thrush.

This design was the third Morris & Co. wallpaper to include birds, and the first by Dearle. His apprenticeship would have included such tasks, as Morris was intent on mastering the art of drawing these feathered friends, having some ten years earlier written to Thomas Wardle: 'I am studying birds now to see if I can't get some of them into my next design.'

102 | John Henry Dearle, *Double Boughs*, 1890/1891, Jeffrey & Co. for Morris & Co.

This block-printed paper was selected by Sir Isaac Lowthian Bell for his three-year refurbishment of the medieval Mount Grace Priory and Manor House, purchased in 1898. For the English Heritage restoration of 2010, the original blocks were used to produce a close replica of the original wallpaper, each roll taking a week to print by hand.

Steel magnate Bell was a wealthy patron of the arts, commissioning Morris together with the architect Philip Webb and the painter Edward Burne-Jones to refurbish his Yorkshire mansions. Aside from his weekend home, Mount Grace Priory, his principal residence was Rounton Grange, the latter a substantial project begun in 1874.

103 | John Henry Dearle, *Granville*, 1896, Jeffrey & Co. for Morris & Co.

As William Morris's protégé in his formative years, Dearle was not only trained by Morris in the art of surface pattern but also in painted glass and tapestry-weaving. It was not until 1887 that Dearle's designs would be transformed from artwork into production. *Granville* and *Double Boughs* demonstrate Dearle's mastery of the Morris style.

Granville was issued in the year of Morris's death. For Dearle, this was not the only change in recent years. The influential business manager George Wardle, joining The Firm in 1866 as draughtsman, book-keeper and block-cutter, retired in 1890. George had installed the indigo vats at Queen Square and introduced Morris to his brother-in-law Thomas, the Leek dyer.

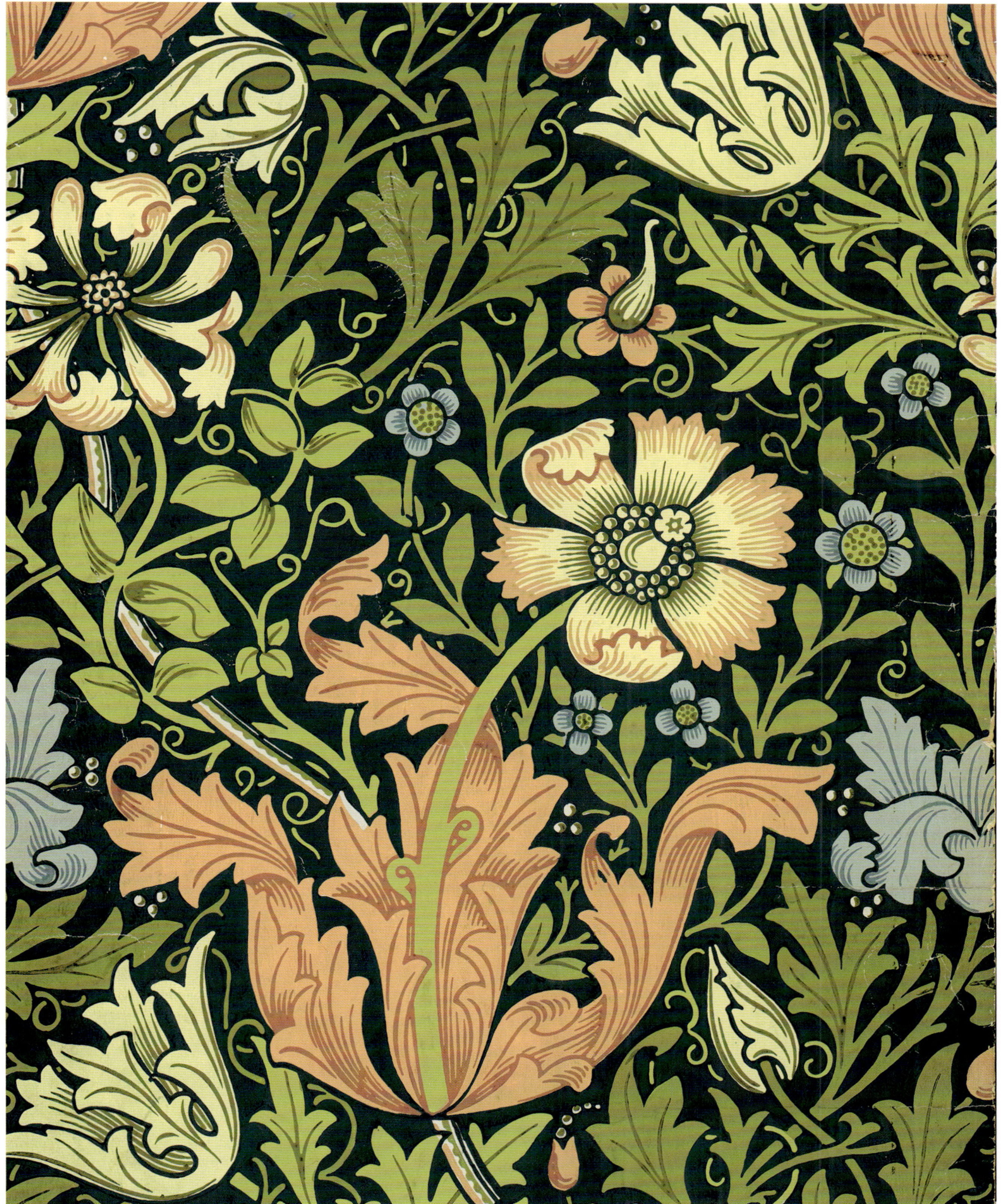

104 | John Henry Dearle, *Compton*, 1896 (registered), Jeffrey & Co. for Morris & Co.

The immense *Compton* pattern, with a height repeat of 84cm (33in) was registered both as a wallpaper and printed textile on 27 February 1896. It is named for Compton Hall in Wolverhampton. May Morris is among those who recorded that this was Morris's last repeating design, but except for the initial discussions he was not involved with the project.

The hall's owner, Laurence W. Hodson, was a patron of the arts and collector of Pre-Raphaelite paintings. He engaged the services of Morris & Co. between 1894 and 1896 to re-design the interior; subsequently the hall's original, and now famous, *Holy Grail* tapestries were donated to Birmingham Museum & Art Gallery.

105 | John Henry Dearle, *Golden Lily*, 1899, Jeffrey & Co. for Morris & Co.

Also attributed for much of its life to William Morris, *Golden Lily* has perhaps been the most enduringly popular design by Dearle. A piece survives in an early 20th-century pattern book that explains how the hand-printed wallpapers 'are produced very slowly... the consequence is that in the finished paper there is a considerable mass of solid colour'.

The design was one of the first Morris & Co. wallpapers adapted to fabric in the 1960s by George Lowe at Sanderson. Nigel Weymouth and his girlfriend Sheila Cohen, at their King's Road, London fashion shop 'Granny Takes a Trip', used it to produce jackets bought by famous pop stars and other celebrities in the music and fashion industries.

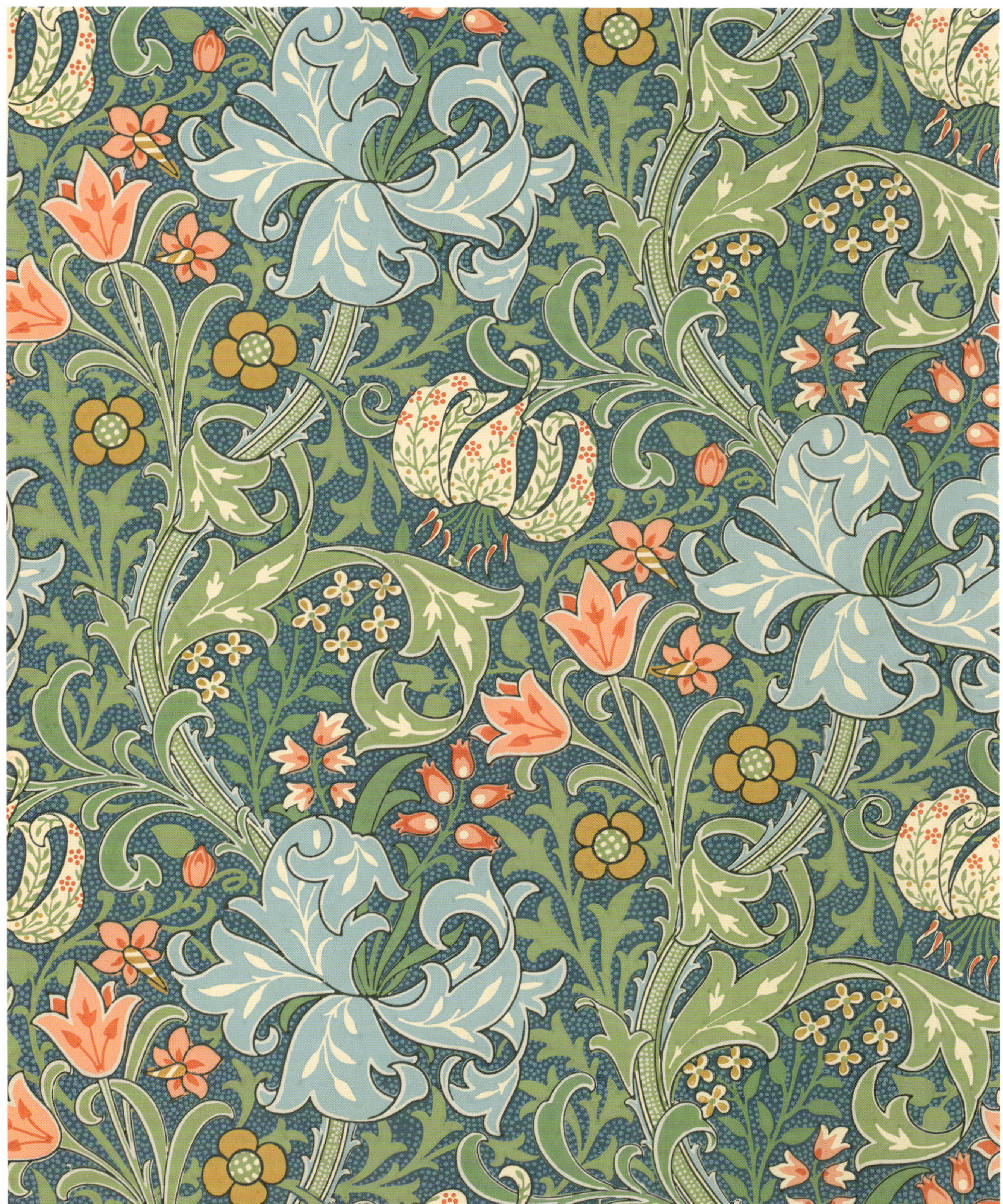

106 | John Henry Dearle, *Golden Lily*, 1899, Jeffrey & Co. for Morris & Co.

Following William Morris's death in 1896, Dearle upheld the creative legacy of Morris & Co. until 1932, serving The Firm for 54 years. In 1899, Dearle created two variants of his *Golden Lily* wallpaper pattern. This more detailed version presents the pattern printed on a refined pinwork ground with miniature floral tracery in the petals of the secondary lilies.

Although designed specifically as a block-printed wallpaper, requiring 11 blocks to complete the pattern, in 1966 Sanderson re-issued *Golden Lily* as a machine-printed wallpaper with matching fabric. It was produced at half the scale of the original and in then-fashionable vivid colours, albeit uncharacteristic of the Morris & Co. ethos.

107 | John Henry Dearle, *Woodland Weeds*, 1894, Jeffrey & Co. for Morris & Co.

It can be assumed that John Henry Dearle's *Woodland Weeds* was designed concurrently with Morris's *Spring Thicket* wallpaper as the resemblance in layout, style and image distribution bear close relationship to each other. The symmetry in both these and the more formal Morris design, *Autumn Flowers*, relates to woven textiles designed by Morris in c.1888.

Since the early-1890s, Dearle had gained both respectability and acclaim for his creativity, just as Morris gradually withdrew from day-to-day engagements. However, Morris retained a watching brief over all creative aspects and for the last five years of his life worked with Burne-Jones and Dearle on a set of tapestries based on the legend of the Holy Grail.

108 | John Henry Dearle, *Single Stem*, 1894, Jeffrey & Co. for Morris & Co.

The composition of *Single Stem* follows the Morris & Co. creative signature characteristics. Its combination of back-print, acanthus leaves and flowing circular form are nevertheless aesthetically different from earlier Dearle patterns. This is the result of the strong colour contrasts used, resulting in a greater distinction between the background and pattern.

It has been suggested that Dearle was endeavouring to create a striking alternative in a larger-scale wallpaper. It may also be that he was influenced by *Horn Poppy*, the 1885 pattern by May Morris. Both share the more open and 'spikey' drawing that is a departure from earlier designs, but at different scales: Dearle's repeat is 65cm high whereas May's is 51cm.

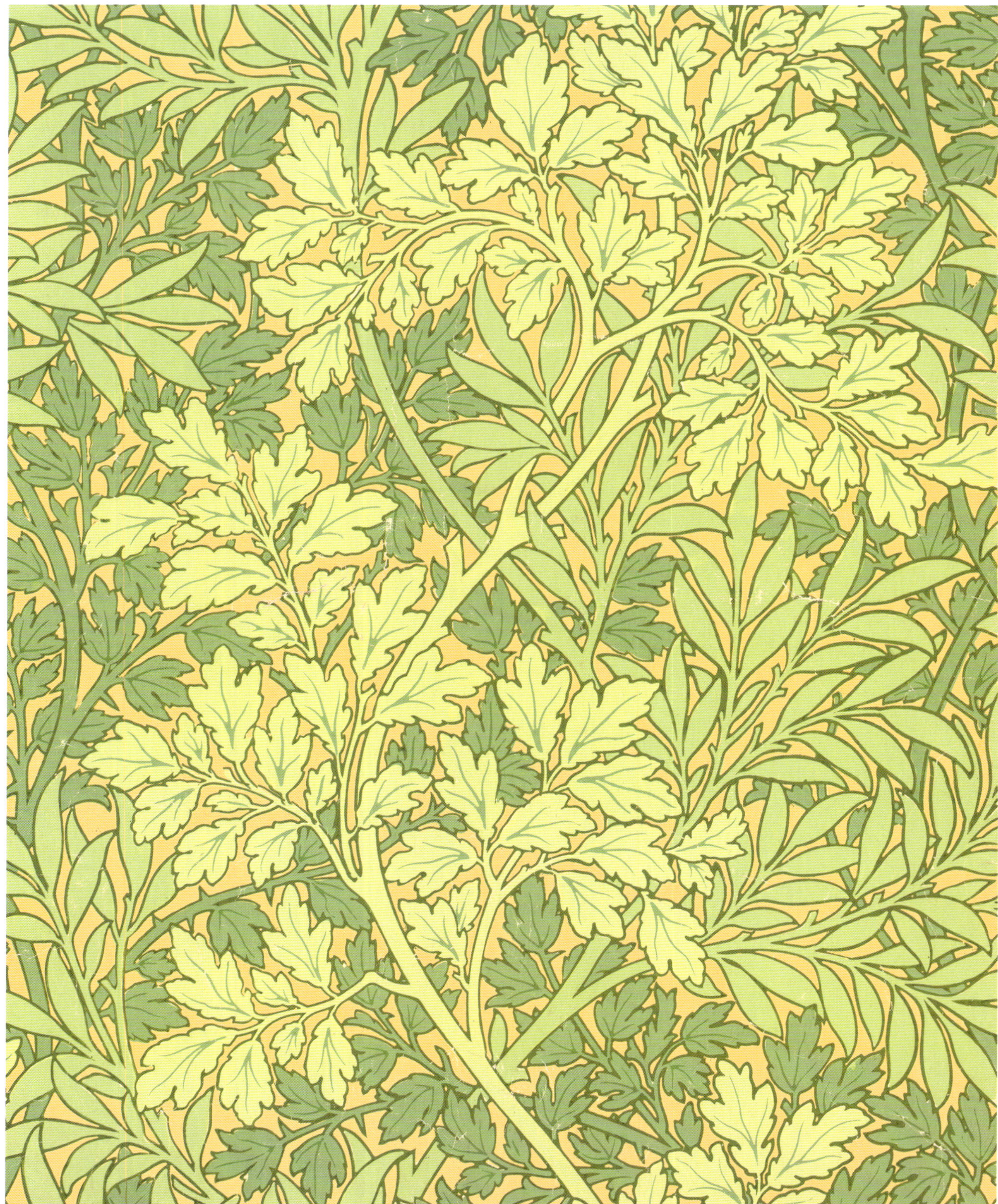

109 | John Henry Dearle, *Foliage*, 1899, Jeffrey & Co. for Morris & Co.

For *Foliage*, Dearle drew upon his considerable experience in the Merton Abbey tapestry workshop, where until 1932 he was involved with every hanging woven there. In the dense overlapping flow of foliage, this design suggests the *Greenery* tapestry, designed by Dearle in 1892. Twice woven, one tapestry is now in the Metropolitan Museum of Art in New York.

Lewis F. Day wrote of Dearle as 'A Disciple of William Morris' in *The Art Journal* (1905, pp.84–89). On Dearle's support of The Firm's ethos, Day observed 'it was only natural that [Morris] should depend more and more upon the assistance of a pupil who entered so entirely into his spirit, that he could be relied upon to do much [of] what he himself might have done'.

110 | John Henry Dearle, *Orchard*, 1899, Jeffrey & Co. for Morris & Co.

This pattern, too, shows Dearle's involvement with Morris & Co. tapestries, which from the mid-1880s incorporated fruiting trees. The depiction of the roots of the tree in *Orchard* is a novel feature in his wallpaper designs and reinforces the pattern's relationship to Dearle designs for panels, including *Owl* (c.1895), which was being embroidered at the time.

A greater apparent solidity of forms also links to the handful of madras muslins designed by Dearle a few years later. These, in which solid woven areas contrast with sheer leno, were woven by Alexander Morton & Co. *Orchard* thus embodies Dearle's sensitivity to the adaptation of patterns to alternative substrates. It was illustrated in *The Art Journal* in 1906.

111 | John Henry Dearle, *Artichoke*, 1898/99, Jeffrey & Co. for Morris & Co.

This boldly scaled, half-drop design of ornamental artichoke flower buds is supported by harebells on a background of willow leaves. In designing *Artichoke*, Dearle might have been reflecting the continued success of William Morris's *Willow Boughs* block-printed wallpaper, created some 12 years previously.

While it conveys simplicity, *Willow Boughs* nevertheless was printed with five wooden blocks. In contrast, Dearle's expansive repeating *Artichoke* pattern atop a willow-like ground required 12 blocks to print the complete design. Despite their different subjects and scale, the layout of *Artichoke* shares an underlying structure with *Willow Boughs*.

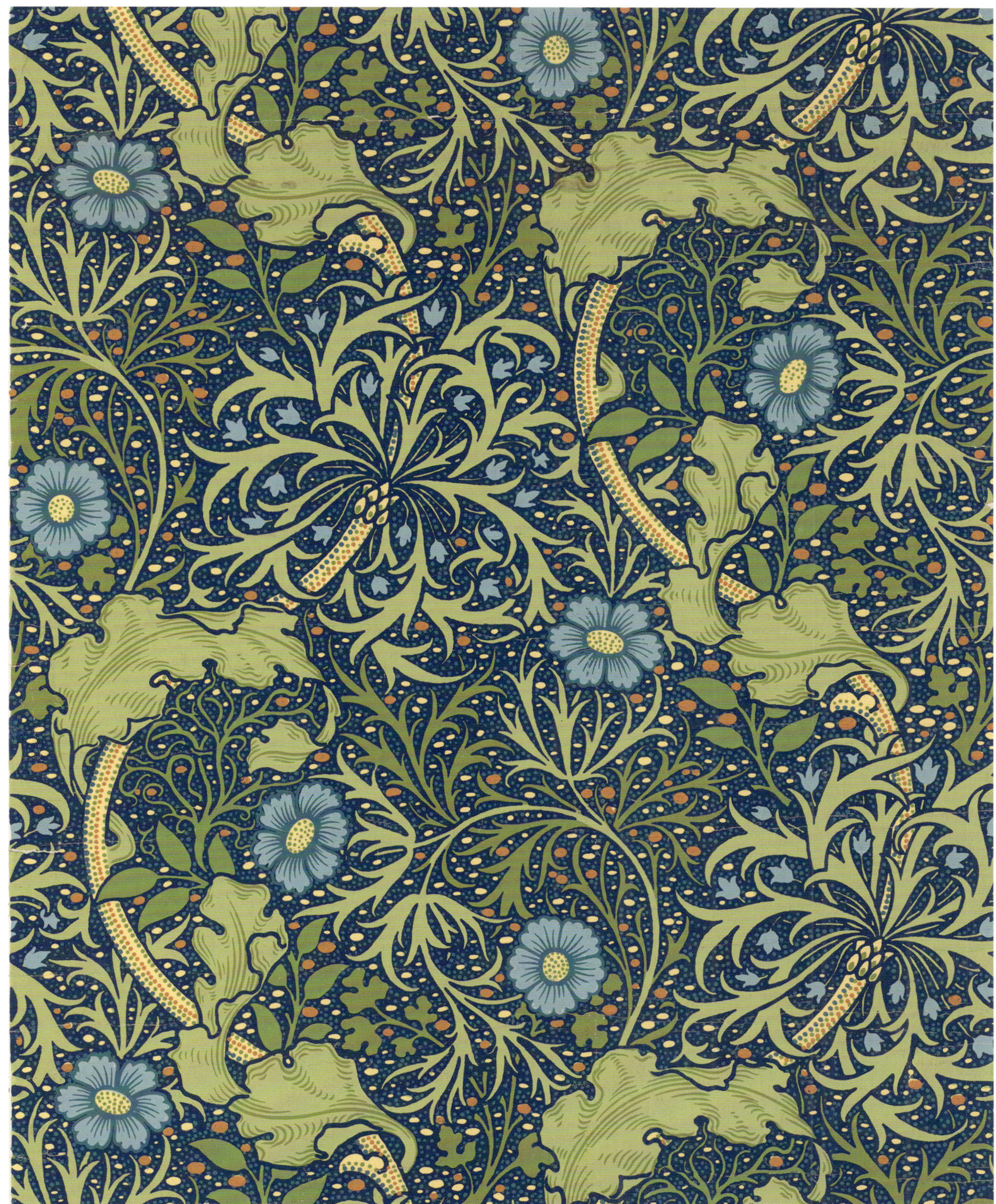

112 | John Henry Dearle, *Seaweed*, 1901, Jeffrey & Co. for Morris & Co.

The seaweed in this pattern appears as the back-print. Although making its first appearance here for Morris & Co., patterns depicting seaweed dating from 1788–92 were created by the calico-printer and designer William Kilburn (1745–1818). As early enthusiasts for late 18th-century designs, Morris and his circle may well have seen similar designs.

In addition, seaweed garnered interest during Queen Victoria's reign (1837–1901), when she and many children and women, including George Eliot (1819–80), went 'seaweeding'. Creating albums of pressed seaweed reflects both the interest in amateur botany that developed in the 19th century and the proliferation of illustrated botanical books.

113 | John Henry Dearle, *Blackberry*, 1903, Jeffrey & Co. for Morris & Co.

As an interior decorator, Dearle understood that the cluttered interiors and dark colours of the Victorian Age were past and a new 'lighter era' would emerge. *Blackberry* reflects this transition from dark to light. It would also have worked well with the Hepplewhite, Sheraton and Regency furniture featured in the Morris & Co. catalogues from the 1890s onwards.

Dearle had also by now become an educator. In 1901, at the age of 42, he began examining submissions to the National Competition of Design, an annual event held at South Kensington. Over the following years, Dearle worked for the Board of Education and with the City and Guilds of London Institute.

114 | John Henry Dearle, *Michaelmas Daisy*, 1912, Jeffrey & Co. for Morris & Co. Decorators Ltd

The light, airy feeling of *Michaelmas Daisy* met the needs of those Morris & Co. customers requiring a pretty and airy design for bedrooms and small reception rooms. Like *Blackberry*, it was not only compatible with Regency revival styles, but chimed with the growing fashion for informal American wicker and rattan chairs.

In the previous year, The Firm had been busy with commissions relating to the coronation service of King George V at Westminster Abbey on 22 June 1911. These included the Chairs of State, for which Dearle passed the bullion work to the Society of St Margaret, and Morris & Co. embroidery of frontal and dorsal fabrics supplied by St Edmundsbury Weavers.

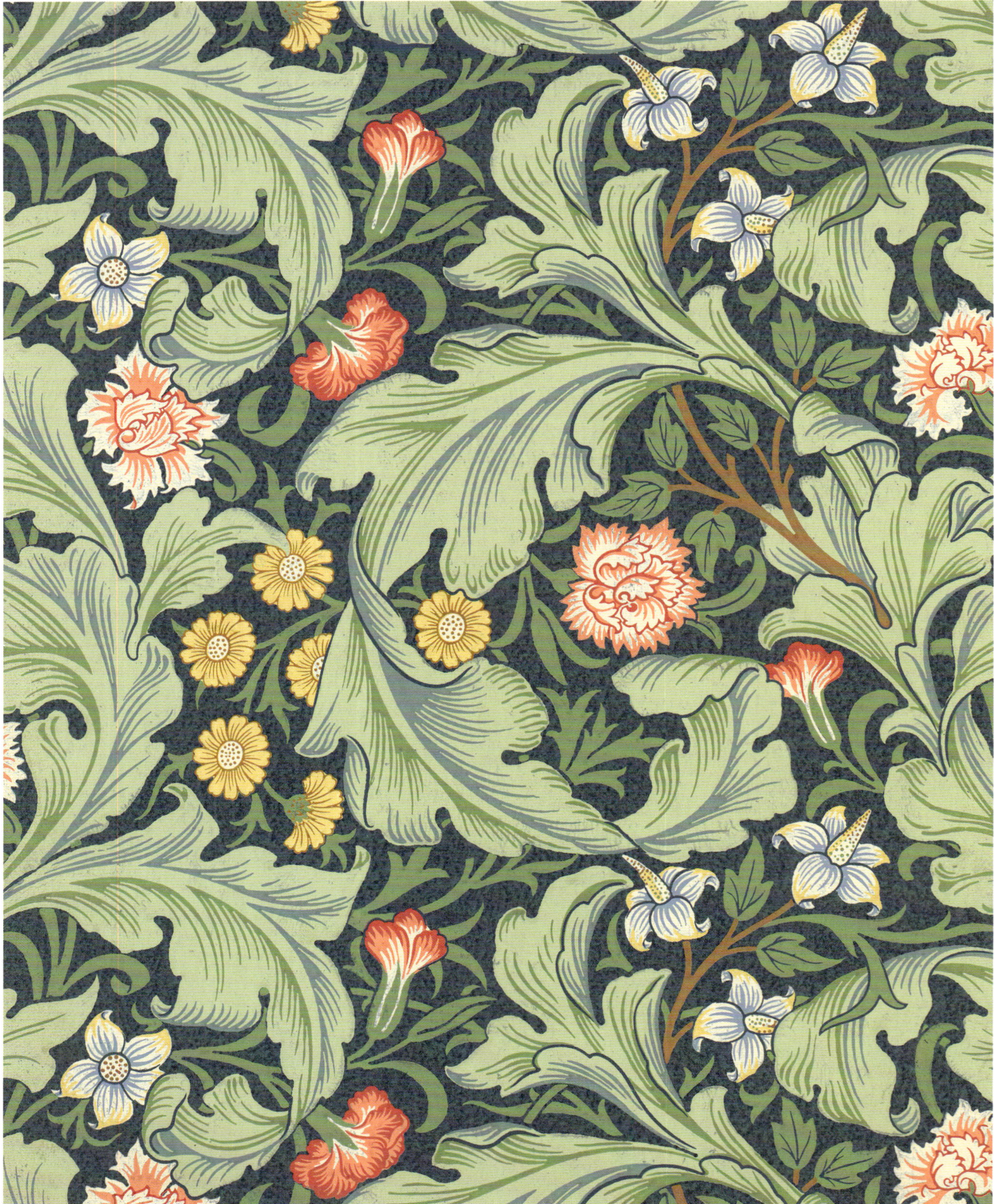

115 | John Henry Dearle, *Leicester*, 1912, Jeffrey & Co. for Morris & Co. Decorators Ltd

Leicester was a late addition to Wightwick Manor, the 'House Beautiful' built by Theodore and Flora Mander in 1887 and extended in 1893. Installed in the Morning Room, it exemplifies one of the important roles played by wallpaper in this period, namely the ease with which it could be replaced when coal fires had darkened the existing paper.

Bequeathed to the National Trust in 1937, today the interior remains one of the finest and most complete examples of Morris & Co. decoration to be found in the UK, displaying examples of wallcoverings, carpets, embroidery and upholstery designed by The Firm. It also houses De Morgan tiles, Kempe glass and Pre-Raphaelite works of art.

116 | John Henry Dearle, *Sweet Briar*, 1912, Jeffrey & Co. for Morris & Co. Decorators Ltd

Sweetbriar takes its name from the wild, invasive shrub that adorns countryside hedgerows. The plant is aptly named after the fragrant 'sweet' smell of the flowers coupled with the thorny 'briar' bush. It is the last Dearle design to continue the use of Morris's parallel meandering vines, as seen in the latter's *Flora* of 1891.

Illustrated in *The Studio Year-Book* in 1913, the *Sweetbriar* pattern was soon used on a printed cotton. Clearly a successful cloth, a sample of the latter is held in the Cooper-Hewitt, Smithsonian Design Museum in New York, dated c.1934. It was donated in 1935 by Cowtan & Tout Inc., who distributed Morris & Co. products in New York.

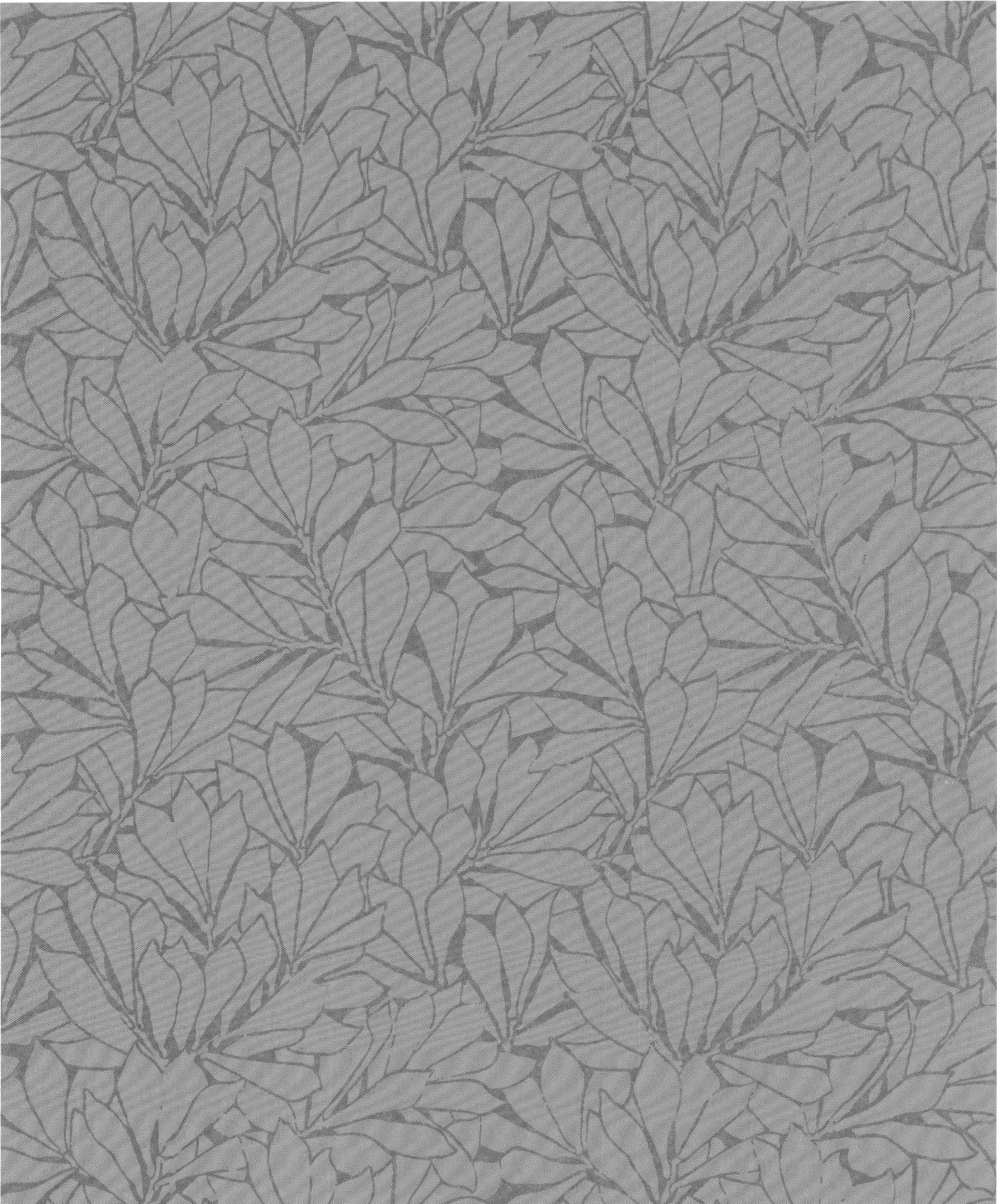

117 | Kathleen Kersey, *Verdure*, 1913, Jeffrey & Co. for Morris & Co. Decorators Ltd

Kathleen Kersey (Mrs Allington, born 1889) was a member of the Morris & Co. design circle on the eve of the First World War. She designed *Verdure* for two uses: as an all-over patterned wallpaper and as a back-print for her *Arbutus* pattern (shown right). However, with the onset of the war, shortages of both staff and paper limited its immediate circulation.

Nevertheless, this wallpaper example was printed in the early-1950s on a duplex ingrain paper, using the original blocks. It shows considerable 'block wear' resulting from extensive use, indicating that *Verdure* was printed many times in the period between 1918 and 1940, a piece of physical evidence that attests to its subsequent popularity.

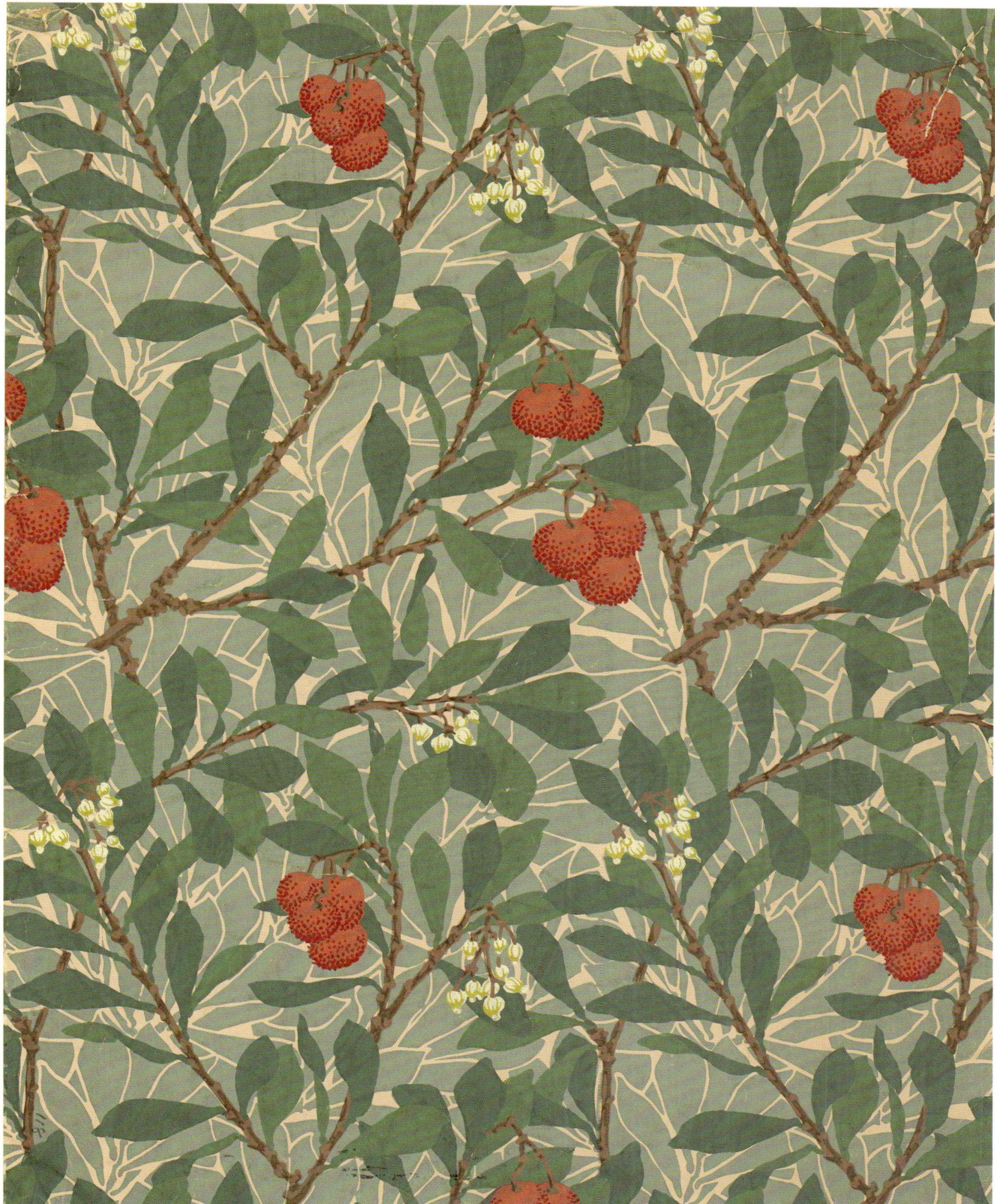

118 | Kathleen Kersey, *Arbutus*, 1913, Jeffrey & Co. for Morris & Co. Decorators Ltd

Kersey's *Arbutus* pattern emulates the creative arrangement and composition of earlier Morris & Co. block-printed wallpapers and one might assume that she studied these as an apprentice designer. Several other designers, including William Arthur Smith Benson (the chairman of The Firm), also contributed designs in the early-20th century.

It was in this year that Jane Morris finally purchased Kelmscott Manor, preserving the house as a memorial to her father. It is now owned by the Society of Antiquaries of London and run as a museum. Also befitting memories of Morris & Co., *Arbutus* was one of several Morris & Co. patterns re-issued in the Archive III collection in 2015.

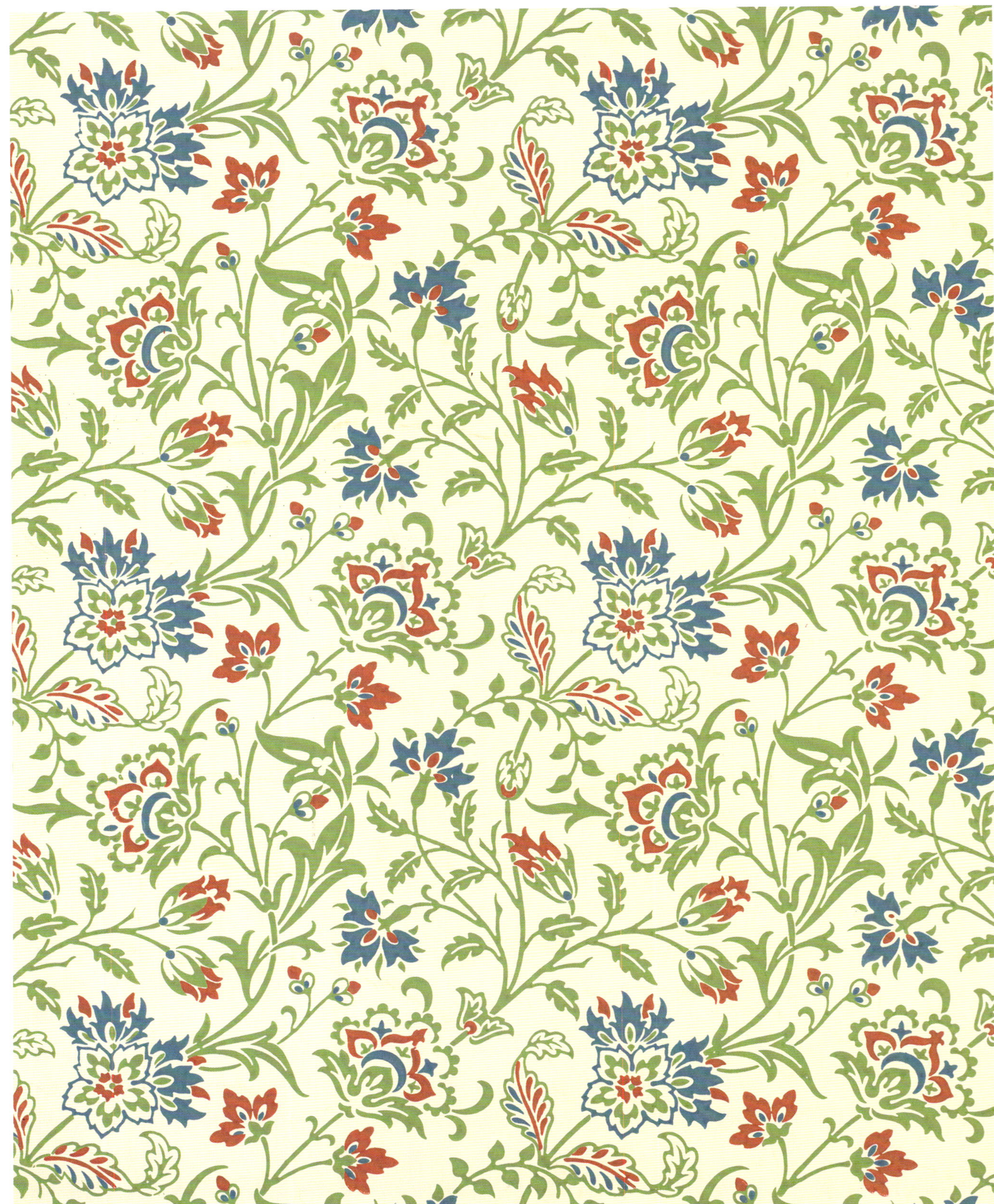

119 | John Henry Dearle, *Brentwood*, 1913, Jeffrey & Co. for Morris & Co. Decorators Ltd

Like Morris, Dearle was a frequent visitor to the South Kensington Museum (now Victoria and Albert Museum) and an avid researcher of antique textiles. This design recalls Indian chintz patterns of the sort that he may have viewed there. It was later printed as a cotton and linen, and several versions exist that were block-printed in the 1950s.

Some say that Dearle named *Brentwood* after the small Essex town 30 km (18.6 miles) from London, which was expanding at this time. However, it is much more likely that he named it after the river that is sometimes given the shortened name, *Brent*. In total, Dearle named some 14 designs after rivers, including four others that are also Thames tributaries.

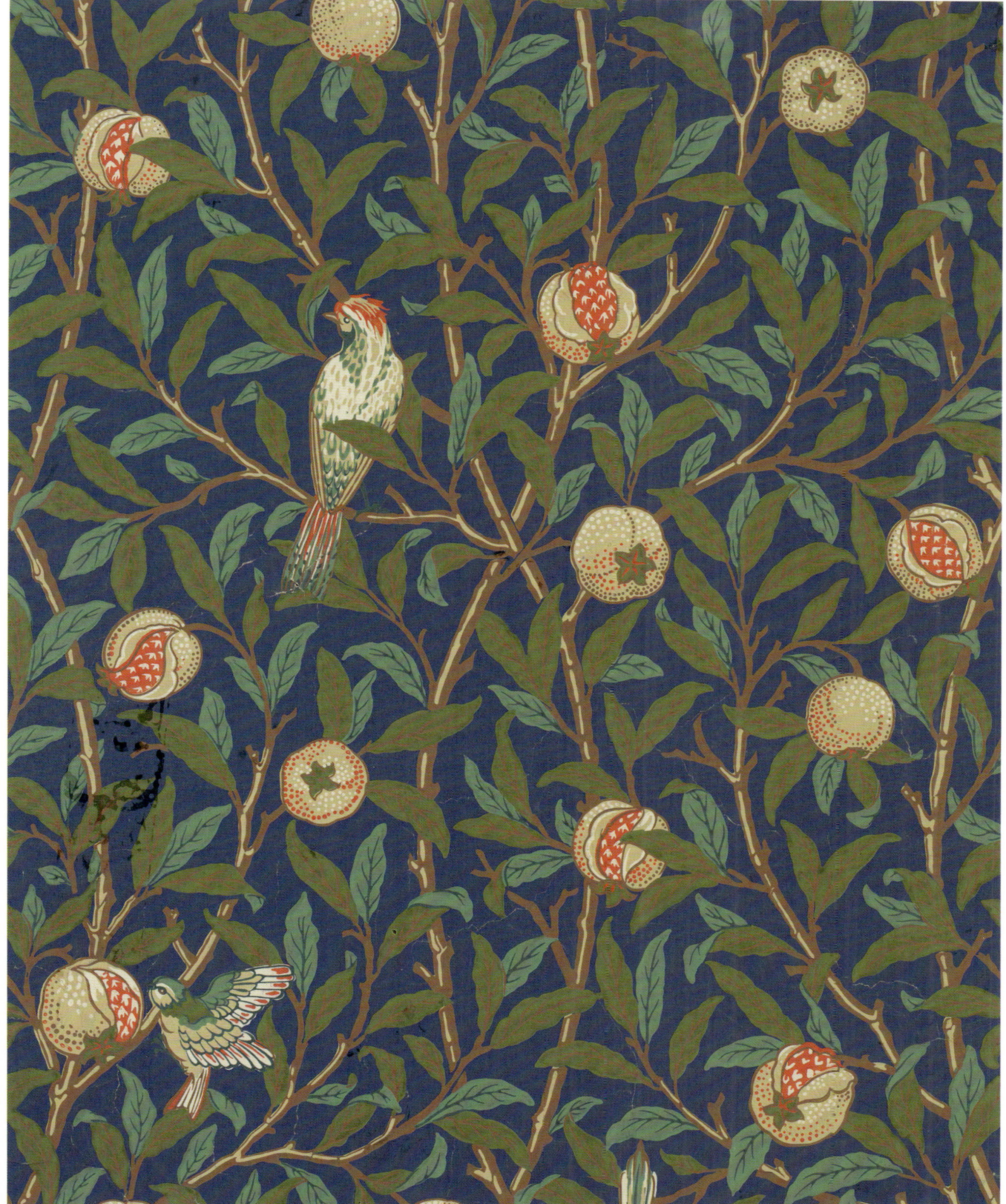

120 | Possibly John Henry Dearle, *Bird and Pomegranate*, 1926/27, Jeffrey & Co. for Morris & Co. Art-Workers Ltd

Bird and Pomegranate was possibly Dearle's last block-printed wallpaper design and, significantly, the last wallpaper to be issued by Morris & Co. Its issue coincided with the year in which, following various commissions from the Royal Household, King George V granted Morris & Co. its first Royal Warrant.

Since 1887, Dearle had created about 60 printed designs for Morris & Co. Some 33 were for wallpaper. With Morris (accounting for 51 patterns) and a handful of others, The Firm created more than 100 wallpapers. While insignificant compared with rival businesses, these continue to influence interior decoration throughout the world today.

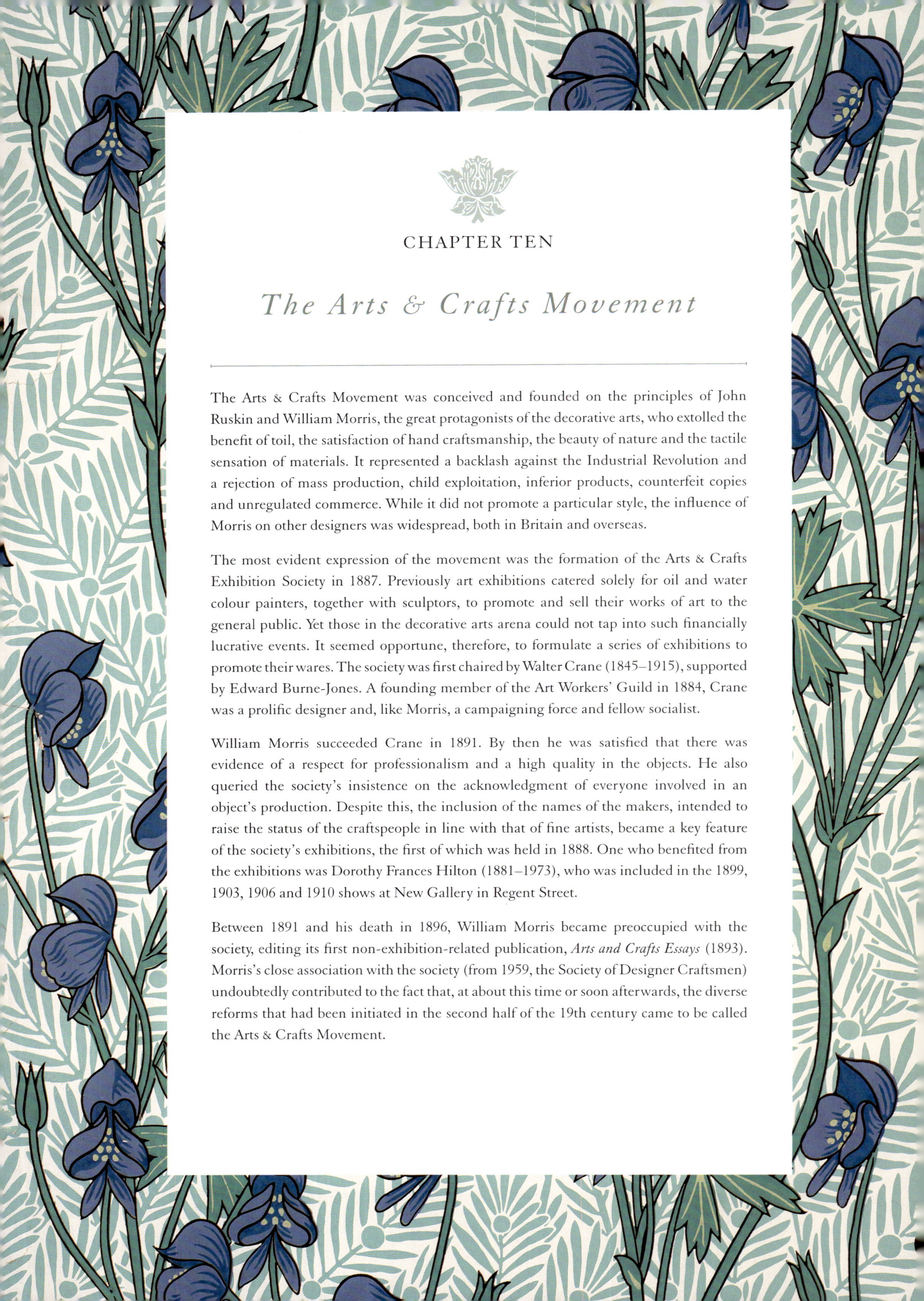

CHAPTER TEN

The Arts & Crafts Movement

The Arts & Crafts Movement was conceived and founded on the principles of John Ruskin and William Morris, the great protagonists of the decorative arts, who extolled the benefit of toil, the satisfaction of hand craftsmanship, the beauty of nature and the tactile sensation of materials. It represented a backlash against the Industrial Revolution and a rejection of mass production, child exploitation, inferior products, counterfeit copies and unregulated commerce. While it did not promote a particular style, the influence of Morris on other designers was widespread, both in Britain and overseas.

The most evident expression of the movement was the formation of the Arts & Crafts Exhibition Society in 1887. Previously art exhibitions catered solely for oil and water colour painters, together with sculptors, to promote and sell their works of art to the general public. Yet those in the decorative arts arena could not tap into such financially lucrative events. It seemed opportune, therefore, to formulate a series of exhibitions to promote their wares. The society was first chaired by Walter Crane (1845–1915), supported by Edward Burne-Jones. A founding member of the Art Workers' Guild in 1884, Crane was a prolific designer and, like Morris, a campaigning force and fellow socialist.

William Morris succeeded Crane in 1891. By then he was satisfied that there was evidence of a respect for professionalism and a high quality in the objects. He also queried the society's insistence on the acknowledgment of everyone involved in an object's production. Despite this, the inclusion of the names of the makers, intended to raise the status of the craftspeople in line with that of fine artists, became a key feature of the society's exhibitions, the first of which was held in 1888. One who benefited from the exhibitions was Dorothy Frances Hilton (1881–1973), who was included in the 1899, 1903, 1906 and 1910 shows at New Gallery in Regent Street.

Between 1891 and his death in 1896, William Morris became preoccupied with the society, editing its first non-exhibition-related publication, *Arts and Crafts Essays* (1893). Morris's close association with the society (from 1959, the Society of Designer Craftsmen) undoubtedly contributed to the fact that, at about this time or soon afterwards, the diverse reforms that had been initiated in the second half of the 19th century came to be called the Arts & Crafts Movement.

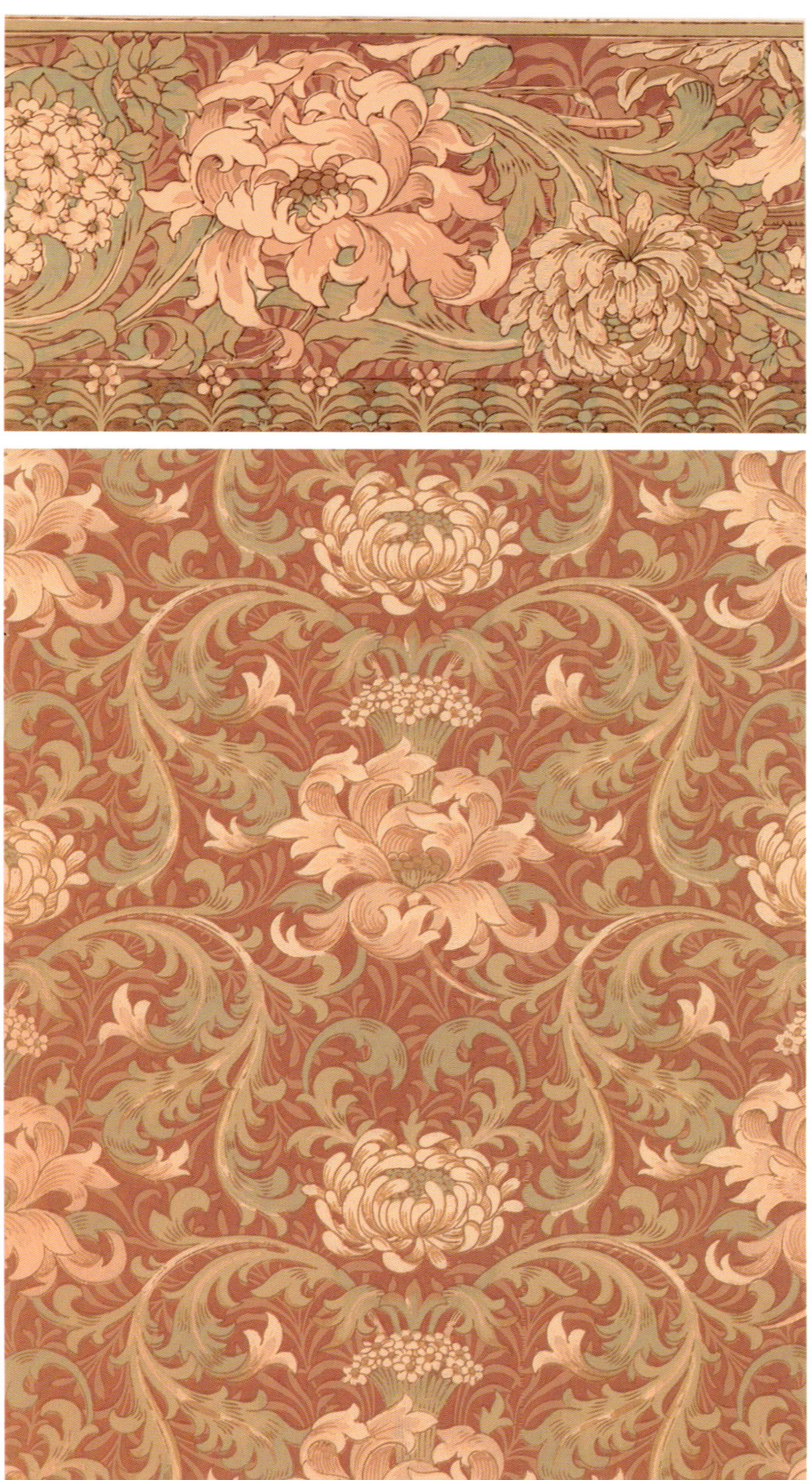

121 | The Sanderson Studio, *The Rossetti*, filling and frieze, 1897, Arthur Sanderson & Sons

The Rossetti, with its accompanying frieze, was designed in 1885. Produced in three colourways, this version, with its rich terracotta-colour ground, shows the perfection of the surface wash-printing by machine at Chiswick in 1897. This is a process in which the ground pigment is sieved to create an overall even finish, something Morris sought to produce but never did.

The pattern's name alludes to Dante Gabrielle Rossetti, who had encouraged Morris to abandon architectural training, writing 'if any man has poetry in him, he should paint it'. Rossetti became a founding partner in Morris, Marshall, Faulkner & Co. and contributed designs for stained glass and other decorative objects.

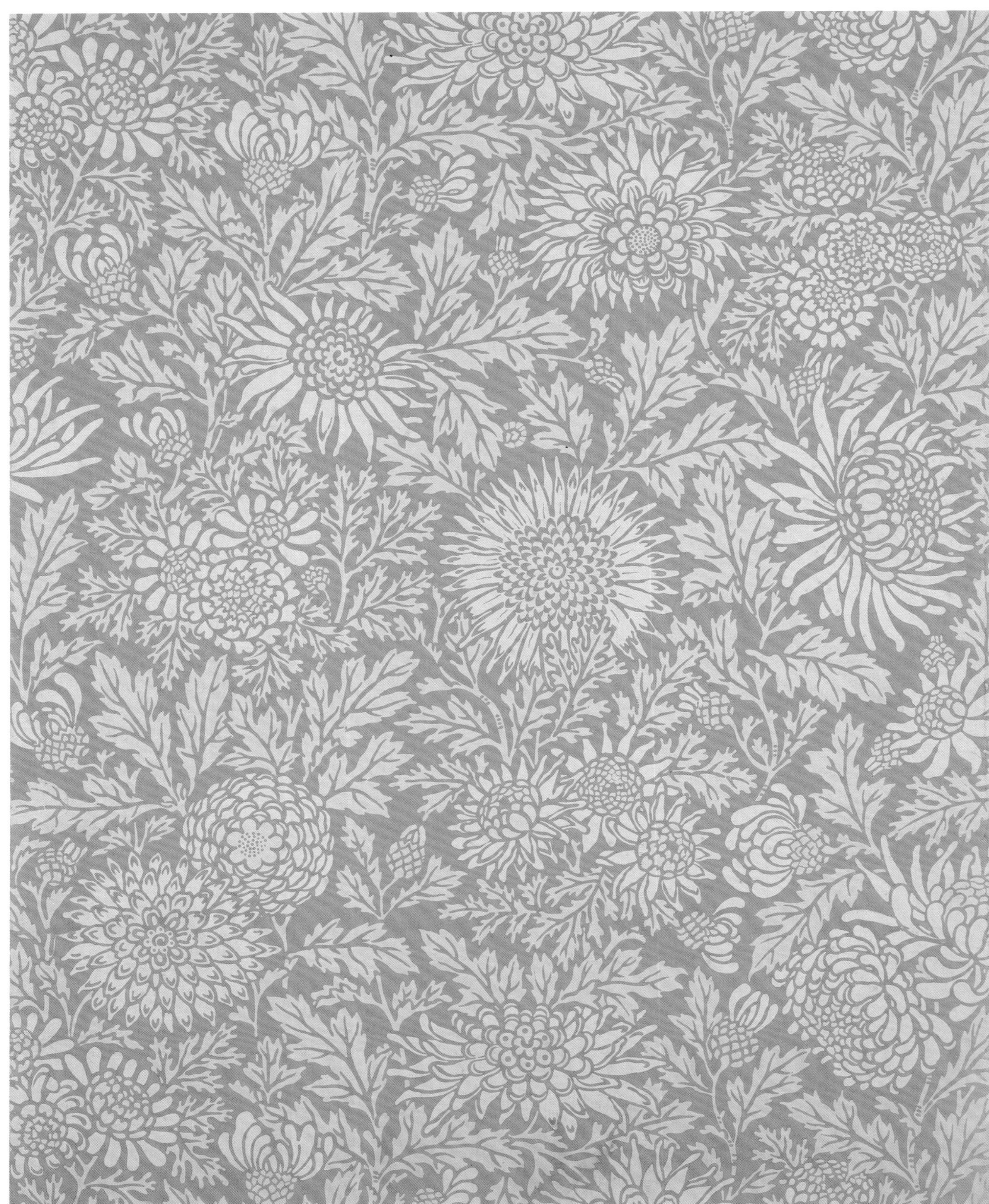

122 | The Sanderson Studio, *Chrysanthemum*, 1880–1900, Arthur Sanderson & Sons

Chrysanthemum's subtle three-colour, block-printed design also incorporates marigolds and thistles. Its linear style, tonal colours and choice of flowers are typical of the 'artistic' wallpapers intended to be hung in a tripartite arrangement of co-ordinating dado, filling and frieze. This is a filling paper, functioning as a backdrop to paintings and other wall decor.

Arthur Sanderson & Sons printed many similar tonally coloured wallpapers that observed shifting tastes in middle-class homes. Having turned away from traditional painterly florals towards Morris-style patterns, by the end of the 19th century tastes had moved towards more linear floral styles. Designs such as this became mainstream by 1900.

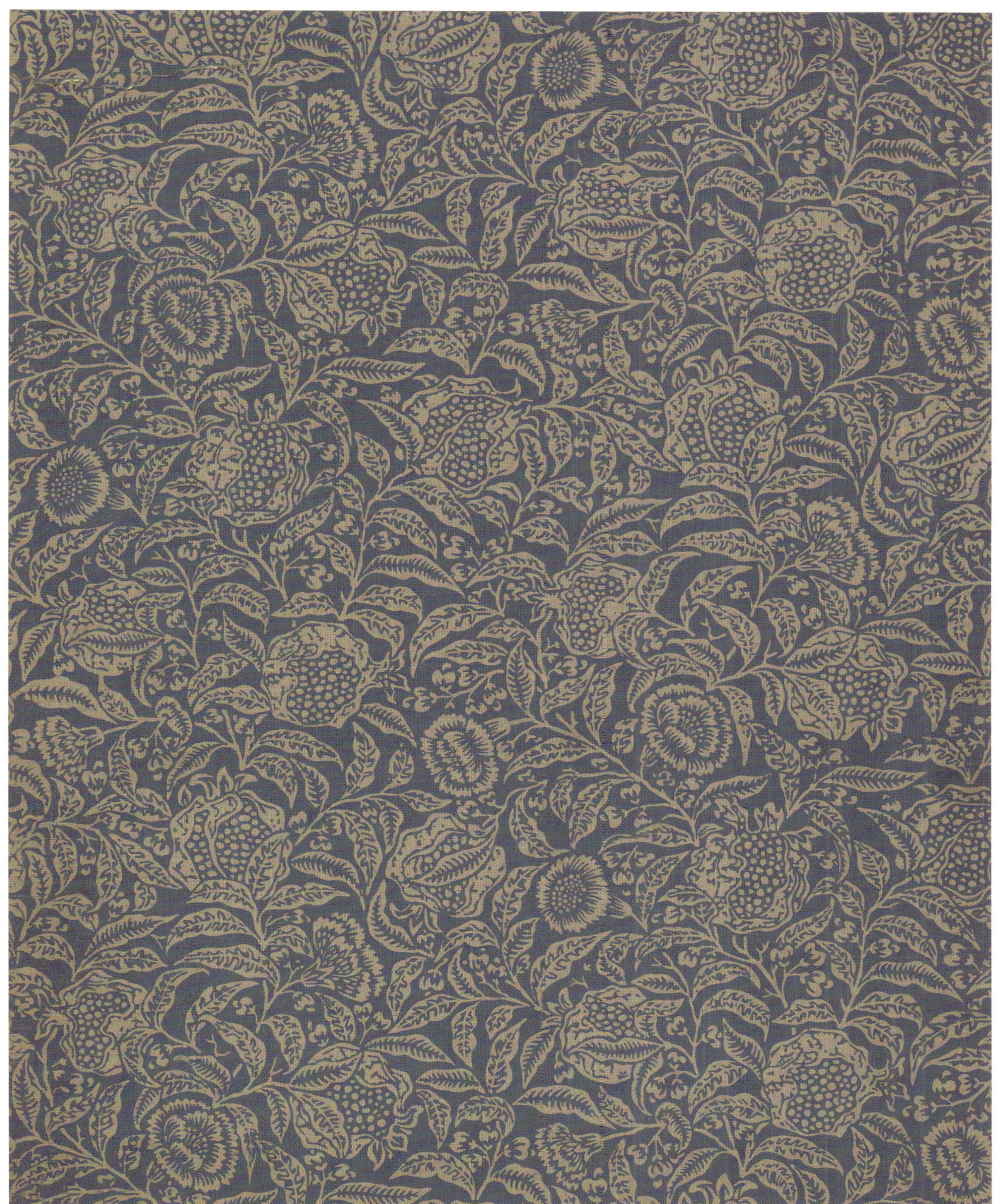

123 | Designer unknown, *The Addison*, c.1885, Charles Knowles & Co.

This example shows that Knowles also printed papers in arts and crafts style. *The Addison* has a hand-crafted 'wood block' feel, accentuated by having only two colours. It is striking because the pattern is defined not by the positive areas of the design but by its dominant background colour. This was to become known as the 'white line' style.

The single printing block used to create this design was purchased by Arthur Sanderson & Sons in 1913 as part of the Charles Knowles & Co. document archive. Knowles's reputation was built on high-quality damask wallpapers, including 'Crystal Damask' and 'Frosted Golds', whereby damask patterns were block-printed on to mica grounds dusted with gold.

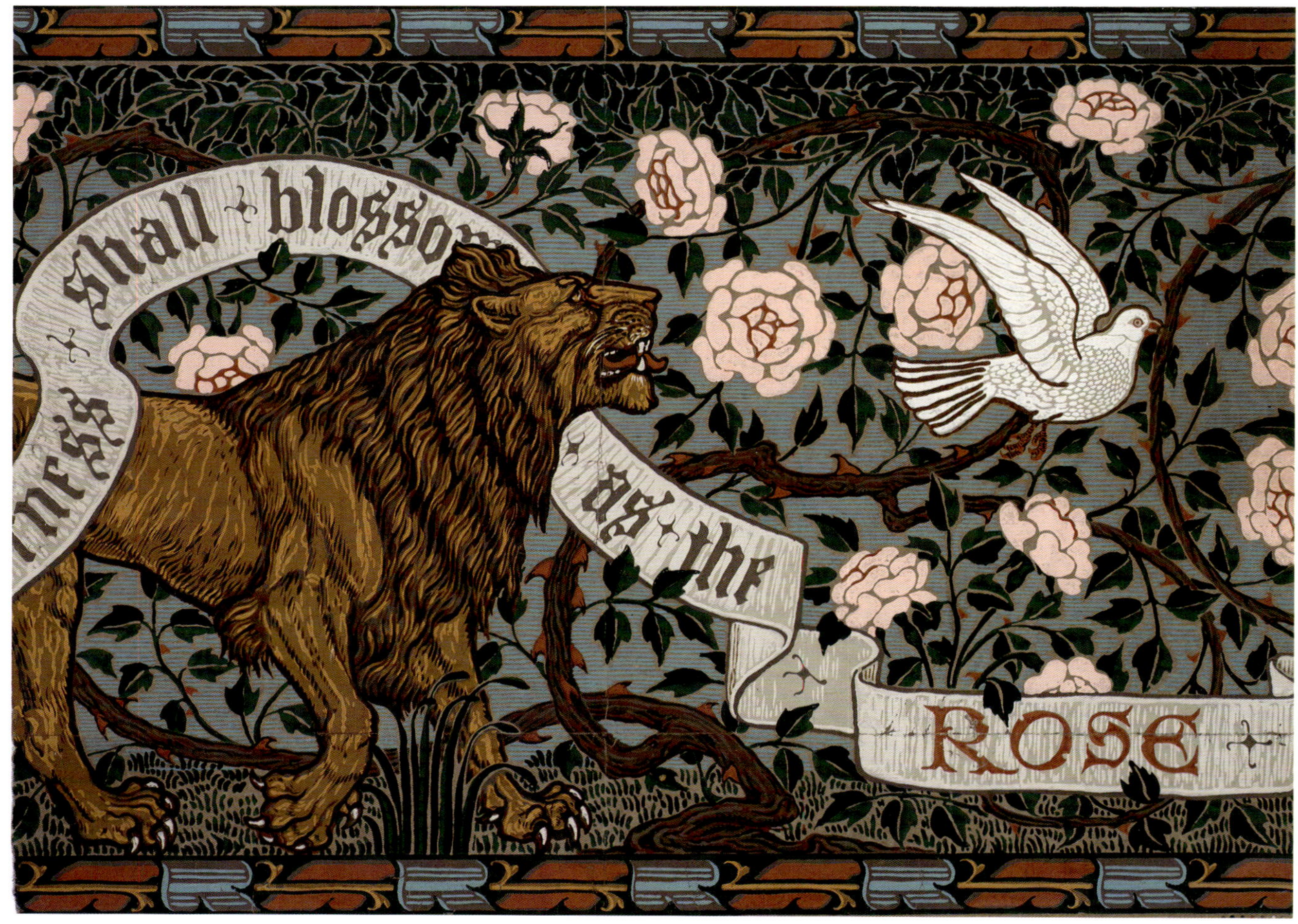

124 | Walter Crane, *Lion and Dove*, 1900, Jeffrey & Co.

This elaborate frieze was designed by Walter Crane (1845–1915) to be used with a filling wallpaper entitled *The Rose Bush*. Both were exhibited at the 1900 Exposition Universelle in Paris. For Crane this was not a new experience, having exhibited at the Philadelphia Centennial Exhibition in 1876, garnering an award and critical acclaim for Jeffrey & Co.

By 1900 Crane was a highly regarded painter, illustrator and designer of mural decoration, stained glass and pottery. With the wood engraver and printer Edmund Evans, he produced several illustrated children's books. Also creating designs for nursery papers, *Sleeping Beauty* (1879) was produced as a washable wallpaper by Jeffrey & Co. in 1885.

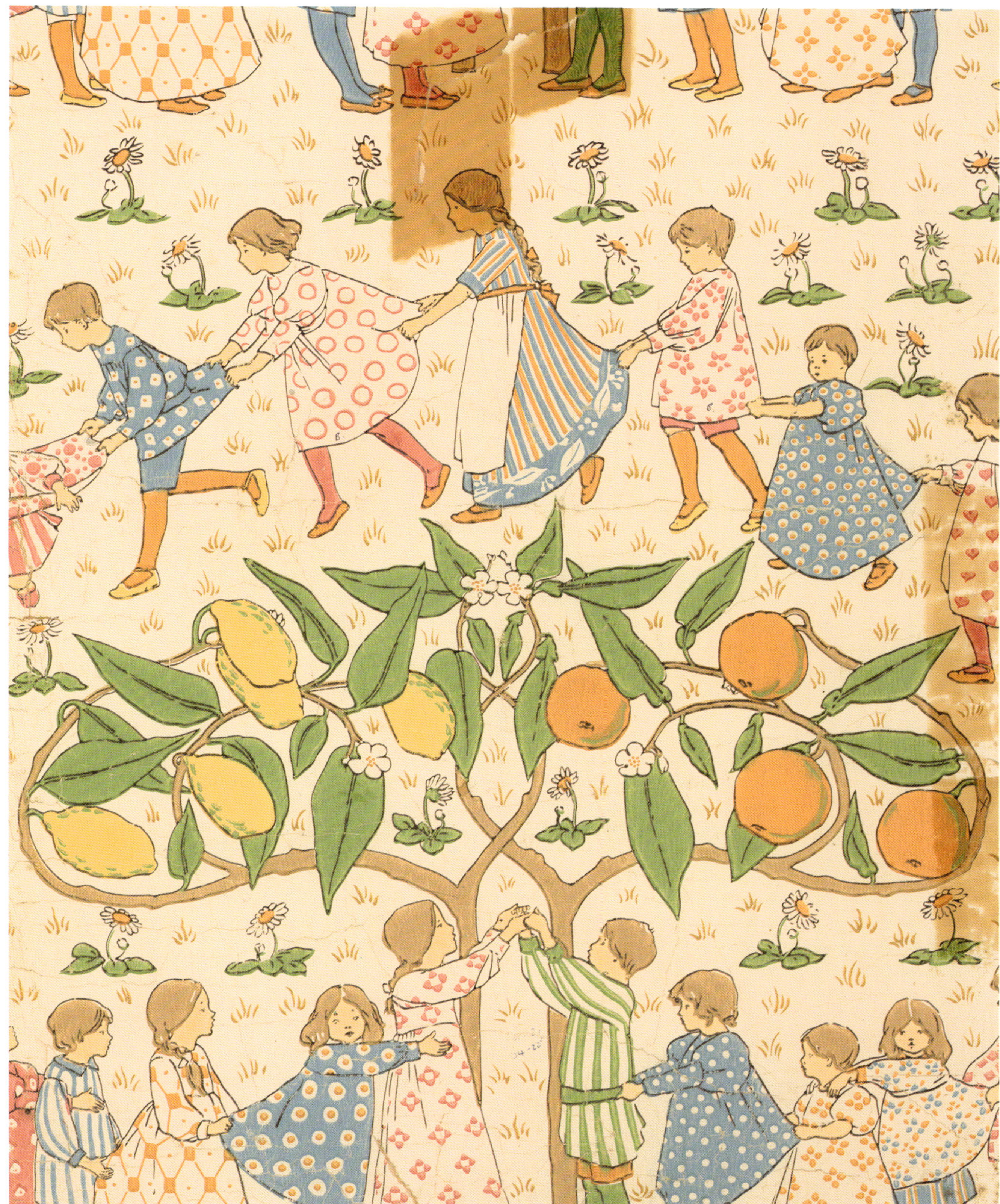

125 | Dorothy Hilton, *Oranges and Lemons*, 1900, Jeffrey & Co.

Following in Walter Crane's footsteps, this nursery wallpaper is typically illustrative, in this case of the traditional nursery rhyme that gives this paper its name. *Oranges and Lemons* was described in a 1902 edition of *The Art Journal* as an 'excellent design' and the promising work of a new designer, who also designed *Banbury Cross* for Jeffrey's in 1902.

The paper was machine-printed by Jeffrey's, as were numerous nursery papers produced in response to growing literacy among children, for whom illustrated books were becoming commonplace. A similar paper entitled *May Day* was reproduced in a 1905 edition of *The Queen* ladies' newspaper, though there is no mention of the designer's name.

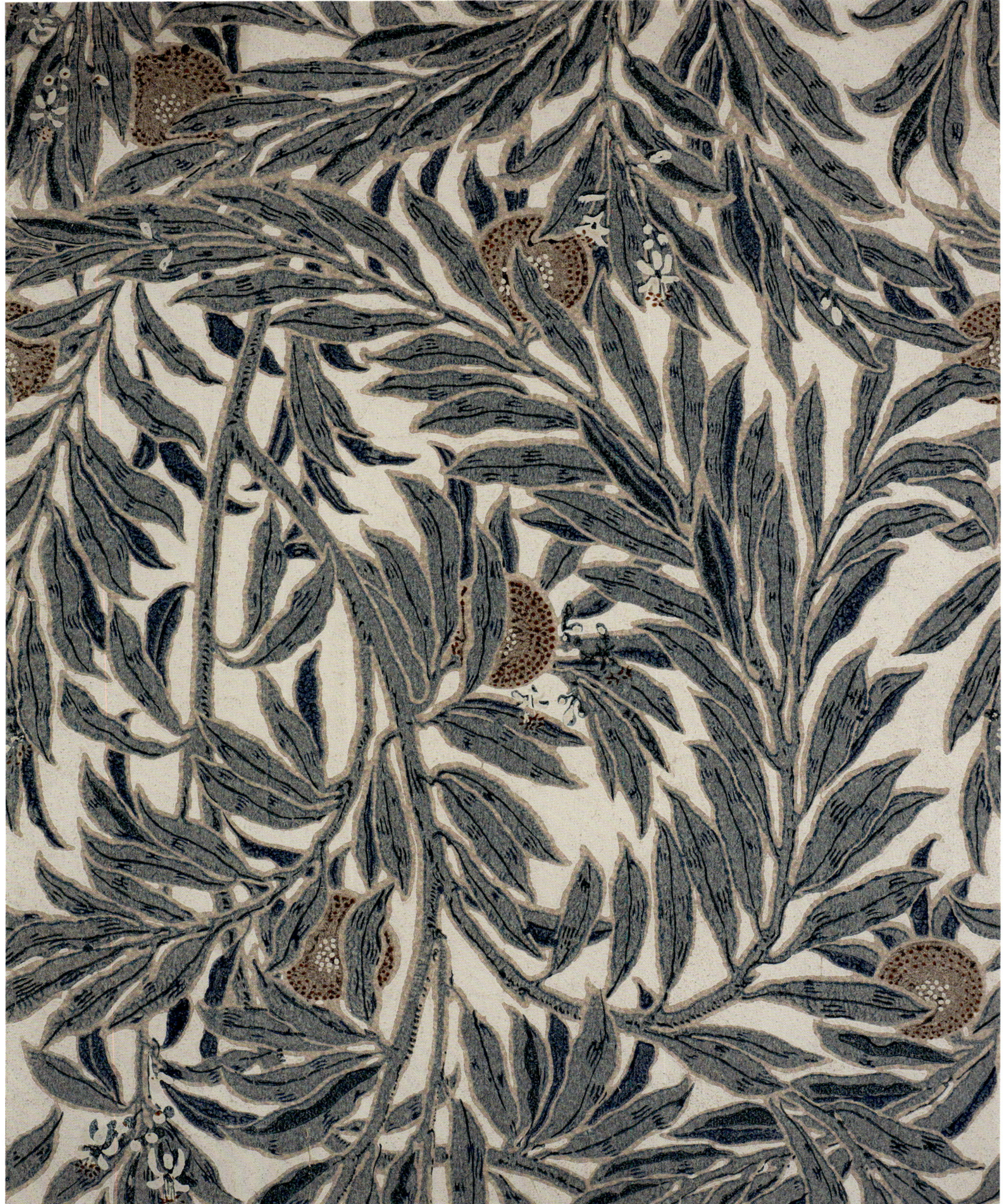

126 | Walter Crane, *The Orange Tree*, 1931 printing of original 1902 design for Jeffrey & Co., Arthur Sanderson & Sons Ltd

Following the move of Jeffrey blocks and machines to Sanderson's Chiswick works, this edition of *The Orange Tree* was printed in 1931 on ingrain paper for a mottled ground effect. With a co-ordinating frieze entitled *Fruit*, it borrows from the all-over, cascading foliage patterns popularised by Morris with *Willow* (1874) and *Willow Bough* (1888).

As early as 1884, the American magazine *Carpentry and Building* could comment on the supply of 'cheap and truly artistic papers' made in response to public demand: 'The paper manufacturers have employed the best artists and have given prizes for good designs. They have taken hints from Morris and his followers.'

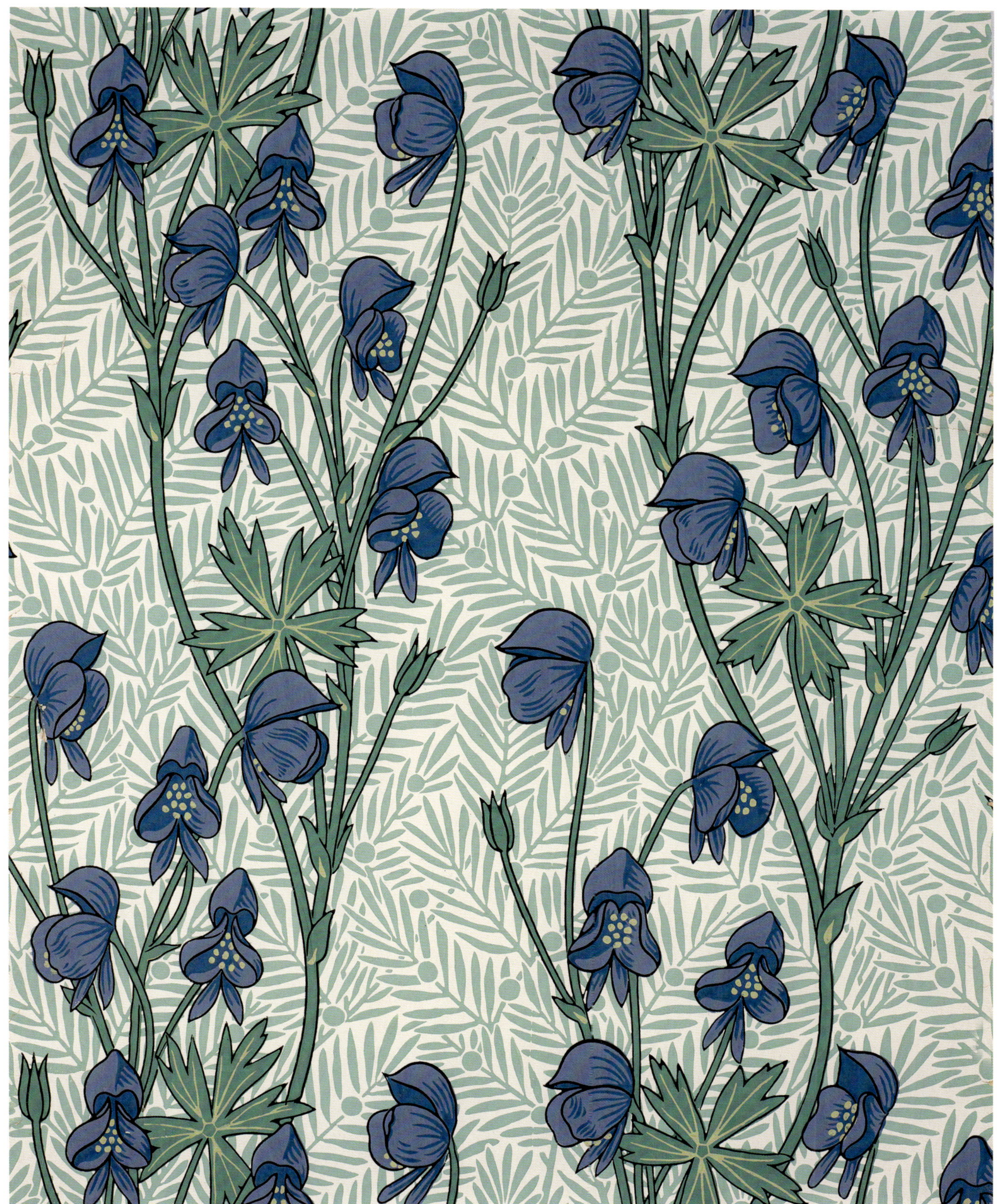

127 | A.F. Vigers, *Monkshood*, 1901, Jeffrey & Co.

Allan Francis Vigers (1858–1921) began his career as an architect but became a successful wallpaper designer and book illustrator. In 1903, he illuminated the Chiswick Press edition of Morris's *The Hollow Land*. Like Crane an admirer of Morris, he numbered among those who contributed to what became recognised widely as a distinctive British design style.

In 1903, the *Monkshood* block-printed wallpaper was shown at the Arts and Crafts Exhibition Society exhibition at The New Gallery in 121 Regent Street. Vigers also produced designs for the firm that were machine-printed with only a few colours but not sold under his name. These made an affordable and artistic offering for a growing middle-class market.

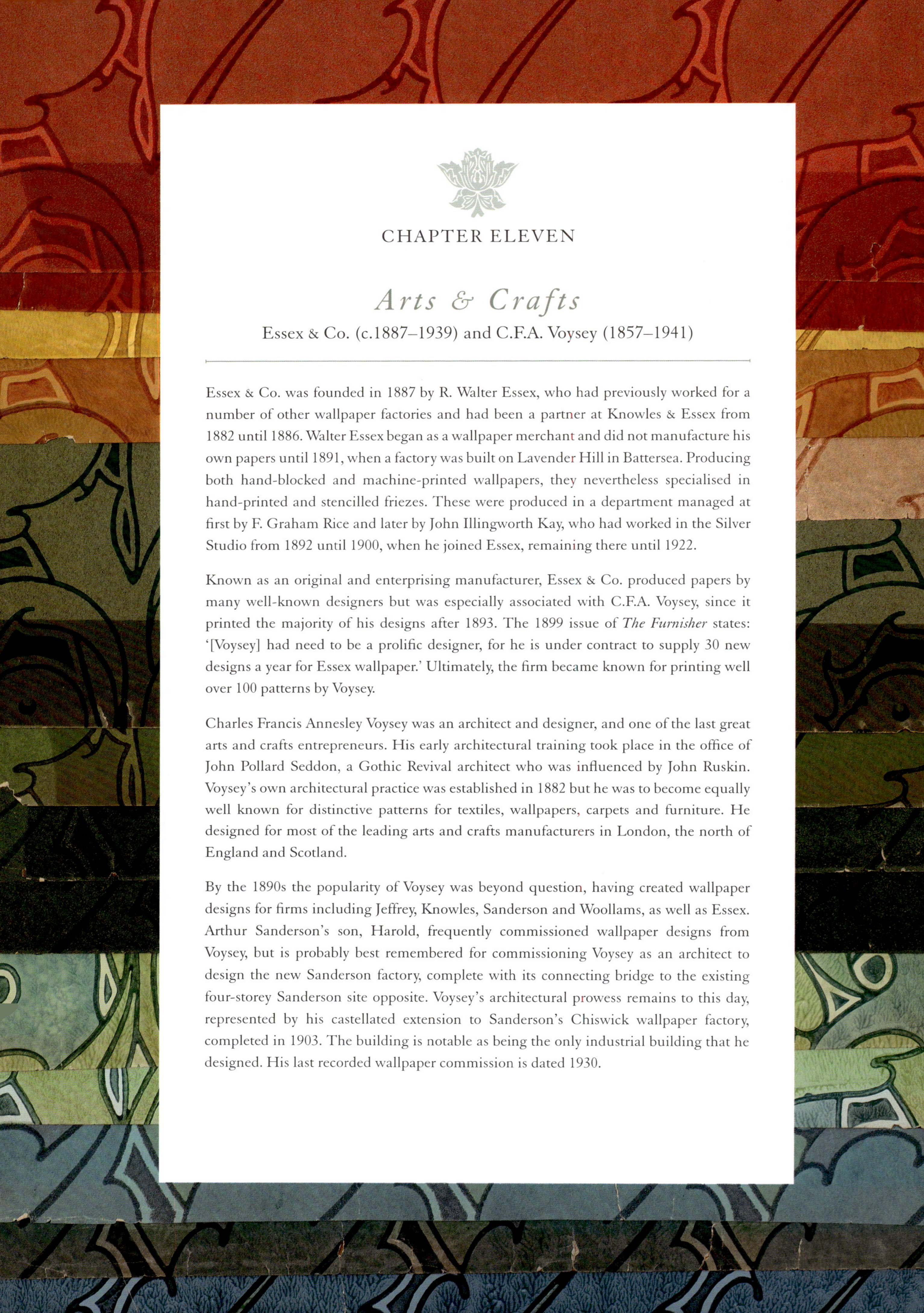

CHAPTER ELEVEN

Arts & Crafts

Essex & Co. (c.1887–1939) and C.F.A. Voysey (1857–1941)

Essex & Co. was founded in 1887 by R. Walter Essex, who had previously worked for a number of other wallpaper factories and had been a partner at Knowles & Essex from 1882 until 1886. Walter Essex began as a wallpaper merchant and did not manufacture his own papers until 1891, when a factory was built on Lavender Hill in Battersea. Producing both hand-blocked and machine-printed wallpapers, they nevertheless specialised in hand-printed and stencilled friezes. These were produced in a department managed at first by F. Graham Rice and later by John Illingworth Kay, who had worked in the Silver Studio from 1892 until 1900, when he joined Essex, remaining there until 1922.

Known as an original and enterprising manufacturer, Essex & Co. produced papers by many well-known designers but was especially associated with C.F.A. Voysey, since it printed the majority of his designs after 1893. The 1899 issue of *The Furnisher* states: '[Voysey] had need to be a prolific designer, for he is under contract to supply 30 new designs a year for Essex wallpaper.' Ultimately, the firm became known for printing well over 100 patterns by Voysey.

Charles Francis Annesley Voysey was an architect and designer, and one of the last great arts and crafts entrepreneurs. His early architectural training took place in the office of John Pollard Seddon, a Gothic Revival architect who was influenced by John Ruskin. Voysey's own architectural practice was established in 1882 but he was to become equally well known for distinctive patterns for textiles, wallpapers, carpets and furniture. He designed for most of the leading arts and crafts manufacturers in London, the north of England and Scotland.

By the 1890s the popularity of Voysey was beyond question, having created wallpaper designs for firms including Jeffrey, Knowles, Sanderson and Woollams, as well as Essex. Arthur Sanderson's son, Harold, frequently commissioned wallpaper designs from Voysey, but is probably best remembered for commissioning Voysey as an architect to design the new Sanderson factory, complete with its connecting bridge to the existing four-storey Sanderson site opposite. Voysey's architectural prowess remains to this day, represented by his castellated extension to Sanderson's Chiswick wallpaper factory, completed in 1903. The building is notable as being the only industrial building that he designed. His last recorded wallpaper commission is dated 1930.

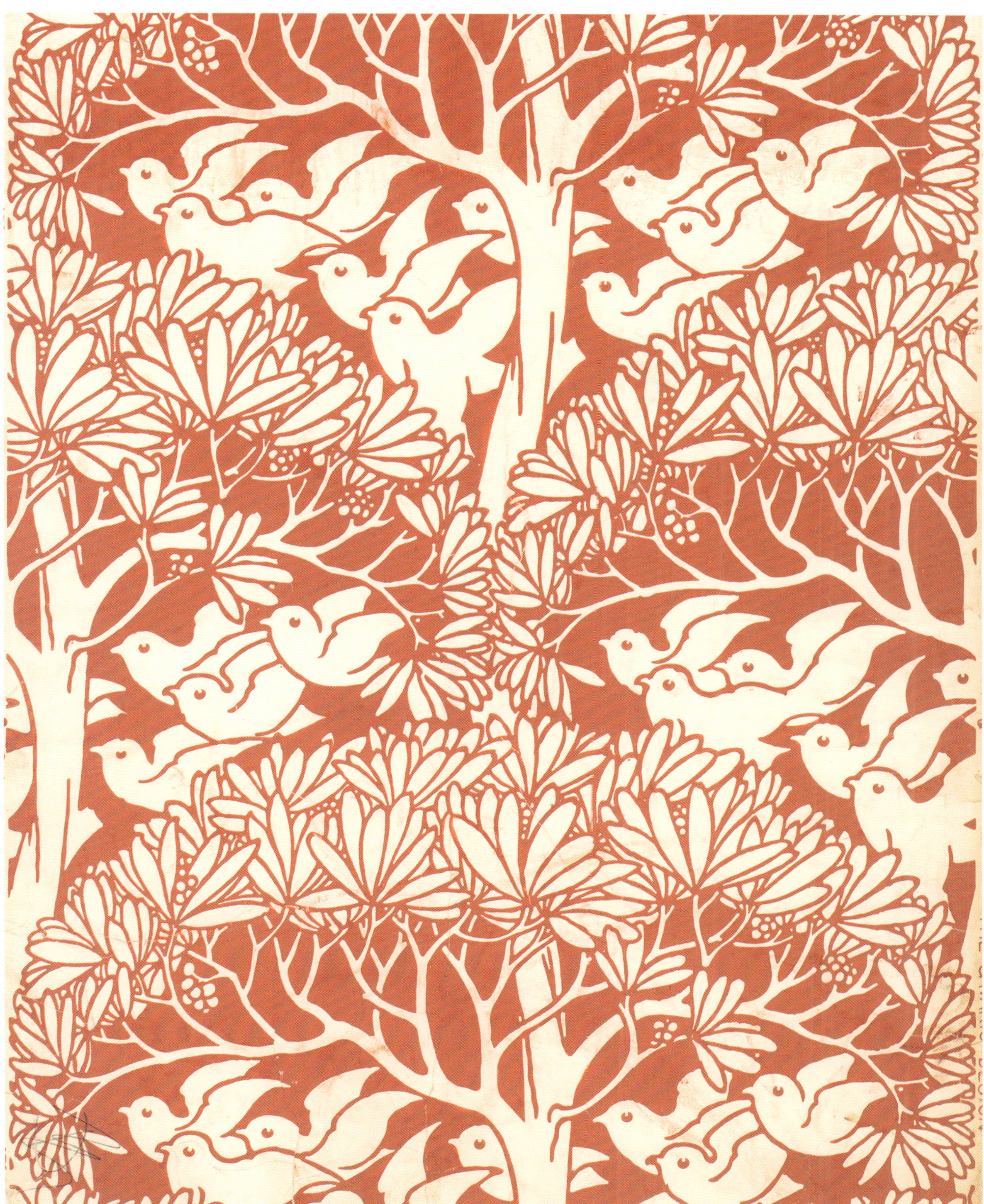

128 | C.F.A. Voysey, *Savaric*, c.1896, Essex & Co.

Savaric wallpaper was used to furnish a bedroom in Hôtel Solvay in Brussels. Solvay House, now a UNESCO World Heritage Site, was designed in 1894 by Victor Horta, Belgium's most influential Art Nouveau architect. His client was Armand Solvay, the son of the wealthy Belgian chemist and industrialist Ernest Solvay. It was completed in 1900.

Voysey's own architectural style combined modern simplicity with the traditions of the British vernacular. Although many of his designs continued to reflect arts and crafts' sensibilities, in *Savaric* the sinuous line in his pattern design shared a common decorative spirit with art nouveau interiors.

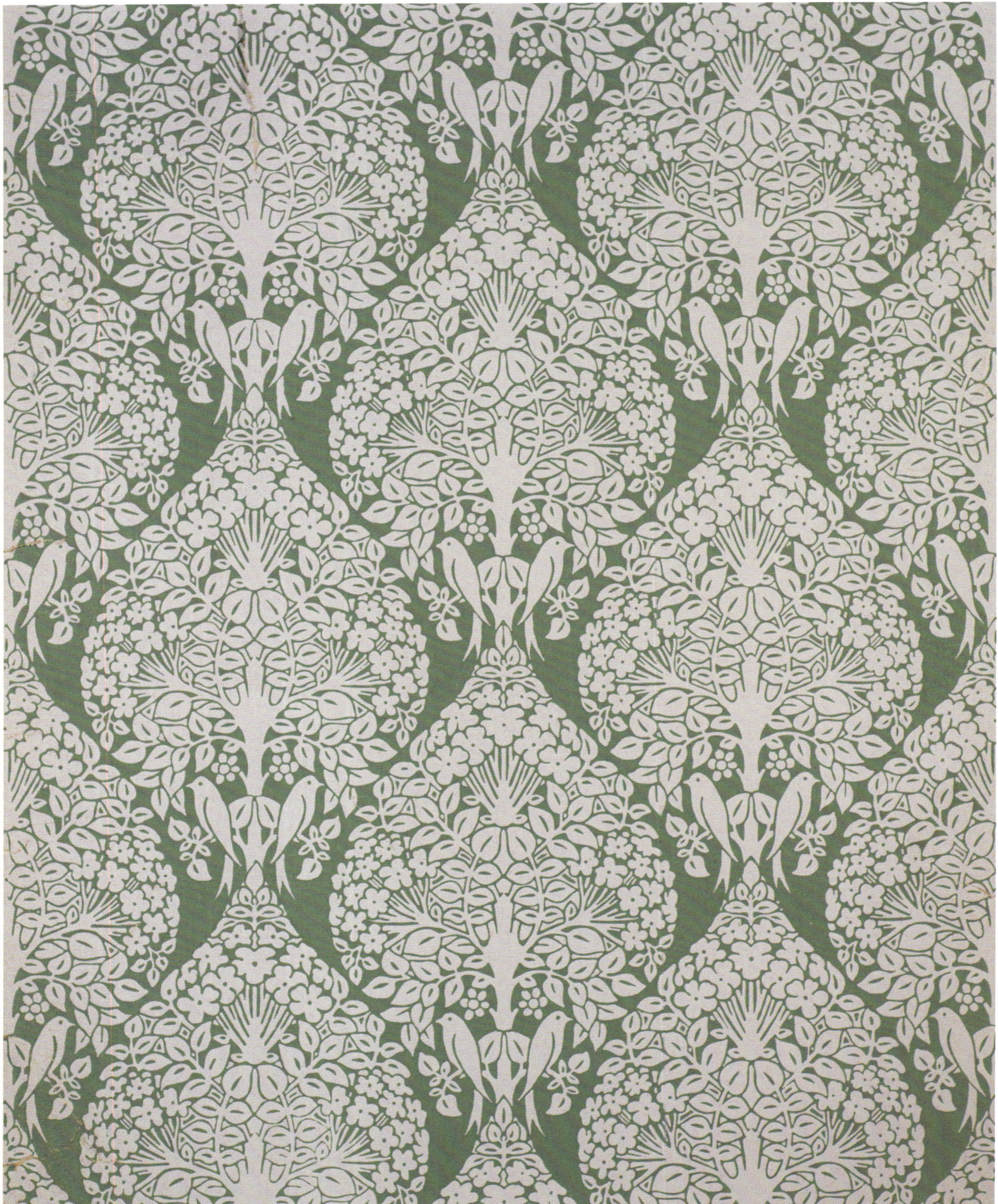

129 | C.F.A. Voysey, *Lerena*, early-20th century printing of original 1897 design for Essex & Co., Arthur Sanderson & Sons Ltd

The structure of *Lerena*, with its tightly interwoven ogee forms, is close to that of a wallpaper of 1851 by A.W.N. Pugin, created for the Houses of Parliament but never installed there. However, its pale celedon green colouration is not a medieval reference; instead, it reflects the fresh tones fashionable when printed by Sanderson in the early-20th century.

Voysey's admiration for Pugin derived from his grandfather Annesley Voysey (c.1794–1839), an architect engineer who constructed the first purpose-built office in London in 1823 and knew Pugin. Voysey's book *Individuality* (1915) praised Pugin's originality and his Gothic-revival style, which he saw as moral, religious and emotional.

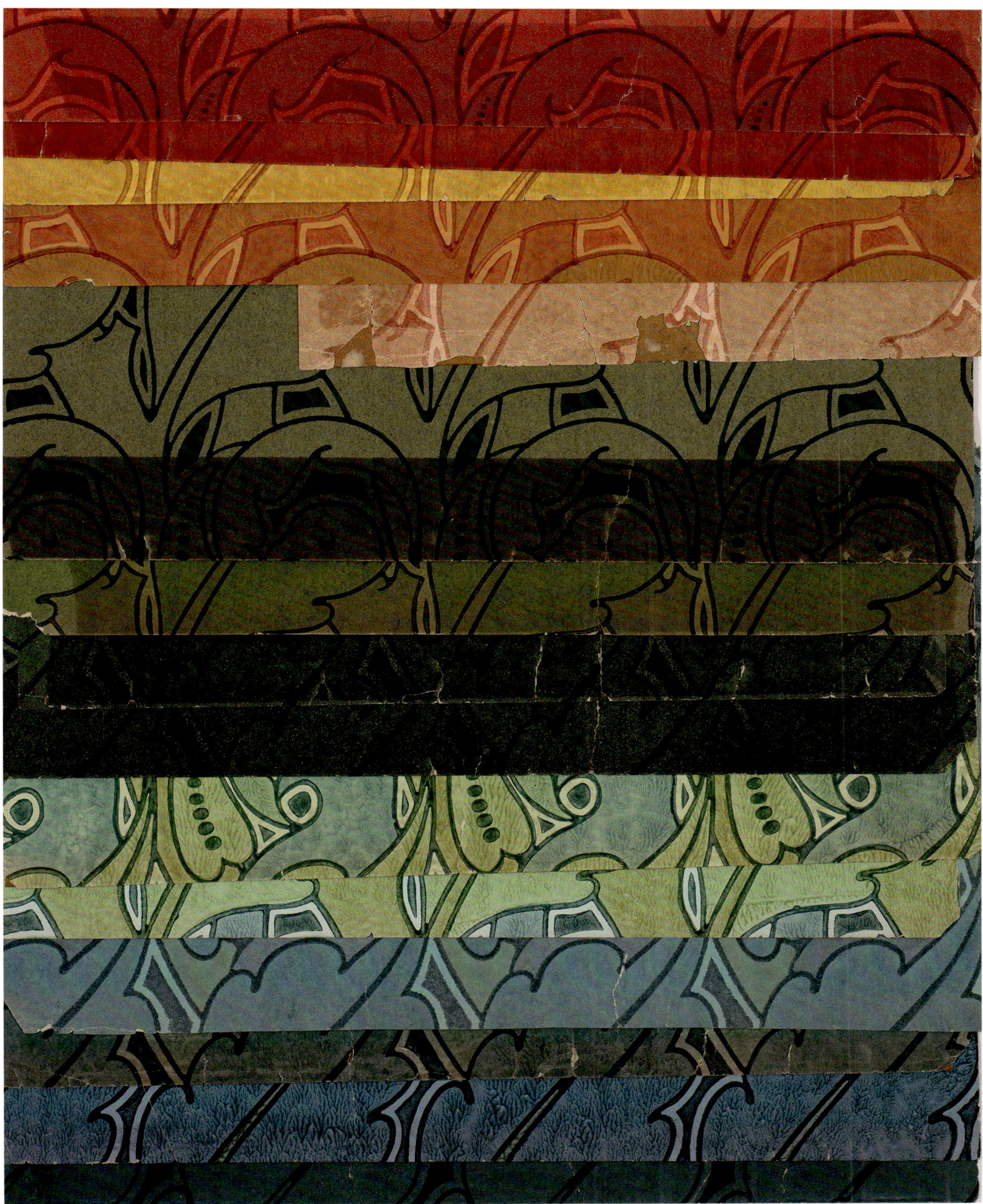

130 | C.F.A. Voysey, *Columba*, c.1898, Essex & Co.

A pattern with closely ranged tones, this design was produced in several colourways, including a red version printed with mica. Both the colours and the added gleam are suggestive of Voysey's designs for tiles, particularly the rich but essentially monochrome earthenware examples manufactured by Pilkington's Tile and Pottery Factory in c.1900.

Columba was illustrated in *The Artist: An Illustrated Monthly Record of Arts, Crafts and Industries* in 1899. Voysey was featured from 1903–12 in *The Craftsman*, the leading journal for the American Arts & Crafts Movement. Its influential editor, Gustav Stickley, described the designer's work in 1902 as 'the most significant and individual in England'.

131 | C.F.A. Voysey, *Sparhawk*, c.1898, Essex & Co.

This four-colour design has limited colours and a flat, stencilled quality. As Voysey noted in *The Journal of Decorative Art* in April 1895, he believed in the careful use of controlled areas of colour to create 'a simplicity and breadth which are an immense relief to the motley collection of forms and colours with which most rooms are crowded'.

Sparhawk is the colloquial name of the sparrowhawk, a small bird of prey native to British woodlands. Native and mythical birds were a favourite Voysey motif; he depicted them in a way that fully expressed their group and individual characteristics. The beady-eyed, sharp-beaked example in this paper is a disquieting force in an otherwise harmonious paper.

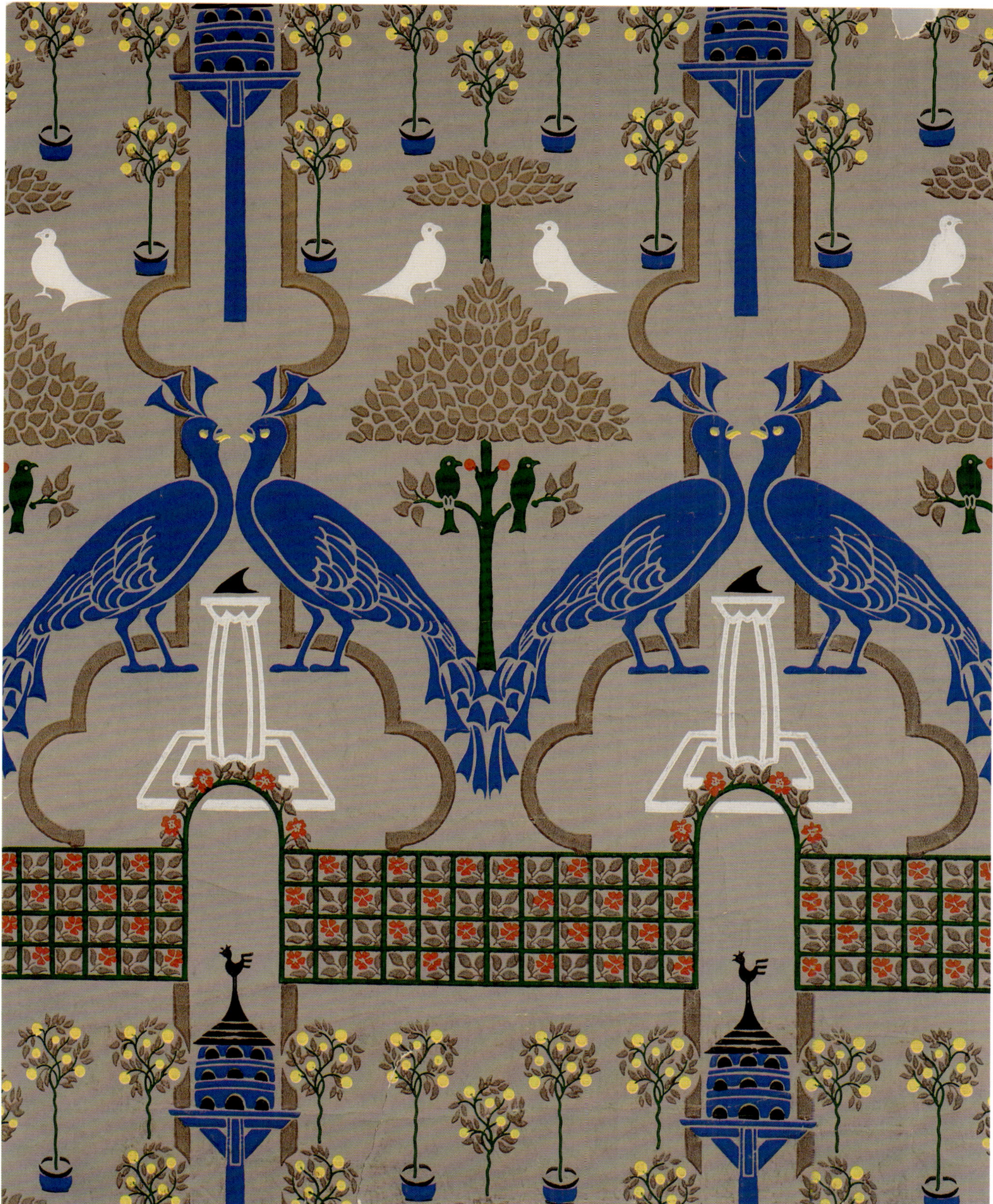

132 | C.F.A Voysey, *Squire's Garden*, 1896, Essex & Co.

This design featuring peacocks, doves and a dovecot in a parterre-style garden of trees was based on an embroidered bed quilt designed by Voysey and worked by Mrs Reynolds-Stephens in 1896. In 1898, it was issued as a machine-printed wallpaper by Essex & Co. and exhibited by them at the 1900 Exposition Universelle in Paris.

The embroiderer was married to the sculptor and designer W. Reynolds-Stephens, who also produced patterns for embroidery worked by his wife. These are discussed in *The Studio* (Vol XVIII, October 1899, pp.184-5) together with two embroideries worked from Voysey's designs, one of which, a circular cushion, is illustrated.

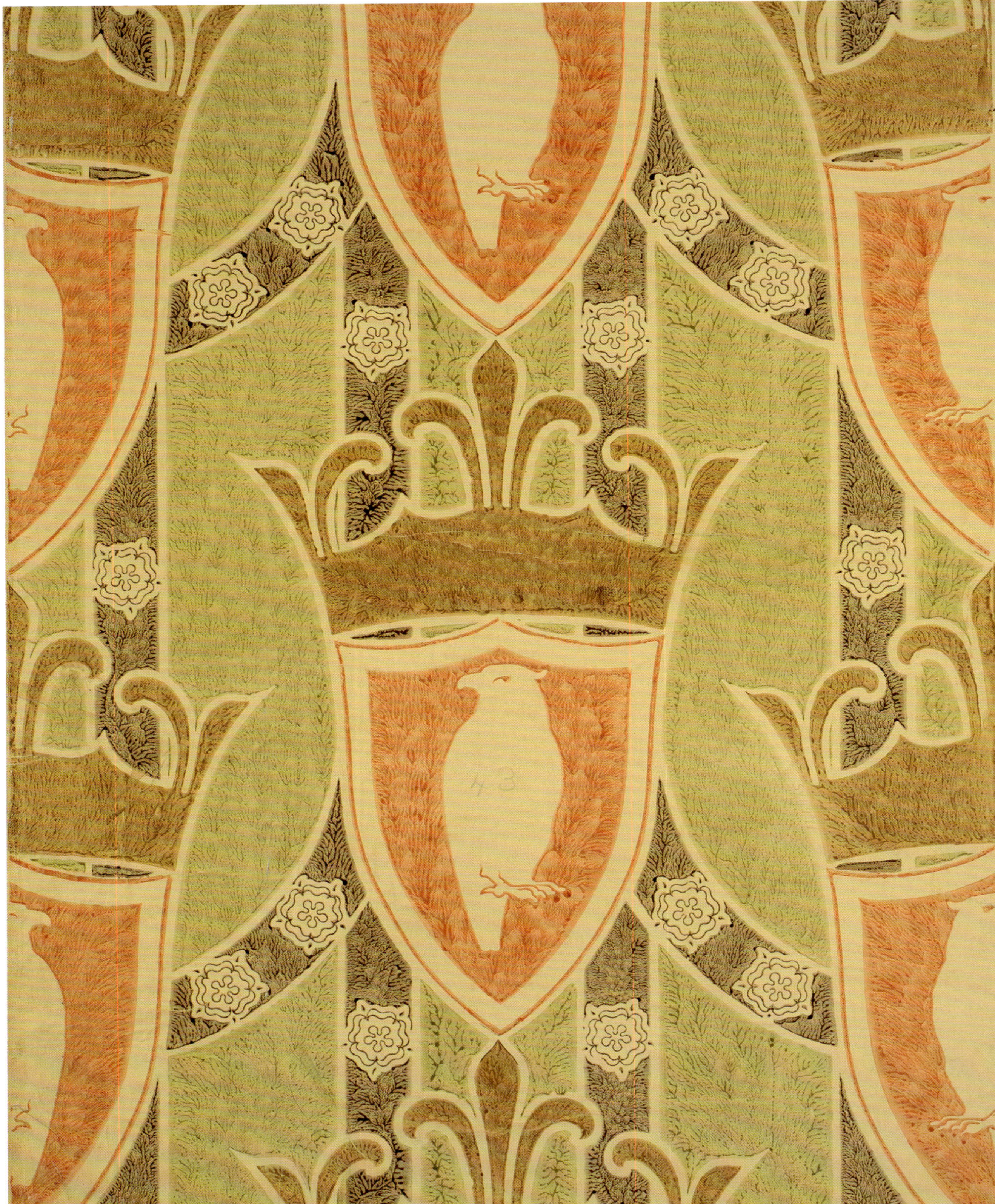

133 | C.F.A. Voysey, *The 'Heraldic' Design*, 1902, Essex & Co.

Like many other designers of the period, Voysey was called upon to design patterns commemorating royal events. This example was undoubtedly created in celebration of the coronation of King Edward VII, who was crowned in August 1902. The original design was painted out in red and two shades of blue on a white ground, echoing the Union Jack colours.

Among Voysey's many designs, there were only a handful to incorporate royal motifs. One with a foliage-surrounded crown was made for Queen Victoria's Diamond Jubilee in 1897. Another incorporating crowns, dragons, roses and thistles was possibly to mark one of the annual visits of King George V to Scotland after the First World War.

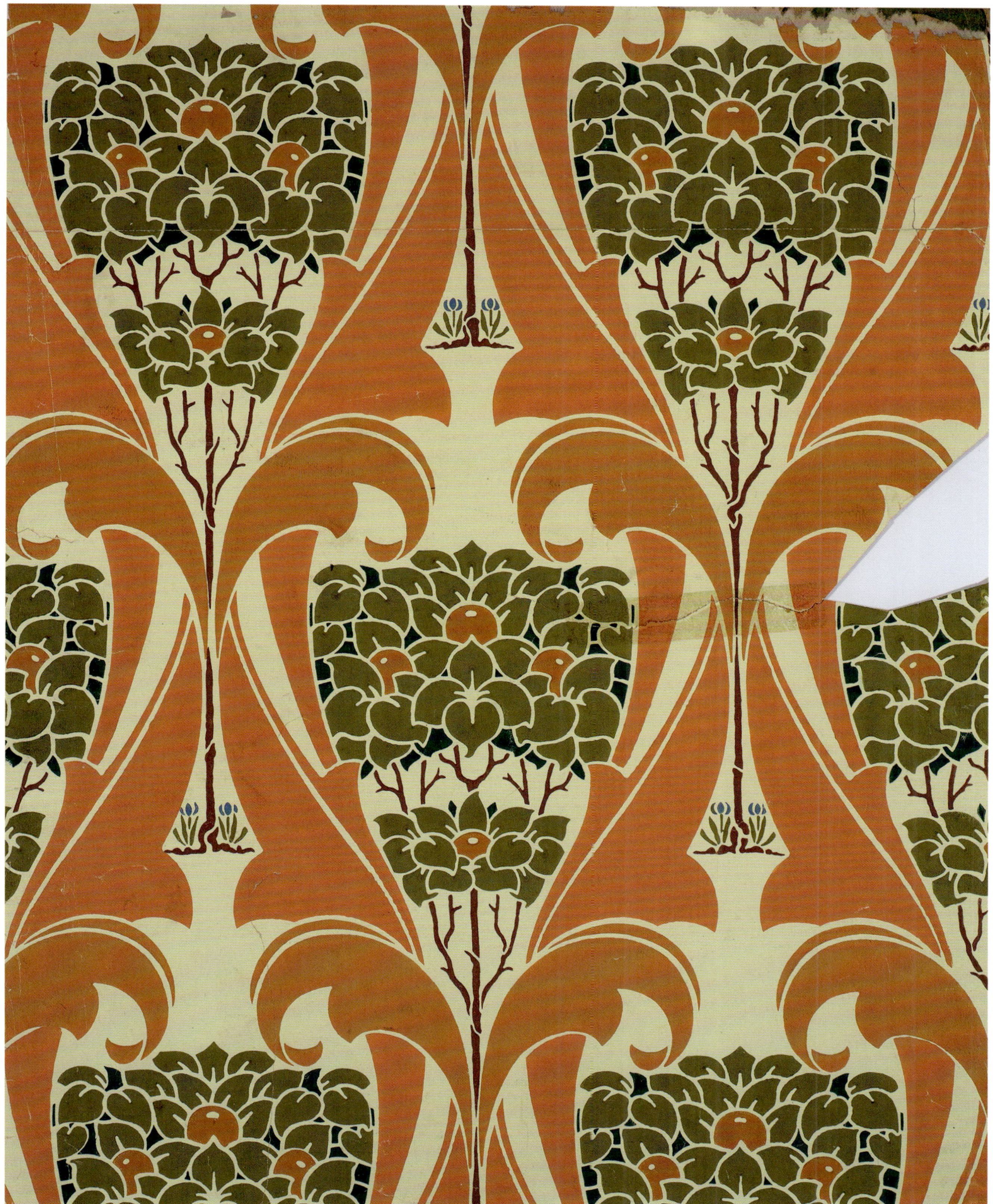

134 | C.F.A. Voysey, *Montreaux*, c.1904, Essex & Co.

In a prolific career that spanned 50 years, Voysey was to become known for his informal, unlaboured patterns. *Montreaux* typifies this intentional lack of rigidity. In its boldness and flat tints of colour, it also typifies the elements of pattern-making that were to influence the early 20th-century emergence of the Modern movement.

Voysey's architectural eye was underpinned by John Ruskin's principles on the moral value of artistic endeavour. In his 1909 lectures on 'Ideas in Things', Voysey urged: 'Let every bit of ornament speak to us of bright and healthy thought.' This quintessentially arts and crafts sentiment also drew from William Morris, who saw nature-based decoration as therapeutic.

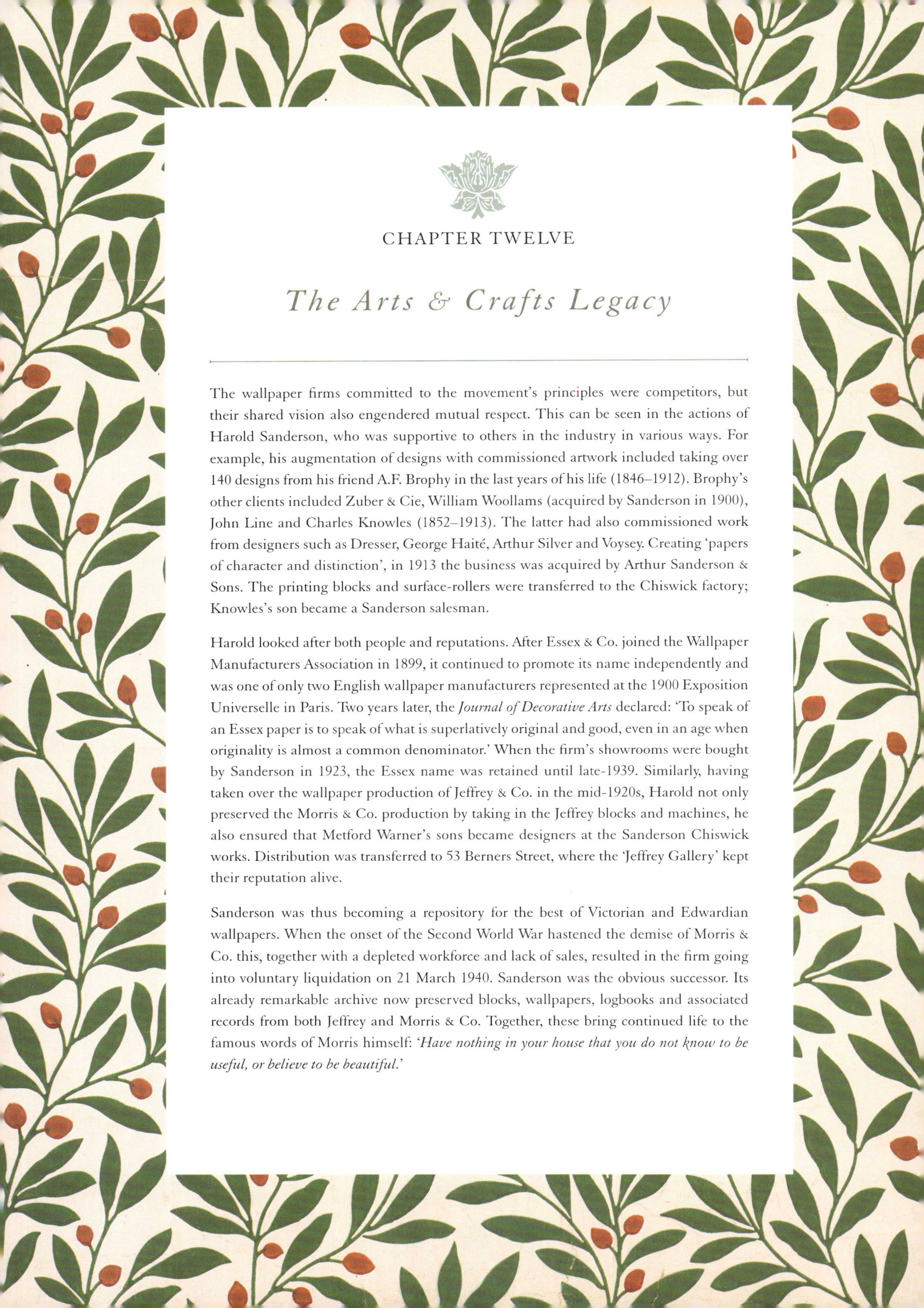

CHAPTER TWELVE

The Arts & Crafts Legacy

The wallpaper firms committed to the movement's principles were competitors, but their shared vision also engendered mutual respect. This can be seen in the actions of Harold Sanderson, who was supportive to others in the industry in various ways. For example, his augmentation of designs with commissioned artwork included taking over 140 designs from his friend A.F. Brophy in the last years of his life (1846–1912). Brophy's other clients included Zuber & Cie, William Woollams (acquired by Sanderson in 1900), John Line and Charles Knowles (1852–1913). The latter had also commissioned work from designers such as Dresser, George Haité, Arthur Silver and Voysey. Creating 'papers of character and distinction', in 1913 the business was acquired by Arthur Sanderson & Sons. The printing blocks and surface-rollers were transferred to the Chiswick factory; Knowles's son became a Sanderson salesman.

Harold looked after both people and reputations. After Essex & Co. joined the Wallpaper Manufacturers Association in 1899, it continued to promote its name independently and was one of only two English wallpaper manufacturers represented at the 1900 Exposition Universelle in Paris. Two years later, the *Journal of Decorative Arts* declared: 'To speak of an Essex paper is to speak of what is superlatively original and good, even in an age when originality is almost a common denominator.' When the firm's showrooms were bought by Sanderson in 1923, the Essex name was retained until late-1939. Similarly, having taken over the wallpaper production of Jeffrey & Co. in the mid-1920s, Harold not only preserved the Morris & Co. production by taking in the Jeffrey blocks and machines, he also ensured that Metford Warner's sons became designers at the Sanderson Chiswick works. Distribution was transferred to 53 Berners Street, where the 'Jeffrey Gallery' kept their reputation alive.

Sanderson was thus becoming a repository for the best of Victorian and Edwardian wallpapers. When the onset of the Second World War hastened the demise of Morris & Co. this, together with a depleted workforce and lack of sales, resulted in the firm going into voluntary liquidation on 21 March 1940. Sanderson was the obvious successor. Its already remarkable archive now preserved blocks, wallpapers, logbooks and associated records from both Jeffrey and Morris & Co. Together, these bring continued life to the famous words of Morris himself: *'Have nothing in your house that you do not know to be useful, or believe to be beautiful.'*

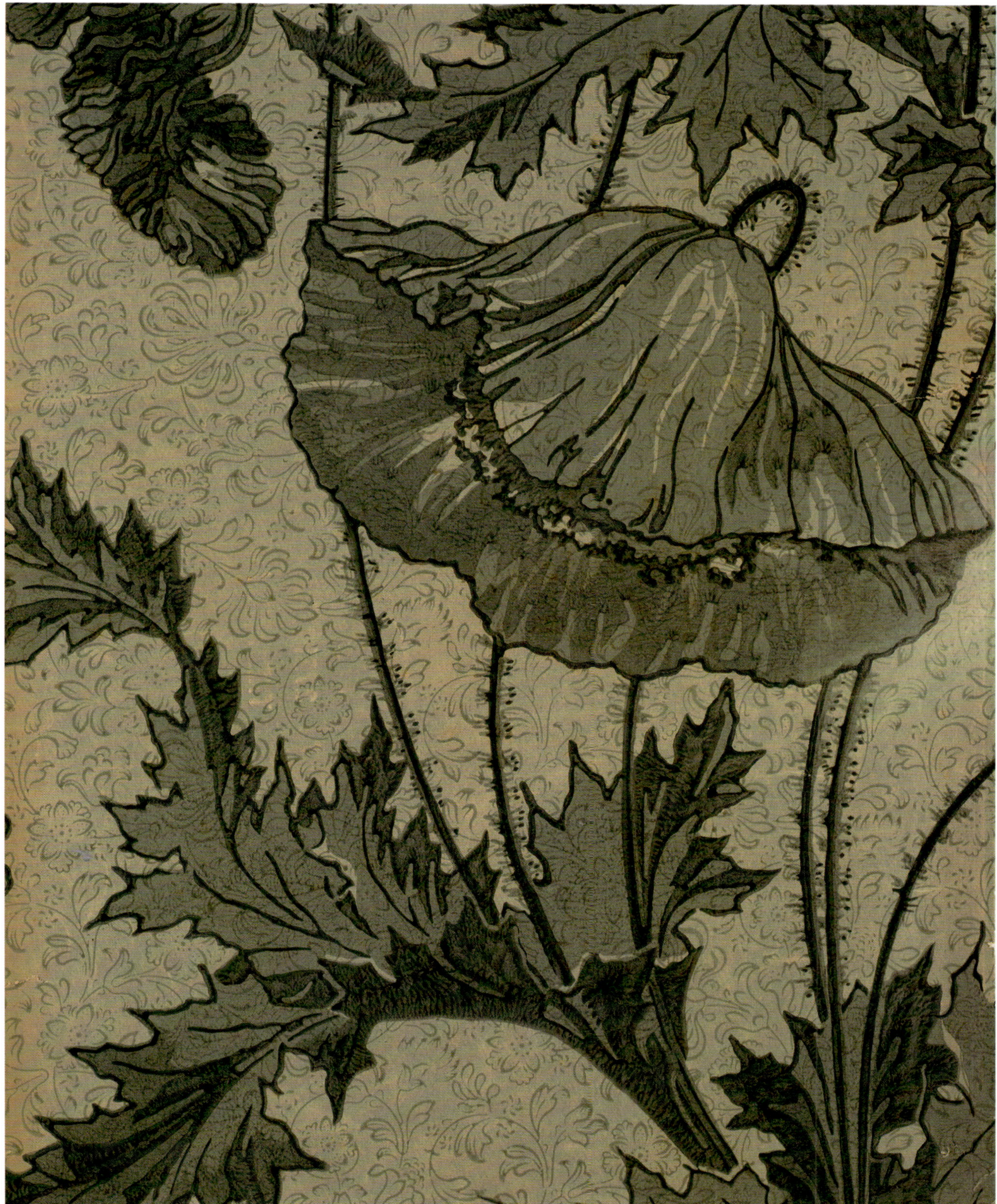

135 | A.F. Brophy, *The Poppy*, 1890, Arthur Sanderson & Sons

Andrew Fengar Brophy was a versatile designer, capable of supplying anything from neo-classical to art nouveau styles. Early successes include contributing to a Jeffrey & Co. paper awarded a gold medal at the Paris Exhibition of 1878. For Sanderson, this large poppy pattern had a 'remarkable run' in 1890 and was continued in several colourways the following year.

Born in Limerick, Ireland and resident in Kensington, London by 1871, Brophy established himself as a freelance designer working in fabrics, furniture, glass and metalwork as well as wallpaper. From 1883, he was headmaster at the training institute for London City & Guilds' qualifications, and was influential in the flourishing of many freelance designers.

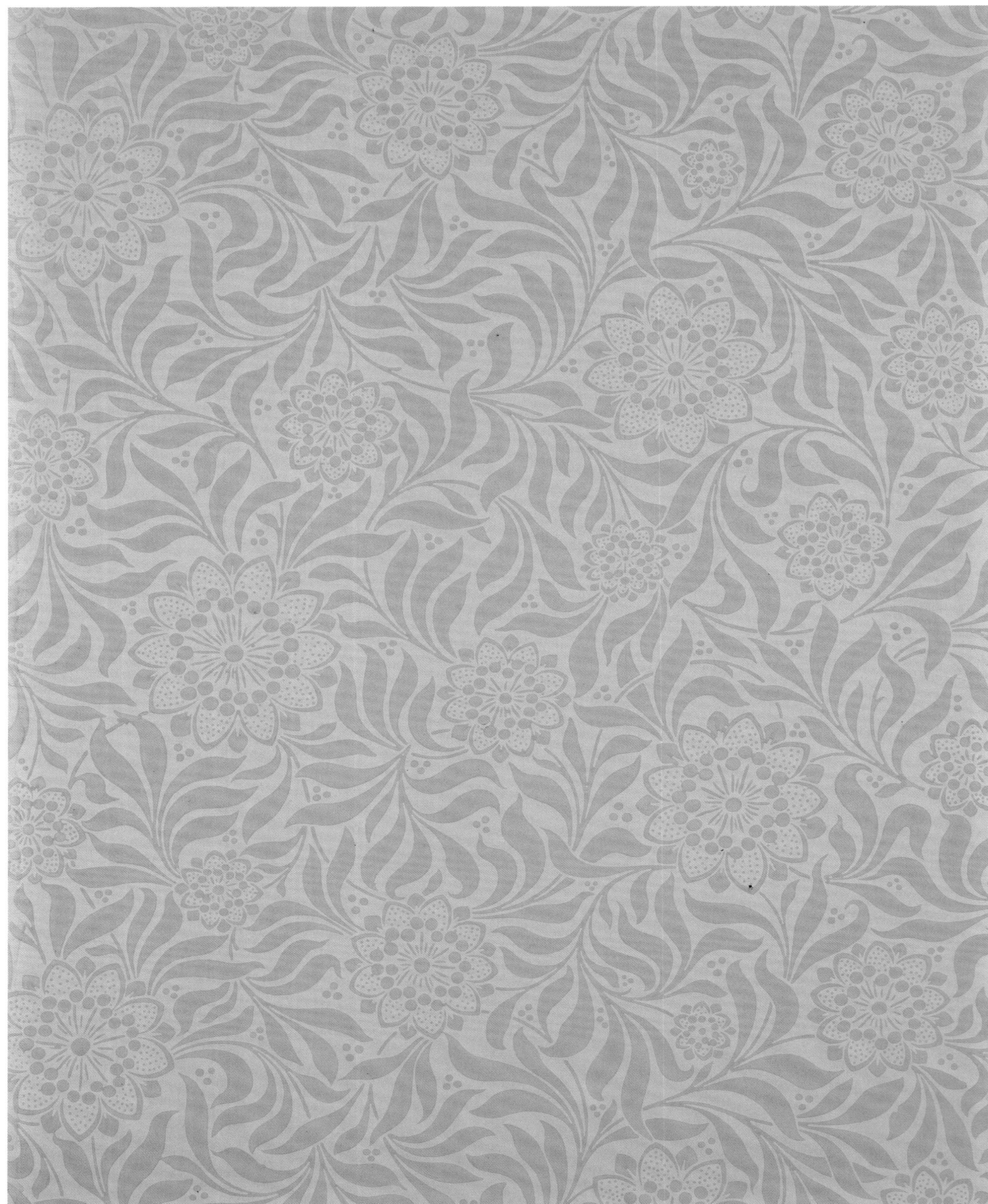

136 | By or after Lewis Foreman Day, *Edelweiss*, c.1890, Arthur Sanderson & Sons

Edelweiss is reminiscent of Day's work for Jeffrey & Co. from c.1887–1900. Day worked freelance for several manufacturers and was author of *Everyday Art* (1882) and *The Anatomy of Pattern* (1887). An active member of the Arts and Crafts Exhibition Society, he firmly believed that good design could reform the products of large-scale industry.

Moot Points: Friendly Disputes on Art and Industry (1906) records a debate between Walter Crane and Day giving the latter's view that 'neither of us wants stodgy, shoppy, spiritless ornament. But I find "joy" enough in trying to solve a problem in design. I am satisfied with the modest ornament which is content to be (much of what it should be) background.'

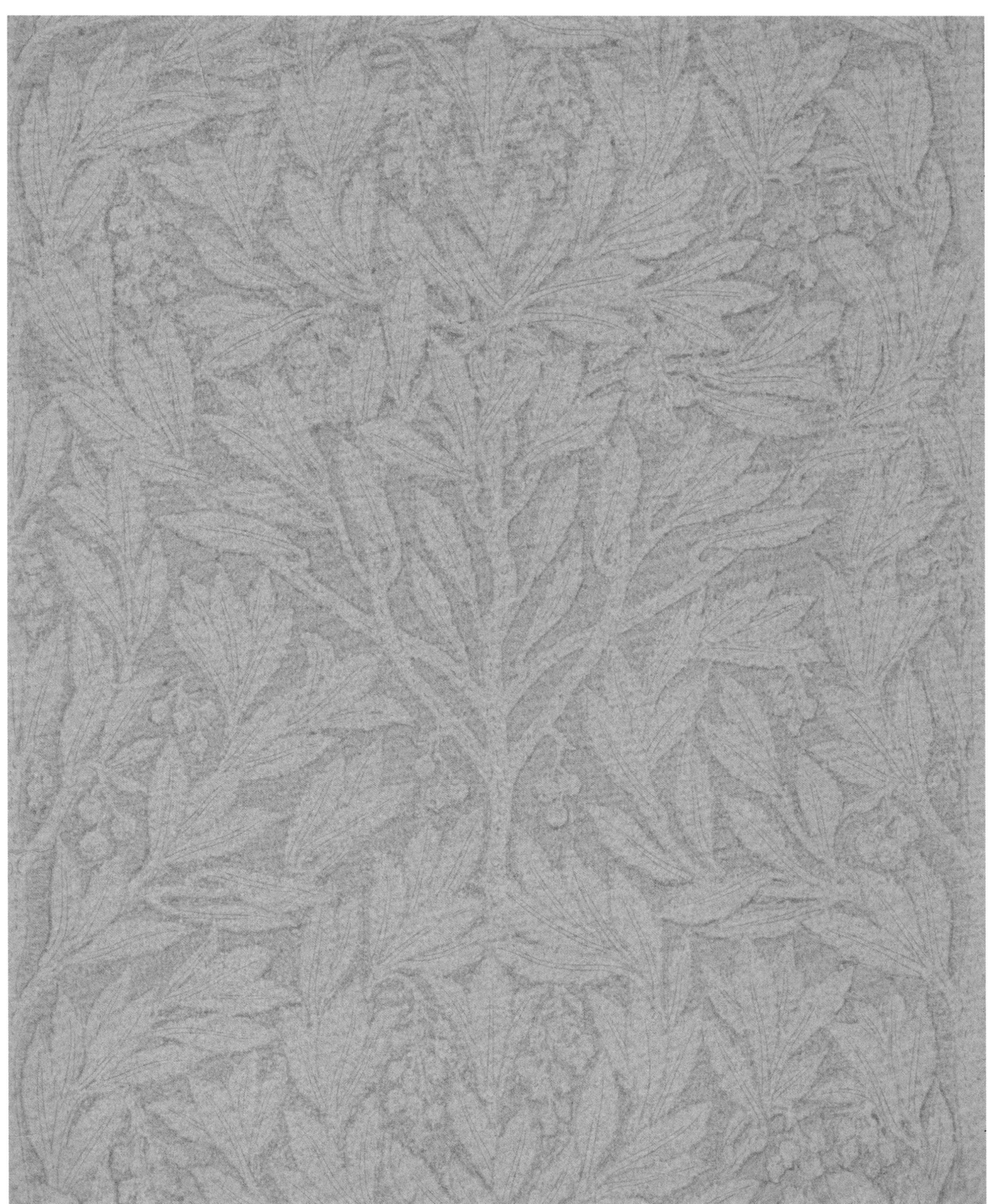

137 | George Heywood Sumner, *Arbutus*, early 1930s' printing of original 1899 design for Jeffrey & Co., Arthur Sanderson & Sons Ltd

Heywood Sumner's design is recorded in the 1899 edition of the Jeffrey & Co. logbook, which documents its printing in strong distemper hues of contrasting green. This subtly coloured version on ingrain paper was probably a post-1929 printing produced at the Sanderson factory after taking in the Jeffrey designs and production facilities.

While respecting Morris's sentiments, Heywood Sumner could never accept Morris's elitist approach to the Arts & Crafts Movement. Therefore, in 1893, he joined with others to form The Fitzroy Picture Society, issuing low-cost decorative pictures, sgraffito panels and illustrations for public buildings, schools and affordable home use: arts and crafts for all.

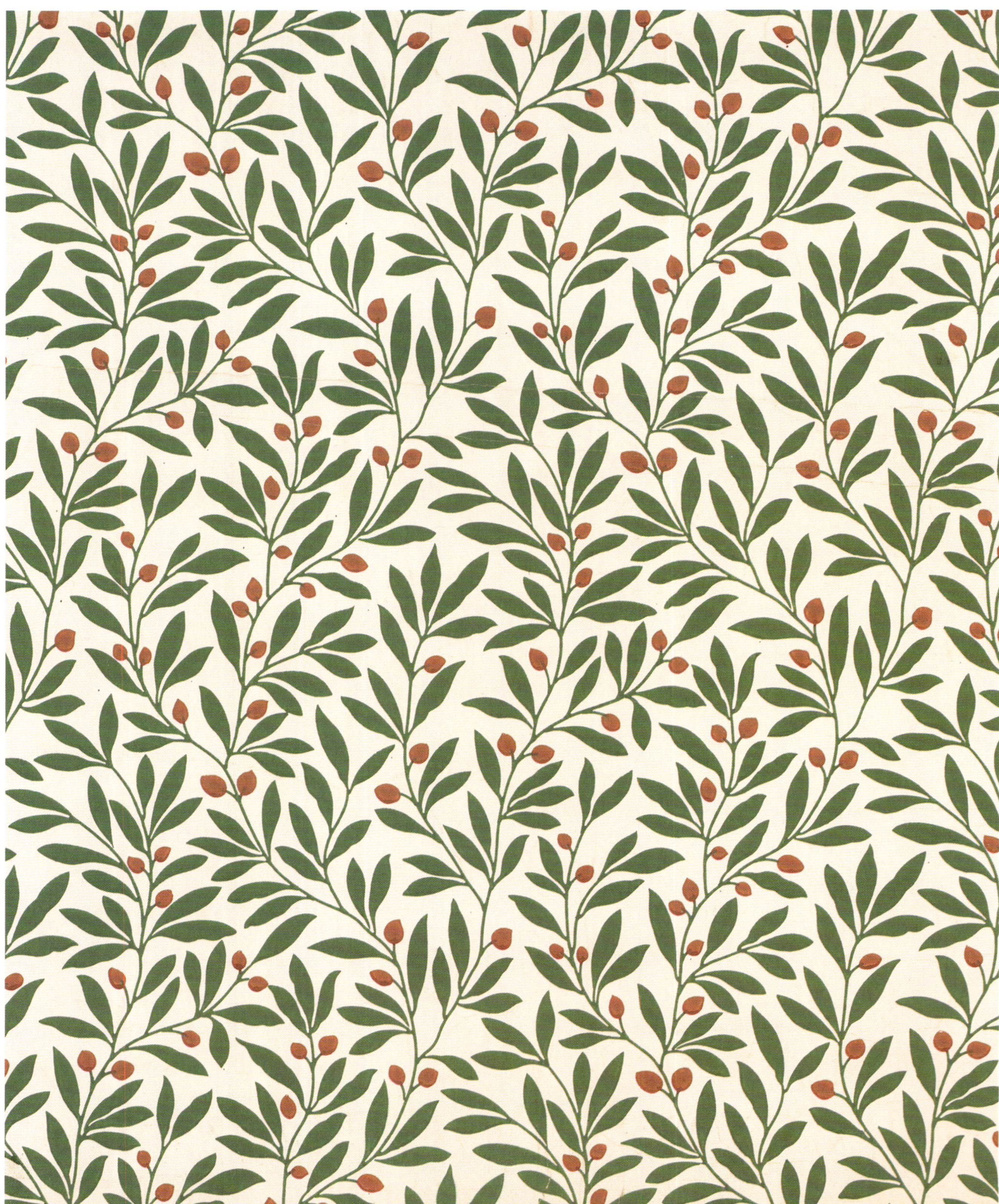

138 | Turner, *The Myrtle*, 1913, Charles Knowles & Co.

This was an affordable, machine-printed paper, printing from 1906. This later version sold for 2 shillings 6 pence per roll (some £10 today). The designer is likely William Lakin Turner (1867–1936), the Lake District landscape painter who also designed papers for the Manchester printer Lightbown Aspinall & Co., and London's Jeffery & Co.

Myrtle was chosen for its meaning within the language of flowers, namely love and fidelity. Its bright leaves, white berries and fragrant flowers made it popular for wedding bouquets, including Queen Victoria's. The tradition among royal brides continued in the bouquets of Queen Elizabeth II, Diana, Princess of Wales and more recently Catherine, Duchess of Cambridge.

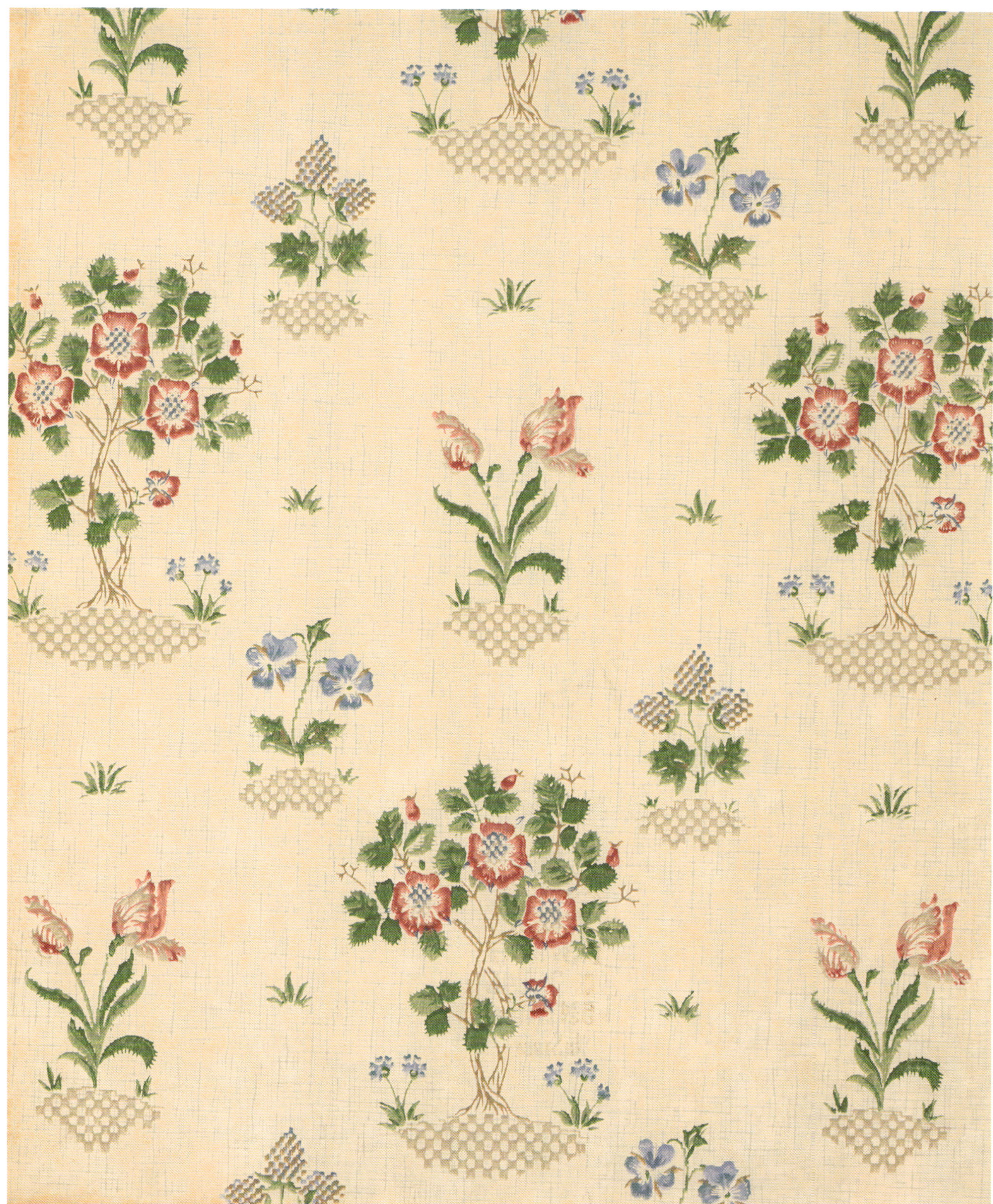

139 | Designer unknown, *Sanitary Paper*, c.1918, John Line and Sons Ltd

Here, the wallpaper printer John Line has borrowed from the simplicity of Morris's *Daisy* to create an understated, pretty pattern with tapestry-style flower sprigs. It is printed on a ground that for decoration and practicality has been given a linen-style texture. With a waterproof finish, such 'sanitaries' remained popular until the early-1930s.

John Line began wholesaling wallpapers in 1880, eventually block-printing and stencilling private designs. After several acquisitions and amalgamations, in 1906 John Line opened a block-print works in Southall reproducing works by Brophy, Voysey and others. Heading the studio from 1907–10 was architectural ceramics designer W. J. Neatby (1860–1910).

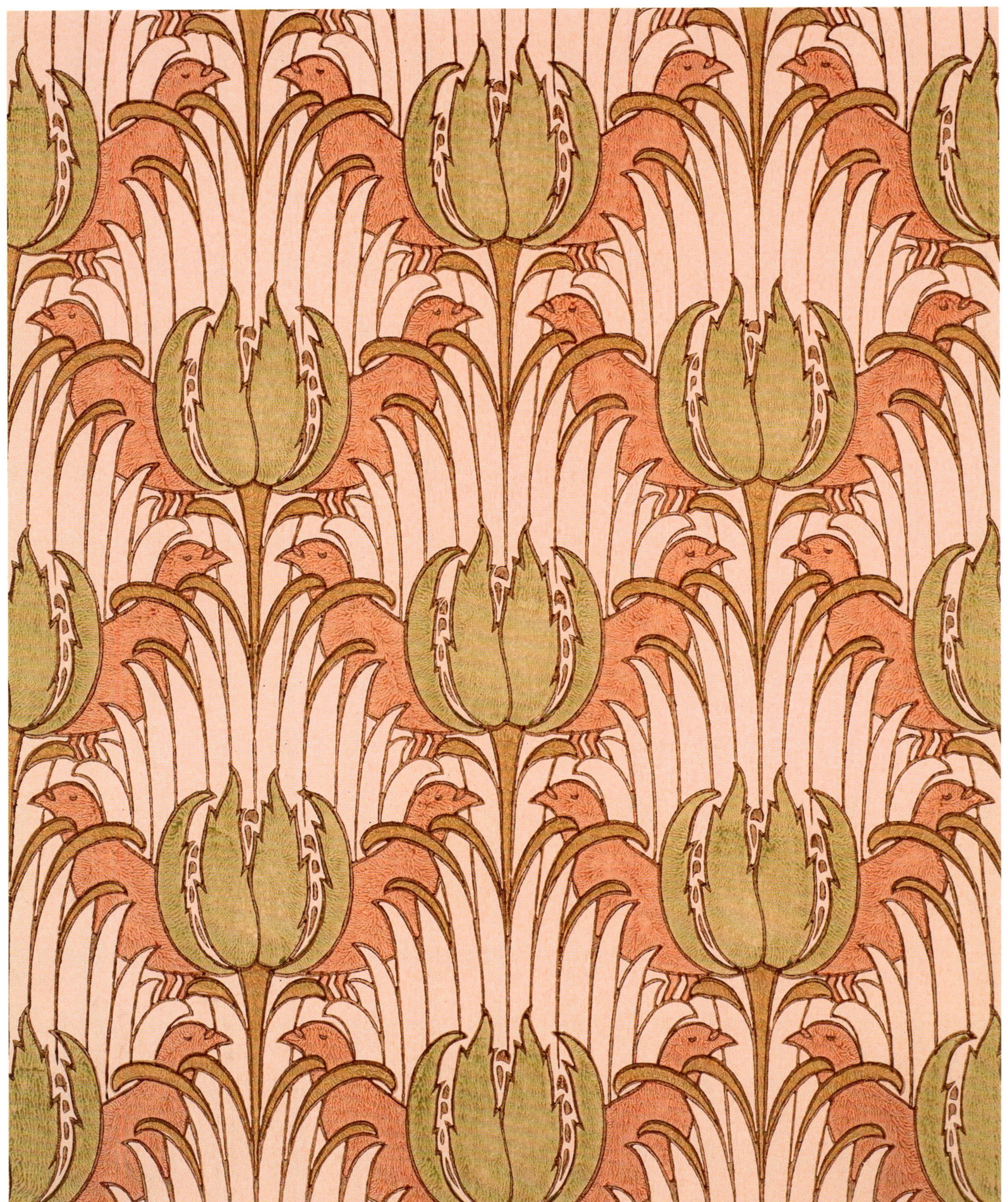

140 | C.F.A. Voysey, *Bird and Tulip*, 1920s' printing of original 1895 design, Arthur Sanderson & Sons Ltd

The wallpaper seen here is a version reprinted by Sanderson, who continued to print Voysey's wallpapers, in some cases in their original colourways as seen here, into the 1920s. It quite possibly dates to the period after 1923, when the Essex & Co. showrooms came to Sanderson, although it may also have been acquired via Knowles in 1913.

In 1896, *The Studio* published an article entitled 'Some Recent Designs by Mr Voysey', including an illustration of this wallpaper with its impressive, large-scale co-ordinating border. In 1897, it was adapted for a woven silk and wool 'loaded leno' cloth by the Scottish arts and crafts manufacturer, Alexander Morton & Co.

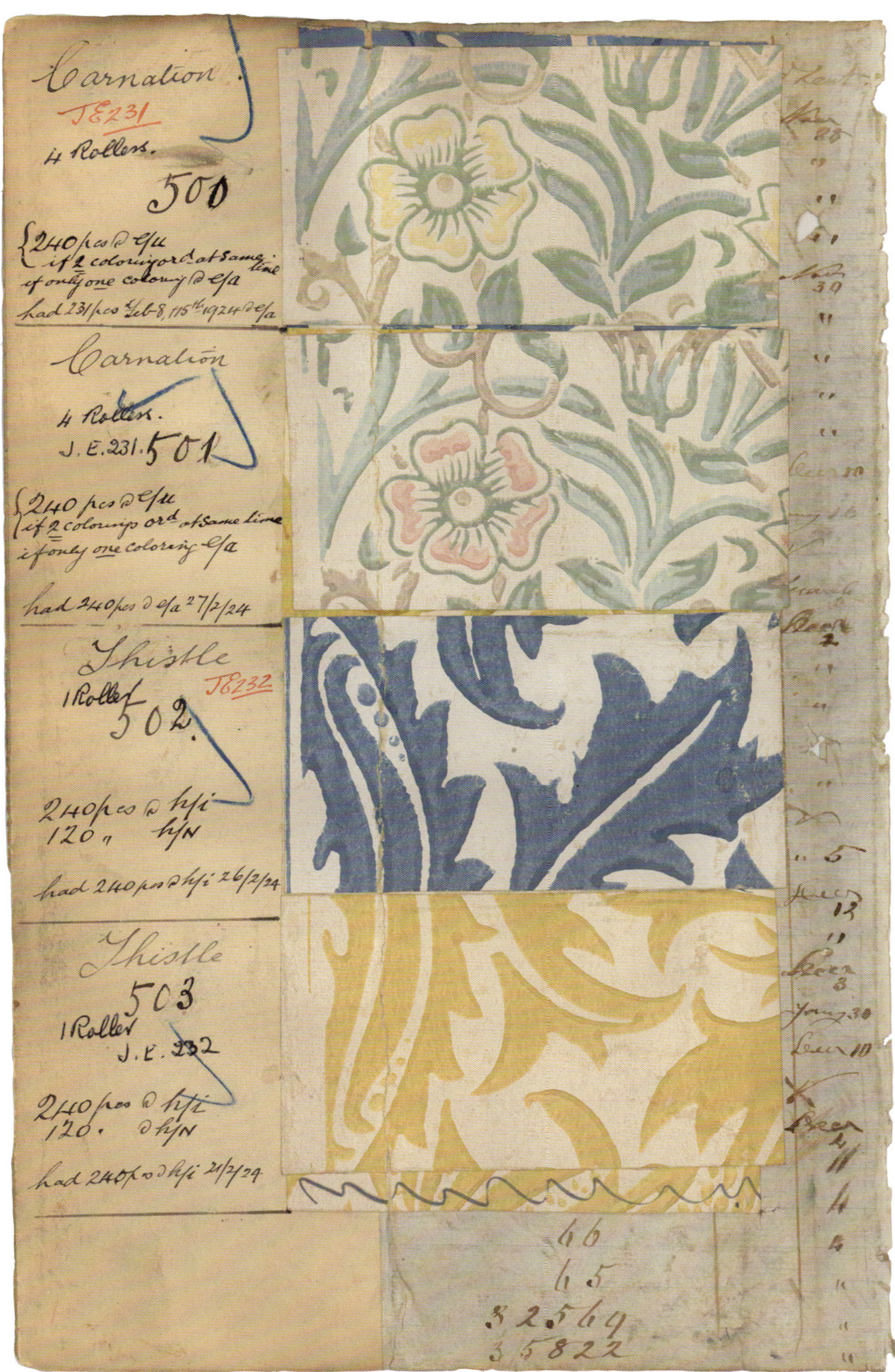

141 | *Logbook*, 1924, Jeffrey & Co.

This page is third from the end of the Jeffrey & Co. logbook and shows two designs printed via surface-rollers, each in two colourways. Both show the irregular deposit of pigments that could be exploited by the use of rollers made from wood, as opposed to those made from engraved copper. This lent a hand-made look to the finished products.

Many manufacturers developed the practice of recording their prices in letter code. Here, one can compare the price of the four-colour design *Carnation* with that of the one-colour pattern *Thistle*. For 240 pieces, the former cost e/a and the latter h/i, meaning that 'e' represented a higher number than 'h'. 'N' pence would have been higher than 'i' pence.

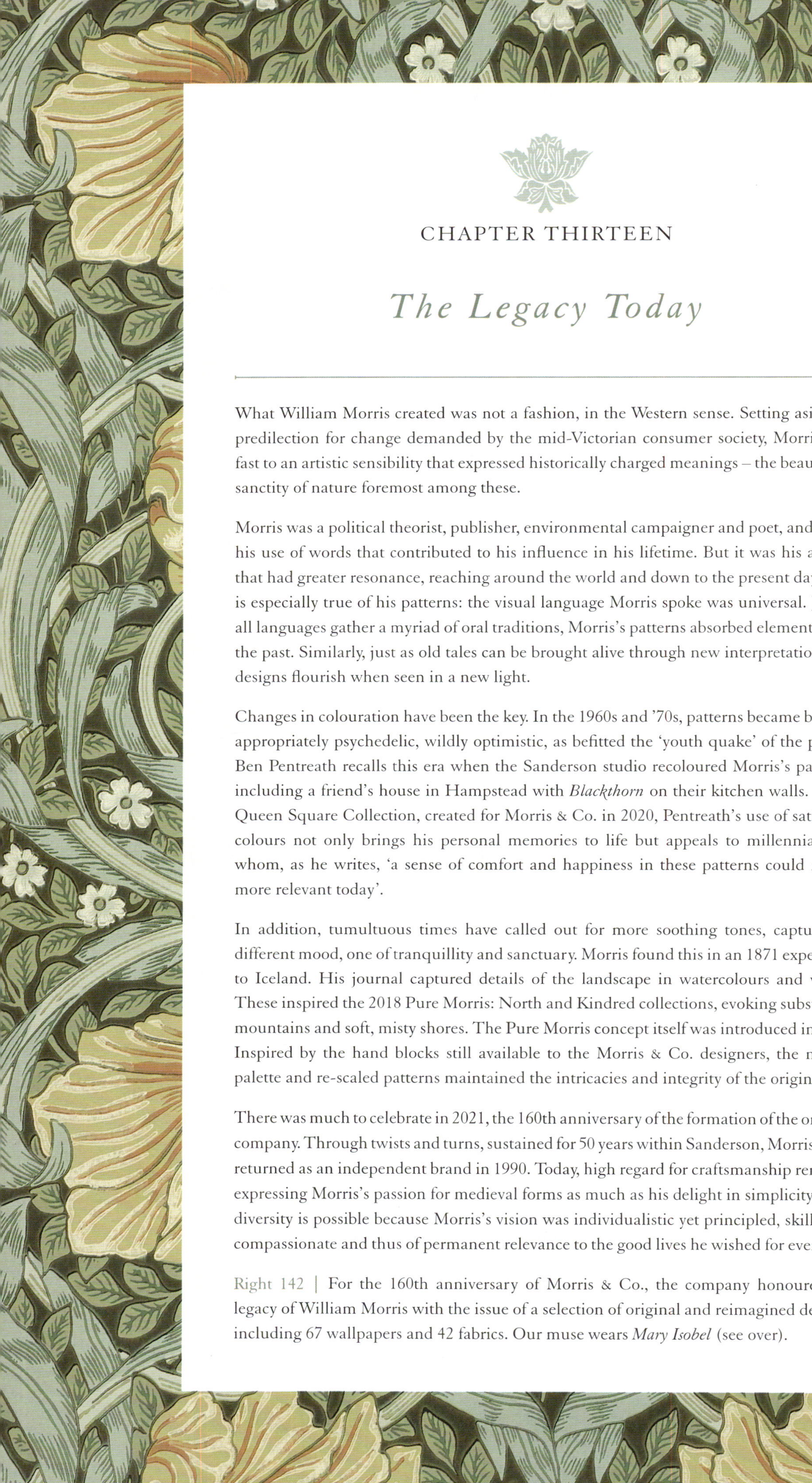

CHAPTER THIRTEEN

The Legacy Today

What William Morris created was not a fashion, in the Western sense. Setting aside the predilection for change demanded by the mid-Victorian consumer society, Morris held fast to an artistic sensibility that expressed historically charged meanings – the beauty and sanctity of nature foremost among these.

Morris was a political theorist, publisher, environmental campaigner and poet, and it was his use of words that contributed to his influence in his lifetime. But it was his artistry that had greater resonance, reaching around the world and down to the present day. This is especially true of his patterns: the visual language Morris spoke was universal. Just as all languages gather a myriad of oral traditions, Morris's patterns absorbed elements from the past. Similarly, just as old tales can be brought alive through new interpretations, his designs flourish when seen in a new light.

Changes in colouration have been the key. In the 1960s and '70s, patterns became brazen: appropriately psychedelic, wildly optimistic, as befitted the 'youth quake' of the period. Ben Pentreath recalls this era when the Sanderson studio recoloured Morris's patterns, including a friend's house in Hampstead with *Blackthorn* on their kitchen walls. In the Queen Square Collection, created for Morris & Co. in 2020, Pentreath's use of saturated colours not only brings his personal memories to life but appeals to millennials, for whom, as he writes, 'a sense of comfort and happiness in these patterns could not be more relevant today'.

In addition, tumultuous times have called out for more soothing tones, capturing a different mood, one of tranquillity and sanctuary. Morris found this in an 1871 expedition to Iceland. His journal captured details of the landscape in watercolours and words. These inspired the 2018 Pure Morris: North and Kindred collections, evoking substantial mountains and soft, misty shores. The Pure Morris concept itself was introduced in 2016. Inspired by the hand blocks still available to the Morris & Co. designers, the neutral palette and re-scaled patterns maintained the intricacies and integrity of the originals.

There was much to celebrate in 2021, the 160th anniversary of the formation of the original company. Through twists and turns, sustained for 50 years within Sanderson, Morris & Co. returned as an independent brand in 1990. Today, high regard for craftsmanship remains, expressing Morris's passion for medieval forms as much as his delight in simplicity. Such diversity is possible because Morris's vision was individualistic yet principled, skilled yet compassionate and thus of permanent relevance to the good lives he wished for everyone.

Right 142 | For the 160th anniversary of Morris & Co., the company honoured the legacy of William Morris with the issue of a selection of original and reimagined designs, including 67 wallpapers and 42 fabrics. Our muse wears *Mary Isobel* (see over).

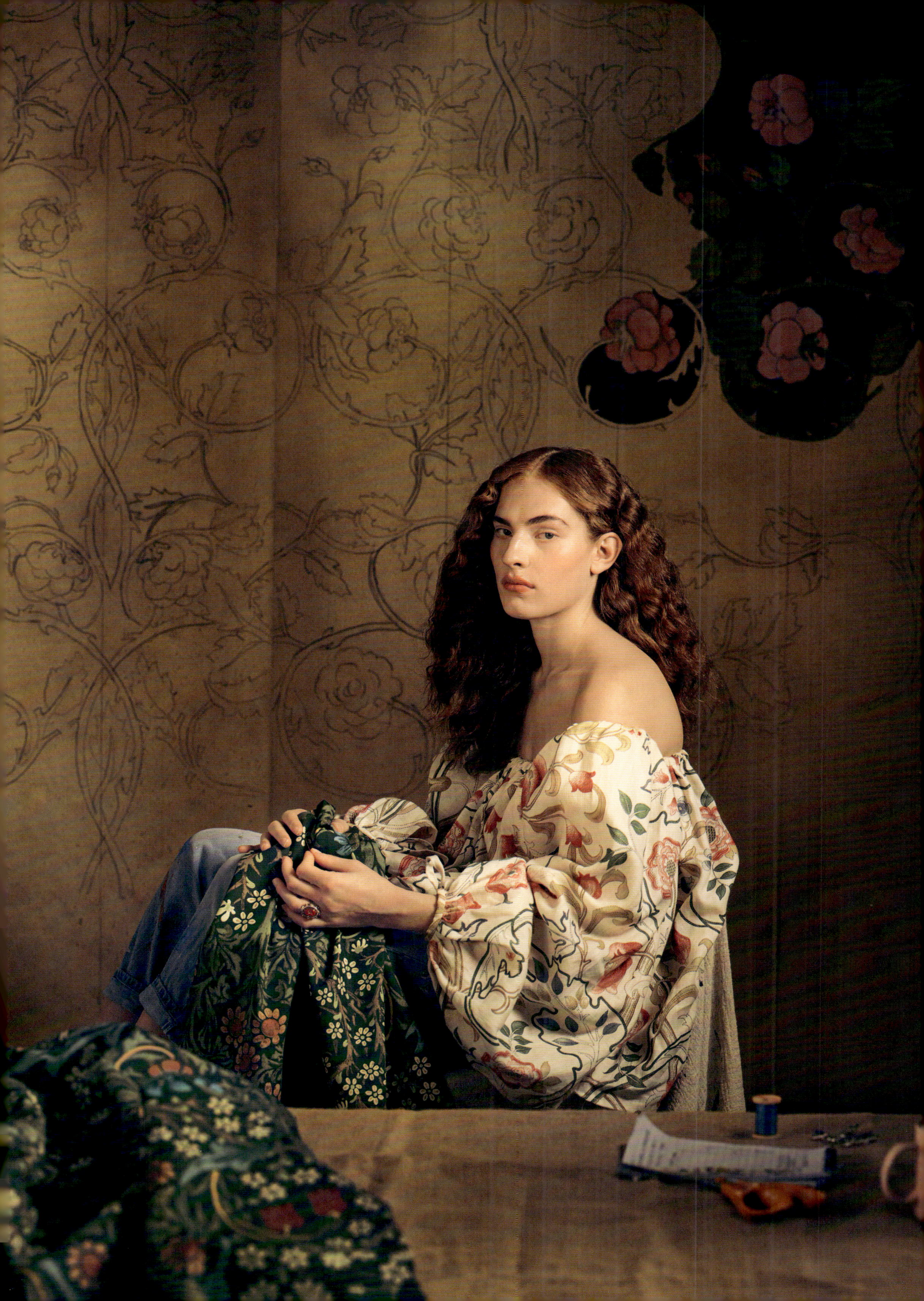

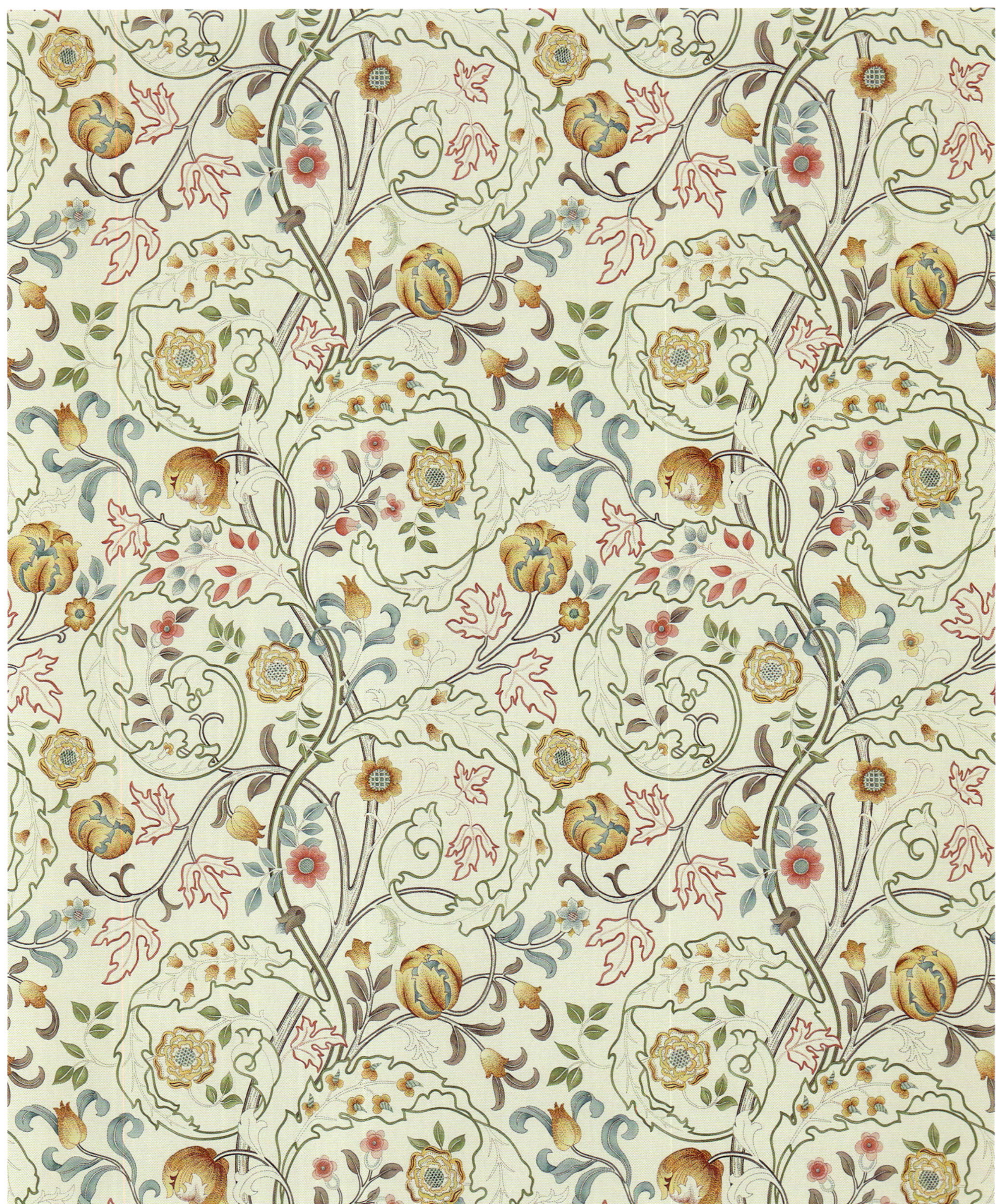

143 | Morris & Co. Studio, *Mary Isobel*, 2021, Morris & Co.

Scrolling acanthus leaves and flowers adorn this wallpaper, adapted from an embroidery designed in the 1890s by John Henry Dearle. Also available as an embroidered silk and linen-blend fabric, it epitomises the on-going evolution of designs that offer new options while remaining true to the Morris & Co. traditions.

Right 144 | William Morris, *Bachelor's Button*, [1892], 2016 re-edition, Morris & Co.

One of Morris's last wallpaper designs, this version has been greatly enlarged from its original scale. In its new dramatic form, it was first offered as part of the Pure range, launched in June 2016. Such was its popularity that it became part of the 160th anniversary collection five years later.

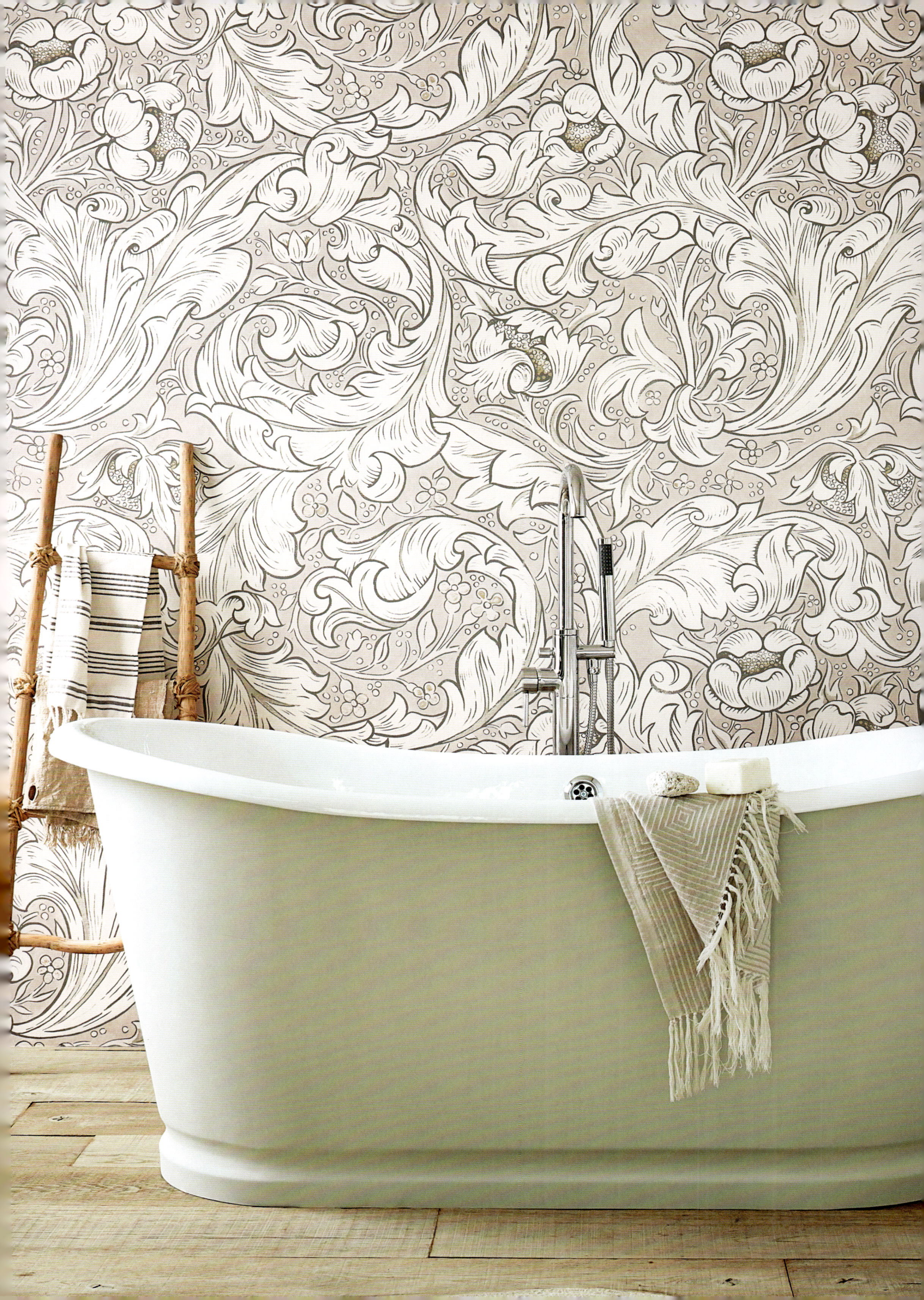

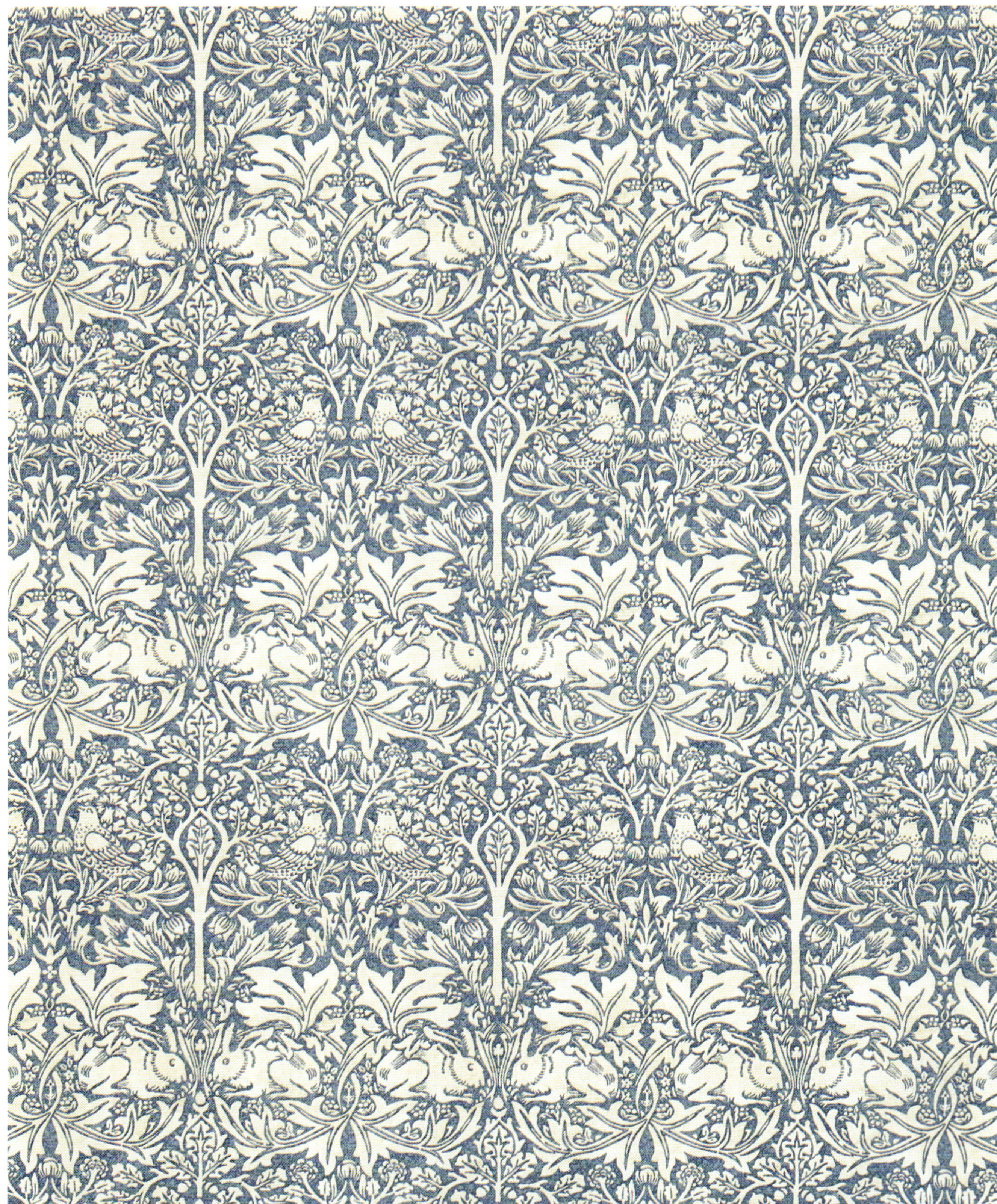

145 | William Morris, *Brer Rabbit*, [c.1881], 2021 transformation, Morris & Co.

Also known as *Brother Rabbit*, the inspiration for this wallpaper comes from an indigo-discharged and block-printed cotton, registered by the company in 1882. It was named after a character in *Uncle Remus, His Songs and His Sayings* by J.C. Harris, which was being read to Jenny and May Morris at this time.

Right 146 | William Morris, *Snakeshead*, [1876], 2021 transformation, Morris & Co.

Designed as a printed cotton and first blocked by Thomas Wardle in January 1877, *Snakeshead* was registered a year later. This pattern was a favourite of Morris himself and its dark overprinted background reveals the influence of Indian patterns, which fascinated him at this time. It first appeared as a wallpaper in a 2017 Archive IV collection, 'The Collector'.

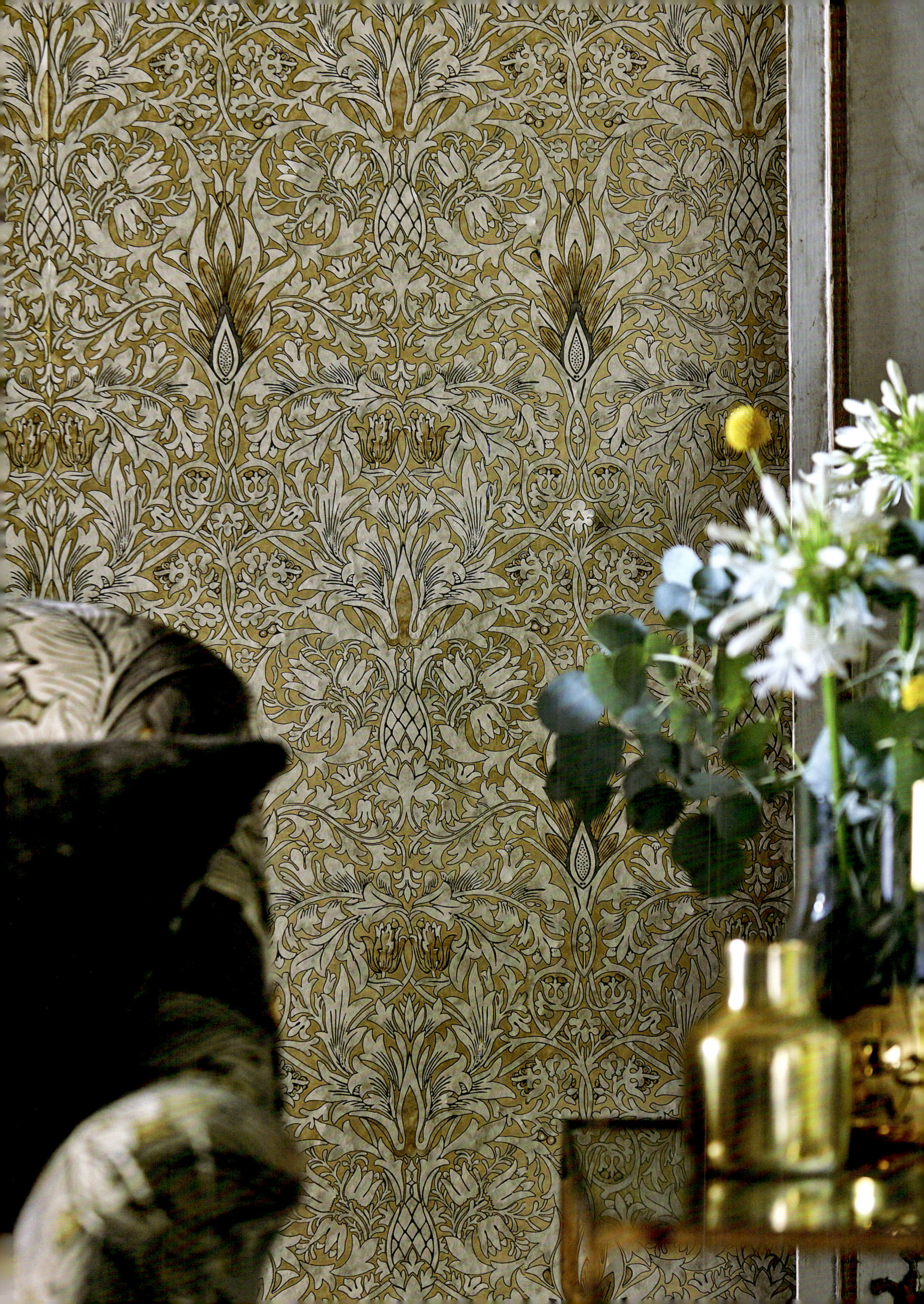

147 | William Morris, *Pimpernel*, [1876], 2021 re-edition, Morris & Co.

Pimpernel is one of the best known of Morris's patterns. It survives *in situ* in Wightwick Manor, the Victorian manor house near Wolverhampton cared for by the National Trust since 1937. It was also selected for the dining room walls at Kelmscott House, where it was overlaid by a wall-and ceiling-suspended Persian carpet.

Right 148 | William Morris, *Willow Boughs*, [1887], 2020 re-edition, Morris & Co.

This wallpaper was one of 18 selected by the interior designer Ben Pentreath for inclusion in The Queen Square Collection of 2020. It was created by surface-rollers to retain the original character of the printing. The collection name alludes to the location of the Art Workers' Guild, above which is the Pentreaths' London home.

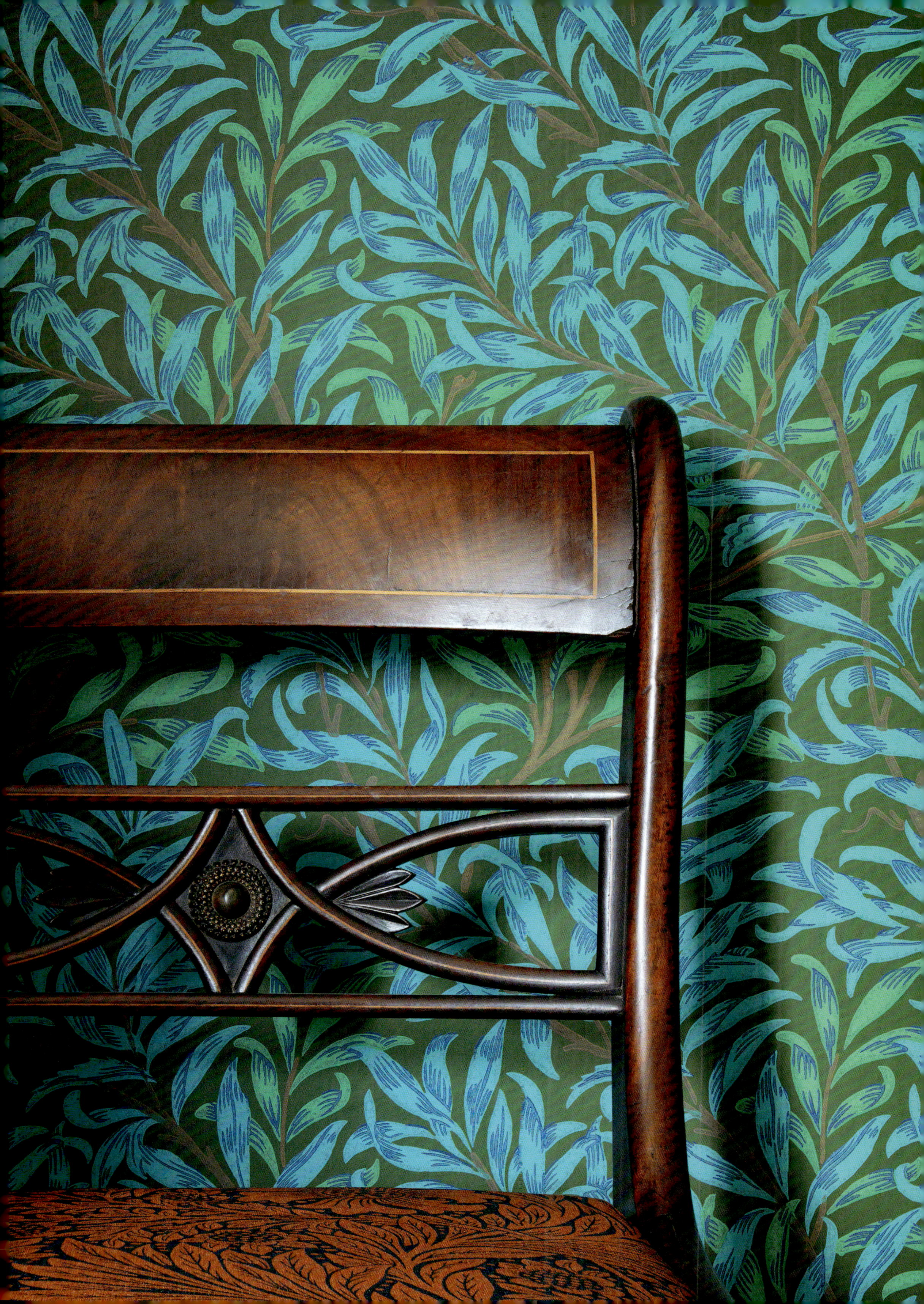

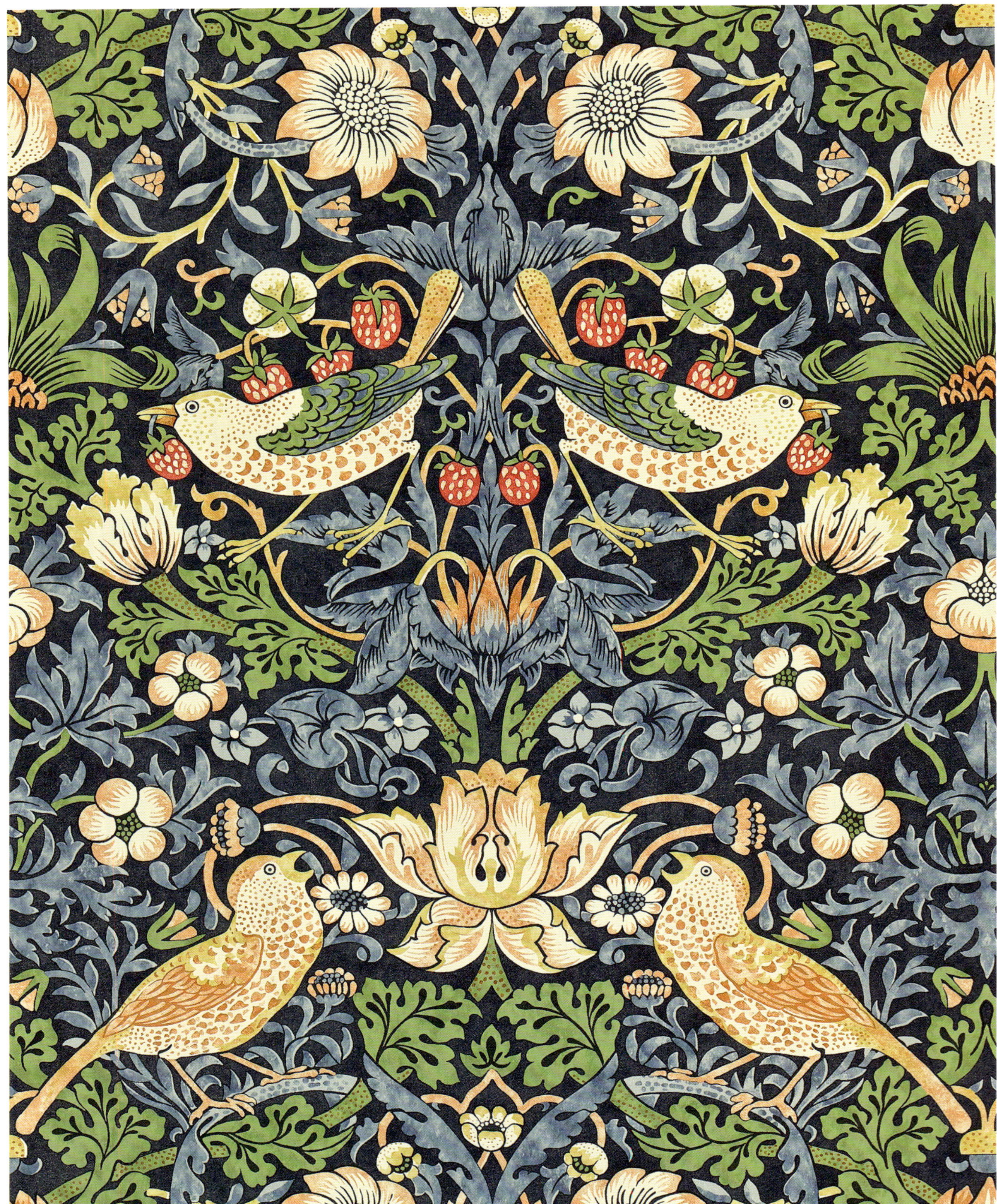

149 | William Morris, *Strawberry Thief*, [1883], 2021 transformation, Morris & Co.

Also beginning life as a block-printed cotton, this wallpaper captures the colouration of the original, which had an indigo-discharged ground and, for the first time in the Merton Abbey works, successfully incorporated dyed red and yellow tones. Used as a chair cover by the influential typographer Emery Walker, it remains today in his Hammersmith Terrace home.

Right 150 | William Morris/John Henry Dearle, *Blackthorn*, [1892], 2020 re-edition, Morris & Co.

Blackthorn was among the Morris & Co. patterns promoted in Sanderson's 1976 Triad collection. It was extremely popular, going on to appear in their Options ranges for about a decade from 1981. As a result of Ben Pentreath's fond recollections of this design, he included it in The Queen Square collection and used it his Dorset home, as seen here.

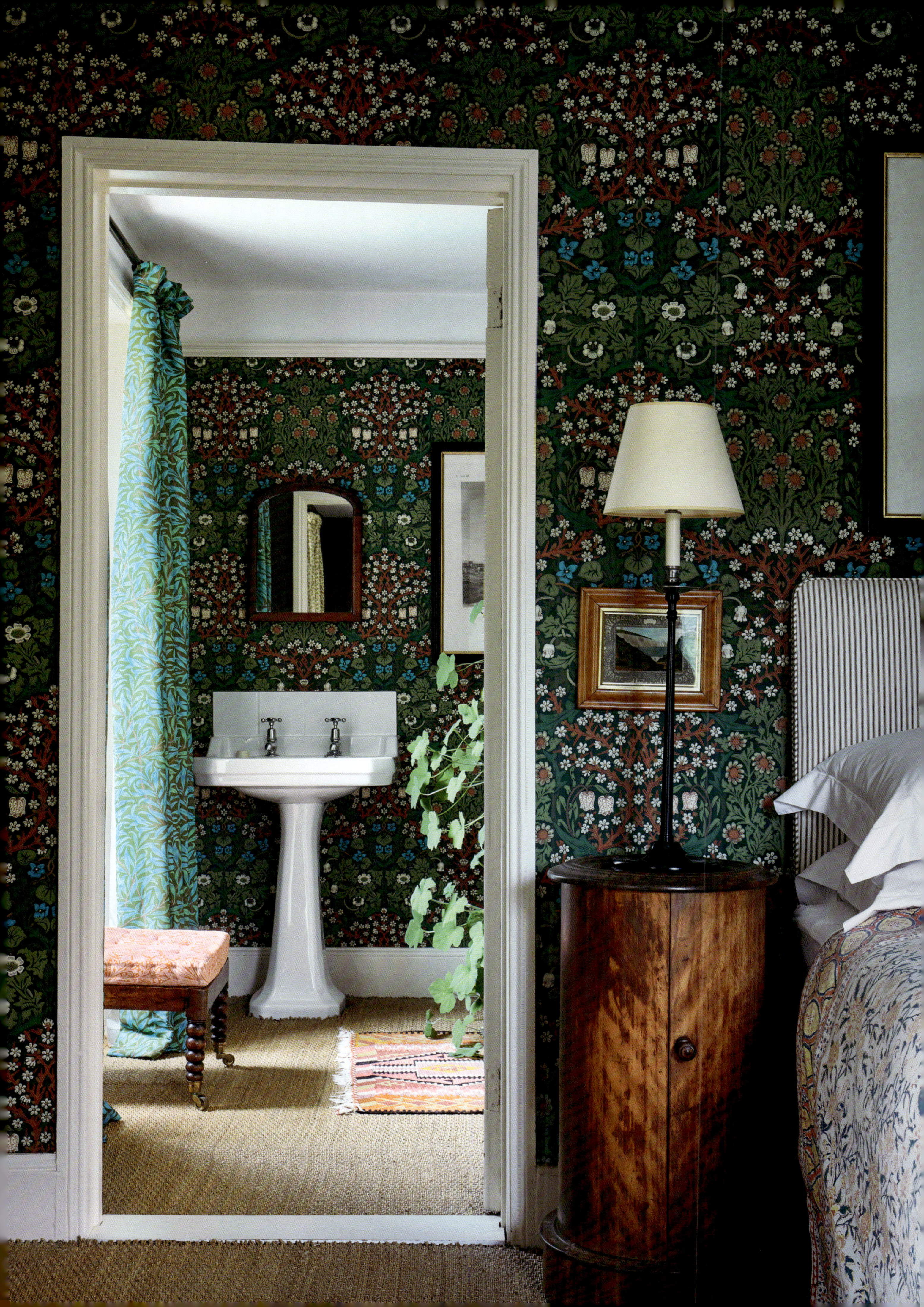

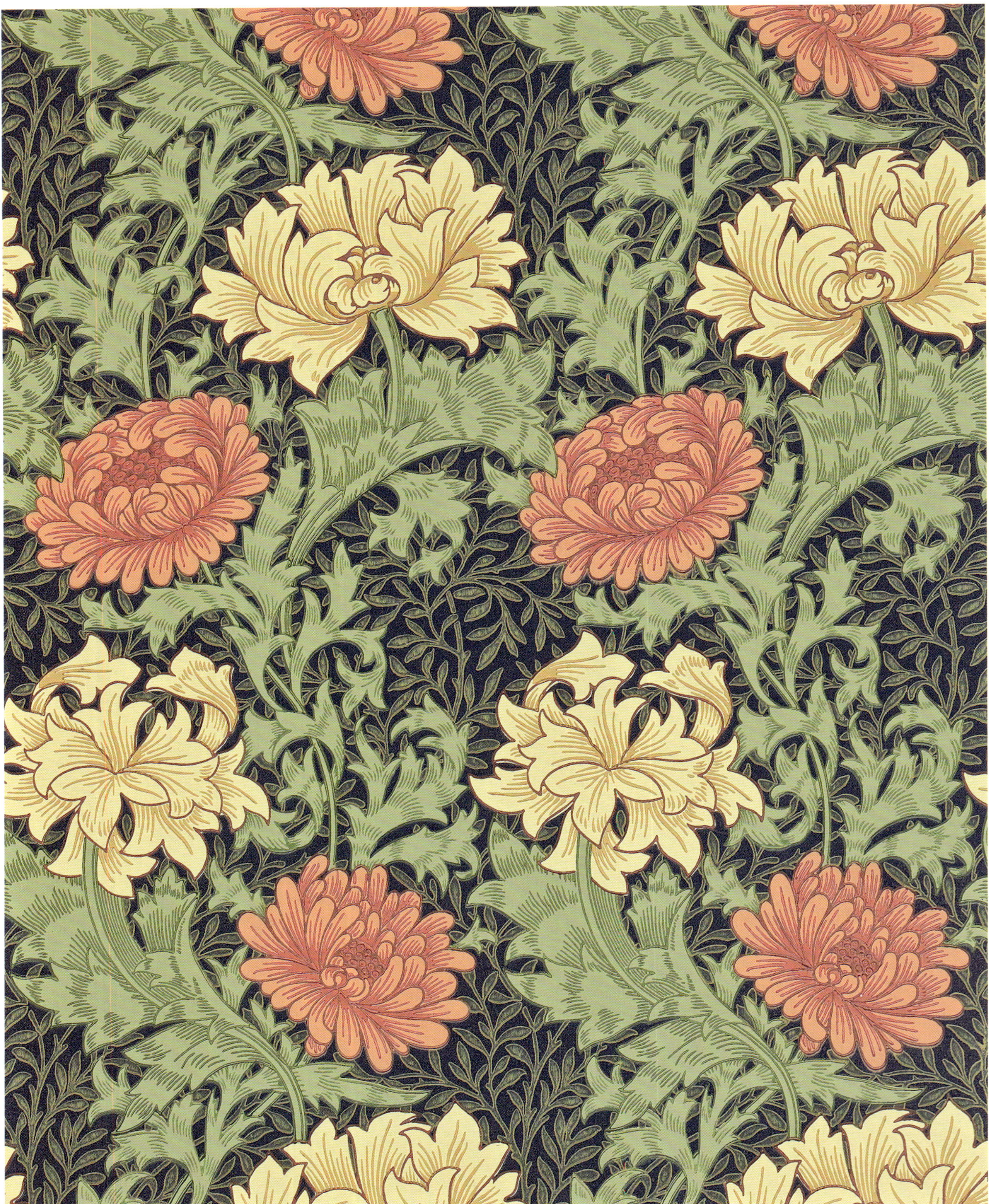

151 | William Morris, *Chrysanthemum*, [1877], 2013 re-edition, Morris & Co.

This pattern was originally printed using wood blocks on pasteboard to emulate Japanese leather papers, a technique perfected by Jeffrey & Co. in 1878. Current versions faithfully reproduce some of the earliest colourways while others incorporate a softer palette with subtle metallic highlights, as seen here.

Right 152 | John Henry Dearle, *Leicester*, [1912], 2013 re-edition, Morris & Co.

This is one of several designs created by Dearle in the years just prior to the First World War. By this time having been with the company for 34 years, and designing wallpapers since 1887, he was so immersed in the Morris style that it had become his own. It was included in The Archive II collection, 2013, and revisited for the 160th anniversary too.

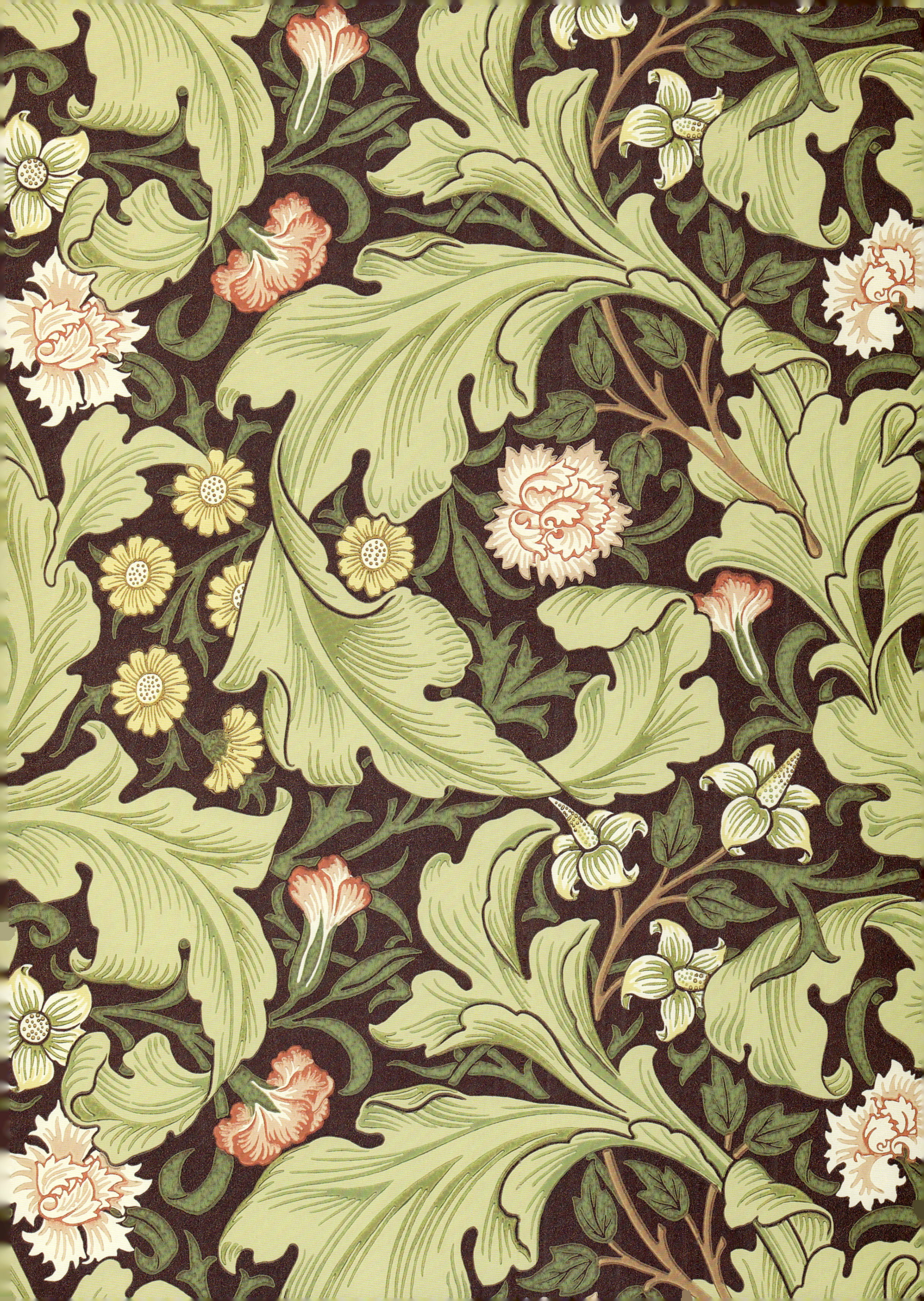

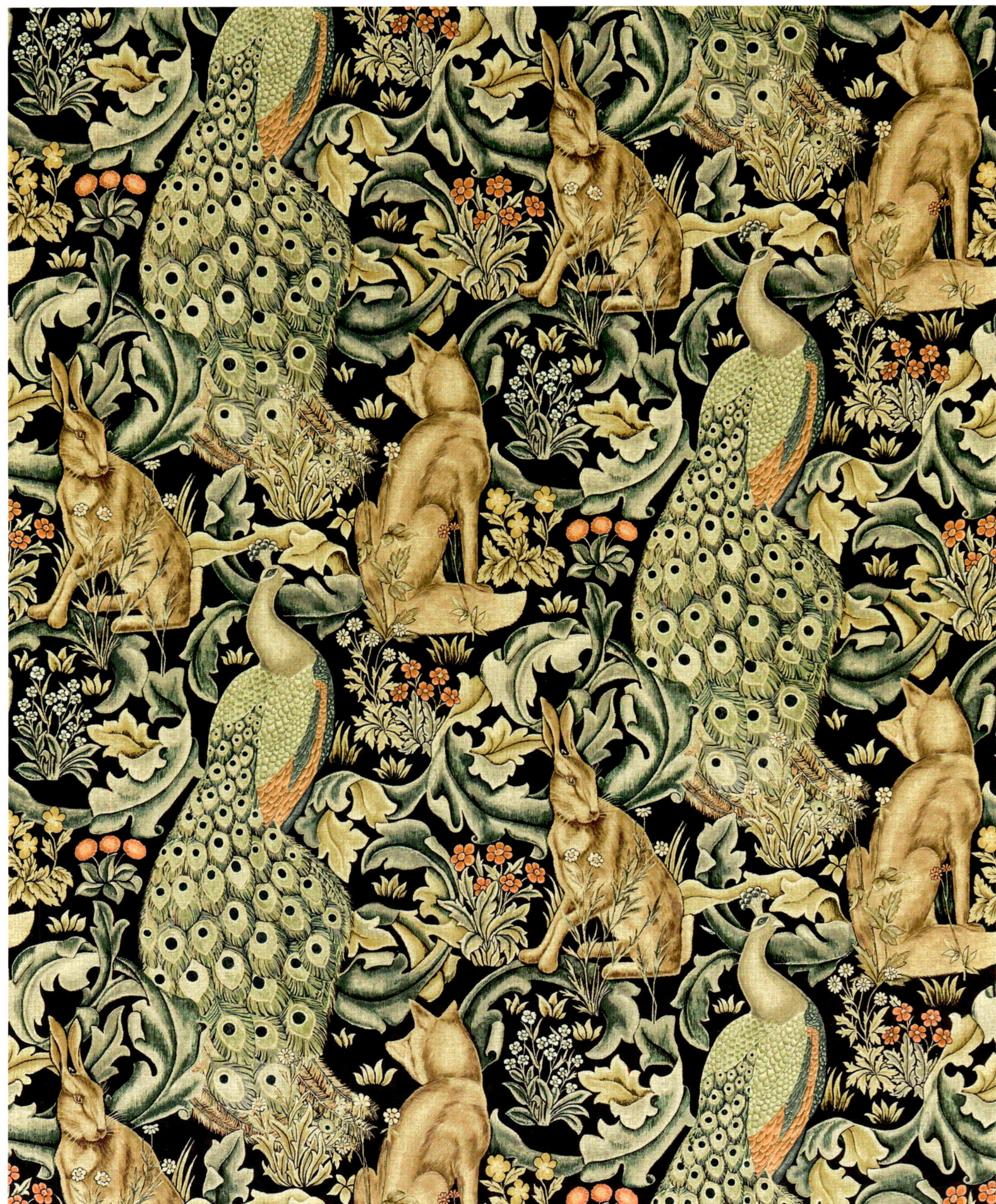

153 | Alison Gee, *Forest*, from William Morris and Philip Webb, *Forest Tapestry*, [1887], 2013 transformation, Morris & Co.

Forest is a digitally printed adaptation, here on velvet, that artfully combines animals drawn by Webb, with Morris's masterful acanthus swirls and *mille fleur*. Considered one of the most successful Morris & Co. tapestries, it hung in 1 Holland Park, London described as an 'epoch-making house', the 'first flower of the "movement" in aesthetic furnishing'.

Right 154 | Morris & Co. Studio, *Owl and Willow*, 2021, Morris & Co.

The inspiration for this digitally printed wallpaper was the *Verdure with Deer and Shields* tapestry, which accompanied the Morris & Co. *Holy Grail* panels first woven in 1891–94 for Stanmore Hall. The original a collaboration between Morris, Burne-Jones and Dearle, this ambitious design is printed in three sections on a single roll to be cut and joined to make a full scene.

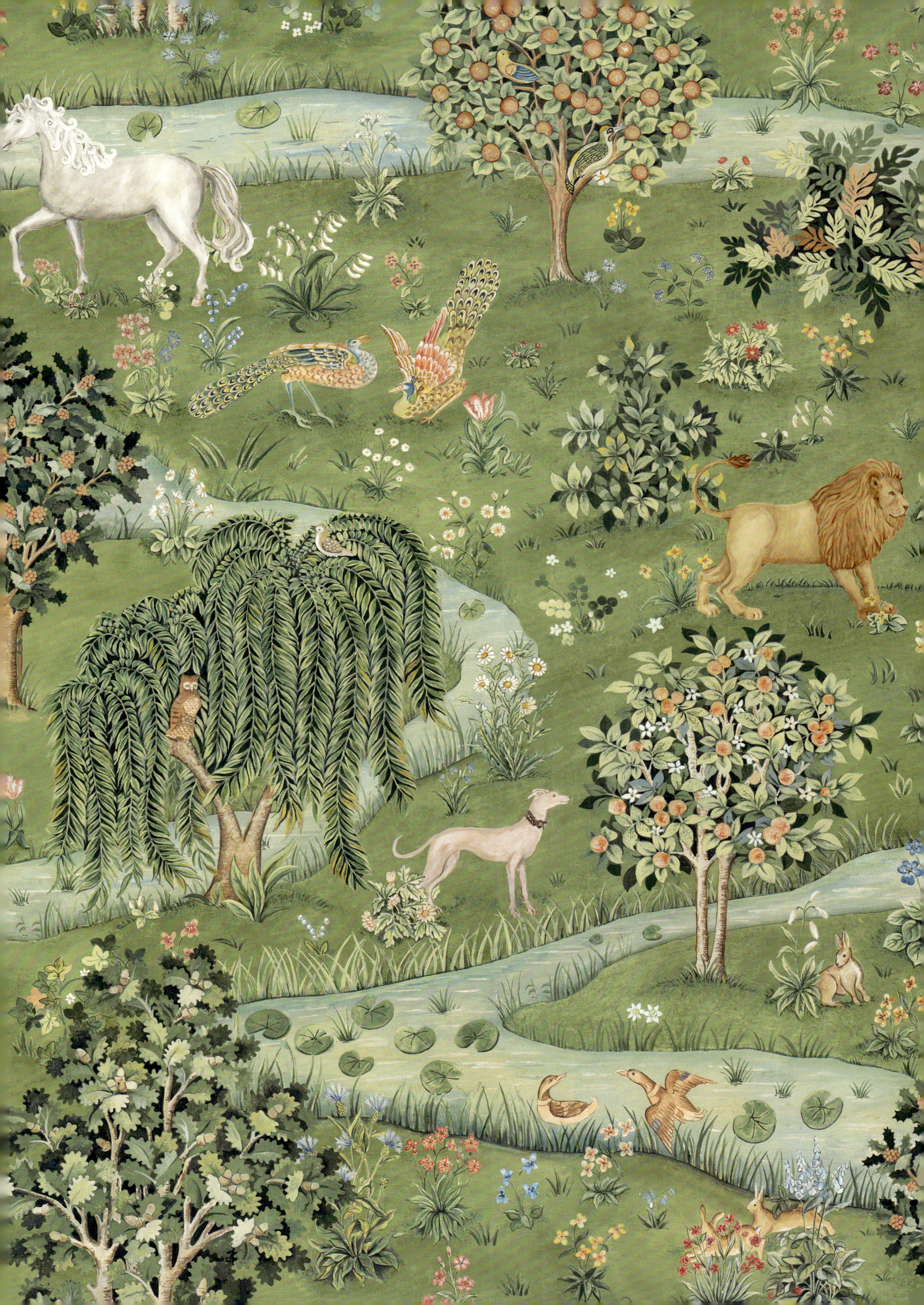

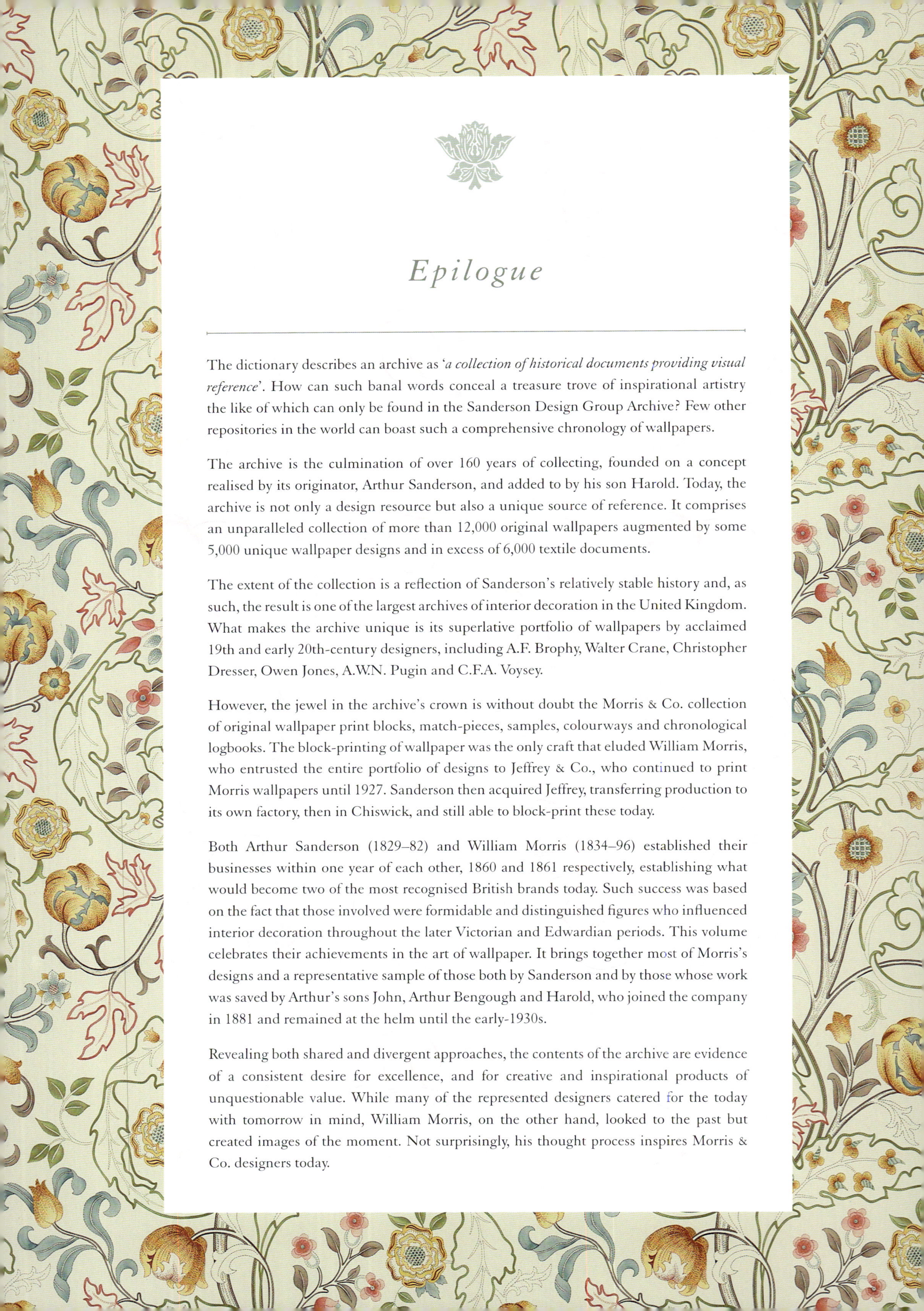

Epilogue

The dictionary describes an archive as '*a collection of historical documents providing visual reference*'. How can such banal words conceal a treasure trove of inspirational artistry the like of which can only be found in the Sanderson Design Group Archive? Few other repositories in the world can boast such a comprehensive chronology of wallpapers.

The archive is the culmination of over 160 years of collecting, founded on a concept realised by its originator, Arthur Sanderson, and added to by his son Harold. Today, the archive is not only a design resource but also a unique source of reference. It comprises an unparalleled collection of more than 12,000 original wallpapers augmented by some 5,000 unique wallpaper designs and in excess of 6,000 textile documents.

The extent of the collection is a reflection of Sanderson's relatively stable history and, as such, the result is one of the largest archives of interior decoration in the United Kingdom. What makes the archive unique is its superlative portfolio of wallpapers by acclaimed 19th and early 20th-century designers, including A.F. Brophy, Walter Crane, Christopher Dresser, Owen Jones, A.W.N. Pugin and C.F.A. Voysey.

However, the jewel in the archive's crown is without doubt the Morris & Co. collection of original wallpaper print blocks, match-pieces, samples, colourways and chronological logbooks. The block-printing of wallpaper was the only craft that eluded William Morris, who entrusted the entire portfolio of designs to Jeffrey & Co., who continued to print Morris wallpapers until 1927. Sanderson then acquired Jeffrey, transferring production to its own factory, then in Chiswick, and still able to block-print these today.

Both Arthur Sanderson (1829–82) and William Morris (1834–96) established their businesses within one year of each other, 1860 and 1861 respectively, establishing what would become two of the most recognised British brands today. Such success was based on the fact that those involved were formidable and distinguished figures who influenced interior decoration throughout the later Victorian and Edwardian periods. This volume celebrates their achievements in the art of wallpaper. It brings together most of Morris's designs and a representative sample of those both by Sanderson and by those whose work was saved by Arthur's sons John, Arthur Bengough and Harold, who joined the company in 1881 and remained at the helm until the early-1930s.

Revealing both shared and divergent approaches, the contents of the archive are evidence of a consistent desire for excellence, and for creative and inspirational products of unquestionable value. While many of the represented designers catered for the today with tomorrow in mind, William Morris, on the other hand, looked to the past but created images of the moment. Not surprisingly, his thought process inspires Morris & Co. designers today.

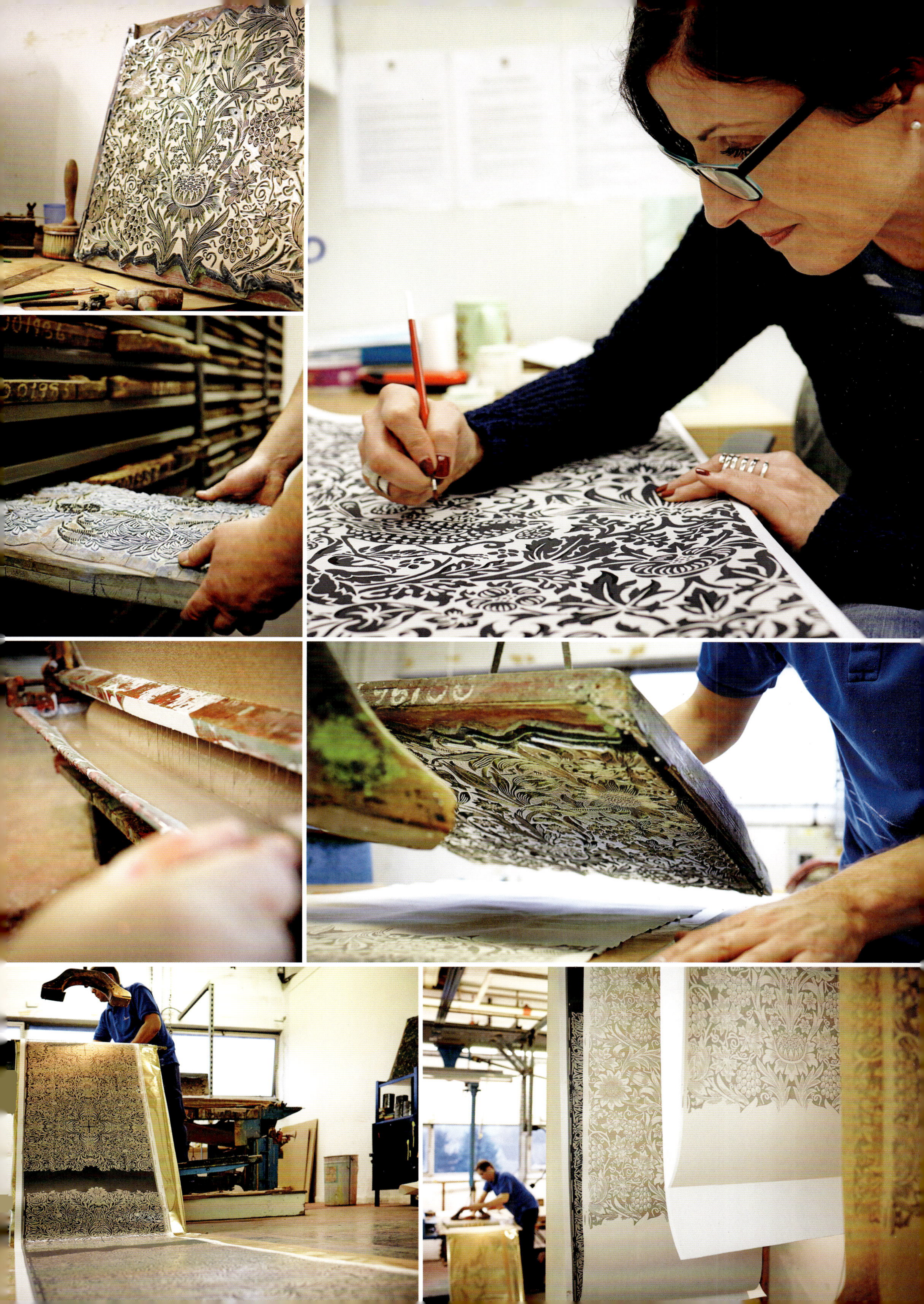

Index

Index of Designs

109 | *Foliage*
John Henry Dearle, 1899 (printed)
73.8 x 57.5cm, 12 print blocks
Jeffrey & Co. (manufacturer)
for Morris & Co.

153 | *Forest*
Alison Gee, 2013 transformation
from William Morris and Philip
Webb's original 1887 *Forest*
Tapestry design
digitally printed
Morris & Co.

014 | *Four Seasons Panel*
19th or early-20th century
122 x 56cm, approx. 31 print blocks
Wm Woollams & Co. (attrib.)

005 | *Frieze with Putti and Jardinières*
Charles-Louis Müller, c.1865
76 x 142cm, multiple print blocks
Zuber & Cie

057 | *Fruit*
William Morris, 1864 (printed)
82.5 x 51.75cm, 12 print blocks
Jeffrey & Co. (manufacturer)
for Morris, Marshall, Faulkner & Co.

081 | *Garden Tulip*
William Morris, 1885 (printed)
74.5 x 57.4cm, 8 print blocks
Jeffrey & Co. (manufacturer)
for Morris & Co.

028 | *The Glenview Paper*
Christopher Dresser (attrib.), 1999
80 x 54.5cm, screen print
(1876 Corbière Son & Brindle
original, 6 print blocks)
Arthur Sanderson & Sons Ltd

105 | *Golden Lily*
John Henry Dearle, 1899 (printed)
75.9 x 55.8cm, 11 print blocks
Jeffrey & Co. (manufacturer)
for Morris & Co.

106 | *Golden Lily (Speckled Ground)*
John Henry Dearle, 1899 (printed)
76.3 x 57.6cm, 11 print blocks
Jeffrey & Co. (manufacturer)
for Morris & Co.

080 | *Grafton*
William Morris, 1883 (printed)
77.3 x 57cm, 3 print blocks
Jeffrey & Co. (manufacturer)
for Morris & Co.

103 | *Granville*
John Henry Dearle, 1896 (printed)
80.3 x 55.5cm, 11 print blocks
Jeffrey & Co. (manufacturer)
for Morris & Co.

088 | *Hammersmith*
William Morris, 1890 (printed)
71 x 56cm, 4 print blocks
Jeffrey & Co. (manufacturer)
for Morris & Co.

008 | *'Henri II' Embroidery*
Wallpaper
Paul Balin, 1877–85
81.2 x 48cm, multiple print blocks

133 | *The 'Heraldic' Design*
C.F.A. Voysey, 1902
57 x 86cm, 4 blocks
Essex & Co.

099 | *Honeysuckle*
May Morris, 1883 (printed)
101.4 x 55.7cm, 8 print blocks
Jeffrey & Co. (manufacturer)
for Morris & Co.

100 | *Horn Poppy*
May Morris, 1885 (printed)
70.8 x 57.3cm, 3 print blocks
Jeffrey & Co. (manufacturer)
for Morris & Co.

094 | *Indian*
George Gilbert Scott the Younger,
1868–70 (printed)
82.5 x 51.7cm, 4 print blocks
Jeffrey & Co. (manufacturer)
for Morris Marshall, Faulkner & Co.

101 | *Iris*
John Henry Dearle, 1887 (printed)
82.6 x 51.7cm, 6 print blocks
Jeffrey & Co. (manufacturer)
for Morris & Co.

036 | *Japanese Staircase*
Chiswick Design Studio, c.1888
77.2 x 50.2cm, 7 print blocks
Arthur Sanderson & Sons

037 | *Japanese Staircase*
Chiswick Design Studio, c.1888
77 x 50cm, 5 print blocks
Arthur Sanderson & Sons

061 | *Jasmine*
William Morris, 1872 (printed)
74 x 57.8cm, 20 print blocks
Jeffrey & Co. (manufacturer)
for Morris Marshall, Faulkner & Co.

044 | *Kinkarakawakami Leather Paper*
c.1885
97.5 x 93.5cm
Rottmann, Strome & Co.

064 | *Larkspur*
William Morris, 1872 (printed)
82.75 x 52cm, 1 print block
Jeffrey & Co. (manufacturer)
for Morris, Marshall, Faulkner & Co.

115 | *Leicester*
John Henry Dearle, 1912 (printed)
74.1 x 56.8cm, 10 print blocks
Jeffrey & Co. (manufacturer) for
Morris & Co. Decorators Ltd

152 | *Leicester*
John Henry Dearle, 2013 re-edition
of original 1912 design
surflex printed
Morris & Co.

129 | *Lerena*
C.F.A. Voysey, early 20th C.
(1897 design for Essex & Co.)
93 x 56, one surface-roller
Arthur Sanderson & Sons Ltd

003 | *Les Vues D'Amérique Du Nord*
Jean-Julien Deltil, 1833 (designed),
1834
4 rolls, each measuring 386 x 50cm,
1,690 print blocks for complete
panorama
Zuber & Cie

065 | *Light Larkspur*
William Morris, 1875 (printed)
87.75 x 56.3cm, 10 print blocks
Jeffrey & Co. (manufacturer)
for Morris & Co.

062 | *Lily - trial sample*
William Morris, 1874 (printed)
62.5 x 69.5cm, proof: 51 x 56.5cm,
letter: 19.5 x 12.1cm, 8 print blocks
Jeffrey & Co. (manufacturer)
for Morris, Marshall, Faulkner & Co.

063 | *Lily*
William Morris, 1874 (printed)
82.5 x 53.1cm, 8 print blocks
Jeffrey & Co. (manufacturer)
for Morris, Marshall, Faulkner & Co.

124 | *Lion and Dove*
Walter Crane, 1900
69.5 x 84.5cm, 12 print blocks
Jeffrey & Co.

095 | *Loop Trail*
Kate Faulkner, 1877
(registered & printed)
82.4 x 51.8cm, 2 print blocks
Jeffrey & Co. (manufacturer)
for Morris & Co.

006 | *'Louis XIII' Embroidery*
Wallpaper
Paul Balin, c.1877
94.7 x 49cm, multiple print blocks

009 | *Louis XVI*
Paul Balin, c.1878–85
49 x 83cm, multiple print blocks

096 | *Mallow*
Kate Faulkner, 1879 (printed)
72.3 x 57.7cm, 1 print block
Jeffrey & Co. (manufacturer)
for Morris & Co.

041 | *The Mandarin*
Louis Stahl (attrib.) c.1915
65.5 x 52cm, 3 print blocks + emboss
Arthur Sanderson & Sons Ltd

143 | *Mary Isobel*
Morris & Co. Studio, 2021
Adapted from John Henry Dearle's
1890s embroidery design
gravure printed
Morris & Co.

114 | *Michaelmas Daisy*
John Henry Dearle, 1912 (printed)
57.9 x 55.5cm, 2 print blocks
Jeffrey & Co. (manufacturer)
for Morris & Co. Decorators Ltd

127 | *Monkshood*
A.F. Vigers, 1901
51.5 x 75cm, 6 print blocks
Jeffrey & Co.

134 | *Montreaux*
C.F.A. Voysey, c.1904
52.5 x 72.7cm, 6 blocks
Essex & Co.

004 | *Music Frieze*
1850–75
93.5 x 117cm, multiple print blocks

138 | *The Myrtle*
Turner, 1913
52.5 x 51cm, 2 print blocks
Charles Knowles & Co.

093 | *Net Ceiling*
William Morris, 1895 (printed)
76.2 x 55.8cm, 3 print blocks
Jeffrey & Co. (manufacturer)
for Morris & Co.

087 | *Norwich*
William Morris, 1888 (printed)
72.5 x 56.7cm, 18 print blocks
Jeffrey & Co. (manufacturer)
for Morris & Co.

126 | *The Orange Tree*
Walter Crane, 1902 (designed) for
Jeffrey & Co., early-20th century
(printed)
68.5 x 55.75cm, 6 print blocks
Arthur Sanderson & Sons Ltd

125 | *Oranges and Lemons*
Dorothy Hilton, 1900
71 x 55.5cm, 9 print rollers
Jeffrey & Co.

110 | *Orchard*
John Henry Dearle, 1899 (printed)
74 x 57.5cm, 10 print blocks
Jeffrey & Co. (manufacturer)
for Morris & Co.

042 | *Oriental Scene Wallpaper*
Chiswick Design Studio, c.1919
71.5 x 51.5cm, 6 print blocks +
emboss
Arthur Sanderson & Sons Ltd

052 | *The Osier*
Metford Warner, 1924
69.5 x 54.25cm, 4 print blocks
Jeffrey & Co.

154 | *Owl and Willow*
Morris & Co. Studio, 2021
Inspired by Morris, Burne-Jones and
Dearle's 1891–94 *Verdure with Deer*
and Shields panel accompanying the
Stanmore Hall *Holy Grail* tapestries
digitally printed
Morris & Co.

017 | *Palace of Westminster Wallpaper*
A.W.N. Pugin, c.1848
104 x 53.5cm, 2 print blocks
Samuel Scott for J.G. Crace

018 | *Palace of Westminster Wallpaper*
A.W.N. Pugin, c.1848
62.5 x 55.25cm, 2 print blocks
Samuel Scott for J.G. Crace

020 | *Palace of Westminster 'Robing Room' Paper*
A.W.N. Pugin, c.1951 reproduction from c.1848 original
111.5 x 57cm, 2 print blocks
Arthur Sanderson & Sons Ltd

051 | *Peri*
c.1885
75.5 x 51cm, 1 print block
Jeffrey & Co.

069 | *Pimpernel*
William Morris, 1876 (printed)
74.7 x 57.2cm, 11 print blocks
Jeffrey & Co. (manufacturer)
for Morris & Co.

147 | *Pimpernel*
William Morris, 2021 re-edition of original 1876 design
surflex printed
Morris & Co.

078 | *Pink and Poppy*
William Morris, 1880 (registered), 1881 (printed)
78 x 51.5cm, 1 print block
Jeffrey & Co. (manufacturer)
for Morris & Co.

026 | *Pomegranate*
In the style of Christopher Dresser, 1876
85.5 x 55.2cm, 5 print blocks
Corbière Son & Brindle

135 | *The Poppy*
A.F. Brophy, 1890
60 x 39cm, 4 print blocks
Arthur Sanderson & Sons

015 | *Ribbons and Bows*
Early-19th century
58 x 52cm, 11 print blocks
Wm Woollams & Co.

070 | *Rose*
William Morris, 1877 (printed)
75 x 56.9cm, 7 print blocks
Jeffrey & Co. (manufacturer)
for Morris & Co.

001 | *Rose Border*
Charles-Louis Müller (possibly), c.1848–70
56 x 87cm, 19 print blocks

012 | *Roses and Azaleas with Gold Decoration, Border of*
c.1846
49.25 x 56cm, 27 print blocks
Wm Woollams & Co.

121 | *The Rossetti*
The Sanderson Studio, 1897
filling: 74.5 x 51cm, frieze: 28 x 59.5cm, surface wash machine print (1885 design, 10 print blocks)
Arthur Sanderson & Sons

139 | *Sanitary Paper*
c.1918
56 x 50.5cm, 8 print rollers
John Line and Sons Ltd

128 | *Savaric*
C.F.A. Voysey, c.1896
89.5 x 56cm, 1 print block
Essex & Co.

060 | *Scroll*
William Morris, 1871 (printed)
73.5 x 56.2cm, 12 print blocks
Jeffrey & Co. (manufacturer)
for Morris, Marshall, Faulkner & Co.

112 | *Seaweed*
John Henry Dearle, 1901 (printed)
72.8 x 55.5cm, 9 print blocks
Jeffrey & Co. (manufacturer)
for Morris & Co.

040 | *Silhouette Wallpaper*
Early-20th century
87.5 x 54.5cm, 2 print rollers
Sanderson Design Group Archive (document)

108 | *Single Stem*
John Henry Dearle, 1894 (printed)
94.4 x 55.3cm, 8 print blocks
Jeffrey & Co. (manufacturer)
for Morris & Co.

146 | *Snakeshead*
William Morris, 2021 transformation of original 1878 (registered) block-printed cotton design
gravure-wide width printed
Morris & Co.

131 | *Sparhawk*
C.F.A. Voysey, c.1898
75 x 52cm, 4 print blocks
Essex & Co.

092 | *Spring Thicket*
William Morris, 1894 (printed)
105.6 x 55.7cm, 18 print blocks
Jeffrey & Co. (manufacturer)
for Morris & Co.

132 | *The Squire's Garden*
C.F.A. Voysey, 1896 (designed), 1898 (printed)
66 x 53cm, 7 print rollers
Essex & Co.

076 | *The St James's Ceiling*
William Morris, 1881 (printed)
71.7 x 57cm, 2 print blocks
Jeffrey & Co. (manufacturer)
for Morris & Co.

077 | *The St James's Wallpaper*
William Morris, 1881 (printed)
101.7 x 55.8cm, 68 print blocks & patches
Jeffrey & Co. (manufacturer)
for Morris & Co.

016 | *Stamped-Gilt Wallpaper*
c.1850
60.75 x 55cm, 1 print block
Wm Woollams & Co.

149 | *Strawberry Thief*
William Morris, 2021 transformation of original 1883 block-printed cotton design
gravure printed
Morris & Co.

075 | *Sunflower*
William Morris, 1879 (printed)
75 x 57cm, 1 print block
Jeffrey & Co. (manufacturer)
for Morris & Co.

002 | *Swags and Jardinières Scrolls with Flower Baskets*
c.1855
63 x 54.2cm, 23 print blocks

115 | *Sweet Briar*
John Henry Dearle, 1912 (printed)
76 x 55.4cm, 7 print blocks
Jeffrey & Co. (manufacturer)
for Morris & Co. Decorators Ltd

011 | *'T' Piece with Roses and Azaleas*
c.1846
69 x 54cm, 22 print blocks
Wm Woollams & Co.

055 | *Trellis*
William Morris, 1863 (designed), 1864 (printed)
82.5 x 53.1cm, 11 print blocks
Jeffrey & Co. (manufacturer)
for Morris, Marshall, Faulkner & Co.

007 | *untitled wallpaper*
Paul Balin, 1863–73
49 x 95cm, multiple print blocks

117 | *Verdure*
Kathleen Kersey, 1913 (printed)
84 x 56cm, 1 print block
Jeffrey & Co. (manufacturer)
for Morris & Co. Decorators Ltd

034 | *Vine*
William Morris, 1873/74 (printed)
93.1 x 55.4cm, 7 print blocks
Jeffrey & Co. (manufacturer)
for Morris, Marshall, Faulkner & Co.

084 | *The VRI Cipher Paper*
William Morris, 1887 (printed)
68 x 66.7cm, 1 print block
Jeffrey & Co. (manufacturer)
for Morris & Co.

082 | *Wild Tulip*
William Morris, 1884 (printed)
82.8 x 52cm, 18 print blocks
Jeffrey & Co. (manufacturer)
for Morris & Co.

066 | *Willow*
William Morris, 1874 (printed)
74.7 x 52cm, 2 print blocks
Jeffrey & Co. (manufacturer)
for Morris, Marshall, Faulkner & Co.

083 | *Willow Boughs*
William Morris, 1887 (printed)
74.8 x 52.2cm, 5 print blocks
Jeffrey & Co. (manufacturer)
for Morris & Co.

148 | *Willow Boughs*
William Morris, 2020 re-edition of original 1877 design
surface printed
Morris & Co.

107 | *Woodland Weeds*
John Henry Dearle, 1894 (printed)
74.4 x 55.4cm, 10 print blocks
Jeffrey & Co. (manufacturer)
for Morris & Co.

068 | *Wreath*
William Morris, 1876 (printed)
86.5 x 55cm, 22 print blocks
Jeffrey & Co. (manufacturer)
for Morris & Co.

Further Reading

Ackerman, P., *Wallpaper: Its History, Design and Use*, New York, 1923
Atterbury, P., *A. W. N. Pugin: Master of Gothic Revival*, London and New Haven, 1996
Coleman, B., *Zuber: Two Centuries of Panoramic Wallpaper*, Layton, 2019
Halén, W., *Christopher Dresser: A Pioneer of Modern Design*, London, 1993
Harvey, C. and J. Press, *Art, Enterprise and Ethics: The Life and Works of William Morris*, Milton Park, 1996
Hendon, Z., *Wallpaper* (855: Shire Library), London, 2018
Hoskins, L. (ed), *The Papered Wall: The History, Patterns and Techniques of Wallpaper* [1994], London, 2005
Jacqué, B., *Le Papier Peint Décor D'Illusion*, Strasbourg, 1989
Jones, O., *The Grammar of Ornament* [1856], Princeton, 2016
Livingstone, K., et al., *C. F. A. Voysey: Arts & Crafts Designer*, London, 2016
MacCarthy, F., *William Morris: A life for our time*, London, 1988
Morris, W., *The Collected Letters of William Morris, Volume I: 1848–1880*, Princeton, 2014
Parry, L., *William Morris Textiles*, London, 2013
Schoeser, M., *Sanderson: The Essence of English Decoration*, London, 2010
Wailliez, W., 'Japanese leather paper or kinkarakawakami: an overview from the 17th century to the Japonist hangings by Rottmann & Co', *Wallpaper History Review*, 2016
The William Morris Internet Archive: Works, at https://www.marxists.org/archive/morris/works/index.htm

Acknowledgements

This book has been a collaborative project. It began as a concept initiated for Japanese readers by Michael Parry as the accompanying text to 'The Art of Wallpaper' exhibition, which toured Japan between July 2018 and May 2020, co-ordinated by The Asahi Shimbun Co. Tokyo. I am grateful to Michael for sharing his work with me. My thanks go gladly to him as well as to members of the Japanese project team, namely Yoko Obuchi of The Asahi Shimbun Co. , Yuri Matsushita, Chief Curator of the Gunma Prefectural Museum of Art, and Mariko Higashi.

Other key contributors were Ben Pentreath, who wrote the insightful Foreword; my own assistant Diane Mackay, whose proof reading was invaluable; and Keren Protheroe, the Sanderson Design Group Archivist who gracefully facilitated my work, providing additional and most welcome details. The contribution of the team at ACC Art Books was most appreciated.
We're all grateful to the Sanderson Design Group for keeping the archive safe and valued, having the vision to celebrate it and sharing their enthusiasm. Finally, Claire Vallis and all in the Morris & Co. design team deserve special thanks for making manifest Morris's idea that 'the past is not dead, it is living in us and will be alive in the future which we are now helping to make'.

ISBN: 978-1-78884-168-9

First published by ACC Art Books in 2022
Reprinted 2024

A CIP catalogue record for this book is available from the British Library.

All photographs by Justin Piperger, or SDG staff, except: Tullie House Museum & Art Gallery Trust (p.64); Jake Curtis (p.157); Andy Gore (pp.159, 161); Peter Dixon (pp.163, 165); Dean Mitchell (p.171)

Graphic Design by Paul Eaton, Redback Visual

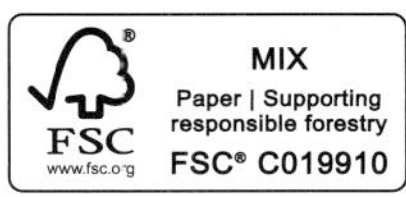

Printed in China
for ACC Art Books Ltd., Woodbridge, Suffolk, UK

www.accartbooks.com

ACC
ART
BOOKS

Front cover | *Pimpernel* [1876] surface-printed 2021 re-edition, Morris & Co., see pp.79 and 162.

Back cover | *Willow Boughs* [1887], rotary screen-printed cotton 2021 transformation, Morris & Co., see pp.93 and 163.